A FINAL GRAIN OF TRUTH

A FINAL GRAIN OF TRUTH

JACK WEBSTER

With best wishes

Jack Webster

BLACK & WHITE PUBLISHING

First published 2013
by Black & White Publishing Ltd
29 Ocean Drive, Edinburgh EH6 6JL

1 3 5 7 9 10 8 6 4 2   13 14 15 16

ISBN: 978 1 84502 710 0

ALBA | CHRUTHACHAIL

Typeset by Iolaire Typesetting, Newtonmore
Printed and bound by ScandBook AB, Sweden

CONTENTS

For Ayliffe

WHAT'S IT ALL ABOUT?

The title of this book alone would tell you, if you didn't already know, that something must have come before. And indeed it did. I first ventured into this territory well over thirty years ago, when I was at the height of a career in journalism, working as a features writer with the Scottish *Daily Express* and coming into contact with some of the most fascinating personalities of the twentieth century. In my earlier days I had presumed to write a so-called autobiography when my life had scarcely begun. Needless to say, it got nowhere. But there is a time for everything and, gradually, as my career developed, it dawned on me that there might now be a book in all this, with so many intriguing tales to tell. So I jotted down the names of my interviewees over the years, wove their stories into the fabric of my own life, including a childhood in rural Aberdeenshire, and presented the manuscript to a publisher. I called it *A Grain of Truth* and on Guy Fawkes Day of 1981 it saw the light of day. Hooray!

It did remarkably well in the bookshops but that seemed like the end of my personal memoirs. Several years later however it happened to be read by the chairman of Collins, the publishers in London, a prominent Scot called Ian Chapman, who promptly bought it up for his paperback company, Fontana. But as part of the deal he insisted that I write another one in similar vein, this time a second hardback to be called *Another Grain of Truth*. That appeared in 1988 and went to Fontana paperback in the following year. But even that was not the end.

The up-and-coming B&W publishing company in Edinburgh wanted to combine the two books in one omnibus volume, which took us into the 1990s. Twenty-odd years after the second *Grain*, by which time I had written seventeen books and lived a great deal more, it occurred to me that there might be a case for *A Final Grain of Truth*. This would be a wrap-up of my life's experience, now viewed from the greater distance of my eighties. I don't feel that age and still travel the world as if I had never been there before. Inevitably there are some stories which will have a familiar ring for those who know my writing. But if it is true that wisdom comes with age then perhaps there will be a fresh slant, as I view my life from a broader perspective.

One criticism of those two earlier books was that I told the stories objectively and revealed very little about myself. It was fair comment. So, putting self-consciousness aside, I have opened up a little on what I feel and think about the people and the world around me. Happily, Campbell Brown and his Black & White Publishing company have shown the same enthusiasm as they did all those years ago. But whatever the results, as you accompany me on this final journey I hope you will find enough interest and entertainment to feel that your time has not been wasted.

CHAPTER ONE

A STICKY START

That summer of 1947 remains in the memory as by far the most glorious of my lifetime, days of heavenly blue skies and golden sunshine that seemed to go on forever. You could have closed your eyes and thought it was California, then opened them to find you were still in the Aberdeenshire district of Buchan, where the gods are seldom so generous. Less welcome, however, that phenomenal summer was in sharp contrast to my prevailing mood, as I lay weak and limp from the effects of a heart condition and pondered the fact that life was not exactly a bowl of cherries.

Out of school at fourteen, it was not long before I found the world closing in on that dream of a life beyond my native Buchan, the name given to the rural area of North-east Scotland which runs eastward from the rivers Deveron and Ythan, with the Moray Firth to the north and the great North Sea to the east. Not that I was unhappy in my village of Maud – it lies twenty-eight miles to the north of Aberdeen – where I was born on the morning of Wednesday, 8 July 1931. On the contrary, I was passionately fond of the place. As a community of just a few hundred people, it lay at the heart of the Aberdeenshire cattle country and could claim to have the biggest weekly livestock market in Britain, rivalled only by that Oxfordshire town which gave us the nursery rhyme about "Ride a cock horse to Banbury Cross!"

The fact that my father, John Webster, was the auctioneer in charge of that cattle-mart complex took me close to the rural life of Buchan, with its long tradition of turning the natural mediocrity of its soil into some of the finest cattle country in Britain. That process, in turn, had produced its own brand of common sense,

1

hard-working, honest, decent folk whose efforts had so ennobled them that they came to personify the very salt of that earth upon which they had toiled. These were my people, including my own father and mother, both bred from small-farming backgrounds just a few miles from Maud. So why could I so love the native corner yet show such little interest in my farming heritage? It was a huge disappointment to my father that his only child was not inclined to become the latest in a long line of farming John Websters, seven of whom were buried in one Buchan churchyard!

There is, of course, no accounting for the permutation of genes, producing such vast differences even within the same family. But the power of genetics is beyond doubt nevertheless. I must therefore look for an answer in my mother's family, which can at least give us a clue. For into the fabric of her farming background comes a rather extraordinary man, her grandfather. Gavin Greig, the forester's son from the Parkhill estate, near Dyce, was himself a product of rural Buchan but, more to the point, he was a brilliant academic and musician, destined for widespread fame as the result of a folksong collection declared by many to be the greatest of its kind in the world.

Gavin Greig was said to have traced his ancestors in two different directions, one of which connected him to the same family as Scotland's national bard, Robert Burns, and the other to the national composer of Norway, Edvard Grieg. Edvard Grieg's great-grandfather was a Buchan man, Alexander Greig (note the different spelling), who grew up on the farm of Mosstown of Cairnbulg, near Fraserburgh, but accepted the offer of a fellow Aberdonian to work in his British Consul's office in Bergen. In time, Alexander himself became the Consul and was followed in that role by his son and grandson. Through the generations, they used to cross in a little boat from Norway to Fraserburgh twice a year for the sole purpose of attending Communion in the local church. Can you imagine it today?

The change of spelling seemed to arise because the continental pronunciation of Greig sounded unpleasantly like "Grige". So by transposing the vowels they at least came a step nearer to the Scottish pronunciation of "Greg".

2

From the same generation, Gavin Greig was writing plays and composing music in the same folk tradition that intrigued Edvard Grieg across that short strip of water to Norway. My grandmother, Edith Greig, the first of Gavin's nine children to be born and the last one to die, told me of her father leaving by train one day to attend a piano recital by Grieg. She thought his destination was Edinburgh. But, in a more respectful age, he did not intrude upon the privacy of his distant cousin to introduce himself. Can't you imagine what a story that would have made in today's world of rampant publicity?

By the age of twenty-two Gavin Greig was out of Aberdeen University and into a headmaster's chair in the parish of New Deer, where he remained till his premature death in 1914. So this family legend filtered into my childhood of the 1930s, not only through my grandmother, who lived into her nineties, but from the many witnesses who were still around to tell me what a remarkable man my great-grandfather had been.

The Robert Burns connection arose from the fact that the poet's paternal family was not from Ayrshire, as is generally assumed, but from the farm of Clochnahill, near Stonehaven, which is still an active farm to this day. His father, William, a major influence in his son's life, was the only one of the family ever to leave the Northeast. He went south to look for work as a gardener and landed in Edinburgh, where he helped to lay out that parkland known as The Meadows, in the shadow of the famous castle. He then went westward to look for more work and landed by chance in Alloway, where his son Robert was born. I suspect that if someone had told him he would build with his own hands a little cottage that one day would rival the great Edinburgh Castle as a tourist attraction in Scotland, he simply wouldn't have believed it, would he? Through his mother's side, Gavin Greig managed to trace his roots back to that farm of Clochnahill.

So that trawl through my mother's background gives a possible explanation of the kind of child she herself had produced. Whereas my father lived for farming alone, ruggedly blunt and down-to-earth, my warm and lively mother, always ready for fun, embraced the finer points of life as well, not least the world of music, which came to her almost exclusively from Broadcasting House in London. As for so many people in saner times, the wireless was her lifeline. In the whole of her rural existence she never saw an opera or attended an orchestral concert, yet she would waltz through her housework on a wave of melody, unbelievably well versed on every word and note – and cherishing the dream that should have made her a ballet dancer. Her taste in music and composers ranged from Tchaikovsky, Rachmaninov, Puccini and Dvorak to George Gershwin, Jerome Kern and Ivor Novello, with Victor Sylvester thrown in for perfect rhythm and Fred Astaire for the subtle majesty of his dancing.

If our family was not familiar with orchestral concert or opera house, we did at least have access to Hollywood, via the fourteen-mile drive to Peterhead on a Saturday night. Lost in the scented atmosphere of the Playhouse or the Regal, I would absorb the magic of Beverly Hills, with its palm-lined streets and sophisticated ladies, entranced by the clowning of Charlie Chaplin, the dancing of Fred Astaire and Ginger Rogers, the skating of Sonja Henie, the voice of Deanna Durbin, the athleticism of Johnny Weissmuller as Tarzan and the sheer craft of Clark Gable and Vivien Leigh, Spencer Tracy, James Stewart, Katharine Hepburn, Greta Garbo and so many more.

Now that we have touched on the unexpected genetic background of my mother, with its hint of Robert Burns and Edvard Grieg, is it any wonder she dreamed of a more romantic life? For her, alas, it was all too late. For me, lying in that pathetic state of 1947, with a weakened heart and a bad stammer, it seemed no more likely, though I did have one driving ambition which had engaged me since I was a little boy. When asked, I always said I wanted to be "a reporter". A reporter? Where did that come from?

I have often wondered if, subconsciously, the child mind sensed that writing was a possible escape to a more glamorous world. From the silver screen could Humphrey Bogart in his belted raincoat and felt hat have put an idea into my innocent head? In the aftermath of the Second World War, however, the men returning from the forces had to get their jobs back. Newsprint was so scarce that the papers were ridiculously small. But there I lay, more in hope than expectation, writing my pathetic little notes to every editor in Scotland.

And there they sat, dictating their bleak replies that were nothing if not consistent. My father was insisting that, if farming was not my choice, then I had better think of banking or something more useful than newspapers. Surely not banking? He sent me to sit the entrance exam which, uncharacteristically, was one of the few I had ever passed. Worse still, in due course I received word to start as a clerk at the North of Scotland Bank in the nearby town of Turriff on Monday, 15 March 1948. Remember the date.

The will to live can so easily ebb away. Was there no way out of this? As a last resort, I put myself in the hands of an uncertain Providence; and from that point onwards I would never again scoff at the power of prayer! For two extraordinary things happened.

After those months in bed, my ailing heart (a mitril stenosis) showed an amazing sign of improvement, due, it seemed, to the healing power of youth. And secondly, there came a phone call from Turriff. No, not from the dreaded North of Scotland Bank. This was the *Turriff Advertiser*. The what? I didn't even know such a paper had come into existence. It must have been the only one in Scotland I hadn't written to. Well, they needed a boy to assist the editor – and they had heard of "a loon Webster fae Maud who was pestering every newspaper in Scotland for a job". Would I come for an interview?

On the very next day I became the first-ever junior reporter on the *Turriff Advertiser*, due to start on a significant date – the following Monday, 15 March 1948! At last the gods had come on my side.

On that Monday morning I hastily passed the door of that very bank which might have sealed forever my dream of becoming a journalist. Instead, a hundred yards further along High Street, I entered the world of newspapers, with whatever joys or sorrows that profession might hold.

CHAPTER TWO

AN EDITOR AT SIXTEEN

The *Turriff Advertiser* was owned by old Willie Peters and his delicate son Bob, both printers not journalists, who had simply added
a small weekly newspaper to their main activity of commercial
printing. They had one Linotype machine, operated by Norman
Murdoch and the rest was achieved by the old-fashioned practice
of picking individual letters from alphabetical boxes, much as we
did when we were children, and forming them into words before
inking them on to paper. As I recall it, the neighbouring *Huntly
Express* was produced entirely by this method. In other words, the
Willie Peters of this world had scarcely progressed beyond the
founding Willie Caxton of five hundred years earlier.

On my first day Willie appeared, complete with his inseparable
hat and pipe, removing the latter just long enough to say, "We
didna speak aboot pey." Pay? Who cared about pay? What did
money matter when you were on the cloud nine of realising your
life's ambition? "We'll just see what you're worth at the end o' the
week," concluded Willie.

That seemed fair – until the end of the week, when Willie assessed
my worth at £1.10s (£1.50p in today's money). I was already committed to £1.15s a week for digs with Mrs Anderson at 31 Woodlands
Crescent. With a few uncomplimentary words about this "damnt
tippence-ha'penny bugger o' a job," my father coughed up ten shillings a week (50p) which covered my digs and the bus fare home at
the weekend, leaving enough for a bag of sweeties.

Matters changed within ten weeks, however, when the editor,
a wee mannie from London with the impressive name of Ronald
Scott Hutton but with no real interest in Turriff, was sacked. Willie

Peters (no fool he) spotted an opportunity for further financial pru-
dence. He could appoint the editorial dogsbody as acting editor of
his *Turriff Advertiser* – and get two for the price of one. Brilliant.

Within weeks I had gone from the depths of depression to the
heights of the impossible dream. It didn't matter that old Willie had
now reassessed my newfound worth at a mere £2 a week. At the
age of sixteen, I sat in the editor's chair, put my feet up on the desk,
puffed on an imaginary cigar and sent my lackeys in all directions
to collect the big news of Turriff.

Of course there was only me, so I returned from fantasy and for
the next two and a half years went running upstairs and down-
stairs like Wee Willie Winkie to collect the news of Turriff which
might, on a good week, amount to a whist drive and a meeting of
the Women's Rural Institute. Oh, and there was a massive appetite
for deaths. In fact I came to the conclusion that deaths were really
the life and soul of the *Turriff Advertiser*.

Post-war Turriff was a bustling little town of 3,000 people, to my
surprise much given to gambling and illicit affairs. It could boast
one of Scotland's finest agricultural shows but gained its greatest
attention – worldwide, in fact – after David Lloyd George, Chancellor of the Exchequer, introduced National Insurance in 1911. A
local farmer, Robbie Paterson of Lendrum, refused to pay the new
tax and one of his cows was impounded in lieu of his payments.
Rural folk are slow to rouse but when the poor beast was paraded
for public sale in the town square, they came in force to create a riot,
pelting policemen with divots and rotten eggs and setting Robbie's
white cow free to run.

It was one of those local incidents which fires public imagination
and the story of the Turra Coo made headlines in every country of
the world. When the animal was recaptured and taken for a more
orderly sale in Aberdeen, local farmers clubbed together, bought
the cow and presented it back to Robbie Paterson, in appreciation
of the stand he had taken on behalf of them all. Four thousand
people turned out for the presentation, when Turriff Brass Band
played "Jock o' Hazledene" and the Turra Coo was handed over by

7

a popular New Deer farmer, Archie Campbell, father of a famous North-east poetess of the future, Flora Garry.

When I was in Turriff there were still many witnesses to the notorious event, including a local auctioneer, Bertie Reid. As a boy, Bertie had been the orra-loon at Lendrum, looking after the famous cow, but when I asked for his abiding memory of the creature he didn't hesitate. "She was a damned puir milker," he said.

In that post-war period of austerity we were still in the grip of food rationing and general scarcity, lamenting that nothing was as good as before the war. In fact "The War" became the great divide of our lives. During that war there was no possibility of overseas travel for civilians and even in those post-war years the severe limit on the currency you could take out of the country made it a doubtful venture. Nevertheless, with my fascination for glamorous cities like Paris, I decided to take my first trip abroad in 1949, though how I managed it on that wage of £2 a week from old Willie Peters I cannot understand.

With a friend from Turriff – and still short of my eighteenth birthday – I set out on the great adventure, by train from Aberdeen, through London to Newhaven, across the Channel and into that great French capital, which remains one of my favourite cities to this day. No fancy hotels, just a bed and breakfast but an entrée to the great wide spaces of Paris – from the focal point of the Arc de Triomphe, up the Eiffel Tower, down the Champs-Élysées to Place de La Concorde, along Pigalle and up to the heights of Montmartre. What a city this was.

The money stretched to the famous Folies Bergère, where I listened to the great Josephine Baker. In the immediate aftermath of that war, in which Nazi jackboots had pounded the Champs-Élysées, Paris still managed to retain an atmosphere of long ago. Even the traditional prostitute, complete with fur cape and cigarette holder, still lingered seductively in doorways (a fair fascination to a loon fae Maud!), and you would not have been surprised to round a corner and come face to face with F. Scott Fitzgerald or even the dwarfish figure of Toulouse-Lautrec, however long gone.

Other legends were still a possibility; Ernest Hemingway was alive, as were Maurice Chevalier and Edith Piaf; Noel Coward might still come from London to hold a rendezvous with his friend Cole Porter.

Full of fantasies, I was now heading for the Longchamp Race-course to see the famous Grand Prix de Paris. There, I had my old Box Brownie camera poised for pictures when who came suddenly into the lens but the most glamorous star from Hollywood. I looked up to find myself face to face with Rita Hayworth no less, linked into the arm of Prince Aly Khan who, I discovered, had become her husband on the previous day. I snapped the honeymoon couple, smiled appreciatively and couldn't believe my luck.

So this was Paris, wonderful Paris. More than sixty years later I made my way to the cinema, attracted by the title of Woody Allen's latest film, *Midnight in Paris*. This came from Woody's own experience of the great city, a little after me, in which he carried the imagination of our mutual fantasies into the reality of film. And yes, delightfully, he was meeting up with all those legends, from Hemingway and Cole Porter to Scott Fitzgerald and Toulouse-Lautrec. Now I didn't feel so ridiculous after all.

Reluctantly, l left the magic of Paris and returned to the no-nonsense world of Turriff where, by the late 1940s, we had not seen a new car since before the war. But suddenly there was a brand new model parked in the town's High Street and crowds gathered round just for the novelty of touching it. It was a Jowett Javelin, all streamlined and gleaming.

As I approached my nineteenth birthday, old Willie Peters put his head round the door once more, still with hat and pipe in place, to reveal his latest calculation of financial genius. After two and a half years he was now obliged to pay me £3 a week. But he had a proposition. Since income tax began at £3 and I would lose one shilling from my new wage, there was surely a better way to do it. If he paid me only £2.19s, I would lose nothing – and he would gain a shilling! I refrained from a round of applause. But it was surely time to move on. With experience behind me, I was now ready for the next step, which in those days meant the nearest daily paper.

That was the *Press and Journal* in Aberdeen, at that time owned by Lord Kemsley in London, but with a fascinating history which made it one of the oldest daily newspapers in the world.

CHAPTER THREE

GIANTS OF JOURNALISM

Printing had been introduced to Aberdeen in 1621 by a German gentleman called Edward Raban, who ran his bookseller's business in Broad Street but also produced books of an astonishingly high artistic standard. There was an attempt at a newspaper in 1657 but the real story began nearly a hundred years later, in the aftermath of the Battle of Culloden, and the man at the very root of today's *Press and Journal* was James Chalmers, whose father was Professor of Divinity at Marischal College. Young Chalmers went off to Oxford University with the intent of following his father's profession but became intrigued by the art of printing. Gathering up some knowledge and experience of the trade, he returned to Aberdeen, set up his own business in Castle Street and successfully applied for the posts of official printer to both the city and the university.

Then came the 1745 Rebellion, when Bonnie Prince Charlie marched south to Derby but was sent into retreat by the dreaded Duke of Cumberland, son of George II, whose royalist troops chased him all the way to Aberdeen. Taking a breather before the final march to Culloden, Butcher Cumberland, as he came to be known, found barracks for his soldiers by commandeering the newly-built but not yet occupied Auld Hoose of Robert Gordon's, the same building which stands as the focal point of that college today. When he eventually set out for the crucial confrontation, he was followed by James Chalmers, who was to become a rare witness to the defeat of Bonnie Prince Charlie and his Jacobites at Culloden on 16 April 1746.

Within two days Chalmers was back in Aberdeen, churning out a news sheet from his Castle Street presses and giving the folk of the North-east their very first notion of a "newspaper". More significantly, it gave Chalmers the idea of doing this on a regular basis.

In 1748 that became the *Aberdeen's Journal*, which held sway for more than a hundred years until it was eventually challenged by an up-and-coming *Aberdeen Free Press* in 1853, based just a stone's throw away on Union Street, in what later became the popular family business of Esslemont and Mackintosh. In 1922 they amalgamated under the compromise of *The Press and Journal*, based in the Broad Street premises of the *Journal*, next door to the Town House.

Into that great history I took my first nervous steps on Monday, 16 October 1950, achieving what had always been my ambition – to be a reporter on *The Press and Journal*. Well, here I was and here I would stay for the next ten years, mainly as a reporter but gaining some experience as a sub-editor as well. Within that period I would spend three years as the staff man in my native Buchan area, covering the fishing towns of Peterhead and Fraserburgh, as well as the rural hinterland.

On a Friday I would cover the Sheriff Court at Peterhead and encounter justice mixed with comedy. A man from one of the strongly Brethren villages between Peterhead and Fraserburgh faced a fairly serious motoring charge one day.

"Don't you have anyone to represent you?" asked Sheriff Hamilton. The accused raised his right hand and said with great conviction, "Your Honour, God is my defender."

Whereupon a puzzled sheriff leaned over the bench and said, "My good man, on this occasion I think you might be better to get someone who is better known locally!"

More seriously, I covered that most devastating of events, the Great Gale of 31 January 1953 which ravaged so much of Scotland. Nine days later came a second Fraserburgh Lifeboat Disaster, in which six men perished at the mouth of the harbour as we onlookers stood in helpless despair. The irony of that tragedy was that the sunny serenity of the day belied the fact that the turmoil of the Great Gale was still boiling in anger a hundred miles out at sea and playing havoc with the more predictable rhythms of the waves which overturned the lifeboat.

Returning from Buchan to the old Broad Street headquarters of *The Press and Journal*, I was learning from some of the greatest journalists I would ever encounter. They were men like George Rowntree Harvey, who had worked as a night sub-editor to pay his way through Aberdeen University and had to be ordered home in the early hours of his final exam day to catch some sleep before his big moment. George sought no favours but he emerged with first-class honours and developed into what many claimed to be the finest music and drama critic in British journalism. In London they could not believe that he would scorn the glory of Fleet Street for his preferred choice of Aberdeen. He also became one of the great eccentrics of North-east life.

There were men like Andrew Ingram, who had worked on *The Times* of India with Eric Linklater before returning to his native corner as a giant of journalism – one of so many whose names would never be known to the wider public. In contrast to the rumbustious Andrew there was the introverted Cuthbert Graham, another giant of his craft who attracted my attention for a very special reason.

When I first arrived in Broad Street in 1950 I was intrigued by several discoveries, one of which was the fact that I was working in the same small reporters' room, at the same old desks, as a man who had become a hero of mine. He was there at the back end of the First World War just as I was in the aftermath of the Second. His name then was Leslie Mitchell but he had become better known as Lewis Grassic Gibbon, regarded by many as Scotland's finest prose writer. Mitchell had struggled with rejection till the last few years of his very short life, when he received the challenge of a newspaper critic to write about his native North-east of Scotland in the way that Thomas Hardy had written about Wessex. Quietly he took up that challenge and began writing *Sunset Song*, the first in a memorable trilogy which would turn him into a novelist of international repute, under his new name of Lewis Grassic Gibbon, just before he died during an ulcer operation. He was not yet thirty-four.

13

The significance of this story is that the journalist who had challenged him towards his destiny, by suggesting what he should write, was none other than the painfully shy Cuthbert Graham, a young man with perception so far beyond his years. Is it any wonder I sat at his feet and coaxed him to tell me all he knew about the man who had also become his close friend? I shall return to Grassic Gibbon later.

Another discovery at *The Press and Journal* was the fact that our national bard, Robert Burns, had visited the old *Aberdeen's Journal* office in 1786, during his visit to the North-east to see his relatives at that farm near Stonehaven from which his father had gone south.

The third thing that intrigued me about *The Press and Journal* was that men were allowed to work into their eighties in those days. I'm thinking in particular of old John Sleigh, who had reported on the Tay Bridge Railway Disaster of 1879, when the bridge blew down in a storm and a train took all its passengers to their deaths – and who was still there at the start of the Second World War. I was just too late to know him but the legend lived on.

John was a tall, distinguished-looking man, dressed in dark suit, white shirt, black tie and bowler hat, who was perfect for reporting on society occasions on Royal Deeside. On this particular day he was sent to report on the funeral of an aristocratic spinster lady whose real age had never been known. So he had strict instructions to look at the coffin lid, which in those days invariably gave the information.

John liked two drams better than one but he was back at the grave in time to hear the minister say, "Earth to earth, dust to dust." John suddenly remembered he had not checked the coffin lid. What follows is a perfectly true story.

Having edged close to the graveside and realised it was too dark to see, he now had no option but to bend down on one knee. With a few drams inside him . . . yes, he toppled over and fell in. Well, you can imagine the stooshie that created on Royal Deeside. But local farmers just nudged each other, winked and said that, as far as they knew, it was the nearest her ladyship had ever been to a man! At least, that's the sanitised version of what they said.

The nature of our journalism at Broad Street, Aberdeen, was of course essentially regional, covering that highly distinctive area of North-east Scotland and stretching to the far North and West of the country. But the quality could stand comparison with the very best in Britain, regional or otherwise.

CHAPTER FOUR

AN EVENING WITH MONTY

Within my ten years at Aberdeen Journals the most memorable encounter came far from our own shores – and in the most unexpected of circumstances. Along with my good friend and colleague John Lodge, a real character from Yorkshire who graduated from Aberdeen University and came straight into local journalism, I took an interest in what was happening in post-war Yugoslavia. The Soviet Union may have been dominating Eastern Europe with its bleak form of dictatorship, but Stalin had no power over Marshal Tito, who had certainly taken part in the 1917 Revolution but was now establishing a more relaxed form of communism in his own land.

In 1953 Tito had become president of Yugoslavia and in that same year John Lodge and I, on our own initiative, decided to see it for ourselves. We travelled by train from Aberdeen to London, en route to Paris once more, where we boarded the Simplon-Orient Express on a Saturday night and arrived in the capital city of Belgrade on the Monday morning. From there we crossed the Dinaric Alps in an old Pionair aircraft, which came bumping down in a field of grazing cattle and horses, which was all that the beautiful walled city of Dubrovnik could offer as an airport in those days, long before it became a fashionable holiday resort.

On our meagre currency allowance we found lodgings and set out to explore this ancient gem of a place, described by Lord Byron as "the Pearl of the Adriatic". For it was here that Tito entertained foreign guests in his magnificent Villa Sheherazade, owned before the war by a wealthy American and now restored to its capitalist best by the communist dictator.

When our landlord told us that our new Queen's sister, Princess Margaret, had been there last week and the current guest was believed to be our own Field Marshal Montgomery, John and I pricked up our ears. Well, it was worth a try. So we approached the formidable gates of the villa and tried to explain to an armed guard that we would like to see the Field Marshal. Not unexpectedly, he was less than helpful but agreed to pass on our request. There would be a reply at a given hour, so John and I were back at the guard room in good time, fully prepared for the rebuff.

To our astonishment, the heavy gates were thrown open and we were marched at bayonet-point down through magnificent gardens, sloping towards the Adriatic in an idyllic setting looking its best on a fine September evening. Already we could see the small figure in the familiar black beret, seated by a spacious patio.

Montgomery rose to greet us, interested to hear we were journalists from Scotland, inviting us to sit at his table and asking what we would like to drink. Before we had time to consider, the teetotal Monty had snapped his fingers at the man in the dark suit and ordered two glasses of vermouth.

We had come to interview Monty but, in his own supervised visit, we soon found he was just as interested in what we, with greater freedom of movement, were able to observe. What about the people in their own homes? What were they saying? So our interests were mutual.

By now the man in the dark suit had served our vermouth from a silver tray, but instead of withdrawing to his servants' quarters, to our astonishment, he boldly pulled in a chair and waited for Montgomery to introduce him – as none other than M. Popović, Tito's Foreign Secretary! No wonder Monty won that vital Battle of El Alamein which turned the Second World War in our favour.

As we renewed our discussion, that was the next topic of conversation. For John and myself this was our first interview with a famous figure and not for the last time I realised how hard it is to fit a legend into the frame of an ordinary-looking human being.

Montgomery was just that but it's what is in the head that counts.

So we covered his war days then sat intrigued as he casually moved on to more mundane, domestic encounters.

"Last weekend when I was visiting Winston he was telling me what he was backing in the St Leger," he said. Of course, Churchill was enthusiastic about his horses, owning them, backing them; but first-hand accounts like that were new to us. Our wartime leader had stepped out of history to a level of everyday conversation.

Then we talked about Lord Kemsley, whose newspaper empire included *The Press and Journal* and whose daughter Pamela came daily to her Aberdeen office from Aboyne. In an unlikely union, the elegant lady had married the less than elegant but highly aristocratic Marquess of Huntly, head of the Gordon clan, indicating that her money and his title could be the most likely explanation of the marriage.

"Kemsley is a good friend of mine," said Monty. "Do tell him I was passing on my regards." And with that he bade us goodbye. Lord Kemsley in London was well out of our reach in Aberdeen but back home John and I wondered if Montgomery was really serious about passing on his regards. However, at the risk of sounding foolish, we did as he asked.

A few days later, Kemsley had another letter on his desk:

My Dear Kemsley,
I was in Yugoslavia the other day and while there I met two young men from the Aberdeen Press of your group, John Lodge and Jack Webster. They asked if they could see me and they came to my villa that evening.

I thought they were both extremely nice young men, very courteous and interested in everything. They told me about their experiences and they had without doubt displayed great initiative in making the journey on a limited amount of currency . . . I told them they were to send you personally my good wishes – and I hope they did so . . .
Montgomery of Alamein

That taught us a lesson about paying attention to detail. He was testing us out. Lord Kemsley sent us his letter, which I preserve to this day. And when I wrote about it all in *The Press and Journal* Monty sent me another letter of appreciation.

Yes, life was fun at Aberdeen Journals which, of course, incorporates both *The Press and Journal* and the *Evening Express*. On occasion I would pass the gates of Robert Gordon's College and shudder a little at the memory of my inglorious exit. Having been sent there from the village school at the age of twelve, I had failed to reach the required academic standard by the time I was fourteen. Nowadays, everyone passes on to higher education, even to college or university, sometimes emerging with fancy degrees but still unable to count or spell or punctuate or write a decent English sentence, all of which I had learned at Maud School before I was twelve. In those days, however, I was shown out through that vaulted gateway with tears on my cheeks and the ring of failure in my ears, back home to Maud in total disgrace. It took years to believe that I was not a moron altogether.

With that unhappy memory of five years earlier I would cheer myself up by repairing to a nearby cafe which had a quaint little sign saying, "Food, drink and a kind word – 1s.2p" (less than 6p today). I ordered a pie and a cup of tea as my food and drink and, as the waitress turned to go, I said, "And what about the kind word?" She cast around to see if the boss was looking, then said, "Dinna eat that pie!" I did eat the pie and survived.

But before we leave that scene can I explode a myth that women were hardly to be found in journalism those sixty years ago and had to fight their way to acceptance. In Aberdeen at least, the editorial floor was joyfully awash with women, prominent by-line names like Ethel Simpson, Helen Fisher, Pearl Murray, Margaret Fleming, Aileen Tough, Margaret McGrath, Muriel Munro and some who escape my fading memory, all welcomed and paid on exactly the same scale as the men.

CHAPTER FIVE

FOUR WEDDINGS AND A FUNERAL?

While based in Fraserburgh in the early- to mid-fifties as *The Press and Journal* staff reporter for Buchan, I used to see an attractive schoolgirl waiting for the bus home to the village of Strichen, about nine miles away. She was different.

In time, there came an opportunity to speak to her, when I discovered her name was Eden Keith, whose father had been principal maths teacher at Fraserburgh Academy before taking up the post of headmaster at Strichen Secondary School. In that brief encounter I arranged to take her out on the following week and on that very evening, our first real contact, we decided to become engaged! And I had always regarded myself a slow worker, especially with women.

Eden was eighteen, I was twenty-three and it caused a bit of a stir when she turned up at the Academy sporting an engagement ring. By then I was on the point of returning to the headquarters of *The Press and Journal* in Aberdeen, which was perhaps just as well, since this was not the way you did things in the Buchan of those days.

We were married on 17 February 1956 in the muckle Kirk of St Nicholas, Aberdeen, on what was evidently recorded as the coldest day of the century to that point. I can vouch for the brass-monkey temperature, which was not helped by the fact that a negligent beadle had forgotten to switch on the heating. Fortunately I had protected the shivering anatomy with a pair of woolly Long Johns, admittedly not the most romantic way to enter married bliss but without doubt the most sensible.

Poor Eden had no such defence, committed to being a white bride, with consequences which, for the duration of the honeymoon, landed her in bed – no, not so much with me as with the flu.

The service was conducted by the Rev. Dr Matthew Welsh Neilson from New Deer, for whom the ordeal must have reminded him of freezing trenches in the First World War, from which he sadly returned with shell shock. Dr Neilson had both married my father and mother and baptised me but we had never subjected him to an ordeal like this.

The reception was held at the Caledonian Hotel in Union Terrace, at that time the social hub of Aberdeen, the height of sophistication with its American bar and cocktail lounge, complete with palm-court trio. This had become my favourite venue for interviewing the stars appearing at His Majesty's Theatre, but now a major crisis was arising. By a serious miscalculation of the time required for interminable toasts, I became aware that bride and groom would have to leave before the reception was properly under way.

The London honeymoon would start from Dyce Aerodrome, as we called it then, and take-off time was speedily approaching. So Eden and I beat a hasty retreat, accompanied by my best man, the same John Lodge of the Montgomery adventure, and Eden's bridesmaid and school friend, Norah Richards, and were just in time to board the old thirty-two-seater Pionair before it took off for Renfrew, Manchester and finally Northolt, which was London's airport before Heathrow.

As a consequence of that icebox called St Nicholas Kirk, we left behind us a trail of pulmonary disaster that went far beyond Eden's dose of flu. From more modern times we'll remember the Hugh Grant film *Four Weddings and a Funeral*. With so many elderly guests at our wedding, including my dear old Granny Webster, we managed to turn that round to Four Funerals and a Wedding.

CHAPTER SIX

TOWARDS THE DAILY EXPRESS

With such a dubious start, we settled into furnished rooms at 13 Kepplestone Avenue, near the headquarters of the Gordon High-landers, with Mrs Margaret Milne, a widow from the First World War – and the same landlady who had welcomed Eden's parents as newlyweds in July 1931. (In the week I was born.) Still driving the same old Ford Anglia (FGD 699) that I acquired after passing my test in 1951, I was happily engaged in my role as a reporter on *The Press and Journal* and *Evening Express*. After all, that had been my boyhood ambition and as yet there were no realistic thoughts of journalism beyond Aberdeen.

By now, as a married man, I was earning £12 a week and head-ing towards the last statutory increment that would take me to £16 when I reached twenty-eight. In this twenty-first century it is worth pausing to consider how we regarded inflation in the 1950s. When I reached that maximum of £16 I remember calculating, realistically by the inflation standards of the day, that when I retired in thirty-seven years' time, I might be earning £25 a week. Then suddenly my world was turned upside down.

Evidently the *Scottish Daily Express* in Glasgow was looking for sub-editors, that breed of desk-bound people who take the writers' copy, check it for accuracy and mould it into the page patterns of the night, complete with headlines that fit the space. Their profes-sional status is exactly the same as that of the reporter though, in a perfect world, it should be superior, since they could be expected to have the know-how of the writer plus the technical ability to display his work.

In his cynicism, the writer is likely to reply that sub-editors,

22

often mistaken for the ones immediately below the editor, are as common as rats in a sewer – and not half as intelligent. Be that as it may, I had just moved to sub-editing in Aberdeen when two of us were invited to join Lord Beaverbrook's *Daily Express*. Duncan MacRae was an established and highly talented sub-editor and ready for the national challenge. In that particular role I was still a novice. The offer of £20 a week was certainly a twenty-five per cent improvement but was it enough to justify the upheaval in our very attractive North-east way of life, so near to my Buchan roots where the whole family lived and nearer still to the civilised tenor of Aberdeen?

Behind the quiet charm of Eden lay a very astute brain, which calculated that no, the £20 was not enough. "But why don't you ask for £25?" she suggested. Twenty-five pounds? It seemed preposterous. That was my ambition for the retirement year of 1996.

"Try it," she said. So I did.

And there wasn't even a murmur at the other end of the phone. "When can you start?" was all they said, as I went into a fair imitation of a faint. Deep down I should now have guessed that such a move had to come eventually, if those early dreams of Manhattan and Hollywood were to be realised.

So that was how I tendered my resignation at Broad Street, Aberdeen, said goodbye to the greatest bunch of journalists I would ever meet – and contemplated a new life at the national level of the *Daily Express*.

CHAPTER SEVEN

THE END OF AN EMPIRE

Leaving the Grampian cocoon of Aberdeen for the perceived rough-and-tumble of Glasgow was not without its apprehension. After all, this was the place I had once described as "that conglomeration of villages, city of golden hearts and stainless-steel razors that guarantees to kill you, with kindness if not with cutlass, city of tongue and twang where even the church organs are liable to have glottal-stops". All that – and Rangers and Celtic too! Not that I was a stranger to Glasgow and its citizens.

I had been going there since 1938 when, for all the impressive spectacles that would follow in an adventurous life, I experienced what I still regard as the greatest of them all. This was the British Empire Exhibition in Bellahouston Park, which ran from May till October and welcomed no fewer than 13.5 million people from all over the world. Kings and queens and Hollywood stars mingled with a mass of humanity in that most picturesque of Glasgow parks, which had been turned into a wonderland of magnificent pavilions, representing every corner of the British Empire in all its colour and diversity.

Singers like Paul Robeson and Gracie Fields came to sing, Sir Henry Wood conducted the orchestras of the world, while the magical funfair was masterminded by an unknown man whose name would soon have the familiar ring of Billy Butlin. To crown it all, the Tower of Empire soared from its hilltop base into the sky, from where the millions could cast an eye over a large part of Scotland.

The lights, the music, the dancing made it something that Scotland had not seen before or since. If it had been left in position, Glasgow could have boasted a permanent attraction that corresponded to the Eiffel Tower of Paris. Any notion that I might simply have been seeing it through the eyes of an impressionable child was cast aside when I saw a colour film which emerged in more recent times, confirming that it was just as magnificent as I had thought.

The only blight was an atrocious summer of rain. But even on the last night, when the heavens released their final torrent, no fewer than 365,000 people linked arms and sang and danced with abandon to the popular tune of the time, "The Lambeth Walk", from Noel Gay's musical *Me and My Girl*.

We should perhaps have sensed there was something else in the air. On that last night, however, what we didn't know as they lowered the lights on the Empire Exhibition in Bellahouston Park was that they were virtually lowering the lights on the British Empire itself, for Prime Minister Neville Chamberlain was on his way back from that meeting with Hitler, waving a useless piece of paper and declaring there would be peace in our time.

The Monster of Munich had duped him with ease – and war was just around the corner. And when that war was over, the British Empire began to fall apart. With the echoes of that last night in Bellahouston Park, Glasgow had witnessed a significant moment in history without knowing it.

CHAPTER EIGHT

THE MANUEL MURDERS

On the day before war broke out, Saturday, 2 September 1939, local men who had joined the Territorial Army were boarding a long train in my native village of Maud, en route to some unknown destination which, in time, would prove to be a prison camp in Germany. For within months those men of the highly rated 51st Highland Division were among those given the unenviable task of holding off the Germans so that the rest of our troops could escape the disaster of Dunkirk. My own future father-in-law, Nelson Keith, was among those who then had no option but to surrender to Rommel's Panzer Division. As he told me later, it was no consolation that Rommel came among them, handing out cigars and expressing admiration for the way they had fought. That was the preliminary to the long march towards German captivity which would last for the next five years.

A few hours after those men left Maud, another train steamed in from Glasgow with two hundred evacuees who had come to escape the bombs that would surely be dropped on Clydeside. They were children from Dowanhill and Hyndland Schools who would double our numbers at Maud School and with whom we would share our homes for as long as they decided to stay. Jimmy and Myer Singer became my "adopted brothers" for the next year – and that was how I came to know more about the style and energy and character of the Glaswegian.

Little did I think that the same Jimmy Singer, a quiet-spoken fair-haired boy whose written verse was declared by Miss Cameron, our English teacher at Maud School, as the work of pure genius, would emerge in years to come as Burns Singer, hailed as the great young Scots poet of his day. His early death brought a spate of books analysing his work. And when I asked the leading Scots poet of the time, Hugh MacDiarmid, what the future might have held for the young Singer he so admired, he pursed his little mouth and said, "He might have emerged as a greater poet than me." Considering the mighty MacDiarmid's well-known opinion of his own talents, that was compliment indeed.

Now, twenty years later, I was arriving in Jimmy Singer's own city to work for the *Scottish Daily Express*. This was the aftermath of the Manuel Murders and, of all places, I had found a bungalow in the Burnside district which became the main stalking ground of the dreaded serial killer who struck fear into the community.

Peter Manuel, who ruled as king of the Glasgow underworld, had murdered three members of the Watt family and three more of the Smarts, in a list that would include Anne Kneilands at East Kilbride and Isobel Cook at Uddingston. The American-born son of Lithuanian immigrants, he was handsome, clever and astute and could have achieved whatever he wished. Ironically, for one so evil, he was christened with the names of three saints, Peter, Thomas and Anthony.

So it was an eerie business coming home on the bus after late shifts on the *Express* and walking that last lap to 93 Calderwood Road, through streets which had so recently been the territory of Peter Manuel.

Oddly enough, before he embarked on his final spree of killing, I had actually seen him in Peterhead Prison in the early fifties when he was serving a previous sentence. An enlightened governor of the prison, Major C.D. Heron-Watson, had broken protocol to give me an unheard-of access to prison life. There I met men like the legendary Johnny Ramensky, a Glasgow safebreaker of such exquisite craftsmanship that he was invariably caught for the sheer perfection of his art. Nobody did it like Ramensky, the police said. A man of likeable disposition, Johnny was put to good use during the war when we dropped him behind enemy lines to blow open safes containing valuable information. He was mentioned in despatches for his bravery before returning to civilian life in Glasgow. But Peterhead was his home from home and that was where I found him in 1952. Before and after the war, however, he proved that his skill as a safebreaker was equalled by his talent for escaping, which he did on a regular basis.

The most intriguing part of my visits to Peterhead Prison, however, was the discussion group, where prisoners debated serious topics, like the problems of juvenile delinquency in society! You would hear the chairman, in all innocence, welcoming a new member, expressing regret at the loss of a valuable one – but giving a "welcome back" to Mr So-and-So. It was later, when perusing the minute book, that I realised the presence of Peter Manuel, who had not yet become the clever barrack-room lawyer of his murder-trial days, when he dismissed his distinguished QC, Harald Leslie, and made an impressive job of defending himself.

The consolation in my late-night walks through Burnside was that I didn't have to worry about Peter Manuel any more. They had just hanged him in Barlinnie.

CHAPTER NINE

I'M ON MY WAY

Stories like that of Peter Manuel were now on my desk at the *Express*, in its black-glass palace in Albion Street, where I was settling into the open-plan chaos of a national newspaper in the role of a sub-editor. Once again, this meant taking the copy of reporters and feature writers, checking it for accuracy, spelling, grammar and punctuation and writing the headline. Prominent by-liners, I discovered, were not always as smart as they seemed and it surprised and delighted me to find that my primary education at Maud School had more than equipped me to put some prima-donnas to rights.

As well as my main job as a sub-editor on the *Daily Express* I had now taken on the Saturday night role of chief sub-editor on the *Sunday Express*. That raised my income to an incredible £42 a week. But there was limited satisfaction in correcting the deficiencies of others when you felt you could have done a better writing job yourself. So I started to produce the odd article and to drop it on the desk of the features editor, Drew Rennie, a blunt, dynamic but humorous and quite brilliant son of a Dundee policeman, whose personality was written all over the success of the *Express* in those days.

Soon my by-line was appearing with such lucrative regularity that the editor, Ian McColl, was preparing to tell me that I must choose the route I was taking – sub-editing or writing. This watershed coincided with a news story, appearing in the paper that week, about a young soldier being court-martialled for deserting the army. His defence was that his stammer had brought him such mockery from army colleagues that he could take it no longer. So he fled in distress. It was a touching story. That day I noticed Drew Rennie pacing up and down with an edginess I hadn't seen before. Finally he plucked up the courage to say what he wanted to say. Full of uncharacteristic embarrassment, he wondered if I could perhaps . . . well maybe . . . would it trouble me to . . .

"Would you like me to write about the trials and tribulations of having a stammer, Drew?" I asked. "Sure. No trouble. How many words do you want?"

I have seldom seen such relief on a man's face. As I had some-times suspected, the bold, blunt Drew Rennie was really a big softy at heart.

So my troublesome stammer had found some useful purpose at last, as the catalyst for my transfer. When Ian McColl's offer now arrived, my answer was ready and, for once, I didn't even hesitate in delivering it. So, having left school at fourteen and spent those early years in learning my craft in Turriff and Aberdeen, I had now found my proper role in journalism. Even then, however, I had no idea that I was about to embark on the most exciting and rewarding phase of my career.

With 2,000 of us employed in Lord Beaverbrook's *Scottish Daily Express* – and linked into his London enterprise – we were part of the biggest-selling daily newspaper, not just in Britain but in the whole world. Even America didn't have papers like this. And with people like Drew Rennie in charge of features, you were given your head. If you came up with ideas and carried them through, that story would lead to the next and the next. It was also my good fortune to have landed at the peak time in the history of print jour-nalism, when money was no object.

There were places in the world I wanted to see and people I wanted to meet, and it is the privilege of a journalist that you can just lift a phone and seek an interview with someone you would like to meet anyway. Not many professions can offer such a natural introduction. So the *Express* became a vehicle, not only for doing my job but for fulfilling many a personal ambition. What an incen-tive to do your best.

In those days I didn't know too many people who had been to New York or Washington, Moscow or Hong Kong, but in a short time I had been to all those places and many more. Any thoughts of Glasgow being a stepping stone to the *Express* in London now disappeared as I savoured my good fortune and realised that such wonderful opportunities would not so readily present themselves in the bigger jungle of Fleet Street.

I look around journalism today and wonder how I would have fared in a vastly different world where there is neither the money nor the opportunity to provide my kind of experience. Young men and women are obliged to sit glued to their desks, dependent on a little screen that provides most of their information and a mobile phone to supply the rest. But the lifeblood and real joy of journalism is getting out to meet the people, face to face. No wonder I sweat a little when I think of it – and count my blessings.

A competent enough writer himself, Drew Rennie was much better at organising other people, spotting their strengths and inspiring them to produce good work. His foresight and intuition for what would make a good feature were uncanny; and the force of his engaging personality brought him into the company of people at all levels.

He once sat down in a nearby pub with the aforesaid Peter Manuel at a time when the police had arrested Glasgow businessman William Watt and kept him in Barlinnie Prison on suspicion of having murdered his own wife, daughter and sister-in-law at their home in High Burnside. Manuel loved to flirt on the edge of his own crimes, getting to know people like Drew Rennie and teasing and tormenting that he might know who had done it. Drew quickly sussed that William Watt was innocent – and that the real killer of the Watt ladies and so many others was sitting beside him.

Just as readily, he would spot up-and-coming golfers like Arnold Palmer, Jack Nicklaus or Tony Lima and sign them up to "write" for the *Express* during the week of the Open. Of course, these golfers had no time to write for the *Express* or anyone else during the Open but they could relax at the end of the day and talk to a journalist.

That was where the ghostwriter came into the picture. My colleague Brian Meek, a keen golfer, would absorb the thoughts and feelings of those personalities and write them into an article as if it had been written by the golfer himself. And on three occasions in the early 1960s, with his instinct for what was likely to happen, Drew Rennie had picked the eventual winner of the Open to be "our man" – and there was that man on the last day, holding up the trophy and telling all about it in next day's paper. The *Express* man had done it again . . . and again . . . and again. It was quite uncanny. But that was Drew Rennie.

CHAPTER TEN

MATT BUSBY'S BIG NIGHT

If golf was Brian Meek's special interest, my own was nurtured on the slopes of Pittodrie Park, Aberdeen, where I had stood as a boy from 1942 onwards, cheering on my beloved Dons as they headed towards their first national trophy, the Scottish Cup victory of 1947. Little did I know that I would one day become the club historian, writing the first-ever book about Aberdeen Football Club in 1978, updating it twice and, of course, following the team all the way to European glory in 1983. But more of that later.

So, happily, I was detailed to many a football assignment, as ghostwriter to sporting stars in moments of glory, ranging from Matt Busby, Bill Shankly, Jock Stein, George Best and the great Pelé to my all-time hero of the beautiful game, the incomparable Stanley Matthews of Stoke City, Blackpool and England. In Stanley's case, I caught up with him in his retirement, which was spent in Malta. And there the two of us sauntered through the streets of Valetta, talking over that remarkable career in which he was still playing at the top end of English football when he was fifty. Even as we met, he was turning out for the Post Office team in Malta – at the age of sixty-four! For here was the ultimate thoroughbred of football, the most perfectly balanced player I ever saw, subtle and graceful in his movement and a thorough gentleman into the bargain. The best compliment I can pay him is to say that he was the Fred Astaire of football. The most shocking fact I can reveal is that, by the strict rules of payment in his day, this idol, who would be a multi-millionaire today, was never allowed to earn more than twenty pounds a week.

But my football assignments were never more poignant than in the case of Matt Busby, the former coal miner from Lanarkshire who followed his distinguished career as a footballer by becoming manager of Manchester United. By 1958 he had moulded a brilliant young team which became known as the Busby Babes and had led them towards the semi-final of the European Cup, as it was then known. But returning from the qualifying tie in Belgrade and taking off on the last lap from a snow-bound Munich Airport, their BEA Ambassador plane crashed, killing seven of the Babes and laying Busby himself at death's door.

The nation was stunned. It was one of those occasions, like Kennedy and Princess Diana, where everyone could tell you where they were at that moment. Busby did survive but there were doubts if he would ever be back in harness again.

It took a long time but through the 1960s he gradually rebuilt from the ashes of Munich. Bobby Charlton, a hero of the rescue attempts, was one of the young survivors upon whom he would depend; the newcomers included a brilliant youngster from Northern Ireland called George Best, as well as my fellow Aberdonian, Denis Law. Ten years after the tragedy, Busby and his team were fighting their way once more towards European glory. By May of 1968 they were ready to meet Benfica of Portugal in the European Cup Final at Wembley Stadium.

What a build-up of interest and emotion. As a feature writer I was sent to catch the atmosphere of it all for the *Express*. So I went to Manchester and interviewed everybody from chairman Louis Edwards, the meat king of the north, to Bobby Charlton and George Best and, of course, the great man himself. I trod the turf of Old Trafford and found, yes sadly, the same Denis Law leaning against a goalpost, desolate but resigned to the fact that he would not be sharing in this historic occasion. Injury had ruled out the bespectacled boy from Powis School, Aberdeen, later voted the greatest Scottish footballer of all time, despite the fact that a damaged eye meant he depended almost entirely for his sight on the other one.

But I reckoned there was one more important person to see. Back home, I went to visit Matt Busby's mother, a dainty little lady who had a story to tell. For she was just seventeen when she gave birth to Matt in 1909 and with the Great War just a few years away she would soon be a very young widow. At seventy-six, however, she was now preparing to go to Wembley for the big occasion. This could be her fifty-nine-year-old boy's greatest moment and she was not going to miss it.

I was there that night as Manchester United faced Benfica of Portugal in a match which ended in a 1–1 draw, leading to extra time. Now there were goals by Bobby Charlton, George Best and Brian Kidd – and United had followed the example of Celtic the previous year and become the top team in Europe. The emotion of the night was palpable. From the tragedy of ten years earlier we were now at the moment of triumph. What a night! And it was not over yet.

As I left the stadium I noticed a lost little figure on her own. I looked again and, yes, it was Matt's mother. She was pleased to see a kent face. But she wanted to see her boy in this special hour of his life. So I took her on tow and headed for the main stand. No officialdom was going to stand in the way tonight. This was Matt Busby's mother and now they were summoning him from the dressing room. I'll never forget the scene as I stood back and watched the two of them coming together. Matt took her in his arms and hugged her then they just stood looking at each other, with a tearful silence that spoke volumes. You could tell what was going through their minds. The common thought was of that man who had gone off to the war of 1914, the father who didn't see his boy grow up but would have been so proud to be here tonight.

We all ended up at the Russell Hotel in the centre of London, where the company divided into two. Through in the ballroom the players and their wives and girlfriends and the younger elements were dancing to the music of Joe Loss and his orchestra. The rest of us were in an adjoining private room, where Matt Busby hosted a dinner before rising to say his piece. He was looking back over his life, not least to those ten years ago when he lay at death's door in a Munich hospital, not yet realising how many of his young players were dead. As well as a night of triumph, he said, this was a time to remember, a time for quiet reflection, and he was just glad to be alive, among so many friends. And, of course, there was a special mention for that little lady who brought him up on her own. Beyond that, all words were superfluous. A few weeks later he became Sir Matt Busby.

That involvement with Manchester United gave me the chance to assess at close range the character of its personalities. The brilliance of George Best as a footballer and the likeable nature of the lad were in sharp contrast to his sense of responsibility. You simply couldn't depend on him. I had an appointment to meet him at a house in London, where we would discuss a lucrative *Daily Express* contract for a George Best column. When I arrived he was not there – and his charming wife, Angie, was full of apologies. Yes, he was due home. So we sat till after midnight when, with no sign of him, I went back to my hotel. When I phoned in the morning to see what had happened, a groggy voice told me he had another engagement – and in any case he wasn't obliged to meet me.

"Perhaps, George. But we did have an appointment," I reminded him. So, grudgingly, he would meet me later in his local pub. By then, he was all charm.

As it happened, my photographer had been in Soho that previous evening and was able to give me a first-hand account of George's other engagement. "He was living it up in a nightclub," he said. No surprise there.

Matt Busby tried to nurture this exceptional talent, one of the greatest footballers the world had ever seen, but found it impossible in the end. George Best should have been playing top-class football till well through his thirties but with his addiction to drink he was out of it by his mid-twenties. What a waste.

By contrast, Busby, the working-class lad from Bellshill, Lanarkshire, was a model of good character and conduct. Indeed he was a modest man of such grand stature and personality that you felt he could just as soon have been a High Court judge or a great statesman. I was certainly learning about people.

CHAPTER ELEVEN

A WEEK WITH MUHAMMAD ALI

Much as I enjoyed the sporting connection, those famous names were far from taking over my career. But before leaving that genre, I can hardly ignore an engagement which took me into the company of the man who, stepping far beyond the boundaries of sport, was generally accepted as the best-known name in the world. Not even The Beatles could compete with Cassius Clay, who was not only the greatest boxer the world had ever seen but a personality who caught public imagination as few had ever done. By now he was under the business management of the Black Muslims in America, whose leader, Elijah Muhammad, had persuaded him to dodge the Vietnam War and change his name to Muhammad Ali.

Now, in 1964-65, he had just beaten, not once but twice, the brutish and seemingly indestructible heavyweight champion of the world, Sonny Liston. The whole world was cheering. In Britain the exciting news was that he was coming over here to show us what he could do. One of his exhibition fights would be at Paisley Ice Rink and, as you could guess, the *Daily Express* would be there too. Once again, Drew Rennie fixed the newspaper deal, for a surprisingly modest sum, and once again I was on my way to a week of ghostwriting that proved memorable.

For a base in Glasgow we took him out of the city centre to the suburban Macdonald Hotel at Eastwood Toll, on the south side. And for the duration of his stay I would collect him each day in the *Express* limousine and take him to wherever he wanted to go. Since he himself had taken to versifying ("I float like a butterfly and sting like a bee"), I suggested a visit to Burns Cottage at Alloway, birthplace of our national bard. On the way, I filled him in on the story of Burns and he was intrigued by the modest surroundings, touching the bed where he was born and sitting proudly into the poet's own chair. I wished I had taken a tape recorder because, with typical Ali flourish, he burst into spontaneous verse about Robert Burns. He really was a very clever man, oozing personality.

Wherever we went the crowds were clamouring to see him, chanting his name. When he wanted to change dollars, we headed into the city centre and tried to reach the Royal Bank head office in Buchanan Street but the crowds were already blocking the way and when the police finally cleared a passage, dozens of them were surging into the bank, where pandemonium broke out. An alarmed manager stuck his head out from his office door and came to the rescue of the young lady clerk, who had become so excited that she couldn't handle the money calculation. No wonder, poor girl.

Back at the Macdonald Hotel, we were having lunch one day when the manager was again trying to keep the invading crowds at bay. I happened to notice a young black girl among those being prevented from entering the dining room. As she waved frantically, trying to attract Ali's attention, he suddenly noticed her and called to the manager to let her in. The excited young lass began explaining herself.

"Remember me, Cassius? I'm Jan Scotland. We used to play together when we were kids in Louisville."

"Jan!" he exploded. "Of course I remember you. Pull in a chair." And the two of them went into reminiscences of their childhood in the back streets of Louisville, where they run the famous Kentucky Derby. In boxing quarters he had become known as the Louisville Lip.

"So what are you doing in Glasgow?" he wanted to know.

She was training as a nurse at the Western Infirmary and had told the matron that she knew Cassius Clay, now known as Muhammad Ali. Clearly, the matron had dismissed her nonsense but little Jan persisted, saying she might be able to persuade him to visit the hospital. This too was ridiculed.

"What are we doing this afternoon?" he asked. I knew what was coming. "Well, it's cancelled. We're going to the Western Infirmary."

So we three piled into the limo and headed across the Clyde, past the Kelvin Hall and into the hospital gate. Somehow, word was flashed immediately inside that Muhammad Ali had just entered.

As we slowly emerged from the car, a gathering of staff assembling at the main door now included Matron, who stood open-mouthed and clearly in need of smelling salts. I left it to Jan to do the introductions. After all, this was her big day.

Yes, this really was the best-known man in the world, Muhammad Ali, and he had come to spend some time with the patients. It was all the work of the little nurse from Louisville, who had been as good as her word.

What an afternoon it turned out to be. As the matron conducted him round the children's ward, he signed plaster casts and shadow-boxed and joked with the kids, who couldn't believe what was happening. And when it was time to leave, he took his farewells, gave his old playmate a huge hug and, as we drove off, he winked and said, "That will do little Jan's career no harm at all." Yes, that was Muhammad Ali.

On the big night at Paisley he fought bouts with two other great heavyweight boxers, Cody Jones and Jimmy Ellis, himself a future world champion.

There is a curious postscript to this story. I accompanied the big man everywhere, except, of course, to his bedroom. But there was much discussion going on in that room during the week. By coincidence, it was the week when America's worst race rioting in twenty years broke out in the mainly black Watts area of Los Angeles. It was sparked off when a police patrol arrested a black man for drunk driving. Within hours, the whole area was in flames, with snipers shooting at the police and firemen trying to tackle a thousand outbreaks. By the time the mayhem had died down twenty-eight people, including children, were dead and around 700 injured, policemen and firemen among them.

I had it on good authority that the phone calls buzzing between a bedroom at the Macdonald Hotel, Glasgow, and the Watts district of Los Angeles were not without guidance to the Black Muslims involved in the riots. None of that, of course, had anything to do with Ali himself but it was the last I saw of the great man for the next thirty years. Within that time he reached the point when he should have been retiring, so well protected by his unique skills that his body was virtually undamaged. Instead, however, it seems that little remained of the money which should have seen him into affluent retirement. He had left all that to his mentors. So he had to keep on fighting into years in which he was not so well able to protect himself. That was when the damage was done.

As his friend Howard L. Bingham later wrote: "I have watched while some have taken advantage of the innocence and kindness Muhammad offered. I watched this with hurts in my heart, powerless to stop their actions."

As we all know, he then fell victim to Parkinson's Syndrome, a variation of Parkinson's Disease, which comes as a result of external damage. His decline was a pathetic sight, as I discovered on the only other occasion we met up. It happened in the mid-1990s when the same Howard L. Bingham, a brilliant photographer, produced a pictorial book on the great man's life. Ali accompanied him on a promotional visit to Glasgow, where they would sign copies at Waterstone's bookshop in the city centre. Once again, crowds blocked the street and besieged the shop, in scenes reminiscent of 1965. Still the hero but unable to write, Ali rubber-stamped his name as the adoring crowds filed past. I stood at a distance, observing the blank look of the man who had once electrified the world.

In my hand was the scrapbook I had kept for all those years. But should I intrude on this sad little scene and risk embarrassment? I took a chance. Without a word, I laid my scrapbook in front of him and slowly turned the pages. There we were in that *Express* limousine of thirty years ago. The pictures now showed him playfully punching me on the jaw. Most memorably, he was seated in the editor's chair at the *Daily Express* office in Albion Street, hilariously conducting the daily news conference.

Increasingly engrossed in what he was seeing, Ali studied the pictures, looked up at me and down at the scrapbook. Life came back into his eyes, for this was a reminder of the great days, a time long gone but now . . . Finally he jumped to his feet, took my head into his embrace – and then began to cry like a baby. He was not alone.

CHAPTER TWELVE

SEEKING CHARLIE CHAPLIN

If Muhammad Ali was the best-known name in the world, there is another interesting fact that has been unearthed by anthropologists. Even today, they say, there are remote pockets of primitive people in the world to whom the names of prominent figures of the past are totally unknown. Astonishingly, they reckoned there were only two names in all history which could be said to have gained recognition from every single soul on earth. Muhammad Ali was one. The other was Charlie Chaplin.

Of course, I knew nothing of that when I set my heart on meeting the great little comic in the 1960s. From a seat in the stalls of the Peterhead Playhouse in the 1930s I had merely warmed to the little tramp like every other child in the world and now, as a journalist, I would certainly have him on my list of potential interviewees. But how easy would that be, considering Chaplin had been hounded out of his adopted land by the notorious "McCarthy witch-hunt" of the 1950s, when Senator Joseph McCarthy chaired a campaign to expel from America anyone with a left-wing view that might pass for communism? Ridiculously, as with many other celebrities, Chaplin was deemed to be in that category and had to bid Hollywood goodbye, relocating himself and family at Vevey in Switzerland – upset with the media and vowing he would never give another interview.

With little hope of success, I just persevered by the various methods that journalists employ to seek out their interviewees. It began in 1964 and I was still in pursuit six years later. But all my approaches had come to nothing. I knew that Chaplin occasionally made very private visits to Scotland, being driven in his limousine up the west coast, with a short stay in Nairn and then disappearing down the east coast before anyone knew he was here.

In August 1970, however, I received a tip-off that he had a booking at the Tor-Na-Coille Hotel in Banchory, near Aberdeen, a fact which they naturally refused to confirm. So I booked myself a room and sat reading in the foyer, day after day, in the hope that one of these days his limousine would appear at the door. And one day it did.

Out stepped the elderly Charlie with his much younger wife, Oona, daughter of American playwright Eugene O'Neill. I watched them checking in but made no move till after dinner, during which I observed with interest the demeanour of the Hollywood legend. From his films, I remembered the way he used to tilt his head and smile when wooing the ladies and was intrigued to see that he used that same mannerism to his wife.

When dinner was over I now had to make my pitch. Because of his age I made my approach to Oona, explaining that this was not a witch-hunt but merely a desire to write about a childhood hero. She reminded me of his antipathy to journalists and, in any case, they were leaving just after breakfast and there wouldn't be much time. But she would ask him and bring his answer in the morning. I was down in good time, when she appeared with the news. No, he would not be changing his mind.

With people like that, if there was an autobiography, I had found they were invariably impressed if you brought a copy. With nothing to lose, I approached Charlie himself and said, "Mr Chaplin, I'm sorry you won't talk to me. I've been trying to see you for six years – so near and yet so far – but will you at least sign my copy of your book?"

Oh, he would do that. So I sat him down on a comfortable sofa. Then I asked if he would sign autographs for my three sons. Yes, he would do that too. So I handed him my notebook, which was no use to me now, and was intrigued to see that he was not only signing his name but drawing for each of my boys a sketch of himself – the bowler hat, moustache, baggy breeks and cane.

While he sketched, I took the opportunity to talk to him, dropping in the odd question and finding, to my surprise, that I was getting answers. In those days I was blessed with a phenomenal memory and knew that, if I could get to a typewriter, I would be able to give a reasonable account of our conversation. I then reminded him that, in the early part of the century, he had appeared at the old Tivoli Theatre in Aberdeen. Yes, he remembered. He was an unknown teenager in the chorus of the famous Fred Karno Troupe. There was someone else in that chorus that might interest me, Stan Laurel of Laurel and Hardy.

"That was before Stan and I went off to America," he said. Charlie Chaplin was speaking to me!

"Well, the old Tivoli is still there," I said, "now a bingo hall but still looking exactly the same as when you left it all those years ago. How would you like to see it on your way through Aberdeen today?"

"Yes I'd quite like that," he said. "Just speak to the chauffeur."

The first thing I did was phone the *Daily Express* photographer in Aberdeen. "Get down to the Tivoli, Ron. I'll be there in half an hour with Charlie Chaplin." I wasn't sure if he had fainted but he was there when we arrived.

On our way to Aberdeen, Charlie began to open up. After all those years of avoiding the press, I think he sensed that there was no harm in a chap like me. When we arrived in Guild Street on a fine summer day there were few people to be seen. But within minutes, word got round that Charlie Chaplin was here – and they seemed to appear in droves from nowhere. At first they were not sure if this old man was really him. But he patted children on the head and soon they were convinced, queueing up as he signed their bits of paper.

The crowd was still growing, to the point that we had to usher the frail old Charlie into his limousine and wave him off. I shook his hand and knew that I had come as near as anyone to achieving that elusive interview.

That experience taught me once again the power of perseverance.

Try, try, try again. At close quarters I tried to piece together the remarkable life story of this poor little lad from the slums of London who came from nowhere to become the greatest comic the world had seen. His alcoholic father died when Charlie was young and he was left to the mercy of a mother who was mentally unstable. I remembered in particular his imitation of another little man with a funny moustache whose name was Adolf Hitler, born in the same year as Chaplin. It was fortunate for Charlie that Winston Churchill had bluffed our way out of an invasion by German troops in 1940 because Hitler was so infuriated by Chaplin's impersonation in his recent film, *The Great Dictator*, that he added his name to the death list which would have followed a victory over Britain.

CHAPTER THIRTEEN

GOOD OLD WINNIE!

Fascination with extraordinary people has dominated the whole length of my career. What makes them different from the rest of us? Even coming face to face with Winston Churchill left me with the dilemma of fitting a legend into the physical frame of that apparently ordinary human being.

I was walking down a long, deserted corridor in the House of Commons one day when I saw this elderly figure coming towards me. I slowed my pace to take it all in, for this was a rich moment, with no one else in sight. This man who would rank with the all-time greats of history could have passed unnoticed if I had not known it was Churchill.

He smiled, said, "Good afternoon" and passed on his way.

I said, "Good afternoon," then turned to watch the progress of the man who had seemed, in my boyhood, to be all that stood between me and Hitler. He would be forever my hero. And I had had a moment of his courtesy.

When he died in 1965 I stood by his coffin as he lay in state in the Great Hall of Westminster, that magnificent symbol of so much history that he himself had helped to create. I wouldn't have missed this moment, and here is an excerpt of what I wrote for the *Daily Express* next day:

From the steps that lead down to the hall, we beheld a scene that was breath-taking in its simplicity. Beneath the amber rafters where they held the trials of William Wallace and Guy Fawkes the coffin of Sir Winston lies upon a bier, three steps high on a crimson dais.

It is covered by the Union Jack and at the corners four candles flicker away the hours. At the corners, too, stand soldiers in full ceremonial dress, heads bowed and still as the swords they rest upon.

Slowly and reverently we begin to flock past, old and young, wistful men with the limp of war and medals jangling on their chests; Beatniks who were not even born; those who suffered in the Blitz and children who were grasping at the reality of history.

Opposite the coffin we pause in the dim light, to glance at the cross above his head and the insignia of Knight of the Garter and to commune, each with himself.

My own thoughts went back to a childhood which felt safe only because the boom of Churchill protected me from Hitler. I remembered the cheers of victory as he drove the length of Union Street, Aberdeen, at the end of the war, when he came to receive the freedom of the city. I managed to run alongside his slow-moving car, reaching out the boyhood hand of gratitude to touch him.

Now the cheers have died away and here we stand, in silent thanks, seeking to absorb a precious moment. It is hard to encompass greatness within the shell of a mortal body. But here we gaze upon the remains of history and suddenly the spirit of wartime is with us again. Cynicism perishes. Men and women weep unashamedly.

The blood and the sweat and the toil are over, only the tears remain – tears of sorrow at the departure, tears of joy for the memory and inspiration of an incredible life.

Above, Big Ben strikes out the hour, echoing eerily through the Parliament buildings. And a policeman says, "Move along, please."

The Guard is changed and the people file past at the rate of 4,000 every hour. At the far end they linger, unwilling to let him go, and turning back for a last glimpse of the man who was their saviour.

No more the booming voice and stirring word, the impish

smile and the big cigar. No more the inspiration of the man who said it was the British people, not he, who were the lion.

Today, in this great Hall of Westminster, the lion stalks quietly by. But the roar is gone forever.

CHAPTER FOURTEEN

AN INVITATION FROM PAUL GETTY

Still in pursuit of extraordinary people, I decided one day that I would like to interview the richest man in the world. At that time the distinction fell to Paul Getty, the American oil billionaire who chose to live in England, on an estate in Surrey called Sutton Place, which once belonged to the Duke of Sutherland. Even then, before the modern strangulation called security, it was not always easy to reach such people. So often they were surrounded by "protectors", and that was the barrier I encountered as I set out to meet Mr Getty.

On the initial call I was greeted politely by a Mr Wallace, who said Mr Getty was busy but if I called in another month he would see what could be done. I was in no hurry. Thus began a ritual of monthly calls, which I observed obediently until it stretched to eighteen, with different reasons why I could not see Mr Getty. But sometimes the gods come on your side. On the next call I asked once more to be put through to Mr Wallace. When the extension answered I said, "Is that you, Mr Wallace?"

"Mr Wallace? No," said the voice, "this is Mr Getty speaking."

"Hello there, Mr Getty!" I exploded. "I've been trying to contact you for eighteen months but can never get past your Mr Wallace." I explained my purpose – to discuss his own fascinating life but also to talk about North Sea in which he had made an initial investment of £100 million.

"You mean you have been trying to get through to me for eighteen months? Well, that's ridiculous. You call Mr Wallace and tell him to get you the first appointment in my diary."

I thanked him and blessed the telephone girl who had put me

through to the wrong extension. This time she made no such mistake.

"Ah, Mr Webster," he said. "Now I'm sorry . . . "

"No need to be sorry this time, Mr Wallace," I interrupted. "You get me the first appointment in Mr Getty's diary – on Mr Getty's instructions!" When he heard the story, there was a clatter at the other end of the phone. I could only assume that he had had a seizure.

More importantly, I was at Sutton Place within a week, driving in through the electric gates, past the guard dogs (and two lions!) and round to the front of the magnificent mansion. I did a rough calculation that Paul Getty's front lawn, which stretched like the gardens of Versailles, was fifteen times the length of Pittodrie Park.

Into the house, there were minders at every bend till I was shown into a small, drab room in which Paul Getty was sat with his shoe and sock off and in mortal agony with some goutish ailment of the big toe, from which he could find no relief. I thought, for the richest man in the world, there must be a moral in that story somewhere. As for the man himself, with a reputation as a serial womaniser and a miser, who allegedly installed a payphone for his houseguests, I took him as I found him. From his early twenties in Oklahoma he had developed a remarkable talent for sensing major oil fields, even where the so-called experts said there was none. He ran his hundred companies by his own judgement alone and developed into the colourful entrepreneur of the oil industry.

With that curious curse of the rich, however, Paul Getty was predeceased by two of his sons and had recently faced a ransom demand from the kidnappers of his grandson, Paul Getty III. With the ransom paid, the boy was returned – minus one of his ears, which had previously arrived by parcel post! All that, plus five divorces. On the personal level I found him a deeply intelligent and cultured man, Oxford-educated and talking in that measured way of great minds. They think before they speak and come away with the kind of thoughts that offer a cue to my original question: What makes them different from the rest of us? Genius is very hard to define.

CHAPTER FIFTEEN

THE GENIUS OF BARNES WALLIS

When I left the grandeur of Paul Getty's estate, I was heading across Surrey for another appointment on that very same day – at a modest little cottage in the village of Effingham. Unlike the richest man in the world, the gentleman who greeted me at the cottage door had gained little material wealth in his lifetime but ranked nevertheless as one of the truly great figures of the twentieth century. In Fleet Street I had been told that Barnes Wallis, creator of the "Dam Busters" of World War II and so much else, was a "difficult man," harbouring a grievance that he had had to struggle so hard to have his inventions recognised. But that turned out to be more of a reflection on the journalists who interviewed him than on the man himself. There is a way of speaking to people.

As we settled to a mug of coffee at his kitchen table I soon realised that this gentle, white-haired Victorian was very different from what I had been told. Of course, by their very nature, inventors were obliged to convince the sceptics that this was not just another crackpot idea. It was a useful incentive to making sure that it worked, and Barnes Wallis accepted that. So we talked through his remarkable career, dating back to the end of the nineteenth century when, as a young lad, he had filed past the coffin of William Ewart Gladstone as it lay in state at Westminster Abbey. Happily he had lived long enough to see the first man landing on the moon

Without an academic background, he merely trained as a practical engineer before letting loose his inventive genius on an unsuspecting world. Rigid airships had become an exciting form of transport and Barnes Wallis turned his mind to their design. The result was the famous R80, built before the First World War and hailed as the most beautiful airship ever seen. (He believed that ugliness was bad engineering.) While working for Vickers Aviation at Weybridge he went on to design the R100, the most successful of all airships, which had its maiden flight in 1929 and then made a memorable crossing of the Atlantic. It was all very exciting. But enthusiasm for airships suddenly evaporated when the R101 crashed on its maiden voyage, with massive casualties. It was not designed by Barnes Wallis.

As he poured another cup of coffee, we turned to more mundane matters, like our mutual affliction with migraine headaches, before heading up to his attic. Here was a revelation. Around the walls were pictures of his inventions – virtually the history of aviation. After airships, he had turned his gift to a wide range of subjects, though, as a Christian with pacifist tendencies, he had never associated himself with weapons of war. But he was also fiercely patriotic and therefore had no qualms about engaging in the battle against Hitler.

As well as joining the much-maligned Home Guard of *Dad's Army* fame, he was soon designing the Wellesley and Wellington bombers and those powerful explosives which destroyed the German warship, the *Tirpitz*, and the sites of the dreaded V-rockets. But his best was yet to come – when he was called to a task that would eventually spread his fame around the world. Much of Hitler's war effort was centred on the Ruhr Valley, with its factories, mines and railways, all so well defended as to make a bombing attack difficult. Churchill turned to the great inventor himself and Barnes Wallis came up with the only likely answer. With planes flying as low as possible to avoid the protective netting, he would try to perfect a bouncing bomb that would skip over the surface of the adjoining dams, like a pebble on water, seeking to burst the dam walls and flood the Ruhr Valley.

So it was that on 17 May 1943 the "Dam Busters," led by Squadron-Leader Guy Gibson, set out for Germany. It was a hazardous operation with no guarantee of success. Flying at a height of only sixty feet above the water, Gibson and his men did indeed burst those walls, releasing 300 million tons of water, which cascaded down that valley, destroying German factories over a stretch of fifty miles. That operation was claimed to have shortened the duration of the Second World War.

And there I was, alone in his attic with this warm and kindly Victorian figure, studying his face and marvelling that, within the head before me now lay that quality of genius for which once again there was no explanation. On his drawing board lay plans for the next idea which, he apologised, had to remain a secret. I later discovered that he was preparing an aeroplane that would rise above the atmosphere and fly to Australia and back well within a day.

As for the "Dam Buster" raid, there was a price to pay for its success. Apart from German casualties, fifty-three of the 133 British airmen were killed, a fact which bore so heavily on Barnes Wallis that he said if he had known what was going to happen he would not have gone ahead with it.

He also told me of another strange happening. In all the German bombing of Britain, from Clydebank to Coventry and the blitz which wreaked havoc on the London area, only one bomb fell on the well-known town of Epsom, best known as the venue of the Derby. That one bomb claimed only two victims – the sister and brother-in-law of Barnes Wallis's wife, Molly. The fates had granted the Monster of Munich an ill-deserved stroke of revenge.

The full story of the Dam Buster raid came more graphically to public attention in 1954 when it was made into a much-acclaimed British film under the same name, with Barnes Wallis portrayed by Michael Redgrave and Guy Gibson by Richard Todd, two of the leading actors of their day. It was written by that great novelist and playwright R.C. Sheriff, who had already given us memorable plays like *Journey's End* and films which included *Goodbye Mr Chips* and *The Four Feathers*. The music was written by that equally distinguished Englishman, composer Eric Coates, whose haunting theme tune remains fresh and popular to this day. But therein lies another tale, which should have been exposed a long time ago.

A year after the *Dam Busters* came to the cinema in 1954 Hollywood produced a Doris Day musical called *Love Me or Leave Me* in which the delectable Doris sang a song called "I'll Never Stop Loving You", with lyrics by Sammy Cahn and music allegedly by Nicholas Brodszky. It was a beautiful song. And no wonder, for the tune was copied note for note from the *Dam Busters* theme tune, the work of Eric Coates. Of course, composers have been known to copy musical phrases from one another but this was the most blatant case of plagiarism. The "coincidence" was later raised on his radio programme by Benny Green, who nevertheless refused to take sides and seemed quite happy to leave it as a puzzle: Who copied who?

When I challenged him to investigate the story properly, the mischievous Benny chickened out. So I pursued it myself. For a start, the *Dam Busters* film came a year earlier, though that alone would not necessarily have proved the point. So what else did I discover? When Eric Coates was asked to provide music for the 1954 film he remembered a composition he had written as far back as 1943, in tribute to Field Marshal Montgomery and his Eighth Army for their victory at the Battle of El Alamein.

In those wartime conditions, the tune had never been published and had little exposure at the time. But it had that rousing, patriotic feeling that, with some minor refinements, would surely be as appropriate for the *Dam Busters* as it was for El Alamein. And that is what happened.

So why did Eric Coates not raise hell? By the time the Hollywood film appeared, sadly, he was in the last year of his life. That apart, he was such a splendid English gentleman that I suspect he would not have relished a public wrangle with a streetwise New Yorker like Sammy Cahn.

The final twist to this shocking tale is that Messrs Cahn and Brodszky were nominated for an Oscar – specifically for their song, "I'll Never Stop Loving You". I hope they at least had the grace to blush.

CHAPTER SIXTEEN

HEADING FOR THE BIG APPLE

My native village of Maud in Aberdeenshire had always seemed a long way from the skyscrapers of Manhattan but I had dreamed of that destination since boyhood. The man who inspired the dream was surely Bertie Forbes, the first millionaire we had ever seen in my corner of Buchan and at whose feet I sat in the 1930s, listening to his graphic description of life in New York. By then, Bertie had become the friend or acquaintance of men like John D. Rockefeller, founder of Esso, Frank Woolworth of "Woolies" fame and the fellow Scot he called "Wee Andy", who turned out to be none other than Andrew Carnegie! For all that, the man he idolised most was still his old dominie in the parish of New Deer, Gavin Greig, who, in the great Scottish education system of its day, was turning out fourteen-year-olds not only with a sound knowledge of all the basics but with the addition of Latin and Greek and an appetite for the great wide world beyond.

One of the ten poor children of a country tailor, Bertie was a classmate of the headmaster's daughter, Edith Greig, the first of nine children to be born and the last to die. She was also my grandmother. Telling little Bertie what he didn't know – that he had a gift for essay-writing – Gavin Greig was guiding him towards journalism, first to the *Peterhead Sentinel* in 1894, at the beginning of a journey which would take him to the heights of that profession. From there he made his mark with the *Dundee Courier* before seeking the adventure of a foreign land.

That destination was South Africa, much in the news with the Boer War, and there he arrived in time to encounter such famous war correspondents as Winston Churchill, who was now heading home to a political career, and Edgar Wallace, the thriller writer who had decided to remain in Johannesburg and revive the ailing Rand *Daily Mail*. Wallace needed an able dogsbody and who should turn up out of the blue but a little butterball of a lad with an Aberdeenshire accent called Bertie Forbes. The timing was perfect.

Bertie would also caddie for entrepreneurs on the golf courses of Johannesburg, where he picked up useful information about the financial world, an area which began to fascinate him. However, if this was to be his speciality, there was only one place to be.

In 1904 he wrote a letter to my family, saying he was coming home to Scotland but only as a stopover on his way to New York. He arrived there, aged twenty-four, without contacts, and finding it difficult to show that he was not some Scottish country bumpkin but a budding journalist with something to offer. When the editor of the New York *Journal of Commerce* asked why he should employ someone who didn't know the difference between Wall Street and Broadway, little Bertie had an answer: "Because, sir, I'll work for nothing."

That took a trick. He was hired at a meagre $15 a week but was soon proving his worth with articles that would revolutionise business journalism in America. His strength was to expose financial dealings that were secretly withheld from the readers in those days – inside information that could move the money markets. There was a storm of complaints to his employers but Wall Street sat up and took notice. This Scottish upstart was telling it as it was. Soon his daily columns were being syndicated around the United States, sometimes under different pen names. William Randolph Hearst, the biggest media mogul the world had seen until Rupert Murdoch, was looking for a top financial writer.

He narrowed his search to two men, both of whom turned out to be Bertie Forbes! He told me later that Hearst had asked him to name his own salary, which put him in a quandary. Throwing caution to the wind, however, he asked for $20,000 a year, a colossal figure in 1912. Hearst told him much later that he had been prepared to pay a lot more but calculated that a Scotsman would tend to under-value himself!

By 1917, Bertie had become such a national figure that he launched his own business magazine, the very first of its kind. *Forbes* magazine became the bible of the financial world, with Bertie hailed as the great humaniser of American business. It survives to this day, now with the third generation of his family, but still providing that inside information and pinpointing the affairs of the world's richest people.

Every two years, he came home to Aberdeenshire to entertain the whole parish to what became known as Bertie's Picnic. It was a fabulous event where, in a field beside his old school, he resumed friendships as if he had never been away.

For my own family, the descendants of Gavin Greig, there was a special place in his affections, remembering what his old dominie had done to set him on the right track. He would come to our house in Maud to play cards with my parents and other friends. It was either poker or solo.

In the pre-war days, he and his entourage stayed at the fashionable Cruden Bay Hotel, a smaller version of Gleneagles Hotel, both of which were owned by the railway companies. Considering what political vandalism was later committed when the branch-lines of Britain were closed forever, it is heart-warming to remember that in those far-off days the well-established Buchan Line from Aberdeen to Peterhead and Fraserburgh was given a branch of its own, from Ellon to Cruden Bay, for the main purpose of serving that magnificent hotel.

Cruden Bay was a village with several claims to fame. Apart from its fabulous hotel and golf course, it had once been visited by Bram Stoker, the Irish writer who so fell in love with the place that he took a cottage there and came back year after year. The story goes that it was while walking along the beach that he set eyes on the ancient Slains Castle and found the inspiration for his most famous tale of *Dracula*.

This corner was also the ancestral home of Rupert Murdoch, whose grandfather, the Rev. Patrick Murdoch, the local Free Kirk minister at the nearby village of Hatton, uprooted the entire family and took them off to Australia. Rupert's great-grandfather had also been minister at Rosehearty. In more recent times, Cruden Bay had become the arrival point for the main pipeline bringing North Sea oil to Scotland.

It was during those visits of the 1930s that Bertie Forbes took an interest in my own future and began to fire my interest in journalism. There I sat, enthralled, listening to his tales of the city that never sleeps – and dreaming that one day I might see New York.

So Bertie was much in my thoughts that summer day in the mid-1960s when I flew from Glasgow to Southampton, took a taxi to the dockland and stood gazing in disbelief at the size and scope of the old *Queen Mary*, built at John Brown's of Clydebank, launched in 1934, and still perhaps the greatest ship that ever sailed the seas. At last, I would step on board the old lady, en route to the New World. Yes, the day had arrived. From Maud to Manhattan, I was on my way.

As we sailed down the Solent and out into the Atlantic, I was going to absorb every moment of this voyage. For ships like the *Queen Mary* were now under threat from the jet aeroplane, which could take you to New York in a few hours. The world was in a hurry.

For my first visit to the United States, however, I was determined to get there on a day-by-day basis, retaining that sense of adventure which would finally deliver me to the magic of the Manhattan skyline. The purpose of my journey was to work for a spell in the New York office of the *Daily Express*. Happily, among all the other plans, that would enable me to take in the fiftieth anniversary of *Forbes* magazine, which would fall on 15 September 1967.

The Forbes building on Fifth Avenue had once been the home of Macmillan the publishers, to which Margaret Mitchell had delivered the manuscript of *Gone With the Wind* in 1936. Now it belonged to the Forbes family but, sadly, there would be no Bertie to greet me. In May of 1954 the night watchman, doing his rounds, was surprised to see a light still showing in the boss's office. As he tapped on the door there was no response. Inside, he found Bertie on the floor, dead as could be. Appropriately in his last moment, he was still clutching a pen in his hand. He was seventy-four.

Bertie had married a stately beauty called Adelaide Stevenson, with whom he had five sons. As the eldest, Bruce succeeded his father and gained a majority holding in what remained a family business. But Bruce died of cancer in his forties, recalling another tragedy in which, as a teenager in 1933, he was driving his first motor car and had to swerve to avoid another vehicle. His passenger was the second son, his brother Duncan, who died instantly in the crash. (Bruce felt his mother never forgave him for the accident.)

Succession therefore fell to the third son, Malcolm, who never imagined what the fates would deliver. He had been through the Second World War, decorated for his bravery at the Normandy landings of 1944, when he was also seriously wounded. Back home, he became a leading light in the Republican Party, the man who suggested that they should enlist Dwight D. Eisenhower, their wartime hero, as candidate for the Presidential campaign of 1952. Eisenhower was still Supreme Allied Commander of Nato forces and Malcolm was given the task of flying to Paris to persuade him towards politics. The man who became known as 'Ike' did indeed become President of the United States for the next eight years.

Malcolm's own star was also rising, hailed as the Republican's answer to the up-and-coming Democrat, John F. Kennedy, who was two years his senior. As a first step towards the White House, he would stand for the Governorship of New Jersey. But a decision to build his famous yacht, *The Highlander*, in Holland was used against him when there were shipyards in New Jersey to think about. As he later joked, "I was edged out by a landslide!" It was Kennedy who went on to succeed Eisenhower.

At least Malcolm was now available to lead the Forbes empire, which he did in spectacular fashion, taking it beyond the realms of publishing and into other ventures, like buying large tracts of America and selling them off in ten-acre lots. His rising fortunes were not at all hindered by his flamboyant personality, which turned him into a record-breaking hot-air balloonist, as well as the owner of eighty-eight Harley-Davidson motorbikes.

So, as the *Queen Mary* ploughed her way towards the New World, my sense of anticipation was mounting by the day. We crossed over with her sister ship, the *Queen Elizabeth*, exchanging waves with the passengers, and then came an eerie moment that Sunday morning when the bells peeled out across the parish of the Atlantic, calling us to worship. By evening, we dined in great style, keeping to the same tables with some interesting people. Each night, an elderly duchess kept pressing me to join her at the bingo table, an invitation I steadfastly refused, with the promise that I would be there in time for the dancing.

On our last night, however, she was so insistent that I reluctantly agreed to sample my first-ever game of bingo. There she sat, giving instructions on how to play this silly game, in which you score off the numbers as they are called. I was down to my last number. "If that one is called you must get up and shout 'Bingo!'" she told me.

Dear God! It happened. As I rose like an idiot, shouting "Bingo!" two trumpeters arrived to escort me to the dais. I had won the week's accumulated jackpot of 160 dollars, a lot of money in the '60s.

Among those cheering me on my way was Tom Stoppard, the playwright, heading for the Broadway premiere of his famous play, "Rosencrantz and Guildenstern Are Dead." When he heard it was my very first game of bingo, he shook his head: "And they say there is no God!"

Well, as you can imagine, the rest of the night was champagne, till I withdrew for a few hours of sleep before the big moment. By five o'clock that morning I was up on the bow of the *Queen Mary*, my bleary eyes scanning the dark horizon to catch that very first glimpse of America. (I'm sentimental about things like that!)

A big American leaning on the railing, complete with an equally big cigar, was ready for my question: "Excuse me . . . that twinkling light in the distance . . . could that be America?"

"Yeah, man, it sure is," he drawled. "That's the lights of South Brooklyn."

I must take in every moment of this. We sailed under the Verrazano Bridge, with the Statue of Liberty appearing on the left. And suddenly, out of the morning mist, came the outline of the Manhattan skyline, so near and yet so silent. Quite magical. It was H. G. Wells who said of that view that New York looked not so much a city as a series of boxes from which a city might be unwrapped.

As the *Mary* edged her way round the foot of Manhattan and into the Hudson River on the west side, I still could not believe the silence of such a city. It was only when she edged into her berth that the cacophony broke suddenly upon us. Yes, this was New York, all right. The farewells over, I headed down the gangway, taking special note of that moment when I placed a foot on the United States of America for the first time.

Stepping into my first yellow cab, I said, "Can you take me to the Tudor Hotel, please?"

"The what hotel?" came the rasping voice that could have been Damon Runyon himself.

"The Tudor Hotel – in 42nd Street," I tried to clarify in my best English.

" There ain't no Tyouder Hotel in New York. Can you spell it?"

"Yes – T-u-d-o-r."

"Oh hell, man, you mean the Tooder Hotel!"

As Churchill said: "Britain and America – two countries divided by a common language!"

So here I was, on my first visit to America, settling in to the "Tooder Hotel" and getting to know my way around the *Express* office, further along 42nd Street. The only familiar face was that of Harry Benson from Glasgow, a wonderfully charismatic guy, as well as a world-class photographer.

On one of my first outings, I followed Harry to the United Nations building on First Avenue, pursuing the Greek actress Melina Mercouri, who was running to make contact with King Constantine of Greece, recently overthrown in a military coup and now about to meet U-Thant, Secretary-General of the UN. In that scramble of reporters and photographers, I had my first taste of daily journalism in New York.

Of an evening I would drop in for a drink with Harry and Gigi in their east-side apartment, not far from First Avenue. Bobby Kennedy lived round the corner and was on such familiar terms with Harry as to call by their apartment on occasion. Little did we realise what lay in store for the man within a few months. With his brother assassinated in 1963 and succeeded by Lyndon B. Johnston, Bobby made a late decision to stand for President in 1968 and arrived in Los Angeles to make an important campaign speech at the Ambassador Hotel. Harry Benson was there, as usual on big stories like this, anticipating that, for security reasons, Kennedy would eventually leave the hotel via the kitchens. Harry's instincts were good.

As Kennedy took his final applause, Harry was already in the kitchen, poised for the entourage as it approached. He raised his camera for an exclusive shot . . . when suddenly there was a shot of another kind. As Bobby Kennedy dropped to the floor, Harry was taking a very different picture. A Jordanian immigrant, Sirhan Sirhan, had fatally wounded the man who hoped to be President. The picture which sticks in the memory is that of Bobby Kennedy's wife, Ethel, holding up her hand in distress, with her dying husband to be seen through her outstretched fingers. It was the picture that went round the world. Needless to say, it was Harry's picture.

For a very different reason, I already knew of the Ambassador Hotel in Los Angeles. If I can add a lighter note at the end of this tragedy, it is just to say that the golf professional at the hotel was a man I had already met, called Emmons Millar – who was brought up by his granny in my native village of Maud! We're everywhere.

So, picking up the vibrations of America, I was now interviewing some of those I wanted to meet. Back home, I had once written in appreciation of his music to Richard Rodgers, who, with his lyricist Oscar Hammerstein II, had given us those great musicals, from *Oklahoma*, *Carousel* and *South Pacific* to *The King and I* and, of course, *The Sound of Music*. In that letter I had emphasised the universal appeal of his music, saying that the wind which swept down the plains of Oklahoma blew just as surely in the far corners of Aberdeenshire, where my mother went about her work in the farmhouse "whistling a happy tune" and spinning around to his *Carousel* waltz. To my delight, Rodgers not only replied but sent a parcel of books, detailing everything he had ever written. So when it came to my stay in New York, there was no difficulty in securing the interview.

Climbing to that fourth-floor apartment in Madison Avenue I was now meeting the man himself who sat behind a desk, rather like a dapper little businessman. His suite was well appointed, with modern paintings on the wall, typically mid-Manhattan, including the splendid Steinway grand piano in the corner. He was quiet and courteous but with little to suggest that he was one of the great composers of the twentieth century. Nor did his working methods live up to my romantic image.

"No, I am not the kind of composer who wakes up in the middle of the night with an idea and springs out of bed to put it down on paper before it disappears," he told me.

As we discussed his famous musicals he explained that he simply waited for Hammerstein to give him the story. Then they would go through it, scene by scene, to establish the mood and rhythm required for each one.

"I then go away and think about it," he said. "I have to sit down and concentrate – and work. And by the time I go to the piano, the tunes are already in my head. I am now ready to play."

It sounded all so clinical but, of course, it made good practical sense. I found myself studying the face of Richard Rodgers, searching again for the emotion and inspiration I thought essential for a man of that genius.

His tunes were running through my head: "Blue Moon", "People Will Say We're in Love", "Some Enchanted Evening", "This Nearly Was Mine", "If I Loved You", "Climb Every Mountain", "Edelweiss" and that international anthem of football, "You'll Never Walk Alone". These distinctive melodies and dozens more had come from within the heart and mind of the modest little man before me. Once again, it was hard to believe.

Having lived with a stammer for so long, I detected a difficulty in his speech which, he then calmly explained, was caused by a cancer of the jaw. He added, "I have not kept it a secret but that was twelve years ago and I had a check-up yesterday. I'm all right." That explained much of his demeanour.

We spoke of his great partnership with that master of words, Lorenz Hart, a devotee of Shakespeare by the time he was seven but a flawed genius in adulthood, a heavy drinker known to disappear on an opening night. Together they had written such shows as *Pal Joey* with songs like "Bewitched, Bothered and Bewildered", and "The Boys from Syracuse" ("Falling in Love With Love" and so much more). But Hart was dead by the time he was forty-eight, having lived just long enough to see Rodgers teaming up with the more reliable Oscar Hammerstein for their highly successful *Oklahoma* in 1943 – and no doubt reflecting on what he himself had just lost.

Hammerstein had come from a partnership with another master of music, Jerome Kern, with whom he had produced the groundbreaking *Show Boat* in 1927. Thus came the familiar sound of "Rodgers and Hammerstein" that would continue till the latter's death in 1960. When I met Richard Rodgers he was sixty-five but in his remaining years he failed to find another suitable lyricist. Even Stephen Sondheim didn't fit the bill.

As we shook hands I felt I was leaving a rather complex, lonesome but thoroughly nice man. My last glance was at the Steinway grand.

Forty years later I came to know his daughter, Mary Rodgers, who lived in an apartment overlooking Central Park, just a few blocks from the Dakota Building, where John Lennon was assassinated. As I entered her drawing room the first thing I noticed was a Steinway grand. Yes, it was her father's one from all those years ago; and yes, I could run my fingers over those ivories from which so many wonderful melodies had been created.

I raised the question of her father's composing methods, to which she added a few surprising memories from her childhood.

"If we heard him in the music room, we knew to stay out, because he was doing one thing only – he was composing. I never once heard him play the piano for his own or anyone else's pleasure," Mary revealed. Very strange.

"By coincidence, I went to school with Irving Berlin's daughters and I would come home and ask my mother: 'Who is the better composer, Mum – Irving Berlin or my dad?'" There had obviously been rivalry in the classroom.

My interview with Irving Berlin was a very different experience. Forever the bouncy little extrovert, he was full of chat, not least when he found I was a Scot. He was fulsome in his praise of our own Harry Lauder, whom he regarded as a great international star, as well as a personal friend.

Unlike people like Stan Laurel and Oliver Hardy, Berlin kept strict control of his own material. Bing Crosby told me of an occasion when he was filming in Hollywood and the Berlin music needed a change of key. It involved the insertion of just one new note but that, said the lawyers, would require the permission of the great man himself.

The phone call to New York was duly made and there was a long pause while Berlin considered the situation. "Yeah," he finally said. "One new note? I suppose that will be all right. But remember, it's MA NOTE!"

Composers have always been my special fascination, ranging widely from Tchaikovsky, Rachmaninov and Puccini to Edward Elgar, Ivor Novello and those American giants of the twentieth century: George Gershwin, Jerome Kern and Cole Porter, as well as Rodgers and Berlin. (Yes, you weren't afraid in those days to admit that your taste in music was exactly like your mother's.)

There was one last story from Mary Rodgers which intrigued me. After *Oklahoma* in 1943, when Richard Rodgers and Oscar Hammerstein were moving on to the next production, their business acumen had also brought them ownership of a story that should make another good musical. Over-committed on their own project, they decided to farm it out to some other composer. It was the true story of a gun-totin' girl called Annie Oakley; the chosen composer was Jerome Kern. Tragically, before he could start on the music, Kern collapsed on Park Avenue one afternoon and was rushed to hospital without any clear identification. Word finally reached both Hammerstein and Berlin, who found one of the world's great composers lying anonymously in that hospital corridor, clearly in a bad way. He died on Armistice Day 1945, at the age of sixty.

So the Annie Oakley story was now offered to Irving Berlin, who overcame his doubts about this kind of Western tale and agreed to try it. Came the day when he sat down at the piano in what he regarded as the awesome presence of Rodgers and Hammerstein for a first hearing of his efforts. With their polite nods of approval, he went off to add the final polish to his compositions, returning some time later with the finished version. But Hammerstein had a question: "There's one tune missing from your previous visit, Irving. What happened to it?"

Berlin confessed that, as he scanned their faces for reaction, he didn't think they had liked it.

"Get it back in!" roared Hammerstein. The missing song was "There's No Business Like Show Business", later personified by the raucous tones of Ethel Merman and destined to become the everlasting anthem of the musical theatre. The show itself, *Annie Get Your Gun*, turned out to be one of the greatest musicals of all time.

Yes, I was having the time of my life. Maud may have been a long way from Manhattan but I was getting the hang of things.

CHAPTER SEVENTEEN

"DIEF" GOES MISSING

The Dominion of Canada was created in 1867 and the arrival of Expo Year in Montreal in 1967 was part of the centenary celebration, with the whole world beating a path to its door. Though Heads of State were queueing up to meet Prime Minister Lester Pearson at Parliament Hill in Ottawa, I had managed to fix my own interview. Or so I thought. But when I arrived from New York to confirm the appointment they had lost trace of it. Apologies were not enough. What were they going to do about it? I was due next day in Chicago. Well, if I left a phone number they would try to find another slot and let me know. I didn't hold out much hope. To their credit, however, they did call Chicago to say the Prime Minister would fit me in next Tuesday if I could make it back to Ottawa.

Meanwhile, two big stories were holding the headlines in Canadian newspapers. In this centenary year the old two-nation problem of French and English had raised its head once more, with a furious outburst against President de Gaulle of France for coming to Canada and stirring up trouble with his "Vive le Quebec Libre!" speech. Premier Pearson himself was under fire for pandering to the French-speaking province of Quebec, where a substantial part of his personal support was to be found.

The other breaking story was that of former Conservative Prime Minister John Diefenbaker, who had been ousted by the Liberal Lester Pearson and had now been ditched by his own party at its annual conference in the Maple Leaf, Toronto. Worse still, he had gone missing after the conference. Journalists trying to track him down for reaction could find him nowhere. Diefenbaker had been a popular and successful Premier in his day and this mystery was causing concern.

Due to return to Ottawa for the Pearson interview, I left Chicago knowing I had to change planes at Toronto. At the transfer desk, the lady said if I took my luggage I could run across the tarmac and get the last available seat in the Ottawa plane (no security in those days).

Breathlessly, I slumped into my seat and found the passengers engrossed in their newspapers. It was all about Diefenbaker – poor old Dief the Chief, great guy, cast out by his own party and now this . . .

As I got my breath back, I looked across the passage – and who was sitting within two feet of me? Yes, the man himself! His wife, Olive, had a consoling hand on his arm and their heavy eyes told of a tearful night. My friends say I'm tarred with luck and I was beginning to believe it as I realised I had a scoop almost literally on my lap. But was this the moment? What reaction would I get? Tempting as it was, better perhaps to wait for our arrival in Ottawa.

For the moment I would just observe at close quarters the private emotions of a great Prime Minister in his hour of personal defeat. We exchanged a smile – and I would stay close by him as we left the plane.

Journalists had been covering every possible arrival point and, sure enough, the television cameras were poised as we reached the terminal. In an impromptu press conference, they were asking some fairly innocuous questions: "What do you intend to do now, Mr Diefenbaker?"

"I guess I'll go out West and do a bit of fishin'," he replied.

I thought he might want to say something more important.

"Mr Diefenbaker, as a journalist from Great Britain, can I ask if you have anything to say to the people of the Old Country in this, your moment of departure?"

He paused. Then turned and said, "Yes. Yes, I do have something to say to the people of Britain; in fact, to the people of the world. I want them to know that, even if I am no longer at the centre of

Canadian politics, I shall fight to the end of my life to preserve a one-nation Canada."

As the cameras whirred, he launched into a spirited speech which found its way across the nation on radio and television that night. As he stepped into his limousine, the media men gave him a sympathetic round of applause. He rolled down the window and said, "Gentleman, you don't know how much that means to me."

It was a poignant, emotional moment. As he drove off, the paparazzi turned to thank me for my question. "Where the hell did you come from, anyway?" they wanted to know.

I gave a casual shrug: "Oh, I just found him sitting beside me in the plane!"

After a night at the Chateau Laurier Hotel I kept my appointment with Prime Minister Lester Pearson, former history professor and Nobel Prize-winner whose niece, Catherine Young, still lived in Scotland, married to the eighth Duke of Montrose. After the string of visiting dignitaries, here for the spectacular Expo event, Pearson seemed glad to relax, drinking coffee from an old blue-and-white-ringed mug. Interviewing people at the top, I have found that you can ask any question and expect an answer.

The state of Canadian politics took its place alongside the rumpus over President de Gaulle; and we also touched on the controversial Scots-Canadian Max Aitken, better known as my old boss, Lord Beaverbrook, owner of the *Daily Express*.

Business apart, while in Canada I did something more personal. Back in 1910 my grand-uncle Jimmy Barron had followed a long Scottish tradition by uprooting his wife and family from the Northeast and taking them off to Guelph, Ontario, where a small farm awaited. Enduring the terror of an Atlantic storm on the way, his ten children vowed that they would never set foot on a ship again, and close on sixty years later they had kept their word. As they arrived at the farm all those years ago, Uncle Jimmy put down his case, scratched his head and left the family in little doubt about his thoughts. Was this much different from what they had left?

The same thought occurred to me as I walked up that farm road in 1967. But there they were, nine out of the original ten children, now aged from fifty-eight to eighty, lined up like a guard of honour to welcome the very first family member from Scotland they had seen since 1910. I felt like the Duke of Edinburgh at an inspection.

Two bachelor brothers now farmed the place, so this was still the family home. And if ever I needed proof of heredity's power, I found it here. As I shook hand after hand I could have been looking into the faces of one relative after another back home. John Barron even had my own first two names and I was instantly at home. Quite uncanny.

The kitchen in the farmhouse still had the old-fashioned stove in the middle of the floor, with the lum going up through the ceiling while, in the barn, I spotted an old initialled kist that had brought their belongings from Scotland all those years ago. It was a heart-warming gathering which stirred my admiration for all those immigrants over the years who had transplanted themselves in another land, to become Canadians, no doubt, but were still Scots when you scratched the surface.

As we rounded off the visit with a few drams and a cake they had baked with an inscription of welcome, they lined up once more to wave me off. It was one of those moments that choke you.

It was also time to head back to New York for what would surely be a highlight of my time in America.

CHAPTER EIGHTEEN

FIFTY YEARS OF FORBES

Forbes magazine, which set the pattern for business journals in 1917, was heading for its fiftieth anniversary that September evening of 1967, with invitations to every American company president from General Motors to Coca-Cola. The Cold War, which put the Communist east and Capitalist west at each other's throats, was then in full swing. Indeed, it was a sobering thought that, if the Soviet Union had been looking for an opportunity to wipe out the business leaders of the United States, the Forbes anniversary would provide a rare occasion when they were all under one roof.

Putting that thought aside, I was being driven from Manhattan on the big night, across the Hudson River to New Jersey and on to the Far Hills estate of Malcolm Forbes, by now head of the family enterprise. Guests were arriving by limousine or private plane and filing through the mansion house for cocktails on the lawn. As I wrote at the time:

> Suddenly the gathering dusk became a glitter of floodlights and across the valley from the trees beyond came a hundred pipers playing "Scotland the Brave". Lips which spell out million-dollar deals fell apart as those giants of Wall Street took in the incredible spectacle and confessed that, while they had seen just about everything in this goddamn life, they had never seen anything quite like this. Hell man, this sure was something.
>
> Up they came to the manicured lawns, this parade of exiled pipers, a resounding echo of dear old Scotland, forming a guard of honour for the guests as they trooped into the massive marquee where the anniversary dinner was being held. It is a well-worn

joke about everything being bigger and better in America but the joke may be on those who don't believe it.

All the superlatives could not do justice to the fabulous event of that evening which began with the mellow strings of Lester Lanin and his wonderful orchestra performing on a stage bedecked with a plane-load of heather flown in from Prestwick.

The guest of honour that night was Hubert Humphrey, the Democrat who became Vice-President of the United States on the assassination of John F. Kennedy and who, a year later, would lose out to the Republican Richard Nixon in the fight for the White House. Even now, it could be said that he was just one shot away from being President.

A brilliant orator, Humphrey paid a very moving tribute to the man without whom they would not have been there that night. My thoughts were drifting back to Buchan, to that little cottage called the Cunnyknowe, which gave us Bertie Forbes, one of ten poor children of the local tailor. Who could ever have guessed that the wee boy who sat beside my granny at Whitehill School would one day take America by storm, so teaching the ethical standards of plain farm folk in Aberdeenshire to the mighty moguls of Wall Street – and exposing their shadier elements – that he had earned that aforementioned soubriquet, "The great humaniser of American business".

At the top of his regular columns he had reminded them of the text he took from the family pew as a boy – and which remained his motto for life: "With all thy getting, get understanding."

Bertie would have viewed this night with a fair amount of disbelief. As Malcolm said of his canny Aberdonian father: "He would have been appalled at the expense – but delighted that we could afford it!" So we ate and drank and danced the night away and enjoyed the spectacular fireworks display that rounded off an experience later voted the greatest social occasion America had ever seen.

Before we left for Manhattan in the early hours, Hubert

Humphrey was keen to hear my first-hand account of the man who founded his own *Forbes* magazine and more about the place that bred him. With a few drams inside us, the Vice-President enjoyed my observation that, in this illustrious gathering of Americans, he and I were the only two people there who were not Presidents!

CHAPTER NINETEEN

THE MAN WHO DREW A LEGEND

This American adventure had begun at Southampton when I sailed on the great *Queen Mary*, first of the three royal trans-Atlantic liners built for Cunard at the Clydebank shipyard of John Brown. She would be followed in time by the *Queen Elizabeth* in 1938 and the *QE2* in 1967, both of which I would encounter in later years. But the Mary was the first and managed to retain a majesty of her own, dating back to her origins in the 1920s.

It was in 1991, nearly seventy years later, that I was invited to a dinner in Glasgow, to be told by my host that I would be sitting beside a rather special man – the naval architect who designed the *Queen Mary*. Such nonsense! How could this be? Such a man must be dead long ago. But I was wrong. For this would turn out to be the start of my friendship with ninety-year-old John Brown, a small, quiet, delightful man whose remarkable story seemed to have eluded me and every other journalist of my time. I could only conclude that his own chronic modesty had managed to conceal his legendary status.

Recovering from the shock of discovery, I began to piece together the career of John Brown, born at 364 Clarkston Road, Muirend, on the south side of Glasgow, and educated at Hutchesons' Grammar School. In 1919 he started an apprenticeship at the Clydebank ship-yard of John Brown – yes, his namesake, little knowing that he would become a much more significant figure than the Sheffield steelmaker who had already left his company before it bought over the Scottish shipyard. That John Brown never saw Clydebank in his life.

In tandem with his apprenticeship, young John Brown stud-ied naval architecture at Glasgow University, emerging as the outstanding student of his day. In 1926, at the age of twenty-five, he was called in by his boss, James McNeill, and told to sit down and begin, very privately, to design the biggest luxury liner the world had ever seen. The order had not yet been received but there was good reason to believe it would come, since Cunard was planning a regular service between Southampton and New York. In the meantime, it would be an exercise in showing what he could do.

As it happened, it took four more years before the Clydebank yard embarked on building ship No. 534 and by 1931 they had run into the Depression, when the work was suspended for more than two years. The Prince of Wales came to Clydebank and, realising the devastating effect on the town, persuaded the government to finance a resumption of work. All was set for launching in 1934 but ship No. 534 still had no name.

With Queen Victoria in mind, the chairman of Cunard went to Buckingham Palace to seek the permission of King George V to name her after "the most gracious queen the country has ever known." King George beamed with pride and said, "My wife will be delighted!" The chairman gulped. There was nothing else to do but walk away quietly and call her the *Queen Mary*.

Long before launching day, the young John Brown was in charge of the entire design team of two hundred architects and draughtsmen. Realistically of course, as he always pointed out, no one man designs a ship. But he was the one who drew up those first outlines of the greatest liner the world had ever seen. By the time of the launch, he was already engaged in similar work for the *Queen Elizabeth*, properly named this time after the wife of King George VI, now better remembered as the Queen Mother. This time they had worked out new boiler arrangements so that the three funnels of the *Mary* could be reduced to two on the *Elizabeth*.

Though launched in 1938, she was not ready for sailing until 1940, when she slipped quietly off to New York, under wartime camouflage, to become a troopship, denied the spectacular departure of her sister, who was cheered from the yard by a million people lining the banks of the River Clyde.

John Brown was en route to the top, becoming managing director and vice-chairman and masterminding everything from the Royal Yacht *Britannia* to securing the order for the third of the royal Cunarders, the *QE2*. It would be his last act before slipping quietly into retirement. Surprisingly, the knighthood which had come to his two predecessors, Sir Thomas Bell and Sir James McNeill, was not forthcoming.

Never having sailed on his beloved *Mary*, he booked a trip to New York as a retirement celebration for his wife and himself. When Cunard accidentally discovered the identity of their special VIP, the Browns were duly welcomed as first-class guests, where the Windsors and Churchills and Charlie Chaplins had gone before. When the *Mary* was retired in 1967 she became a hotel and tourist attraction at Long Beach, California, twenty miles south of Los Angeles, where she remains to this day.

Having met John Brown at that Glasgow dinner in 1991, I set out to give him some of the public exposure that had been denied him through all those years of retirement. I was in the midst of my television phase and knew that a special anniversary celebration was due at Long Beach. As the *Mary* entered her sixtieth year, wouldn't it be wonderful to take him to California? I suggested a John Brown documentary to the BBC but for once they could not find the finance. Time was not on my side. So I crossed to the opposition at Scottish Television, where David Scott, a former colleague on the *Daily Express*, quickly cottoned on to the possibilities but could offer a limited budget of £22,000, which was not enough. A desperate call to that great gentleman, Lord Macfarlane of Bearsden, guaranteed the remaining balance and I could now put together a television crew and fly them out to California.

As John Brown stepped aboard the ship he had not seen in all those years, the crew formed a guard of honour for a very special VIP who was now the centre of the whole celebration. The royal suite, which had been named after the Duke of Windsor, had now been renamed the Churchill Suite and for the duration of his visit it was occupied by John Brown. What's more, he had brought with him the little box of instruments with which he had drawn those early outlines of the ship. These instruments were bought with the prize money he received as top student of his year at Glasgow University and now he was presenting them for permanent display on board the *Queen Mary*.

We filmed all that, with a final scene of John Brown taking one last look at his favourite creation. It was a deeply moving moment, rounding off a documentary directed by my friend Mark Little-wood. Against all the odds, it went out on Scottish Television, with much help from STV's Anita Cox, under the title of *John Brown: the Man who Drew a Legend*. She managed to sell it as far away as Australia. But still no sign of an honour.

By 1999 John Brown was in his ninety-ninth year. Time was running out but having failed in my previous approaches, I was determined to make one last attempt, greatly encouraged by Ronald McNeill, son of his former boss, Sir James, who wrote, "I'm delighted with your endeavours to achieve recognition for a man who has been so disgracefully omitted. If you do succeed I shall be your friend for life."

Stating the case for a knighthood on one sheet of A4 paper, I took it to the office of Donald Dewar, who had just brought about the first Scottish Parliament in 300 years. I showed it to his right-hand man, David Whitton, a former journalist, who agreed that the case seemed unanswerable. They put it down the line to Downing Street and suddenly there was a response.

We were heading for a new century and surely this would be an appropriate time to recognise a greatly neglected Scot. I received a very private phone call one day to tell me: "Your man is getting his knighthood." Like a young kid, I physically jumped for joy.

In the Millennium Honours List, the man I met at that Glasgow dinner became Sir John Brown and enjoyed his title for a year. We bade him a last goodbye at Broomhill Church, Glasgow, on 3 January, 2001, four months short of his centenary.

CHAPTER TWENTY

THE ROAD TO HONEYNEUK

From that first contact with America, when I fell in love with New York, it was back to Scotland and back home to Maud, where my father, John Webster, had extended his life as an auctioneer to that of a farmer.

As a boy brought up on the farm of Backhill of Allathan, New Deer, he had been deprived of a father in the most extraordinary of circumstances. My grandfather, a tenant farmer, went to mend a fence which had been knocked down by one of his cattle and in doing so, he cut his forearm on the barbed wire. Unknown to him, the animal had also bled itself on the fence. That same animal was suffering from the dreaded disease of anthrax, which entered my grandfather's bloodstream. He died of anthrax. So my father, aged eight, was left to look after his mother and young brother. While neighbours came to his aid, they were astounded to find that he was managing to muck out the cattle and do so many of the tasks that fall to farm folk.

By the time he was a teenager he was visiting the cattle mart at Maud, four miles away, and becoming entranced by the role of the auctioneer. With that in mind, he became a drover of cattle to the mart, as a first step towards his ambition. Then he was taken on as a clerk and finally as a young auctioneer, mounting his motorbike and canvassing for cattle to his own mart, which was in competition with two others. In time, he became one of the best-known faces in the Buchan district, an authority on livestock and a bit of a character with his humorous comments from the rostrum.

His one remaining ambition was to own his own bit of land and that opportunity presented itself in the summer of 1952. The village

of Maud sat on the edge of the Brucklay estate, owned for generations by the aristocratic Dingwall-Fordyce family who lived in its
magnificent castle. But in the post-war difficulty of maintaining
large estates, Brucklay was offering some of its farms for sale and
that included the 200 acres of Honeyneuk, set attractively within
half a mile of the village.

By no means a man of capital, my father borrowed the money,
put in a successful bid and he and my mother moved up to Honeyneuk in September 1952. By then I was twenty-one and no longer
living at home, off to this worthless job of journalism which so
disappointed my father in his one and only son. There came a time,
however, when a quiet acceptance seemed to be creeping into his
attitude. At least that was the impression of my observant mother,
who would overhear his conversations with farmers on the phone.

They were apparently reading of my various travels and exploits
in the *Daily Express* and showing some pleasure in what I was
doing. My father's response would hardly have sounded like an
endorsement, except to those who understand the psyche of the
Aberdonian male.

"Oh ay," my mother would hear him say, "the loon's deein' nae
bad for 'imsel." And the more it happened the more my mother
could sense the beginnings of something that resembled pride.

By the time I returned from America, there was even a suggestion that maybe, just maybe, I had done the right thing. That was
the greatest acquiescence I would ever have expected. I think he
now accepted that we must each follow our own path.

My mother, on the other hand, had been with me all the way, an
unpretentious country body like my father but a soul mate with a
gift for words and music that set the pattern of my own interests
and enthusiasms for life.

Back on my native heath, it was time to take a fresh look at this land
which had bred me. For every town, village and small community
there is a reason for its existence, and my own village of Maud was
no exception. There it lay in a gentle valley, twenty-eight miles to

the north of Aberdeen and fourteen miles inland from Peterhead, wedged between two long-standing parishes but with no parish of its own.

Though largely disregarded by her two neighbours, I rather liked the idea that my lady Maud nestled between her Old Deer and her New Deer and triumphed over both for one particular reason. Whatever she lacked in terms of their history, she happened to occupy the precise centre-point of that Buchan region of Aberdeenshire well known for its beef cattle. Indeed the very name of Maud is said to mean "meeting place", and that is what it became for a variety of reasons. First there came the arrival of railways in the mid-1800s and eventually a line from Aberdeen to Buchan, which was planned to run through Kittybrewster, Bucksburn, Dyce, Parkhill, Newmachar, Udny, Logierieve, Esslemont, Ellon, Arnage and Auchnagatt. But somewhere soon they would need to split the line into two branches, one heading for Peterhead to the east and the other for Fraserburgh to the north, the two main fishing ports of the North-east. Well, for this major junction where else would they choose but Maud? And that was the real beginning of a village which had been no more than a hamlet called Bank, in the parish of Old Deer.

As the village was now spreading across a little burn into the parish of New Deer it would take on the name of New Maud, as it was still called in my childhood of the 1930s. With a regular flow of goods and passenger trains, Maud Junction now became the busy focal point of this young village, an exciting contact with the outside world, even incorporating a John Menzies bookstall run by Tibby Bruce and, quite uniquely, a restaurant-cum-public house called The Refresh, conducted by two splendid ladies, Lil and Lena Murison.

Maud was now clearly the centre of Buchan, accessible from all points by train and soon to become that "meeting point" for bodies like Deer District Council and Deer Presbytery. More commercially, it had become the natural marketing place for the beef cattle and other livestock, which could be so easily entrained for the south.

In that latter half of the 1800s no fewer than three competing companies established marts, providing that opening which so attracted my father to the job of auctioneering. At first he joined Middleton's Mart and then the Central and Northern Farmers Mart, always in keen competition with the family firm of Reith and Anderson. With a large spread of buildings and pens for the animals, these mart companies came to dominate the appearance of Maud. Wednesday became the big day, as cattle floats came streaming into the village and farmers and butchers came in their hundreds to buy and sell in an atmosphere of bustle and excitement. The outcome was that Maud, with no more than 700 inhabitants, became the biggest weekly cattle market in Britain, providing meat for such establishments as the Dorchester and Savoy Hotels in London.

One thing led to another and soon they were erecting Maud's most impressive building, the Buchan Combination Home, better known as the Poorshouse but later to become one of the finest hospitals in Aberdeenshire. Houses and shops arose in abundance, including a post office, a hotel and no fewer than three separate banks. A handsome new church was built in that original part of the village and now there were children to be educated. So a school for boys was built directly opposite the church (it later became the Freemasons' Lodge), while the educating of girls fell to a certain Miss Paterson, who ran a highly successful school within the home of her father, which was the same Honeyneuk Farm my father was to buy more than a century later.

That was followed by a Dames School nearer the village (it later became Willie Ogston's Smiddy) but all this informality was brought together in April 1896 when a splendid new Maud Higher Grade School was built to serve a wide area, with Mr John Law taking over as the first headmaster. That building remains as Maud School today, albeit now reduced from senior to junior status. And that was where I started school in April 1936.

So the village I came to know as my home was at the height of its prosperity, with trains and cattle marts, a Pleasure Park with a magnificent bowling green – and a police station complete with cells which were mainly occupied, we liked to make clear, by the rowdier elements from surrounding villages like New Deer and New Pitsligo!

Who would have believed that anything could happen to disturb this idyllic setting of my childhood? Well, by the time I returned from the United States in 1967 the danger signal had arisen in the person of just one man. A certain Dr Beeching had been instructed by the government to mastermind a huge reduction in the number of railway stations. The entire Buchan Line from Aberdeen was high on his list and the whole vibrancy of Maud Junction was soon to be reduced to a pathetic state of dereliction, silent and dead.

One thing leads to another. In an age of centralisation, the cattle marts of the North-east, by now known as Aberdeen and Northern Marts, were being brought under one roof at a place called Thainstone, near Inverurie. So the infectious bustle of Maud on a Wednesday – the biggest weekly cattle market in Britain – was gone forever. The rot had set in. Soon the three banks were disappearing, followed by three baker's shops, three butchers, three joiners, two shoemakers, the plumber, electrician, tailor, chemist, cycle agent, dressmaker – and the most famous sweetie shop in Buchan, run by the legendary Lizzie Allan, who ran her business from a wheelchair, on account of the fact that she had no legs. That left the wonderful haven of the elderly, Maud Hospital, but it was not too long before the powers that be managed to close that too.

So Maud was reduced to a pale shadow of its former self, a dormitory for Aberdeen and Peterhead, the kind of fate which befell so many villages around the country for which the railway station was the heart and soul of the place.

Dr Beeching, it could be said, became the major catalyst of destruction for rural life in Scotland. And the irony of his activity as far as the Buchan Railway Line was concerned was doubly disastrous. For he had no sooner wielded his axe than North Sea oil and gas heralded the biggest industrial event in Scottish history. The main supplies would come ashore on the Buchan coast at Cruden Bay and St Fergus, on either side of Peterhead. So for years to come, those lorry loads of pipes would have to be transported from Aberdeen, adding further congestion to roads which were wholly inadequate, when they could have so easily gone by train to Peterhead.

In recent times there has been talk of reopening the Buchan Line, which has been reduced to a cycling track. But too late, I suspect. Too late.

CHAPTER TWENTY-ONE

A MOTHER AT DEATH'S DOOR

In time, I realised just how lucky I was to have my mother, prompted by the visits to our home in Maud of a certain Dr Robert Henderson. It was quite a story. With my difficult birth of 8 July 1931, my mother was immediately rushed to the City Hospital in Aberdeen, suffering from peritonitis, almost invariably a fatal condition at a time when that great Scotsman, Alexander Fleming, was still struggling with his discovery of penicillin. By chance, my mother had once been a nurse in that same hospital and was well aware of the procedures. In her semi-conscious state, she realised that she had been moved to the end of the ward, a precaution taken with dying patients so that there would be minimum disruption when the moment arrived. Aware of her condition, as she told me later, she simply gritted her teeth and vowed that she was not going to die. She was going home to that baby.

Dr Henderson was doing his best to keep her alive but, as he would later confess, it was going to take something like a miracle. The fact that she lived had astonished him to the point that, never having seen survival in a patient so close to death, he came to visit her some time later, just to make sure that all was well. He greatly enjoyed her scones but his subsequent visits were much more to do with celebrating her survival.

He had never forgotten. And he put it all down to her own will-power, that spirit and determination which on rare occasions can see us through when all else is lost. There may, however, have been more to his own credit than even he realised. For the same Dr Henderson was on his way to distinction as one of Britain's medical pioneers of the twentieth century.

The son of the village blacksmith at Clatt in Aberdeenshire, Robert Henderson left school during the First World War to become an apprentice in a local garage. It was one of his teachers in Huntly who pointed out to his father that Robert should be doing something more than this, even suggesting that he was cut out to be a doctor. How inspirational were some of our teachers. Special tuition was arranged so that he could enter medical school at Aberdeen University, from which he graduated in 1929. Around the time of my birth, as it turned out, he was already working on an idea which required some basic hardware from a ship's chandler.

With the help of engineers at the City Hospital he put it all together on the base of a children's cot – and within four weeks his invention was saving the life of a ten-year-old boy who was suffering from infantile paralysis, now better known as polio. What Robert Henderson had created was Britain's very first "iron lung" that came to be known as Henderson's Respirator. Enclosing the patient from the neck down – and by creating a vacuum within the chamber – he was forcing the lungs to expand and fill with air before releasing the vacuum for "breathing out".

By sheer coincidence, that ten-year-old boy whose life he saved was a close acquaintance of my family, Charles Forbes, a farmer's son from Whitehill of New Deer. He survived into middle age and, from personal experience, I remember him as a crack hand at the very English game of croquet, which, curiously, was a highly popular pastime in rural Buchan.

Still at Aberdeen's City Hospital, Dr Henderson then fell victim to the kind of petty bureaucracy that takes the breath away. Having just saved the life of a polio sufferer – the first of so many successes of its kind in Britain – he was disciplined for using hospital facilities to build his machine. Instead of taking pride in what this young doctor had achieved, the local medical officer of health condemned the nationwide publicity which the invention had attracted! How small-minded can people be?

As a result, Dr Henderson's draft paper on his invention was not published and, quite disillusioned, he moved off south from his native North-east. By 1938, however, he was invited to join a committee of the Medical Research Council to impart his expertise on "breathing machines". Out of this, Lord Nuffield, that great philanthropist (and himself the creator of the Morris Oxford car) offered to manufacture Henderson's respirators and supply them free of charge to any hospital in Britain and throughout the Empire that wanted them. Appropriately, seventy-five of the machines came to Scotland and continued to save the lives of polio sufferers thereafter.

Robert Henderson proceeded to a distinguished career in England, directing several hospitals during the Second World War, and was named a Commander of the British Empire in 1947 for his services to medicine. That first iron-lung patient, Charles Forbes, enjoyed his bonus years of life but when he died in the 1950s, his brother Ian spotted a stranger among the mourners. It was none other than Robert Henderson, who had come up from London especially for the funeral.

I never forgot his visits to our house in Maud nor my mother's gratitude for what he did all those years ago. But much of this story was unknown to me until 2000, when I opened the paper one day and read that the same Dr Henderson had just died – while approaching his ninety-ninth year. How much I would have liked to meet him again and tell him of my own undying gratitude. If only I had known that he was still alive.

An interesting footnote to the obituary told of his days as superintendent of the 1,700-bed Southern Hospital in Dartford, Kent. Evidently, a 1985 biography of Prime Minister Margaret Thatcher claimed that Dr Henderson had once been a notable rival to her eventual husband, Denis Thatcher. That rather took his breath away. He conceded that they had once been very close friends. "But I never courted Margaret nor proposed to her," he said.

1934 – Awaiting ice-cream man

Father and
Mother

1937 Coronation – Rajah boy

1948 – First job, *Turiff Advertiser*

1949 – Longchamps Racecourse, Paris

1950 – Joined *Press & Journal*

1950s – My wife, Eden

1956 – Our wedding day, the coldest day recorded in
years, and they forgot to put the heating on in the church!

1967 – My sons Geoffrey, Martin and Keith

Gavin Greig, my great-grandfather

B. C. Forbes (Forbes Magazine) with my parents

My parents' home, Honeyneuk House, with croquet-green

My native village
of Maud

1964 – Chief Sub
at *Sunday Express*

1973 – At Princess
Anne's wedding

1986 – Me

1984 – Ayliffe and Eden at Penina

With Eden, Ayliffe and Walter at Wokingham

Adolf Hitler with his mentor Putzi Hanfstaengl

Me, with Putzi Hanfstaengl
in Munich

With Sophia Loren

With Charles Aznavour

With Bing Crosby
at Turnberry

With Charlie Chaplin
in Aberdeen

With Bob Hope at Gleneagles

1965 – In limo with Muhammad Ali

Ali socks me one

Ali takes over *Express* conference

CHAPTER TWENTY-TWO

DISCOVERING GRASSIC GIBBON

For those of us who aspire to writing as a career the obvious first step is to find if we can do it. But having ended my schooldays before I was fifteen and with no further guidance in my education, I had given myself a handicap. Of course if you are a natural reader you can make good the deficiencies, since reading will almost certainly make you a better writer. But I wasn't a reader. Nor were my father or mother, though the latter wrote me letters that were impeccable in their grammar, spelling and punctuation, as well as imaginative and highly readable, suggesting that she would have made a good journalist.

By good fortune, however, when I was nineteen I did happen to read one book that would virtually change the course of my life. That was *Sunset Song*, by Lewis Grassic Gibbon, the man whose earlier presence at Aberdeen Journals had so intrigued me when I found myself in the same small reporters' room a generation later. Up to that point I had simply plodded along, acquainted with the basic rules of English but without the courage to venture beyond its boundaries. Then suddenly I was reading and rereading and analysing the writing style of this man, Grassic Gibbon, wondering how he got himself into the frame of mind that would produce this particular form of words.

As I would soon discover, he had created a style that was uniquely his own, flirting outrageously with language but producing such a rhythmic flow that punctuation was often rendered unnecessary. To all intents and purposes he was writing in English but by some magical means, he managed to make it sound like Scots. The fact that he, like me, was out of school by the age of fifteen encouraged me to persevere. And gradually I picked up a rhythm of writing and set out to find more about the man himself. As mentioned earlier, at Aberdeen Journals I had a splendid witness in his critic and friend, Cuthbert Graham, the man who challenged him to write about the land he knew so well and without whom we may never have known *Sunset Song*.

The first discovery, of course, was the tragic fact that he was dead before his thirty-fourth birthday. Then I contacted his widow, Ray, and his old headmaster, Alexander Gray, the man who first noted the genius of the twelve-year-old at Arbuthnott School, to the south of Stonehaven, in 1913.

Mr Gray was by now retired in Stonehaven, though still teaching Greek at the nearby Drumtochty School, and together we wandered over that land of the Mearns that had been Grassic Gibbon's inspiration, past the croft where he had grown up, into the school he attended and finally down to his grave in the kirkyard of Arbuthnott. In those days of the 1950s there were still plenty people who remembered him and we would stop to speak to a farmer here and there. Oh ay, they remembered him well, though I suspected they didn't quite understand him.

His real name, of course, was Leslie Mitchell, born in 1901 on the edge of my native Buchan at the farm of Hillhead of Seggat, Auchterless, between Fyvie and Turriff. By the time he was eight his father had taken the family across Aberdeenshire to the Mearns, to the small holding of Bloomfield, high on the Reisk road and almost within sight of Clochnahill, the farm where Robert Burns's father was born and grew up. His father was James Mitchell, originally from Insch, and his mother was Lilias Grant Gibbon from Kildrummy. But his grandmother was Lilias Grassic Gibbon – and it was from her that he would eventually take the pen name of Lewis Grassic Gibbon.

From Arbuthnott School he went to Mackie Academy in Stonehaven, a disastrous venture in which he could not believe "the gaping ignorance and shoddy erudition of some of my teachers". What's more, he told them so. In a row one day he just walked out and said he would never go back. And he never did. That led to the Aberdeen Journals where, at the time of the Bolshevik Revolution in 1917, his news editor sent him one evening to report on the formation of an Aberdeen Soviet.

With no sign of him returning, the news editor went to see what had happened and couldn't find him at the press desk. Oh no. In his first flush of young idealism, Leslie was on the platform, addressing the comrades as a newly elected council member of the Aberdeen Soviet. He didn't last much longer at Aberdeen Journals.

By the age of eighteen he had joined the Army but was having little success with the short stories he was writing. Then he joined the Royal Air Force, around the same time as Lawrence of Arabia, with whom he had much in common. He sent a story to H.G. Wells, who took an immediate interest in him and, at last, when he was twenty-seven, he had his first novel accepted by Jarrolds of London.

But the turning point in his career didn't come until 1932, when he took up that challenge from Cuthbert Graham to write about his own home area. Within a few weeks he had written *Sunset Song*, a story of the men of the Mearns who went off to the First World War, four of whom did not return. It was powerful stuff but the folk of the Mearns took ill with some of the observations and some of the language. From his dour, critical father, who thought he should be at home working on the farm, there was nothing but bleak opposition, to the point of hurt.

Sunset Song was the first part of the trilogy called *A Scots Quair*, written in the closing years of his tragically short life. In that time he had written no fewer than seventeen books, with immediate commissions for a million more words. Like many a North-east body he worked himself too hard and on a February night in 1935, he was rushed to hospital in Welwyn Garden City which had become home to Leslie and Ray, now with two children, Rhea and Daryll. He underwent an operation for a perforated ulcer, which would be a routine matter today. But, as with my own mother three years earlier, peritonitis had already set in and Leslie Mitchell, alias Lewis Grassic Gibbon, died on the operating table.

There was an outpouring of public grief, not least from his fellow novelists. As Neil Gunn said: "Of all our writers he is just the man we could least afford to lose." And as I walk by his grave even now I can so easily picture the scene at his burial in Arbuthnott Kirkyard on a cold February day.

Most of all, I can picture the dour figure of James Mitchell, the father who gave his son nothing but disapproval. Only at the last minute did he realise that, yes, he had indeed bred a genius, one of Scotland's greatest sons. I'm told that he quietly broke his heart and within a year had curled up and died at seventy-four. Leslie's mother, Lilias, lived on at Bloomfield but later moved to Stonehaven, where she died in 1953, in her eighty-first year. His wife Ray, with whom he had been a classmate at Arbuthnott, lived on in Welwyn Garden till her death in 1978. But I kept in touch with his daughter, Rhea, a brilliant scholar, also in Welwyn Garden, and his delightful son, Daryll, a successful businessman who lived at Tavistock in Devon, and looked very like his father.

CHAPTER TWENTY-THREE

MY FIRST STAGE PLAY

For what I owed to Grassic Gibbon, without whom I might never have been a writer, I always vowed that one day I would repay that debt by putting him on stage to speak for himself, for he was the man who not only pointed me in the right direction as a writer but had opened my eyes and ears to my own surroundings. After all, we had both grown up in that same North-east corner of Scotland and within a matter of days that whole scene had gained new meaning for me. The plodding ploughman was now the symbol of a deeper life; the land that lay so still began to yield more than crops. In other words, my heritage had come alive.

Since then, during an adventurous career in journalism, I had gained enough confidence to write seventeen books and a string of television documentaries which had given me an entrée to a whole new world. But could I write something for the stage? I was going to have a damned good try.

I kept remembering how Scots actress Vivien Heilbron had won her fame through the televising of Grassic Gibbon's trilogy in the '70s and '80s. But for all the acclaim of his books, very little seemed to be known about the man himself. So I wrote a script in which Vivien (if she would do it) would take the stage with Grassic Gibbon himself in what the drama world calls a two-hander. As a further impertinence, would her partner in life, Aberdonian David Rintoul, consider playing Grassic Gibbon?

When it was finished I sent Vivien a copy, asking coyly if this might ever interest her; if not, just to forget about it. You can imagine the joy when she came on the phone to say she would be delighted. Unfortunately David was tied up for two years with

Dirty Dancing in London's West End. But on a Sunday, his only day off, the two of them would fly up at their own expense to test out my play at the Grassic Gibbon Centre at Arbuthnott, focal point of his life and work.

And so it was, on 19 August 2007, that Vivien and David took the stage in front of a full house, Vivien the narrator, David representing Grassic Gibbon himself. Nervously I sat there, trying to absorb the vibrations of the audience, watching their faces for reaction. Thankfully, I need have had no worries. You could have heard the proverbial pin dropping, such was the silence of their attention. And when it was all over, the deafening applause was a sure sign that we had a success on our hands. On top of that, I was called on stage for a standing ovation. So late in life, that novel experience rather choked me up and ranks with my most memorable moments.

The audience that night included Duncan Hendry, manager of His Majesty's Theatre in Aberdeen, who took the play as an in-house production and gave it its professional premiere in the following year. There were folk from all over Buchan in the audience that night, former classmates from Maud School and a couple of old girlfriends, all wishing me well. In the absence of David Rintoul, Vivien Heilbron was joined by Michael Mackenzie as they started out on an extensive tour which took them from Aberdeen to venues around Scotland that included the Theatre Royal, Glasgow, and the Festival Theatre, Edinburgh. In addition, two other splendid actors, Eileen McCallum and Steve Robertson (from *Scotland the What?*) embarked on a North-east tour which took them from Peterhead to Maud (where else?!) and on to Haddo House, Inverurie and Aboyne, where there is a delightful little theatre.

And that was not the end of it. The BBC then bought it up for adapting as a play on Radio Scotland, which was broadcast on 7 February 2010, the seventy-fifth anniversary of Grassic Gibbon's death. For the concluding words in *The Life of Grassic Gibbon* I focused on the funeral of Ray in 1978, for which daughter Rhea and son Daryll brought their mother's ashes back to lie with those of her husband:

The mourners sang 'The Lord's My Shepherd' and the service closed with 'The Flowers o' the Forest,' just as Grassic Gibbon had closed *Sunset Song*, with the piper playing the lament up there by Blawearie Loch.

They looked again at the gravestone, with its inscription coming straight from that closing passage of *Sunset Song*: 'The kindness of friends, the warmth of toil, the peace of rest.'

And they turned their gaze across those rolling acres of the Mearns, with its modest crofts reaching to the foothills of the Grampians and rising into the western horizon of an early evening. Rising into the glow of a sunset song that echoes . . . like a distant melody . . . in the human heart.

Those final words, delivered by Vivien Heilbron, gave way to the soaring music of "Crimond", the psalm tune composed in that little Buchan village by Jessie Seymour Irvine, daughter of the local minister.

As the curtain lowered I felt that, after all those years, I had finally gone some way to repaying the debt to my literary hero, Lewis Grassic Gibbon. His son, Daryll, had come to Aberdeen to see my play and his subsequent letter gave much pleasure: "Having learned of the similarities you shared with my father, in education, background and profession," he said, "it is a pity you never met because I think you would have been good friends."

CHAPTER TWENTY-FOUR

A BOOK AT LAST

Long before I tackled that dramatic tribute to Grassic Gibbon, however, his example had given me enough confidence to try my hand at writing a book. It's an exercise that needs perseverance, especially if you have listened to the cynic who said, "There's a book inside every one of us – and that's exactly where it should stay!" Nevertheless, I took the first faltering steps when I was thirty-two, jotting down some thoughts with a view to writing my memoirs. Memoirs at thirty-two? I might have known the omens were not in my favour. The other event of that weekend in 1963 was the assassination of President Kennedy!

However, I forged ahead, completing the manuscript and sending it to Hutchinson the publishers in London. With an almost indecent haste, they sent it back. But I remembered that, for Grassic Gibbon's first novel, *Stained Radiance*, he had suffered no fewer than twenty rejection slips. Perhaps I should try someone more local. So off it went to Paul Harris, an up-and-coming publisher in Aberdeen, who took only slightly longer than Hutchinson to come to exactly the same conclusion.

Grassic Gibbon must have had real faith in his manuscript to keep going. I was made of lesser stuff. Did my premature dismissal from Robert Gordon's College give me an early complex? Whatever the reason, I suspect I had an in-built fear of rejection, whether with words or women, and promptly tossed the so-called memoirs into a drawer.

Several years later a commission to become ghostwriter to that most famous of all Celtic footballers, Jimmy Johnstone, after his team beat Inter Milan to become the first British team to win the European

Cup in 1967, would at least give me the experience of writing a book, albeit someone else's book. So I went to Jimmy's home in Viewpark, Uddingston, week after week, piecing together the life story of the Wee Man who was still only twenty-four years of age. Jimmy's memory was not as good as his feet and he would even forget I was coming. But I could always depend on his boss, the legendary Jock Stein, to fill me in on the kind of interesting detail which only a man of that perception could have supplied. So in 1969 we published *Fire in My Boots* and I didn't see much more of Jimmy until those later years, by which time he had developed the dreaded motor neurone, that most ghastly and immobilising of all diseases.

How sad to find the great Jimmy Johnstone now sipping liquid through a straw and incapable of moving. For the very first time I was seeing his bare feet, two nondescript lumps of flesh, which once had teased, tormented and triumphed over the greatest football defences in the world. His charming wife, Agnes, loving and attentive as always, was by his side as time ran out. Poor Jimmy died soon afterwards.

Still on the theme of football, by the mid-1970s it struck me that no one had ever bothered to write a book about Aberdeen Football Club, the long-standing passion of my life. So with the seventy-fifth anniversary of the club due in 1978, I wrote to chairman Dick Donald, suggesting that, as a writer and a fan, I might just be the man to tackle the history. Though shrewd in most matters, Dick made one of his more doubtful responses, saying it would be better if I waited until the centenary in 2003. When I reminded him gently that some of us might not be around in 2003 and that it would cost the club nothing, he said I was perfectly free to go ahead with the book if I wanted. So that is exactly what I did.

This would be my own project but, thankfully, I was no sooner into the research than Dick's vice-chairman, former Dons player and able administrator Chris Anderson, was aligning the club with the book. Chris would become my close friend but, by cruel coincidence, like Jimmy Johnstone he too would fall victim to that dreaded motor neurone disease, still in the prime of his life.

As for the book, a careless official at Pittodrie had once thrown out a mass of the club's records and what was left was of little use. So over a period of two years I was to be found in the vaults of the public library on Clifton Road, reading every single day's sports pages of Aberdeen Journals from the beginning of the century until the 1970s, piecing together the arrivals and departures of players and all they did in between. At other times I was scouring the country to stir the memories of former players, right back to Matt Forsyth from the First World War and through all the ups and downs of the club's history.

From 1931, the year I was born, there had been much talk of an alleged scandal in which a number of players were said to have been placing fixed-odd bets on the outcome of their own matches. As a sign of the very different times in which we live, I could find nothing explicit in the newspapers, except the odd paragraph to say that five players had been dropped from the first team. They included Black, McLaren and Hill, one of the finest half-back lines in British football, and the diminutive Benny Yorston, who had scored an astonishing forty-six goals in the previous season. Along with David Galloway, they were each shown the exit door of Pittodrie – and still the media of the day was reporting nothing except a brief statement from manager Paddy Travers, to the effect that it was on account of "some domestic trouble". So, for all those years, the public was left with nothing but rumour. In the interests of the club history, however, I was determined to get to the bottom of it.

The ringleader was thought to have been Benny Yorston (he was a second cousin of Harry Yorston's father) and I tracked him down to a bleak flat in Chelsea. Benny had built a property business in London's South Kensington but once again had fallen on hard times. He prefaced our discussion by telling me of a wartime knock on the head, which was a handy excuse for the fact that he could not remember why he left Pittodrie. So he denied all knowledge of corruption and had no memory of the mystery I was talking about. I turned to his wife, who put up as good a pretence as Benny – and, as far as I know, she didn't even have the excuse of a bang on the head.

Back home, I got the full story from former teammates, like the patently honest and decent Willie Cooper, whose reputations were endangered by association. So, when that first-ever history of the Dons of Pittodrie was published and serialised in 1978, it was the very first time that the real story had ever appeared in print – forty-seven years later!

The launching of *The Dons* in August of 1978 was an astonishing event, when two thousand supporters crowded into the Capitol cinema in Union Street, waving their red scarves, singing to the music of Jack Sinclair and his band – and greeting on stage a parade of players from past and present that virtually personified the entire history of Aberdeen Football Club. I looked at that array of talent and realised that this illustrious gathering would never be together again. It justified those two years of sweat that had taken me to all corners.

My own original copy of *The Dons* tells its own story when I give you just some of the autographs that adorn its pages from that memorable night. Older readers in particular will have their memories jogged by this list: Matt Forsyth and W.K. Jackson from the earliest days; Willie Mills and Matt Armstrong, the great partnership of the 1930s; Johnny Pattillo, Archie Baird, Tony Harris, Willie Waddell and Percy Dickie from the 1940s; Fred Martin, Harry Yorston, Don Emery, Archie Glen, Jackie Hather, Chris Anderson and Teddy Scott of the 1950s; and from more recent times, Willie Miller, Gordon Strachan, Steve Archibald, Doug Rougvie, John McMaster, Stuart Kennedy and Chic McLelland. They were all there that night, and the book was also signed by chairman Dick Donald; former chairman Charles B. Forbes; that remarkable chief scout, Bobby Calder; and greatest of referees, Aberdeen's own Peter Craigmyle – not to mention a few scrawls I cannot decipher.

One more autograph from that evening in 1978 marks a coincidence that I could never have foreseen. It belonged to the latest employee of Aberdeen Football Club, who had just taken charge of his first match. Alex Ferguson came quietly upon the scene, interviewed by the BBC reporter (my own cousin, Arthur Argo, as it happened) who asked what he thought of this great occasion. Modestly, the man who had just been sacked by St Mirren expressed his pleasure and said he must try to "emulate those great feats of the past". Great feats of the past? How was I to know that, within the next few years, this new manager of the Dons would treble the "feats" of the previous seventy-five years, dominate Scottish football for most of a decade and take the club to the unimaginable heights of winning the European Cup Winners' Cup, beating the world's greatest football club, Real Madrid, in the final? On top of all that, the Dons would beat the European Champions, Hamburg, in the final of the ultimate Super Cup, to be declared the top team in Europe in 1983.

A minor consequence of that fairy tale was that the first history of the Dons was rendered out of date within a short time. It was nevertheless a great pleasure to rewrite that history after the staggering reign of Alex Ferguson came to an end in 1986. It would now reflect the glory of Gothenburg, that Swedish city where Aberdeen floored the mighty Real on the evening of Wednesday, 11 May 1983. Fourteen thousand fans arrived in fifty plane-loads, as well as by car, coach and the P&O ferry St Clair, taking over the city in their splashes of red and gaining the heart-felt warmth of the local people. By contrast, the result had seemed such a foregone conclusion that no more than 4,000 Spanish supporters bothered to come. They certainly missed a downpour of rain but that was hardly noticed by the legion of delirious Aberdonians who celebrated into the early morning.

With two of my sons, Geoffrey and Martin, and my *Herald* colleague Harry Reid, I joined the victory spree at the team's hotel, one of those occasions that stay with you forever. All Europe was stunned by the final score of 2–1. Where was this Aberdeen, anyway? For the first time the Dons of Pittodrie were now firmly on the football map of Europe.

Two remarkable photographs appeared in next morning's *Press and Journal*. The first showed the main thoroughfare of Union Street at eight o'clock the previous evening. Not a single soul was to be seen. An entire city was glued to the television. The second showed the same street at midnight, by which time they were out in their thousands, jumping with delight, car horns blaring.

Next day I flew in the team plane, home to unprecedented scenes of jubilation, 100,000 people lining the streets, all the way from Aberdeen Airport through Bucksburn to Anderson Drive, down Queen's Road and Albyn Place to Union Street, where the greatest concentration of people that street had ever known roared their appreciation. The tribute was wildly acknowledged by the players from their open-topped bus as they displayed the trophy to many a loyal supporter whose joy was tempered, I suspect, by the fact that they weren't in Gothenburg to see it. But they followed the team to Pittodrie, spiritual home of the Dons, where, I must confess, I had my own moments of quiet reflection. I had been coming here since 1942, from that cloth-cap era of decent folk whose loyalty to the Dons over a lifetime had never wavered, though they had yet to share the joy of even a single trophy.

Most had not lived to see this moment, the highest point of all. And as I looked at this mass of humanity I knew that we would never know this height again. The romance of a fairy tale had come to our beloved Pittodrie, giving us a memory that would never fade.

Alex Ferguson remained with Aberdeen for three more years before accepting the reward he was due. The prize job in British football management was Manchester United and that was where he landed in 1986, leading his team to such heights that he has been acclaimed as the most successful British manager of all time.

Unlike any other manager, he reached the top in both Scotland and England. And in the case of Scotland he did it outwith the dominant force of Rangers and Celtic, the so-called Old Firm of Glasgow, whose head-to-head sectarian adherence to Protestantism and Catholicism had given them a massive fan base that no other club could possibly match. The result had been a farcical imbalance that made a mockery of Scottish football. But the man they called Fergie proved that the slender sling of David can, on rare occasions, overcome the brute strength of Goliath. Back in Aberdeen, however, the succeeding generation has been known to regard the glory of Gothenburg as an albatross round the neck of later teams. But if they had been told fifty years earlier that one day they would have the choice of such glory just once in a lifetime, would they seriously have chosen to reject it?

For my part, I returned to Sweden for the tenth anniversary in 1993 to make a video film, *The Glory of Gothenburg* – and went on to write the official club history for the third time, on this occasion to mark the centenary of 2003, another memorable milestone which was celebrated with a grand banquet at the Aberdeen Conference Centre.

I can add one footnote to the story of Alex Ferguson as he rose to pre-eminence in the history of football. Sixteen years after he left Pittodrie I went to visit him at the magnificent new training ground at Carrington, on the outskirts of Manchester. I was accompanied by my eldest son, Geoffrey, and grandson, Jack, who thrilled at the chance of meeting David Beckham, Ryan Giggs, Peter Schmeichel and all the other stars of that time.

Fergie was then into his sixties and as we strolled around the ground I risked the question of when he might be thinking of retiring.

"Ah, well," said Alex, "I was speaking on the phone to Jean Stein the other night and she said, 'Now, Alex, just remember what happened to my Jock.' And she was quite right . . . "

What happened to the great Jock Stein, by then manager of Scotland, came at the very moment of victory when his team was beating Wales to qualify for the World Cup. Seconded by Aberdeen to be his assistant manager, Alex Ferguson was seated next to Big Jock as he suddenly keeled over. He was sixty-three. And he was dead.

I gathered that Fergie had taken the hint from Jean Stein and that it would not be long before he decided to call it a day. So imagine my surprise a few weeks later when he signed another substantial contract with Manchester United. In fact, it was ten years later – 2013 and into his seventy-second year – before he finally announced his retirement. Several factors were involved, mainly that his wife, Cathy, was mourning the death of her sister.

The man himself was also due to have a hip operation, which would take him away from the training ground for several months. So Fergie was going but not too far. He would take his seat as a director and become an ambassador for Manchester United.

Having been served so well by Scots like Busby and Ferguson (and players like Denis Law from Aberdeen), it was appropriate that United should turn to another of the breed, David Moyes, to follow in the footsteps of Alex Ferguson.

CHAPTER TWENTY-FIVE

A GRAIN OF TRUTH

Having completed that first version of *The Dons* in 1978, my thoughts turned once more to those memoirs of 1963. Where had I put them? And what would I think of them? There they were, still in the same old drawer, but the answer to the second question was "Not very much!" However, by now I had lived through the excitement of the *Daily Express* years with so much more to tell – and that was my incentive to rewrite the early version.

On completion, I thought I would repeat what I did the first time – send it to Hutchinson the publisher in London. Well, if nothing else, they were a model of consistency. Back came the rejection slip. So, having reopened this farcical procedure, I might as well continue the pattern of the 1960s. Off it went again to Paul Harris, who had by now relocated himself in Edinburgh. With co-director and author Trevor Royle, he was now ready to accept my book for publication. Titles have never been a strong point, so I consulted my good friend Don Whyte of the *Express*, son of Ian Whyte, composer and founder-conductor of the BBC Scottish Symphony Orchestra.

Don, whose autobiography was the brilliant *On the Lonely Shore*, came up with the suggestion of *A Grain of Truth*, linking words to the grain of my native cornfields. That was good enough for me and that was how it made its first appearance on Guy Fawkes Day of 1981, prompting the hope that it would not turn out to be a damp squib.

I need not have worried. The first edition was sold out by Christmas and *A Grain of Truth* was on its way to a successful life. Sadly, my mother didn't live to see the books, which would have pleased her so much. Among her favourite pieces of music had been

Dvorak's "Going Home" from his New World Symphony, and that title had some significance.

"I want it played at my funeral," my mother would say; and so it was. She was well known and loved in our rural area of Aberdeenshire, where she would answer the daily phone calls for my father and give an articulate response to many a small farmer who just wanted a bit of advice.

For all the breadth of her musical knowledge, she had seen so little of the professional stage. As a good dancer, she was delighted when I took her to see the ballet *Coppelia* at His Majesty's Theatre, Aberdeen, and again to a personal meeting with her operatic heroine, that great Australian soprano, Joan Hammond, who was staying at the Caledonian Hotel.

But her time ran out and it was no surprise that her funeral brought an astonishing gathering of eight hundred people. On that bleak January day we buried her up there in the kirkyard of Culsh, a high point of Buchan from which I could see in the distance Mains of Whitehill, the small farm where she was born. Below us was the village of New Deer, where she went to school, and further down those rolling acres I could see my native village of Maud, where she had spent her married life from 1931 to 1971.

Back home in the farmhouse at Honeyneuk the women served tea in the best room, as we called it, where the radiogram and her records still lay and where Mam herself had lain till that very day. Then they all left till there was only Dad and myself.

As I recorded at the time:

Next day I was to drive away south and the parting was bound to be hazardous for two Buchan men, father and son, whose tradition gives them little practice in the art of communication, especially on matters of tenderness.

So we stood in the farm close, awkward and embarrassed, neither knowing what to say to the other. Emotionally we had been strangers, my father and I, uneasy with each other's company, but now, in the moment when we had lost our common bond, forced into the contact of two little boys who had suddenly been orphaned.

In the platitudes of goodbye we fell into a silence, standing side by side then, as if jogged by the woman who was gone, we acted in one movement and clasped each other by the hand. It was hopelessly out of character, daft-like and bizarre for Buchan men, and I wondered when I had last as much as touched my father's hand, for it was not in the nature of the creatures to do so.

There we stood without words but not without tears till we regained our composure and self-respect, for Buchan men do not cry. Then I stepped into the car and drove out of the farm close towards Aberdeen and the south, leaving behind the place of my roots and deepest affections.

The setting of my childhood was still there before me in all its familiar landscape but suddenly its meaning and bare beauty had drained to a deadness. For landscapes and what they mean to us live mainly by the people who inhabit and enrich them.

Dad lived on at Honeyneuk, looked after by Helen Beaton the maid, but on Burns Day of 1976 his life virtually ended when the clogging of a cerebral artery became complete and he never again uttered a sensible word. He lingered for another sixteen months.

The farm was carried on by two faithful employees, Charlie Fraser the grieve and Jimmy Mutch the cattleman, tending those 200 acres which he had bought in 1952. Through fifteen years of blasting he had cleansed his land of boulders and turned it into a most fertile and desirable farm, looking down that half mile to the village I knew so well.

I arrived from Glasgow in time for his last few hours and witnessed the process of dying for the very first time. I had always regarded "the black crow of death" as an old wife's tale but, in those final moments, I could hardly believe my eyes. The dreaded bird did indeed settle on my father's window sill. It was all over.

I kept Honeyneuk for eight more years, giving a livelihood to

Charlie and Jimmy, but long-distance ownership is seldom recommended. So in 1985, with the two men fixed for other employment, I decided to sell. Little did I know the indirect effect that this decision would have on my writing career.

CHAPTER TWENTY-SIX
WEBSTER'S ROUP ON TV

On a glorious June day of 1985, with the farm of Honeyneuk already sold to Jim and Belinda Muir from Orkney, we held the auction sale, which in Scotland is more commonly known as the roup, when the livestock, implements and all moveable effects go under the auctioneer's hammer. In this case there were four auctioneers, all of whom had worked under my father, John Webster, the Buchan Auctioneer at Maud Mart. A thousand people flocked to Honeyneuk that day, some to make a serious purchase, others to collect a souvenir of the man who had been a friend to many a crofter and small farmer, giving the kind of advice on which they could depend.

Sensing that there was a deeper significance to this day, however, I suggested to the BBC that a documentary film might be an idea. For, more than just a roup, this was the moment when I was severing my ties with the land which had bred me. Generations of John Websters had tilled the grudging soil of Buchan and here I was, breaking the tradition and walking away from my heritage. It was the tale of a human dilemma.

The BBC responded immediately, suggesting that I should write the script and present the programme myself. After all, it was my story. This would be a new experience, something different from newspaper columns and books. But television? I hadn't thought about that. In fact, I wrote the script in one evening and the BBC crew filmed the whole documentary within twenty-four hours, at the cost of a mere one thousand pounds. I could not have anticipated public reaction.

Webster's Roup was nominated in the following year's television awards and, by a casting vote, was beaten to the top place by a documentary which cost a million pounds. I thought we should have had it for economy alone! It was a simple film which struck a chord with a massive audience. Auctioneer Charlie Morrison took a trick, not only with his verbal gymnastics but with his huge tackety boots which an astute cameraman featured in a musical accompaniment. That was brilliant.

The camera roamed over good country faces, honest, decent folk, some of my own generation who, strikingly, had grown into the exact mould of their fathers. And as the last traces of my Honeyneuk heritage disappeared in a thousand directions, I was wondering what my down-to-earth father would have thought of the decision to sell.

In a final scene for that day, I went back to the Hill of Culsh and stood by the resting place of my parents. A sudden crack of thunder raised the question of my father turning in his grave. For the closing moments we played once again those haunting tones of Dvorak's "Going Home". They tell me there wasn't a dry eye across the country. For all the millions of words I have written in more than sixty years, nothing has captured public imagination so much as that documentary.

More than quarter of a century later I still get letters from people bemoaning that somebody has taped *Coronation Street* over *Webster's Roup*! "Is there a DVD?" they ask. Happily, I can tell them that such a creature does now exist.

This was just the beginning of a whole series of documentaries commissioned by the BBC, for whom I became a kind of flavour of the next seven years, until they lost interest in documentaries. But *Webster's Roup* had an immediate effect on my life. By now a columnist on *The Herald* in Glasgow, I was due to write a profile of Ian Chapman, chairman of Collins the publisher in London.

When he phoned to confirm my appointment he said, "That's not a Glasgow voice?"

"No. I come from Aberdeenshire."

"Where in Aberdeenshire?"

"Oh, just a small village called Maud," I said.

"I know Maud!" Mr Chapman exclaimed.

"Surely nobody in London has heard of Maud?" I questioned. "There are folk in Maud who have never heard of London!"(Just a joke.)

"My father grew up on a farm at Artamford, between Maud and New Deer," he replied.

"Yes, I know the Chapmans at Artamford. But how come that I don't know about you?"

"Well my father was the one who left the farm and became a minister at St Fergus, near Peterhead, where I was born."

Well well, it's a sma' world.

CHAPTER TWENTY-SEVEN

ENTER ALISTAIR MACLEAN

Before leaving for London I suggested to Eden that I should per-haps take a video tape of *Webster's Roup* to show Mr Chapman some scenes of his childhood days. At the end of our interview I passed over the tape with due modesty, saying he might care to watch it and send it back. In my London hotel that evening I had a call from Eden in Glasgow. Mr Chapman had been on the phone, anxious to know if I was still in London. He wanted to see me again next morning. Evidently he had gone home that evening, switched on the tape so that he could send it back immediately – but got so caught up in the emotion that he wanted me to write a book for Collins.

When I turned up at his office next morning, he was waiting with a pen and a contract. "That film is the basis of a book you must write for us, telling about life in the North-east of Scotland and . . . "

"But Mr Chapman, the book you describe has already been writ-ten. It is called *A Grain of Truth*. You will not have heard of it in London but it is doing very well in Scotland."

There was no stopping him. He would buy the paperback rights of that book and I would write a second one – *Another Grain of Truth*. He even had the title.

I sat down and signed his contract for a substantial sum – and I did indeed write *Another Grain of Truth*, published in 1988. The book now in your hand completes the trilogy, albeit a whole gen-eration later.

In the years between, there have been many more books. But Mr Chapman was not finished with me yet. As chairman of Col-lins worldwide, he had been fighting a takeover bid by Rupert

Murdoch, that other Buchan man whose grandfather, the Rev. Patrick Murdoch, was the Free Kirk minister at Hatton of Cruden, a few miles on the other side of Peterhead from where Mr Chapman's father was minister at St Fergus. How close can you get? Murdoch's hostile bid would inevitably give him control of Collins but Chapman had to oppose it for the sake of his shareholders. In doing so, he pushed up Murdoch's buying price by a very substantial sum.

So one of the new owner's first acts was to part company with Mr Chapman, who had been there for forty years. Still a fit man in his early sixties, however, he and his wife, Marjory, decided to set up their own publishing business, which emerged with a splendid address, "Chapmans of Drury Lane". One of his first thoughts was to commission a biography of Scottish thriller writer Alistair MacLean, who reigned for years as the biggest-selling novelist in the world.

Back home from serving in the Navy during the war, MacLean had taken a degree at Glasgow University and was teaching at Gallowflat School, Rutherglen, when he decided to enter a short story competition in the *Glasgow Herald*. From 1,000 entries, the winning story was published in the paper in March 1954, by which time Ian and Marjory Chapman were both young editors at the Collins headquarters in Cathedral Street, Glasgow.

Having read the winning story, they were so impressed that they made contact with the author to suggest he should write a novel for Collins. Over dinner in the city's Royal Restaurant, however, this rather dour Highlander expressed little interest in novels, contenting himself with the odd short story. He did, however, mention his wartime experience on the notorious convoys to Russia, which prompted the Chapmans to enthuse about that as a subject for a novel. MacLean still showed little interest and they did not hold out much hope.

But less than ten weeks later there was a phone call: "Do you want to come and collect that thing?" That thing? Yes, Alistair MacLean had written his book. Ian Chapman hot-footed it to the furnished rooms at 343 King's Park Avenue, where MacLean and his German wife, Gisela, had just had their first child. In a downpour of rain, Chapman was left standing on the doorstep, viewing an array of nappies while MacLean fetched his manuscript. Back home, Chapman peeled open the sodden package on his kitchen table – and there before him was the title page of *HMS Ulysses*, destined to be one of the biggest best-sellers of all time.

When MacLean heard that his book was being accepted he wondered if it would earn him enough to put down a deposit on a new house of their own, at Hillend Road, Clarkston, on the southern border of the Glasgow area heading out towards Eaglesham. Those detached bungalows being built in 1955 were costing £2,750 and the Collins advance was already £1,000. But Ian Chapman's private calculation that within a short time MacLean would have grossed £100,000 was not misplaced. He could then have bought not only No.16 but the whole damned street!

It was just the start of a remarkable career that would produce thirty books with titles like *The Guns of Navarone*, *Where Eagles Dare* and *Ice Station Zebra*, all ready-made for filming and taking him through from the '50s to the mid-1980s. All had seemed set for an idyllic life, gone from the staffroom at Gallowflat School with the envy of many a teaching colleague who could only dream of such an exit.

After a nomadic life around Europe, Alistair settled with Gisela and three sons in the picturesque Villa Murat, in the village of Celigny, overlooking Lake Geneva. But heavy drinking was just the beginning of the problems. When he later eloped with a would-be French film producer and actress called Marcelle Georgius, who turned out to be no less than a gold-digger, his German wife Gisela divorced him. Alistair and Marcelle were married at London's Caxton Hall registry office on Friday, 13 October 1972, an ominous date which didn't take long to prove its validity.

On the first night of their honeymoon in Amsterdam they had a drunken row on the banks of a canal. Alistair had a quick solution to the dispute. He threw her into the water – and it was left to someone else to save her from drowning. Things went from bad to worse. After they split up, the tragic Marcelle was found in a Los Angeles doss-house, a down-and-out and homeless junkie surrounded by young hangers-on, with whom she had squandered £100,000 on cocaine for herself and the so-called friends. When she died in May 1985, aged fifty, MacLean paid for the funeral. But he himself didn't have much longer to go. As his triumphs turned to misery, he desperately wanted to remarry Gisela, who was prepared to renew their friendship but no more. What a fool he had been.

At least, whenever he wished, he could now go back to Villa Murat, which Gisela had gained as part of her divorce settlement in 1972. In addition, the family would always get together for a New Year holiday.

Over the festive season of 1986 they gathered in the Black Forest, when he was in one of his abstemious periods. But it didn't last. Meeting up with an Irishman who had a hard-luck story to tell, he handed him £15,000 as they embarked on the mini-bar of their hotel rooms. There he suffered several strokes and died in the University Hospital of Munich on 2 February 1987. He was sixty-four. Such was the mysterious nature of his movements that not much of this story was known, even to his friends, when Ian Chapman called me on the phone one day.

As the man who discovered MacLean and without whom his career might never have happened, he was asking if I would write his biography. Now running his own publishing business in London, he was offering me a staggering sum to take on the commission.

CHAPTER TWENTY-EIGHT

EDEN'S DECLINE

That phone call from Ian Chapman brought a major dilemma. For one thing, I had never read an Alistair MacLean book. And though I had met many successful novelists in my time, from Compton Mackenzie and Eric Linklater to John le Carre and Jack Higgins, they did not include the fellow Scot who had risen to such heights of fame in recent years. However, there was a much bigger issue than that. My wife, Eden, had developed breast cancer in her late forties and, into her fifties, matters became much worse.

I now suspected that her time was limited so the dilemma was quickly resolved. Of course, I could not possibly accept this commission, however tempting it would have been in normal circumstances. That was my reply to Mr Chapman. He then asked me to delay a decision until I had discussed it with Eden. That evening I told her casually of the phone call and how I had turned it down, never having read MacLean – and having no interest in that kind of book anyway. But that didn't wash with Eden, herself an avid reader, who quickly sensed the scale of this offer. "But why on earth would you turn down an offer like that?" she wondered. "You will never get a better opportunity."

Without revealing my knowledge of her condition, I had no convincing answer. So by the end of that evening I had little option but to accept that I would be writing the story of Alistair MacLean, still wondering how I could cope with my role as a columnist on *The Herald*, a major biography that would entail much travelling – and the looming tragedy of Eden in the prime of her life.

With Alistair MacLean already gone, I would have to depend mainly on his family and most of all on first wife, Gisela, to explain the basic structure of his life, which, from early research, seemed to be one of constant movement. His surviving brothers, Ian in Ross-on-Wye, Herefordshire, and Gillespie in Muir of Ord, would cooperate on family background and personal memories. But Gisela would prove a major problem.

That warning came from Ian Chapman, who knew her very well and had to give me the news that she and at least two of the three boys simply did not want the book. I would just have to do my best. So I gathered dozens of names, friends and film producers and directors like Alexander Mackendrick and J. Lee Thompson, who would have to be tracked down in places as far apart as Hollywood, where MacLean had stayed in Marilyn Monroe's old home, and the Yugoslavian resort of Dubrovnik, where he spent the last eight years of his life as a recluse. But what was I going to do without Gisela, the only person who could piece it all together as a cohesive story? Even the brothers could not explain his meanderings.

There was only one way to go. Using the old *Daily Express* technique of "door-stepping", I simply had to confront her at home in Switzerland. That could be combined with tackling another mystery: Why had most of MacLean's books been turned into successful films while the first and best of them, *HMS Ulysses*, had not? The key to that question would lie with the person who must surely hold the film rights but who, for some strange reason, had never made the film. That person turned out to be a rather brusque Italian aristocrat, Count Giovanni Volpi, who would not speak to me on the phone but might reconsider it if I came to see him in Venice.

I was on my way. First stop, Geneva Airport, where I boarded a taxi for the village of Celigny. Since taxi drivers know everything, I explained my mission and, sure enough, my man knew Mrs MacLean but also knew that, as a German, she spent most of her time back home in the Fatherland. I would be lucky to find her at home.

Approaching Villa Murat, I asked the taxi man to give me ten minutes before driving off. By then I would know the score. By good luck, Gisela was at home, naturally taken aback by my visit and flapping around in her confusion, as I tried to make a brief explanation of my mission. Yes, I understood she didn't want the book but could I just come in and talk to her. I had at least come to show face, in an honest attempt to write the biography of one of Scotland's most successful writers. If I didn't write the story someone else most certainly would. And that would likely be some fly-by-night from London who wouldn't even bother to consult her, concentrating instead on the more sensational, less savoury, aspects of her husband's life, over which she would have no control. I intended to write a balanced book; so the choice was hers.

After considering all that, she allowed me over the doorstep and as we sat down in a highly charged atmosphere, I asked what her worry might be.

"I would be afraid of the questions you might ask me," she said.

"Well, if I ask a question and you don't wish to answer, I promise I will never ask that question again. So on that understanding, will you talk to me?"

We settled on a basis of trust and proceeded to a conversation which could not have been more surprising. My questions were not as difficult as she had feared; indeed, as the talk stretched into its second hour Gisela was volunteering the kind of information I would never have expected, warts and all. Piece by piece she was completing the jigsaw of her husband's life with a clarity that could not have come from anyone else. I suspect that this outpouring was turning into a therapeutic release.

Beyond that, she was producing the photo album, including pictures of the couple being introduced to Her Majesty at the London premiere of *The Guns of Navarone* in 1961. There was so much to talk about. By chance, there was a time when their village of Celigny was also the home of Richard Burton and Elizabeth Taylor. Not that Burton and MacLean had much contact, except that the actor had starred in *Where Eagles Dare*, one of MacLean's most successful films in 1969.

There was at least one other contact, however, which caused a stir in the Dorchester Hotel in London's Park Lane. On this occasion the two men embarked on a drunken brawl which ended with the slightly-built MacLean landing a right hook to Burton's nose, sending him sprawling in a state of unconsciousness.

Having missed the London premiere of *Where Eagles Dare*, Gisela had never actually met Richard Burton. But while dog walking in Celigny she would find him out exercising his Pekinese, when he would pass her by without any inkling that she was the wife of the man who knocked him cold.

Through all this, a glance at my watch told me it was time I was heading for Geneva Airport to catch my next flight to Venice. Would Gisela be kind enough to call me a taxi? That would not be necessary, she said. She would drive me to the airport.

On the way, I said, "Well, Mrs McLean, are you not pleased that I came to see you and to allay your fears about the book?"

"Yes," she smiled. "I am."

What a relief. I knew my biggest hurdle had been overcome. Realising that I had now gained her trust, I asked if I could come back another time, since there was more to discuss.

Yes, that would be fine.

On that subsequent visit to Celigny she asked if I would like to visit Alistair's grave. So we wandered along to the local cemetery, an unpretentious little place where the first grave on the left might have belonged to a local labourer, except that the headstone told a different story: Richard Burton.

Across the narrow pathway, just a few yards away, we came upon that other stone, marking the last resting place of that warm, wayward, fallible human being: Alistair MacLean. No more fisticuffs. And there they lie in peace forever, near a waterfall which tumbles down a ravine like a sparkling Highland burn.

Gisela was now delivering me to Geneva Airport as I headed for Venice to meet the enigma that was Count Giovanni Volpi. There I would seek to solve the mystery of *HMS Ulysses* and why it had never been filmed. But little did I know that another sensational story would also land on my lap.

CHAPTER TWENTY-NINE

THE DUCHESS WAS A WHAT?

Alistair MacLean's very first novel, *HMS Ulysses*, suggested to him by Ian and Marjory Chapman when they met in Glasgow's Royal Restaurant in 1954, showed a command of language that put him immediately into the top bracket of thriller writers. It was based, of course, on his own experience as a sailor during the war, going through the frozen hell of the Arctic and back, facing hurricanes, mountainous seas and German U-boats to take supplies to Murmansk so that the Russians could fight off the Nazi menace. Land in the water and you were lucky to survive for five minutes.

As a novel, it had an advance sale to the shops of 134,000 hardback copies and within a few months had sold 250,000, a phenomenal experience for a first-time, totally unknown writer. The film rights were originally snapped up by Associated British Pictures for an equally impressive £30,000 and it would surely be just a matter of time before the film was made. Thirty years later, there was still no film.

We touched down at Venice Airport and a water-taxi took me speeding towards the Grand Canal, where I was delivered to the jetty of Palazzo Volpi and shown to my room. The Count would call me to his study when he was ready.

So what was the story? From an old Venetian background, Count Volpi's father had made his fortune from insurance, property and hotels like the famous Danielli in the early part of the twentieth century. He was also a well-known Fascist in the days of Mussolini, leading the fight to regain Italy's control of Libya and then becoming its Governor-General. More to the point of this story, however, as a man full of ideas he founded the Venice Film Festival in 1932, the first of its kind in the world. The Cannes Festival and all the others did not arise until after the Second World War.

That was the father. The son now weighing me up in the study of his grand palace had other interests, like building racing cars; but browsing at a bookstall in Venice Airport one day, en route to Libya, he picked up a paperback by an author whose name meant nothing to him. It was *HMS Ulysses*, which so intrigued him that, by the end of his journey, he felt a compulsion to make it into a film. Even without the contacts of his late father, Count Volpi managed to acquire the film rights and engaged David Osborn, a well-known writer, to produce a screenplay. MacLean himself was delighted with it but Volpi was not, and the whole project ran into stalemate. He was very frank about the failure: "It was in the wrong hands, including mine," he told me. "I wasn't a professional. So why did I go out of my way to buy the film rights? I did it like I might have bought a painting."

With his inexperience of the film world, Volpi then proceeded to pass up another golden opportunity to salvage *HMS Ulysses*. Having just won an Oscar for that great British film of 1982 *Chariots of Fire*, producer David Puttnam was looking for a successor. His first choice was *HMS Ulysses* and he went as far as to have two screenplays written. But Volpi was now making another admission of failure: "I made a major mistake. I knew if I settled for a share of the profits I would never see a penny. So instead, I demanded a share of the gross takings and David Puttnam couldn't promise me that.

"I now realise it was more important to make the film than to make money. I should have taken the risk because David Puttnam was a guarantee of the quality I had been looking for. Instead, he went off and made *Memphis Belle* – and that could have been *HMS Ulysses*." As a result, his gloomy conclusion was that his film would never be made.

At that point he announced that we were going for supper at the home of friends along the Grand Canal. His speedboat delivered us to a most impressive building, rather like a cathedral, all broad stairways, crystal chandeliers and priceless paintings. In fact it was a family home, owned by one of the Merchants of Venice. It had not occurred to me that such families still existed.

The hostess was having a few guests for supper, a mixture of Venetian wealth, a professor from Berlin and the inevitable lady from America. Volpi did his best to explain my existence. He was also telling the American lady and me about the Duke and Duchess of Windsor, friends of his parents who used to stay at their home in Italy. Of course the whole world knew the story of Edward VIII, due to become king on the death of his father, George V, in 1936 but who turned down the vacancy for the love of an American double divorcee, Wallis Simpson, who he intended to marry. It was the major sensation of my childhood and if I didn't understand it, I certainly remembered the furore. His brother had to take the throne as King George VI, to be followed in 1952 by the king's daughter, Queen Elizabeth.

What we didn't know, however, was the story our American lady was about to tell us. She had a friend who was driving into Paris one dark, wet night when she came upon an elderly lady in distress because her car had broken down. Knowing something about cars, she stopped to help the poor soul, who was so grateful that she invited her to come for coffee at her home, just a few miles along the road. The Windsors had also lived on the outskirts of Paris and the lady in distress had been a nurse to the Duchess. There was obviously some exclusive piece of knowledge she wished to pass on before departing this earthly scene. And it might as well be told to a stranger. It was simply that the Duchess of Windsor, formerly Mrs Wallis Simpson, was not the woman she was supposed to be. In fact, she wasn't any kind of woman. She was a man!

Now, this is not the kind of news you expect to hear in the home of a Merchant of Venice. Shakespeare might have lapped it up for his next play but I just choked on my champagne. Of course this must be the ramblings of a deranged old woman. Or what was her evidence? Well, in the later years it had been part of her daily duty to bath the Duchess and from simple observation she could see that the vital parts she was regularly sponging were not those of a woman. Swear to God, she could guarantee that her story was true.

Sorely tempted as my journalistic instincts were, I was not going to spread this intriguing piece of news without some better evidence. But that was soon forthcoming – from Michael Bloch, the man engaged by the Duchess's lawyers in Paris to edit the Windsor papers. As he approached his task, he had evidently been told by Dr John Randell of Charing Cross Hospital, London, an authority on sexual matters, to keep in mind that Wallis Simpson was really a man. Dr Randell was given the details by a colleague who had actually examined her. Bloch's further inquiries revealed the condition as Androgen Insensitivity Syndrome, by which children are born genetically male but develop outwardly as female. Though they can be sexually attractive as women, their reproductive organs don't exist.

Medical people are aware of this rare condition and cite Queen Elizabeth I as an example. As for Wallis Simpson, her Christian name was also that of her father, surely confirming her male status at birth. Then came further evidence from author Donald Spoto, who reported that, on the eve of her wedding to the Duke of Windsor, the Duchess told her closest male friend, Herman Rogers, that she had never had intercourse with either of her first two husbands. Her French lawyer, Suzanne Blum, conceded that she too was convinced that her client remained a virgin to the end.

Wallis Simpson was of course a powerful personality, whose dominant role seemed to suit the peculiar tastes of the Duke of Windsor. In addition, while in the Far East she had evidently acquired an extensive knowledge of how to stimulate a man sexually. A very strange story but one I could then reveal to my reading public with a fair amount of certainty that it was true.

As for Count Volpi, his aristocratic inscrutability took a fair old dunt from this revelation, almost enough to put *HMS Ulysses* out of his head. But not quite.

Before that evening was over – and with a relaxing amount of claret consumed – Count Volpi had a proposition for me. Whereas he had given up all hope that his film would ever be made, he was prepared to change his mind on one condition. He needed two film stars, Sean Connery and Mel Gibson. Did I know these people? Well I had had some encounters with Connery.

"If you can get them for me, we could still do it," he barked.

After my biography of Alistair MacLean was published I was flying to Los Angeles one day when I saw Sean Connery boarding our plane and turning left to his first-class seat. Was this my opportunity? With a nine-hour flight ahead of us, could he perhaps spare me a few minutes to hear of Volpi's proposition? I scribbled a note to that effect and, along with a copy of the book, asked a stewardess if she would kindly pass them on to Mr Connery in his luxury apartment up front.

Some time later, she returned with both book and note, apologising that our so-called most famous Scot was not prepared to see me, even for five minutes. Not the most gracious of responses but that did not entirely surprise me.

And there were far more important matters than Sean Connery to think about.

CHAPTER THIRTY

THE CRUELTY OF FATE AND IN COURT WITH BADER

As I came to the end of my research for the MacLean book, I had appointments in that delightful resort of Dubrovnik, where the author had spent his last eight years. It was essential to piece together that part of the puzzle.

Back home, Eden's decline continued. But she had always wanted to see Dubrovnik, where I had interviewed Field Marshal Montgomery in those early years, and this would be a wonderful opportunity to take her with me. At the last moment, however, the doctor would not allow it. I went alone and left her to the care of the nursing staff, as well as the close attention of our neighbours and best friends, Walter and Ayliffe Macphail. We had been a happy foursome for twenty-eight years, sharing a holiday home at Penina in the Algarve and with children who grew up together.

With a husband and three sons, Eden had always longed for a girl in the family but that was not to be. However, two of the boys were already married and their wives were on the point of producing the first grandchildren. As we entered the autumn of 1990 we clung to the hope that there might yet be a girl in the family. Geoffrey's wife was first to give birth: a son, called Jack. Eden held him in her arms and was delighted. But now her time was running out. Meanwhile, Keith, a journalist in England, was running between Glasgow, where his mother was dying, and Oxford, where his wife was going into labour. His joyous phone call telling me that the baby had just arrived – and yes, she was a girl! – was the same phone call I had to tell him that his mother had just died. She would never know about Sinead, and I wondered how cruel the fates can really be?

As if all that was not enough, our good friend Walter Macphail collapsed and died of a heart attack in the same week. In complete bewilderment, we were twice at the Linn Crematorium within days.

After the Glasgow ceremony, the boys and I drove north for a service at Crimond Parish Church, between Peterhead and Fraserburgh. For it was here at Crimond that Eden's father, Nelson Keith, had grown up as a crofter's son, a brilliant academic who served as a captain in the 5th Gordon Highlanders during the Second World War, only to be captured at St Valery in 1940. It was also here at Crimond in the later 1800s that the minister's daughter, Jessie Seymour Irvine, had composed that psalm tune which would be sung in all corners of the earth to the words of "The Lord's My Shepherd". The Queen chose it for her wedding in 1947. Understandably, Jessie called her tune "Crimond" – and standing beside her in the church choir when it was first aired was a young lad called Alexander Keith, none other than Eden's grandfather.

We sang it again on that sad day, when her Guide mistress, Patty Russell, not only played the organ but gave a most moving eulogy from which our three sons gained a new picture of their mother as a little girl in Fraserburgh. With a heavy heart, I looked at Geoffrey, Keith and Martin and thought that whoever created the cliché about no one in this world being indispensible must surely have forgotten about mothers.

Eden had been one of a generation of children who found themselves without a father from 1939 until 1945. She shared the dilemma of so many youngsters when this strange man of whom she had no memory reappeared from a German prison camp to change the domestic scene. It took time to accept this intrusion and several more years to appreciate the true worth of this remarkable man, a typical lad o'pairts, with whom she really had so much in common.

By then, the wartime wounds and deprivations of Nelson Keith were leading to a premature death, which left Eden devastated and now with an urge to see where he had been during those missing years. It would help to fill that gap in her own life. So we spent several years with our three boys in the back seat of the car driving across Germany from one former prison camp to another, talking to local people who remembered the Scottish soldiers so well.

Back home, she had fallen heir to a very secret diary which Nelson Keith had kept, against all orders. His writing had to be small but what a story he had to tell. As a fluent German speaker, among so many other academic talents, he had been called as interpreter for the much publicised Douglas Bader, who had lost both legs in 1931 but still managed to become a legend as a fighter pilot during the Second World War. Ending up in a prison camp in Germany, the legless pilot still had an unthinkable penchant for escaping. Back in custody, he would then face court martial – and that was where Nelson Keith came to interpret.

In answer to questions from the German judge, he would instruct my father-in-law to "tell the old bastard to go to hell", with an assortment of other such sentiments! In his attempts to soften the language, Nelson Keith was himself being checked for accuracy by a German interpreter – and was promptly sentenced to solitary confinement for his troubles. Needless to say, the great Douglas Bader was not his favourite person who, for all his bravery in the air, was fairly widely disliked. I once met his own brother-in-law, Laddie Lucas, another heroic pilot, who couldn't stand the sight of him.

Nelson Keith's diary gave graphic descriptions of his capture at St Valery on 12 June 1940 and of those years of misery in which, as an officer, he was not allowed the privilege of other ranks who could work in the fields as a semblance of normality. But there was no more poignant passage than his description of the final hours of captivity when the Germans faced defeat and our soldiers awaited the moment of liberation. The Germans began to move their prisoners on forced marches when suddenly American planes came flying overhead – and mistook our Scots lads for enemy soldiers:

Saturday, 14 April 1945: We were fired upon by American bombers. About twenty of our lads killed and thirty wounded. After five years of captivity, waiting for release, what an irony!

Monday, 23 April 1945: Still on the march. Just about reached lowest pitch of misery in all the five years. Cold, sleety morning; everything filthy. Was suddenly greeted by George Davidson, an Aberdeen doctor I hadn't seen for years. He'd lost a tremendous amount of weight.

An amazing coincidence. One of the American airmen who shot us up a week ago on Saturday was himself shot down and brought into the camp. He was horrified when he heard of what had happened.

Sunday, 29 April 1945: It seems the Americans have arrived at last and we should be liberated some time today. Much to my surprise, my feelings at being released are non-existent. It's very noticeable that the people least concerned are the five-year POWs.

The recent captures have gone daft. Personally I shan't feel free until we are clear of all the filth and squalor. One thing strikes me as funny. This morning we had armed German guards all around – and now Allied POWs are in the sentry boxes, cutting holes in the wire. The German guards were taken prisoner and marched off.

Nelson Keith returned to his job as head of maths at Fraserburgh Academy before taking over as headmaster at Strichen Secondary School. But his time was soon up. And, as if he had not suffered enough already, he died the excruciating death of pancreatic cancer and was taken back to the kirkyard of Crimond, the parish where his life began.

That recent mention of Jessie Seymour Irvine and her psalm tune called "Crimond" uncovers another of those stories where injustice spurred me to action. Jessie was not completely satisfied with the harmonising of her tune and sought help from Aberdeen tobacconist David Grant, a well-known figure in the local music scene, who obliged with a few minor alterations.

Grant's close friend was Aberdeen journalist William Carnie, another music man in the city, who was then compiling the *Northern Psalter*. Jessie was delighted to hear that her tune had been included in the new publication – except that the composer was given as David Grant! If there is no record of her protest at the time, it seems that this gentle lady of the Manse thought her simple little tune hardly justified a rumpus.

Jessie died in middle-age but a successor of her father, the Rev. Robert Monteith, conducted his own investigation and could produce a letter from her sister Anna, explaining how it had all happened. Mr Monteith lived to a ripe old age and as a young journalist I managed to interview him – and to see the letter. He had plenty other witnesses to the fact that Jessie had written the tune. But in the hymn books, David Grant's name remained as the composer and it was not till much later that I saw a television programme which finally raised my dander.

The Rev. John Bell of the Iona community was telling us categorically that this famous psalm tune had been written not by Miss Irvine as some people thought but by, yes, David Grant. I wondered if Mr Bell could tell us why the tune had been called "Crimond" in the first place – and how a modest Victorian lady had come to be credited with its composition if she had nothing to do with it.

I put the questions to BBC Television and drew an interesting response. The producer, Dr Ian Bradley, author of the Penguin *Book of Hymns* and a respected voice on church music, took full responsibility for John Bell's words. He was, however, prepared to hear the other side of the story. As a result of our exchanges he wrote to tell me: "I am now inclined to change my mind. I think I have been hoodwinked by the musical establishment. The more I reflect on it the more I think the story you have told me is the correct one. I can now see how it all happened and I will take the first opportunity to put the record straight."

I think Jessie Seymour Irvine deserved no less.

CHAPTER THIRTY-ONE

I MEET HITLER'S FRIEND

In the seventh decade of a writing career I am still asked to name the most fascinating personality I have ever met. The expectations can range from Muhammad Ali, Charlie Chaplin, Bing Crosby and Elizabeth Taylor to Paul Getty, Margaret Thatcher, Ian Paisley – and Christine Keeler! All worthy candidates. The honest answer, however, usually comes as a complete surprise since most people have never heard of him. His name was Dr Ernst Hanfstaengl, a charismatic figure of German society, distinguished historian and brilliant pianist, who became the friend and mentor of Adolf Hitler and who, along with his beautiful wife Helene, could unwittingly have changed the history of the world. It takes a bit of explaining but in the post-war years I gained a whiff of his significance, to the point of tracking him down to his mansion in an exclusive suburb of Munich and getting to grips with his remarkable story.

Usually known as Putzi Hanfstaengl, this giant of a man was born of a German father and American mother and in 1906 was sent to Harvard, where his many friends included the future President of the United States Franklin D. Roosevelt. With his charismatic gift he was soon mixing with people like William Randolph Hearst, T.S. Eliot and Walter Lippmann.

The Hanfstaengls were prominent in the world of art reproduction, with shops in Munich and New York, where Putzi remained after graduation to run the business on Fifth Avenue. His customers included great names like Caruso, Toscanini and Paderewski, as well as Henry Ford and Charlie Chaplin. By 1921, however, he reckoned it was time to return to the Fatherland, back to his native Munich, which was by then in the throes of Communist agitation and other political stirrings. With his vast range of contacts it was no surprise when he had a call one day from the American Embassy in Berlin, which was sending an attaché to assess what was going on in Munich. So, with his local knowledge, would Putzi point him in the right direction?

On the attaché's last day he called to say he had met a rather remarkable chap who was to be speaking in a beer hall that evening. His name, as yet unknown to Putzi, was Adolf Hitler. Would he oblige by going to the meeting and sending a report on what he thought of him?

As he opened our second bottle of wine, Hanfstaengl was telling me how he arrived at the Kindlkeller beer hall to find a placard saying, "No entry for Jews." Inside, there were three men on the platform. He had to ask which one was this man Hitler.

On this occasion he evidently gave a well-reasoned speech about the plight of Germany after the First World War and impressed the audience with the power of his oratory. Putzi may not have known Hitler but when he went to introduce himself at the end, it was obvious that Hitler knew the significance of the Hanfstaengls. Their home was comparable to that of the Astors in England, and when he was invited to one of their social gatherings he could hardly believe his luck. For this was where he would meet the whole spectrum of influential people in Bavaria, from businessmen and politicians to editors, writers and powerful aristocrats – exactly the people he needed to court for acceptance, so far from the gutter where most of his contacts were to be found.

Unwittingly, Putzi Hanfstaengl had opened society's door for the man who would one day become the dreaded dictator of Germany, leading the Nazi Party to power and plunging the world into the biggest war it had ever known. In the beginning, however, Putzi became his friend and mentor, intrigued, I suspect, by the thought of hitching his wagon to the rising star of his own native land, who was two years his junior. As a world-travelled aristocrat himself, he could guide him on the international scene, of which Hitler had very little knowledge. He had been as far as the trenches of the

First World War but no further. He wanted to know about America and had at least heard of the Ku Klux Clan, which he admired, and Henry Ford, because of his allegedly anti-Semitic views, not to mention his potential as a source of funds.

Their connection blossomed, at meetings in the Café Neumaier or back in the grubby little flat which Hitler rented at 41 Thiersch Strasse, where he would pace up and down in his braces, rehearsing his speeches, and where his books ranged from *A History of the Great War* to *The History of Erotic Art*. [At a later date I found my way to that flat in Munich and could not equate the nondescript setting with the man who was ready to rule the world.] Musically, he disliked Bach and Mozart but was always delighted when Putzi sat down to play the prelude to Wagner's *Meistersinger* which, interestingly enough, came to reflect the rhythms of his own speeches. A shrewd observer of the human condition, Putzi was getting to grips with the mystery of Hitler's sex life.

He recorded his thoughts at the time: "It was gradually being borne in on me that Hitler was a narcissus type for whom the crowd represented a substitute for the woman he didn't seem able to find. For him, speaking represented the satisfaction of some depletion urge and to me this made the phenomenon of his oratory more intelligible. The last eight to ten minutes of a speech resembled an orgasm of words."

That conclusion was supported by the evidence of Putzi's beautiful wife, Helene, who had first-hand experience of Hitler's attempt at intimacy. She was able to tell her husband that the Fuhrer was in fact a neuter, capable of falling in love but not of performing. Although he was believed to have had an affair with his deputy, Rudolf Hess, his tendencies were neither fully heterosexual nor homosexual and he suffered complexes from the time he caught a bad dose of syphilis in his native Vienna in 1908.

Hanfstaengl was now more and more involved in Hitler's political activities, a superior figure standing above the surrounding rabble who resented his high intellect, glorious presence and influence – and the fact that he could say anything to Hitler and get away with it. However, events were now geared towards Hitler's domination of Bavaria, as that first step towards Germany and the world. His Nazi aspirations burst onto the streets of Munich in 1923, with a putsch in which Hanfstaengl was the second gun behind the master himself, clearly his immediate escort. But in fierce street battles with the police, in which Herman Goering was shot in the groin, the whole violent revolution ran into serious trouble. It was time to run for their lives. For now at least the putsch had failed. Putzi Hanfstaengl would flee across the border to Vienna, where he sheltered with Hitler's sister and her daughter, Geli Raubel.

Hitler himself would find no better haven than the Hanfstaengl country house at Uffing, where he would have the consolation of Putzi's wife, Helene, for whom he still had that infatuation. The Bavarian police were on his track, however, and Hitler was convinced that he would be captured and shot. He was determined that that should not happen and Helene became alarmed at his demeanour, not least when he went quietly up to his room. She crept upstairs, in time to see him open a drawer and take out a pistol. By chance, she had recently taken instruction in ju-jitsu. As he raised the gun to his temple she dashed into the bedroom and disarmed him, persuading him not to be foolish.

At that moment the gorgeous Helene Hanfstaengl held the future history of the world in the palm of her hand. Had she not interfered in that suicide attempt it is almost certain that we would not have had the Second World War. The rest of his rabble would not have survived without the irresistible power of the master. It was as chillingly simple as that.

The police duly arrived and arrested Hitler, who was given a fair trial and sent to Landsberg Prison, where he wrote his much-publicised book, *Mein Kampf*. On his eventual release, he went straight to the Hanfstaengl home at the fashionable Pienzenauer Strasse for a celebration. Free once more and now becoming an intriguing figure on the German scene, having greatly benefited from the publicity of his trial, the likelihood that his day was yet to come did not escape his attention.

And here I was in that same Hanfstaengl home, hearing the story from this extraordinary man, powerful in voice, hilarious in mimicry, a kind of jester at the court of Adolf Hitler who occupied a unique vantage point for assessing one of the most evil men who ever lived.

When Hitler eventually gained control of Germany in 1933, democratically elected by the people, he took Hanfstaengl with him to Berlin, in a dual role as his foreign press chief and private pianist. Putzi would give me an insight into the Fuhrer's behaviour. For example, for all his power and bravado, he was a nervous man who constantly bit his nails and found it hard to sleep. On those restless nights he would send the chauffeur to bring Putzi to his room to play him to sleep.

I guessed he would want Wagner.

"No no," said Putzi. "On those occasions his favourite request was 'The Russian Lullaby', composed by Irving Berlin – a Russian Jew!"

Aware of the Fuhrer's excesses but not yet of his evil intent, he would use the tenderness of those musical moments to suggest moderation.

Knowing my own fascination with piano music, he was now crossing to the keyboard. I stood behind him, intrigued by the movement of those massive hands as they drew the most magnificent sound from the Steinway grand. Yes, he would play me Hitler's favourite lullaby. And as he did so, I glanced at a photograph on the wall and froze at the sight of it. For here it was in the 1930s, this same room, the same man playing the same piano and, standing exactly where I stood now, were Hitler, Goering, Goebbles, Hess and Eva Braun, enjoying the same music, like ordinary civilised people.

"That was Hitler's chair over there," said Putzi. "And that was where Eva Braun sat and Goering and Goebbels . . . "

In this very room so much of Hitler's future had been mapped out. And here I was, enclosed by four walls that had such a story to tell, if only walls could speak. It was a classic example of how the most powerful moments in history are sometimes enacted in the most mundane of surroundings.

I thought back to my boyhood in Maud, those wartime days when the Nazi spectre loomed so large and threatening. As a young lad in one small corner of rural Scotland, how could I have guessed that I would ever have such an immediate and chilling contact as this? As we wandered through the French windows to a spacious garden I was hearing one fascinating tale after another. None intrigued me more than that of how Hanfstaengl contrived to bring Hitler into contact with Winston Churchill.

With his vast array of international connections, he was already a constant visitor to Britain from the 1920s and the Churchill family were among his London friends. Even through Winston's wilderness years Putzi had already sensed his potential place in world politics and thought he had found a perfect opportunity when the future Prime Minister, with his wife, Clementine, and son, Randolph, arrived in Munich in 1931, keen to see what was happening.

Putzi's suggestion to Hitler that he should now take this chance of meeting Churchill was firmly rejected, mainly on the grounds that he was a man of no consequence. Disheartened, Putzi nevertheless went along to have dinner with the Churchills at the Continental Hotel. During dinner, he excused himself from the table, determined to make one last plea by phone. And to his astonishment, who was standing in the foyer but Hitler – taking his farewell of a Dutchman, who had been financing the Nazi Party. Had he changed his mind? For here he was, within yards of Britain's future man of destiny, and surely this was a moment for history. But no. In his customary green hat and dirty white raincoat Hitler said he was unshaven and, in any case, he had too much to do.

Despairing of a lost opportunity, Putzi watched as Hitler disappeared, returning to the Churchill table and wondering if by chance, at a distance of only fifteen yards, the two men had caught sight of each other. It was the closest they would ever come. We are left to ponder what might have happened to the shape of twentieth-century history if they had actually met. We'll never know.

As if all that were not enough, Putzi had another significant story to tell me. It concerned Unity Mitford, one of that bevvy of aristocratic English beauties, five sisters who were seldom out of the news for one reason or another. Jessica Mitford became a distinguished writer, with books like *The American Way of Death*. She also became a communist. Meanwhile, at the other end of the spectrum, the stunning Diana married Britain's fascist leader, Oswald Mosley. Sister Nancy wrote witty novels and set tongues awagging with *Noblesse Oblige*, in which she established rules of language and behaviour into categories of "U" (for upper class) and "Non-U" for the rest. But it was Unity who capped them all by declaring that she was going to pursue her admiration for Adolf Hitler. And that was what she did, travelling to Germany, finding his favourite café and sitting there in the hope that he would notice her.

Once more, whatever his own deficiencies, Hitler was intrigued by an attractive woman and it didn't take long before she was summoned to his table, a first step on the way to his inner circle. But then the Mitfords had a way of getting what they wanted and Unity came to serve a purpose within the Nazi hierarchy. Her own ambition was to become Hitler's wife. There came a time, however, when he needed breathing space and there was only one man to turn to. "Just get her off my back," was his instruction to Hanfstaengl. Putzi duly obliged and became her escort, wining and dining her and keeping her at arm's length from the Fuhrer.

Increasingly concerned about the man's behaviour, however, he now began to distance himself, realising that his moderating influence was having little effect. His big mistake was to air his criticisms to Unity. To ingratiate herself with Hitler, she was now carrying tales of what Putzi was saying. And that was the end of the special relationship between the two men. A furious Hitler had his own idea of a solution.

During the Spanish Civil War in 1937 Putzi received an order to fly to Spain and complain to Franco that German journalists were not gaining access to the war front. It seemed an odd mission but he was still at the Fuhrer's command – and a private plane awaited him. On his arrival at the airfield, he found others in the plane. The pilot was a man he knew well – and his whispered message was that this was an attempt on his life.

Two different versions of the story later appeared in books by Goebbels and Albert Speer but it seemed the Gestapo were to throw him out without a parachute. The pilot said he would land the plane with an alleged fault – and Putzi could then run like hell! And that is what happened. He made his escape and fled to England, arriving on his fiftieth birthday, saying goodbye to the Fatherland for the next ten years and making the most of his London friendships.

When war broke out in September 1939 he was rounded up, like all other Germans in Britain, though in his case he was sent to Canada and kept under house arrest. While there, he managed to send a message to the White House in Washington, to his old Harvard Club friend, Franklin D. Roosevelt. The President could hardly believe his ears. Yes, it was Putzi all right, and he had a proposition. He was offering to become a political and psychological adviser to Roosevelt.

When he heard the full story – and having gained clearance from the British government – the President promptly arranged for a limousine to transport him to Washington, establishing him in a villa outside the capital (complete with Steinway grand piano) and for the rest of the war employing him as his personal adviser on Hitler's mentality. What might the monster of Munich be planning next? No one was likely to guess better than Dr Ernst Hanfstaengl, surely the only man in the world who could claim friendship with three of its most powerful men – Adolf Hitler, Winston Churchill and Franklin D. Roosevelt. His forecasting was said to be highly impressive.

At the end of the war he was delivered back to the custody of Great Britain, from which he was quietly released in 1947, back to that same mansion house in Munich's Pienzenauer Strasse, where so much of Hitler's planning had taken place all those years ago. And here I was in that historic room, hearing the whole story from the man who, with his wife Helene, could have made it all so different. By then, we were all too familiar with what Hitler had been up to. His intention of exterminating all Jews, Gypsies and anyone who disagreed with him was planned to every detail. But the full horror of the concentration camps was revealed to us only at the end of the war, when our troops came across Belsen and Buchenwald and Auschwitz. Even then it was hard to grasp.

So as recently as May 2013 I decided to see it for myself, flying to the beautiful Polish city of Krakow, which lies near to Auschwitz. And until you enter that vast complex of gas chambers and crematoriums you have very little idea of how horrifying it really was. That such brutality could have been inflicted on innocent human beings within our own lifetime defies all understanding. And that Hitler could find thousands of German people to join in his murderous plan simply adds to the bewilderment.

Back in Putzi's Munich mansion I had one more question: whatever happened to Unity Mitford? She was still in Germany on that September day of 1939 but the thought of her homeland being in a world war with her beloved land of adoption was too much to bear. On 3 September, the very day war was declared, she went into the Englisher Garten in Munich, took out a pistol and shot herself in the head. She did not die but inflicted severe damage from which she never recovered.

If anything can be said in favour of Hitler it was that he found time on that historic day to take personal charge of the tragedy, arranged for her to be taken to the neutrality of Switzerland, and sent a message to her mother, Lady Redesdale, to say where she could be collected.

By now the Mitfords owned the Scottish island of Inchkenneth, within sight of Mull, and it was from there that her mother and sister Deborah went to bring her back home. Unity spent her last years on Inchkenneth, flying the Swastika and playing Nazi tunes on an amplified gramophone, much to the astonishment of passing yachtsmen. As her condition deteriorated she was taken to hospital in Oban, where she died in 1948, aged thirty-four.

Into the twenty-first century I crossed in a little boat to her island and found, within that magnificent house, her gramophone, records, pianos and books still intact. As I write in 2013, the last of the Mitford girls, Deborah, who became the Duchess of Devonshire, is still with us, at the magnificent Chatsworth estate in Derbyshire. I went to visit her not so long ago. As for Putzi Hanfstaengl, he lived in that same Munich mansion until 1975, when he died at the age of eighty-eight. As I said, he was quite the most intriguing figure I ever knew – and we kept in good contact till the very end.

CHAPTER THIRTY-TWO

BOOTHBY: THE GREAT ORATOR

If Putzi Hanfstaengl topped my list of interviewees, he was closely followed by the greatest orator I ever heard, Robert Boothby, who, by chance, was the Member of Parliament for my native constituency of East Aberdeenshire. By further coincidence, he was also a long-standing friend of the aforesaid Hanfstaengl, a fact which did not surprise me since both were larger-than-life personalities, exuding charisma on the grand scale, and both with that roguish element that rather added to their appeal. Already pinpointed as the up-and coming star of British politics by Winston Churchill, who had appointed him as his Parliamentary Private Secretary at the age of twenty-six, Robert Boothby was soon in demand as a speaker, not least in Berlin, where he would meet up again with Hanfstaengl.

Hitler had been following his speeches and wanted to meet him, so Boothby turned up at the Esplanade Hotel, which was then the Fuhrer's headquarters. He later told me of how he entered the room where this short, dark figure with a small moustache jumped to his feet, clicked his heels, raised his arm and shouted, "Hitler!"

"I was taken aback so I just clicked my own heels and shouted 'Boothby!'" he laughed. "It didn't go down well." [Putzi Hanfstaengl verified the story for me.] So what was the background of this impressive figure, all bow tie and flowing hair, who could charm the women and gain the admiration of the men?

Robert Boothby was born in Edinburgh in 1900 and grew up in a large house known as Beechwood on the slopes of Corstorphine Hill, with a fine view of the Pentlands. His father was manager of Scottish Provident and a director of the Royal Bank of Scotland and from a well-connected family, young Robert went to school at Rottingdean in Sussex, where he once had tea with Rudyard Kipling, who lived nearby. He then went on to Eton and Oxford. By the age of twenty-three he was ready to stand for Parliament and appeared as the Conservative candidate in an Orkney by-election. It so happened that a group of Tory farmers from East Aberdeenshire were there for the annual cattle sales and, with nothing better to do of an evening, went along to hear him speak.

As I once wrote, "They went in search of bullocks and came back with Bob Boothby. As good livestock men, they checked his pedigree and, though he failed against the Liberals in Orkney, he was just the chap the Tories would need to oust the same party in Buchan." And that was how it happened in 1924. At the age of twenty-four he embarked on a Westminster career in which he would keep his massive majority for the next thirty-four years.

Twice a year or so he would come to our village hall where, as a schoolboy, I would sit entranced by his flow of language and his potted versions of what was going on in the world. This was education as no school could provide it. Older people of all political persuasions and none came to listen, convinced that party labels didn't matter when you heard a man of such knowledge and personality and possessing the most golden voice they had ever heard. This was a phenomenon called Boothbyism, radical and independent, that would guarantee his seat in the Commons for as long as he wanted. As a spokesman for the farmers and fishermen of Buchan he was an incomparable champion.

When fascinating radio programmes like *The Brains Trust* transferred to the novelty of television in the 1950s, massive audiences were intrigued to put faces to those well-informed voices which had entertained them for years. Top academics like Professor Julian Huxley, Professor C.E.M. Joad, Dr Bronowski, Sir Denis Brogan and Robert Boothby were guided by chairman Gilbert Harding into discussions of the highest order. We ordinary mortals were given the taste of a world beyond our ken, inspiring us to thoughts far removed from those brainless chat shows that pass for television entertainment today.

Boothby therefore became the first politician to star on television, with shrewd judgements to match those of his former master, Winston Churchill. For example, he came back from that meeting with Hitler and warned his party that they would soon be dealing with a madman. But for the rest of that decade very few were prepared to listen.

If wise judgements prevailed in his political life, however, they were less apparent in his private one. In fact, his love life was a shambles, centred largely on a lifelong affair with Lady Dorothy Cavendish, daughter of the Duke of Devonshire, who had married the future Prime Minister, Harold Macmillan, but soon realised what a ghastly mistake she had made. I had it on the authority of Boothby's very able biographer, Robert Rhodes James, that even if Dorothy was not exactly beautiful she was a highly-sexed and powerful personality.

"It was Dorothy who seduced Boothby," he explained. "He not only fulfilled her sexually but gave her the fun, glamour and exciting company that her husband was unable to do. Also, Boothby was clearly a rising and successful politician of the time, whereas Macmillan showed no such promise."

The liaison, which had developed into a genuine love affair, was well known in London society but it is a measure of how times have changed that not a word appeared in the press. As Harold Macmillan refused to grant Dorothy a divorce, a stalemate developed, during which the Aberdeenshire MP now found himself falling for an old friend, Diana Cavendish, another aristocratic lady, who happened to be a cousin of Lady Dorothy Macmillan! What a mess. Meanwhile Boothby, who valued his political career, was in tenterhooks that all this might leak out – and cause shock to the good folk of his Aberdeenshire constituency.

In March 1935, however, he and Diana were duly married, once she was convinced that the Dorothy affair was over. The wedding presents included a very handsome cheque from his constituents in Aberdeenshire, as well as a gift from Churchill, who still regarded Boothby as his blue-eyed boy and was delighted that he was marrying Diana. But Dorothy Macmillan reappeared on the scene, unwilling to give up her love affair, and the whole crisis blew up again. Torn between his two genuine loves, Boothby was joined by his new wife Diana in accepting that their brief marriage was not tenable and, incredibly, they agreed on an amicable divorce – and remained affectionate friends till the end of their days. We ordinary mortals may find it hard to understand such "civilised" attitudes (Winston Churchill was furious) but Boothby's fears of a reaction from his constituents were without foundation.

His biographer quoted what I later wrote: "The folk of East Aberdeenshire winced but granted that his private life was his own, even if divorce was hardly known among the farming fraternity at that time. Irreconcilable couples tended to thole each other, no matter how deep and interminable the misery, rather than be dragged into the shame and prominence of the Court of Session."

That divorce of 1937 received its share of publicity but was rather overshadowed by the bigger event of the Duke of Windsor and his determination to marry the American divorcee, Mrs Wallis Simpson, which brought about the sensation of his abdication.

Robert Boothby and Lady Dorothy Macmillan continued their association till the end of her life, when the whole melodrama took a turn towards the bizarre and then to farce, if not to outright comedy. In the basement of his plush flat at No.1 Eaton Square, London, Boothby gathered more than seven hundred of her letters and burned them in an incinerator. Meanwhile, Harold Macmillan, who had indeed become Prime Minister, was discovering a huge number of Boothby's letters to Dorothy. He, too, decided to have a bonfire but, never having lit an incinerator, he ran into difficulties. Seeking the privacy of his back garden, he had scarcely begun when the wind got up and letters were flying in all directions, as he frantically chased them before the endearments of his wife's lover could escape for public consumption. (On reflection, I wondered if he remembered his famous "Wind of Change" speech in Cape Town in 1960!) He later told Boothby that he didn't want some professor writing a thesis about the two of them. Considering their history, they remained on surprisingly good terms. By then, I'm told, Macmillan did manage to see the comical side of it. He was just relieved that, having staved off divorce, he had at least preserved his political career. It would take the notorious case of Christine Keeler and the Profumo scandal to prise him out of 10 Downing Street in 1963.

Sadly, Boothby's own prospects of Downing Street were now on the wane, while still in his thirties. His career took a further severe, if undeserved, blow in the early months of the war when he spoke in the Commons in support of freezing Czechoslovakian assets in Britain to repay Czech exiles whose assets had been lost in Hitler's invasion. The fact that he did not declare an alleged financial interest in such a move was jumped upon by his political opponents, who made the most of it. In fact, a declaration of interest was not required unless the matter went to a vote – and there was no vote.

So, strictly speaking, he did nothing wrong. But as so often in this world, some of the mud is bound to stick. He went off and joined the RAF, serving in a squadron whose motto was "There's Always Bloody Something". It could well have been Boothby's motto too. For such a lady's man (yes, there were other associations) he even had to endure hints of a homosexual past and an association with the criminal Kray brothers – and again when he entered into a happy second marriage with the beautiful Wanda Senna there were vicious rumours that because of her Sardinian background she had connections with the Mafia. There seemed no escape for Robert Boothby.

After the war he gave splendid service to the Council of Europe in Strasbourg and continued to look after his constituents in Aberdeenshire, who stood by him through thick and thin and were just pleased to have such a major figure as their Member of Parliament. When he left them after thirty-four years, honoured first with a knighthood and then a peerage, there was a celebration dinner in Aberdeen, which I attended as *The Press and Journal* reporter. That evening I listened to the two greatest speeches I have ever heard. His old friend, the novelist Sir Compton Mackenzie, proposed the toast of Robert Boothby, mixing fact with hilarity in a tribute of sheer brilliance. Then, for the last few minutes, he turned seriously to "the farce of the Czech assets" and lambasted those who sought to damage his name. In reply, Boothby gave the kind of speech for which he had become famous and confirmed that view that he was the greatest orator I had heard.

In later years I sat with him in his Eton Square apartment, which now bears the blue plaque of his fame, as he talked frankly of his extraordinary life. Though a Conservative, he readily rose above party politics to the extent of counting Labour Prime Minister Harold Wilson as a close friend and lamenting the disappearance of those revolutionary Red Clydesider MPs ("Where are the Wheatleys, the Maxtons, the Kirkwoods, the Geordie Buchanans today? They served a useful purpose in the Commons by expressing Scotland.")

At the same time he criticised his own Prime Minister, Edward Heath, for his lack of warmth and wondered where all the personalities had gone.

"The First World War destroyed a generation but the Second World War destroyed Western civilisation as we knew it," he added.

Did he regret that he became more of a television entertainer than the great statesman the pundits had predicted?

"I could never have remained in government for any length of time," he boomed. "I was too strongly opposed, for example, to appeasement over Hitler and to the Suez invasion. Being a rebel comes naturally to me. I have been a Radical Tory in the tradition of Joseph Chamberlain."

Having been groomed for stardom in the footsteps of Churchill, how did their rift come about?

"At first we worked well together over questions like re-arming. Churchill gave me office when he became Prime Minister but there was a row between us. I tried to tell him how to run the war – and he didn't like it! Nobody more than I admired his conduct in 1940 but he became more and more dictatorial and difficult to serve."

These are just glimpses of our conversations. Boothby was

still the rumbustious man of wit and wisdom but the overriding impression remained: what a waste of a great talent, a figure of stature, intelligence and personality who was surely the greatest Prime Minister we never had. People of his day, like Anthony Eden, Harold Macmillan, Harold Wilson and Edward Heath would shrink into insignificance by comparison. For once I would agree, in politics at least, that they simply don't make them like that any more.

CHAPTER THIRTY-THREE

A WASTED TALENT

Having pinpointed two of the most distinguished figures of my experience, I am tempted to add one more name to that top bracket of Putzi Hanfstaengl and Robert Boothby, even if his name will hardly register with anyone still alive. But to me, Allan R. Taylor lingers in the memory as an extraordinary human being, a great Victorian figure combining such outstanding brain power, judgement, personality and humour as you seldom find in a lifetime.

As an Aberdonian who sampled journalism first on the old *Aberdeen Free Press* and then in Liverpool, he could have gone on to be editor of *The Times* of London – or to a major position in many another profession. But instead, incredibly, he returned to the North-east to become editor of the *Laurencekirk Observer* and finally the *Buchan Observer* in Peterhead. With no disrespect to those two papers, they had no right to expect a man of that stature.

As a young journalist I made it my business to visit him as often as possible in that Peterhead office, trying to absorb the essence of the man and knowing I was unlikely to meet another of his kind. There he sat, quiet of manner but with a face so full of character that you were not surprised when he engaged you into the most fascinating discussions, revealing a knowledge and power of observation that opened up new worlds in your imagination.

By now I should have mentioned his brilliance as a writer, producing weekly columns for the *Buchan Observer* that should have had an international readership. At least his name was known at Westminster, where Robert Boothby was among his greatest admirers and many others marvelled at his grasp of international crises and his ability to forecast the outcome. When he died in

1957 at the age of seventy-four, never having earned more than ten pounds a week, a perceptive obituary writer remembered him as a Chestertonian figure. If cricket was his abiding passion then the theatre came next. With the way he thought and wrote, I was always reminded of Henrik Ibsen, who happened to be his idol.

Considering his literary skills, I once asked him why he had never written a book or a play, something more permanent than the newspaper columns. He confessed that, during his time in Laurencekirk, he did become keenly aware of the fact that the Mearns was an area calling out for an author. Its very atmosphere was the stuff that inspired great literature. So quietly he got down to writing about it, taking his time over a number of years.

Then he broke off to tell me of an earlier time when, travelling on the school train between Stonehaven and Laurencekirk, he used to notice a young lad who always sat quietly alone, never joining in the boyhood banter. He had a face you would remember. Then came the day when Allan Taylor picked up a new book. It was about the Mearns. And yes, it was called *Sunset Song*. It was not long before he identified the author as that young lad on the train.

"I always knew there was something special about him," he told me. "And I just marvelled at the skill of one so young. He had achieved what I would have liked to achieve; and he had done it to perfection. I reached for my desk and tore up my effort."

Much as we appreciated Lewis Grassic Gibbon's masterpiece, how unfortunate that it should have come in time to discourage the author of what might have been another great book about the Mearns.

Allan R. Taylor gave much of his time to looking after his wife, who was stone blind. Together they mourned the tragic loss of their only daughter. I doubt if Peterhead fully appreciated the level of genius which served its local paper for more than thirty years.

CHAPTER THIRTY-FOUR

WRITERS I HAVE KNOWN

From these recent chapters, Hanfstaengl, Boothby and Taylor were all historians and writers of talent. But moving into poetry and fiction, I was also lucky enough to encounter some other great names of the twentieth century.

Robert Graves

Robert Graves was regarded as the leading love poet of his day and writer of some of the finest lyric verse in the English language. When I met up with him in the 1970s he was paying his first visit to Scotland for nearly sixty years. In that year of 1916 he had been left for dead at the Battle of the Somme, his colonel having written to tell his mother of a son who was "glorious and heroic", so heroic, as it turned out, that he came back from the dead. His mission to Scotland had been as a military escort to another great poet of the First World War, Siegfried Sassoon, who had suffered a total breakdown, like so many more in that dreadful war.

Craiglockhart Hospital in Edinburgh was a major destination for those men in need of psychiatric attention and it was there that Graves met yet another of his poetic breed, Wilfred Owen. Owen was cured, in time to return to the battlefields of France, only to be killed one week before the Armistice was signed.

In those post-war years Graves had escaped to the greater peace of Majorca, where he then spent most of his life, regarded as something of an historic monument, with tour bus guides stopping to point him out. Now he was back, at the age of seventy-seven but still a giant of a man with the head of a Roman emperor. As we mounted the staircase of Glasgow's Central Hotel he paused to take in the marble pillars and general grandeur and said he had quite forgotten that places like this existed. He was here to talk about the continuing relevance of our national bard, even in a world far removed from the days of the Cotter's Saturday Night.

"Yes, Burns remains a great poet of Scotland, just as Shakespeare is of England, but then you are a poetic nation," he reminded me. "Three hundred years before Burns, William Dunbar was the father of Scottish poetry. To me, however, the most extraordinary thing about the Scots is that they have a strange power to give life to inanimate objects. Kipling was wise enough to spot this and to emphasise it.

"If you have a breakdown with your car the Scot will somehow manage to get it to a garage. That has an engineering application, of course, but it is far more a poetic power than an engineering one. It is a kind of driving force, a form of magic which no other nation in the world possesses. I cannot explain it; it is quite strange but it is true."

From one of the great poets, it was just one of several observations that intrigued. It was after writing his famous autobiography *Goodbye To All That* that he chose to live in Majorca.

"I went on the recommendation of two people," he said. "They were Lawrence of Arabia, the most extraordinary man I have ever known, and Gertrude Stein, who told me, 'Majorca is a paradise, if you can take it.'"

By that time it was no longer paradise. But it was still his home.

However, if Robert Graves was English there were plenty distinguished writers nearer home to demand my attention before it was too late.

Hugh MacDiarmid

Christopher Grieve became better known as Hugh MacDiarmid, a strange mixture of the kindly and the cantankerous, believed by some, including himself, to be a greater poet than Robert Burns. He may well have been more of an intellectual, producing some gems like "A Drunk Man Looks At The Thistle" but writing from the head has an uphill struggle against what comes from the heart, and that was the strength of Robert Burns, whose translation of everyday thought and observation into simple but beautiful language appealed to the emotions of a worldwide audience.

I have sat by MacDiarmid's fireside at his little cottage near Biggar and studied the demeanour of the man who undoubtedly achieved his own level of greatness. Possessed of a small mouth, which my father would have likened to a sow's backside, he tended to strangulate his vowel sounds to the detriment of his delivery. And while Burns shared his concern for the welfare of the masses, he would never have aligned himself with the communist philosophies that dominated so much of MacDiarmid's thinking.

He and I once had the task of judging the Scottish Poetry Competition, held in the Ayrshire town of Irvine, a stronghold of the national bard with its own substantial Burns Club. At the end of it, no doubt wishing to acknowledge such a rare visit from MacDiarmid, the club members invited the two of us to round off the evening at their club premises. Seated at the top end and furnished with our own private bottle of whisky, we were faced with a formidable array of doughty custodians, ranged around the large table, eagerly awaiting the pronouncements of Scotland's second-best poet. With one last swig, the great man launched into his assessment of Robert Burns. Well, that was what they were there for.

"Robert Burns was no poet at all!" he blasted. "No poet at all." And if that was the preamble, it didn't get any better. Even those strangulated vowels could not camouflage the serious intent of his message.

The evening ended in a disarray of embarrassment. I pitied the local plumber, who was chairman of the Burns Club and had the unenviable task of giving him a bed for the night. I drove them to his home and didn't see the plumber again for some time. When I did, I was anxious to know how he had coped. Well, he had shown MacDiarmid to his upstairs bedroom but, realising his state of inebriation, kept a watch as he crossed to the bathroom in case he should fall down the stairs.

"He appeared in his communist-red pyjamas," said the plumber, "and I gathered that, once in the bathroom, he was having some difficulty in finding his private apparatus. So I called, 'Do you need any help?' to which he replied indignantly, 'Are you a qualified doctor?' I said, 'No. But I am a qualified plumber!'"

That put a farcical end to a disastrous evening. At the *Daily Express* I had worked with Michael Grieve, MacDiarmid's only son, the same age as myself and very like his father in appearance but much more likeable. As for the great MacDiarmid, I never saw him again.

George Mackay Brown

If our last man was not short of ego, there was simply no trace of it in George Mackay Brown, for here was one of the rarest, most natural individuals I ever met, free of the guile and self-importance that mark so many people today. Instead, his quiet-spoken presence left the impression that he belonged to another age, even another world, quaint in his conversation and hard to fit into our modern scene. Yet the simple power of his writing washes over you, leaving no doubt that here is one of the great Scottish wordsmiths. To meet him in person left me refreshed and feeling full of joy that such a man could still exist in our cynical and seriously troubled times.

Home for George Mackay Brown, born in 1921, was the Orkney town of Stromness, where he grew up and which he left only when it was absolutely necessary. On my first visit, there was no reply at his upstairs flat. But everybody looks out for you in a place like Stromness and the woman from the wee shop called up that George had gone for his messages but, "Oh, here he comes down the street." I prepared for my first sight of the man as he came round the corner and noted at the time that he was a lean and rustic figure in a big bonnet, with the gait of a shy boy, yet an old face, old as the hills and crags and battered shores of the land that bred him. He was, in fact, fifty-one at the time.

The truth was that he had forgotten I was coming and was upset and embarrassed by what he thought was a lack of courtesy. But how could that small matter affect your impression of such a man? It took him some time to recover but he made me a coffee and settled into his rocking chair. I studied the flat cheekbones and jutting jaw and the crescent moon of his kindly face, as we moved gently into our interview.

It was here in this picturesque wynd that he grew up as the youngest of five. His father was the local tailor-cum-postie. George's early days were dogged by tuberculosis, with long spells in a sanatorium, during which he could at least read and find his inspiration in people like W.B. Yeats, T.S. Eliot and Gerard Manley Hopkins. He managed to leave Orkney long enough to study at Newbattle Abbey College, where he came under the influence of that other great poet from Orkney, Edwin Muir, and to gain an honours degree in English at Edinburgh University before scampering back to his native island. He seldom left thereafter. In his middle years that ill health settled into chronic bronchitis, which did not hinder a productive flow of sea tales and stories based on the folklore of Orkney.

By the time we met he was telling me that the well of poetry had somehow dried up. "But then you couldn't keep a cat on what you make out of poetry anyway," he said. He was writing a novel about St Magnus, the patron saint of Orkney, and a book of short stories and one for children; he had finished a television play and the Strathclyde Theatre Group was coming to Orkney that week to present two of his pieces, *Witch* and *Return of the Women*. So he was not idle.

Material gain had no real place with George Mackay Brown but he did agree that there were spells when it was hard to survive. The Arts Council Literature Prize for his 1969 collection of stories, *A Time to Keep*, was a help.

"At present I can exist on the sales of my work," he said. "Of course it might be different if I had a wife and children to support but I'm myself and it's a fairly simple life. I write between breakfast and lunch for five days a week, write letters on Saturday and maybe have a couple of pints on Sunday."

Without making any great song about it, he also went to Mass when he could, having gained strength from his conversion to the Roman Catholic faith, unlike his parents, who were strictly Church of Scotland.

"It's a good place for working up here," he adds. "Plenty of peace and not many distractions."

This gentle genius wrote what he honestly felt, without thought of fashion or cult. Meeting him was a kind of haunting experience. Leaving him was not like leaving any other person you would meet in a lifetime. It is impossible to explain.

He took his farewell at the door but was still there, waving gently from the window until you were out of sight. A man from another world.

Eric Linklater

If George Mackay Brown was hardly of this world, Eric Linklater most certainly was. He was barely out of Aberdeen Grammar School when he was deep in the glaur of the First World War, fielding a German bullet which went through his tin helmet and into his skull – before exiting both skull and tin helmet at the other side! Miraculously avoiding the brain, it nevertheless left him with a permanent wound in his head, the memento of a helmet with two holes, and a title for his later autobiography which he called *Fanfare for a Tin Hat*. Linklater's taste for adventure was surpassed only by another North-east man – and former pupil of the same Grammar School – whose real name was George Gordon, to become better known as Lord Byron.

With that wartime behind him, Linklater returned to study medicine at Aberdeen University but was more successful as the leader of the most riotous collection of students that institution had ever known. They had survived the most fearful of all wars and were determined to celebrate the fact that they were still alive. (My own father-in-law, arriving as a young student from Fraserburgh Academy at the end of the war, gave me a graphic description of the antics.) Linky, as he was called, switched from medicine to

English and proceeded on the great adventure of life, landing in America in time for Prohibition and onwards to Bombay, where he became assistant editor of *The Times of India*.

After the Second World War I was there to report on his return to Aberdeen University, scene of those riotous days, but this time to be installed as its Lord Rector. I ran alongside as he was carried shoulder-high to the Upper Kirkgate pub by a new race of high-spirited students. By then he had already distinguished himself as one of our wittiest writers, still remembered for titles like *Juan in America*, *Private Angelo* and *Poet's Pub*.

It was much later before I actually spoke to the man, by which time he was into his seventies and settled in a delightful cottage within the picturesque estate of Haddo House, the North-east home of Lord Aberdeen. Still in good fettle, he was now taking a more serious view of life, adding wisdom to his wit as he gave warning of dangers that lay ahead. He had deep concerns about the pace of oil development in the North Sea, much of which was bound to be experimental. Long before any disaster had struck he was telling me, "No one has had the experience of drilling in seas as rough as they will find off Shetland. And I believe that the dangers of serious accident could be greatly reduced."

Then he drew a sweeping hand across the view from his window and invited me to share his enthusiasm for the absence of people. His horror of an overcrowded world, with numbers doubling within another lifetime, was heightened by his return to Bombay, which he knew as an attractive city but was then bursting at the seams. Calcutta was even worse.

A generation before our modern contact with *War Horse*, he was recalling his experience of those screaming, wounded animals on the battlefields of France. The noise and stench still lingered with the man whose recourse to the comic situations of life in his writing seemed to me now like an escape from it all.

Critical of the amount of careless writing in the modern world, he also had a word of advice for budding authors: "I have always made it my habit to read aloud to myself what I have written because I believe that writing should have a natural rhythm and that if you cannot speak it easily and naturally there is something wrong with it."

Neil Paterson

Just as Lewis Grassic Gibbon became the most eloquent voice of the North-east's landward area in the early 1930s, there was a post-war stirring of excitement for another local writer who looked as if he might perform the same service for its coastal region. Neil Paterson was the son of a solicitor in Banff who gained a huge following for books like *The China Run* and *Behold Thy Daughter*. Some enthusiasts went as far as to hail him as Scotland's greatest storyteller since Robert Louis Stevenson. But it all dried up in 1953 when the novelist disappeared, only to re-emerge in a different guise – as one of the world's most successful screenwriters.

This astonishing transformation began when he tried his hand at writing a film called *The Kidnappers*, starring that great Scots comic, Duncan Macrae, and two Aberdeenshire schoolboys, Vincent Winter and Jon Whiteley.

"I found that I could do this kind of thing," he told me later, "so I went on to films like *High Tide at Noon*, *The Shiralee* and *Innocent Sinner*."

Then he hit the heights in 1958 by turning John Braine's novel *Room at the Top* into a film, for which he won the Oscar. Neil Paterson was now established in another world.

Had he no regrets, I asked, about forfeiting a place among the immortal writers for the greater rewards of Hollywood?

"I never saw it like that," he said. "I have no great message to give, no windmills to tilt which are not being tilted all the time. I was not seduced by Hollywood; it is just that I am a storyteller. Dialogue has always been the strength of whatever talent I may possess and I have simply been telling stories on film.

"Of course, it is true that I am a professional writer and novels tend to be poor reward for your efforts. You can make fifty times more from a film."

Despite all the overtures to make Hollywood his home, however, he resolutely refused to go, limiting himself to an essential three months out of every twelve in Tinsel Town, where his friends included stars like Cary Grant and Stewart Grainger. Away from that hurly-burly, the perfect place to work was the charming Perthshire town of Crieff, which remained home throughout his career.

A man of distinguished appearance, Neil Paterson had some interesting sides to his life. For example, as a fine footballer, he was captain of Dundee United by the age of twenty. I was also intrigued to find that Mr Kerr from Banff, the man who gave us Kerr's pink potatoes, was Neil Paterson's grandfather.

In those early days he was a prolific writer of short stories for the DC Thomson magazines in Dundee. And in that connection, his close friend and colleague was another highly talented Northeast writer, Jimmy Young from the village of New Deer, who wrote under his middle names of Martin Douglas. I used to class them as equals, one living in Crieff and the other in nearby Coupar Angus. But Jimmy died in his forties, now a forgotten man, while Neil went on to fame and fortune and died in 1995 at the age of seventy-nine.

David Kerr Cameron

It would not surprise me if this is a new name to many a reader. But if there is any justice at all, David Kerr Cameron will eventually take his place among the leading Scottish writers of the twentieth century. Like many rural Scots, too respectful to push their own case, he came late to the field of writing; indeed he was fifty before giving notice of a new literary talent with a book called *The Ballad and the Plough*.

It so happened that I had a hint of it more than twenty years earlier, when he was still a young man working as an agricultural engineer but submitting freelance articles to *The Press and Journal* in Aberdeen. As a minor journalist, standing in for the agricultural editor, I had no doubt that this unknown name had talent – but no idea that I was handling the work of a man who would rise to the heights of Scottish literature in years to come.

David Kerr Cameron had been born in March 1928 and went to the village schools of Tarves and Pitmedden in Aberdeenshire, catching the tail-end of a crofting way of life that would soon disappear altogether. It would become a central theme of his writing. His grandfather was farm grieve to Lord Aberdeen at that same Haddo House estate where Eric Linklater eventually settled, while his father was a typical horseman of those vibrant farming days.

A good essay writer at school, young David had never forgotten his headmaster's hints of a career in journalism and, like many more of us in that generation, was finding inspiration in Grassic Gibbon and his unique style of language. He made a gentle start in full-time journalism with the *Kirriemuir Herald* before joining the sub-editors' desk of the same *Press and Journal* where I first encountered him.

But it was his move to the *Daily Telegraph* in Fleet Street that saw him blossom into a writer of style and elegance, not only in his journalism but in the books which came belatedly from the power of his pen. Titles like *The Cornkister Days* and *A Kist of Sorrows* were matched by *Willie Gavin, Crofter Man*, part of a classic trilogy which helped to establish his readership.

If the move to London gave him confidence, his long absence from the Scottish scene may explain why he is not as well known in his native land as he ought to be. But it is never too late. *Willie Gavin* is a good starting point, following the trials of the crofter in his struggle to make fertile a soil that was too often thin and stony. David Kerr Cameron paints a vivid picture of how the crofter took on his thankless task, "stitching the quilt of the landscape" in those folds of the countryside where "small fields fought for a foothold with the whins and broom, forever in danger of losing ground as they supported their inmates in that special thraldom of hope that distils slowly to the acuteness of despair."

David blurs the identity of the real life Willie Gavin but he later told me that he was writing about his own maternal grandfather, Willie Porter, a typical North-east crofter. Willie and his way of life were coming to an end together. When Grannie Gavin went to call him in for his dinner one day she found him sprawled between the drills. They brought him home in his barrow, not yet dead but near enough. Whatever his end, he had lived, like most of his breed, with a rare dignity. David himself died in 2003, aged seventy-four.

David Toulmin

If David Kerr Cameron came late to the scene, he could hardly compare with David Toulmin, who was nearer sixty when he made himself properly known. Both were of a similar breed and background in the Buchan area of Aberdeenshire but whereas Cameron did claim his destiny and become a journalist, Toulmin worked out his entire life as a farm servant (as they were called) and market gardener. Writing remained a hobby, though, one which, ironically, brought him a higher profile than Cameron, mainly because he never left the North-east. To complicate matters, Toulmin was just his interesting choice of a pen name, which had a better ring to it than "Johnny Reid".

Born in 1913, the son of a farm servant, he became a dairyman at Newseat of Peterhead, delivering our daily third-of-a-pint to Maud School in the 1930s. Articles in the local weekly paper were just about his stretch until that late stage when he burst upon the scene with *Hard Shining Corn*, followed by his first novel, *Blown Seed*, and *Harvest Home*, another collection of short stories. *The Sunday Times* was moved to hail him as "a born writer, a natural who creates with intense vividness the incredibly hard, rough life of farm workers in North-east Scotland, an artist to his calloused fingertips . . . his pages brim with life – moving, tender, astonishing, funny and grim". Johnny and I marvelled at the fact that both of us, who left school at fourteen, stepped up to receive the same honorary degree from Aberdeen University.

But there is one more story to tell. In 1988 I was standing by that infamous Bridge on the River Kwai in Thailand, contemplating the extent of Japanese atrocity in the Second World War as they drove countless thousands of our soldiers to work in unbearable heat. Men of the Gordon Highlanders and the Argylls were among those dropping dead from disease, starvation and sheer exhaustion. I walked into the nearby Kanchanaburi cemetery of 6,500 graves, wondering if I might find anyone from my own corner of Aberdeenshire. There were certainly Gordon Highlanders with familiar names but a disappointing lack of further information. I was leaving when suddenly I spotted a plaque with an address: Private R.W. Willox, died 7 June 1943, aged 25. Remembered by his father, mother and family at Sandford Lodge, Peterhead.

Sandford Lodge? It was a farm my father knew well. Could this young man have been a farm servant there before the war? He would now have been seventy. So, would there still be a relative to whom I could bring back pictures of his grave? Here was a Buchan loon like myself, far from the rolling fields of that countryside we had both known so well. I felt compelled to stay and keep him company. Then I took some pictures and knew that there was one small corner of Thailand that would be forever Buchan.

Back home, I wondered who might remember a farm servant from the Peterhead area of fifty years ago. Then I remembered Johnny Reid (David Toulmin). His wife, Margaret, answered the phone but passed it over to Johnny, to whom I told the story. By chance, did he remember an R.W. Willox of the Gordon Highlanders?

There was a pause before Johnny spoke. "That'll be Rob Willox ye're speakin' aboot. Ay, man, I kent him fine. In fact, he was my wife's brother!"

So Margaret came back on the phone to tell me about her beloved brother Rob, one of the ten children, a thoughtful lad who never forgot a kindness to his mother. Off he had gone to the Bridge of Don Barracks in Aberdeen but was back home for the hairst before being posted to Singapore. When that fell to the Japs in 1942 our men were moved to the infamous railway. There was a Christmas card and then a long silence before the Red Cross announced that Rob had died of the dreaded beriberi. His mother broke her heart and died in the prime of life.

As I have already shown, coincidence has followed me to the ends of the earth. But none touched me more deeply than that quiet grave in a faraway jungle.

John R. Allan

No account of my writing acquaintances would be complete without a mention of John R. Allan, farmer at Little Ardo of Methlick and one of the finest wordsmiths of last century. An illegitimate child deserted by his mother at birth, as she disappeared to Canada, he had the good fortune to be retrieved from an institution by his grandparents, who brought him up on a farm near Aberdeen.

In my youth I happened to discover his short classic, *Farmer's Boy*, published in 1935 as a mixture of fact and fiction and hailed by such novelists as Howard Spring. His name had already registered, as a Buchan man back from the war with the courage to stand as local Labour candidate against the formidable Robert Boothby in the General Election of 1945. Before all that, he had gone from an honours degree at Aberdeen University to work as a journalist on the *Glasgow Herald*, then married into the well-known Maitland Mackie family and settled in one of their farms near Methlick. [His son Charlie became another popular writer.]

Having founded *The Maud Review* as a teenager, I plucked up enough courage to knock on his farm door one day to ask if he would write an article for my village magazine. His kindly interest was an inspiration – and he did indeed enhance my modest journal with the power of his prose.

It was into the 1950s, however, before he produced his masterpiece, *North-east Lowlands of Scotland*, written originally as part of a national series of guidebooks but standing out so far as a worthy piece of literature that it remains after all those years as one of the great Scottish publications.

The appeal of John R. Allan's writing apart, he also sought to correct that ridiculous myth, perpetuated in ignorance even by our own people, that Scotland is divided into the Highlands in the north and Lowlands in the south. In reality, that separating line places them more properly into west and east, so that the Lowlands run all the way from the Borders, through the Lothians, Fife, Angus and Aberdeenshire to that northernmost point of John o' Groats. Glasgow in the south-west is therefore quite a Highland city and Aberdeen most certainly a Lowland one. The last of the invading Highlanders were chased out of the North-east at the Battle of Harlaw, near Inverurie, in 1411, an encounter in which the Provost of Aberdeen, Robert Davidson, lost his life and lies buried in St Nicholas Churchyard.

John R. Allan put his own slant on this delicate matter when he wrote: "Nothing so annoys a true native of these Lowlands than the suggestion that he is a Highlander. Even when it is meant as a compliment – and it always is – we know it as a deadly insult."

That "deadly insult" frequently comes with the suggestion that we Lowlanders are *teuchters*, a word that belongs exclusively to Highlanders, especially Gaelic-speaking ones, with disparaging connotations of the uncouth, as any Scots dictionary will tell you. This equates to that other insult when foreigners, in their ignorance, believe that Britain can be called England.

William McIlvanney

If Willie McIlvanney happens to come last in this list it is no reflection on the position he holds among Scottish novelists. Indeed, the second half of the twentieth century produced no greater writer than McIlvanney, born in 1936 to an extraordinary family in a miner's cottage in Kilmarnock. It raises curiosity about the genes of a working-class couple, Conn and Helen McIlvanney, who raised four children of such distinction that we are reminded of a generation that was denied its full potential. For years the family's name and fame belonged largely to Willie's older brother Hugh, who became simply the greatest sports journalist of our time.

Outwith the immediacy of newspapers, it took the public longer to learn about Willie, who followed a substantial career as an academic before devoting himself to novels. Among his early books was *Docherty*, a brilliant portrayal of an Ayrshire miner, which

159

recognised his own background in much the same way as Grassic Gibbon had done for the crofters of the North-east. That promise was fulfilled as he proceeded to novels like *The Big Man* and thrillers with the Glasgow detective Jack Laidlaw, as well as volumes of poetry. By then the well-known name of McIlvanney belonged as much to Willie as to brother Hugh. The power of his intellect and highly original use of the English language had placed him in the top bracket of Scottish writers.

If there have been complaints that there was too much time between his books, it is not only a sign of his popularity but a clear indication that this is not an author who writes to order. With genius of this calibre, the commercial market must wait for the man's own moments, in the knowledge that the moment will be well worth the wait.

Returning to the family genes, Willie McIlvanney has in turn passed them on to two brilliant children, Liam and Siobhan, both of whom gained doctorates at Oxford. Liam became a very young lecturer at Aberdeen University before moving to a professorship in New Zealand.

In 2013 Canongate of Edinburgh was preparing to republish the full scope of McIlvanney's work, offering a welcome reminder of where he stands in Scottish literature. This tribute is not before its time.

In telling of distinguished writers I have met, there is one common factor: they are all men. And that needs to be remedied.

CHAPTER THIRTY-FIVE

MAUD GIRL HITS THE HEIGHTS

It has always surprised me that the great composers of the world have included so few women; indeed it is hard to think of any that come into the category of a Mozart, Beethoven, Handel or Tchaikovsky, Rachmaninov, Elgar, Grieg or dozens more. In that same vein, women have tended to be a minority in Scottish writing, when greater emancipation should have corrected the balance. Not that we have been without talent, with names like Nan Shepherd, Catherine Gavin, Agnes Mure Mackenzie and Rachel Annand Taylor. And there are at least three others in whom I take particular pride since they all came from within a few miles of my own village. The first, in fact, was born and brought up right there in Maud, where her father, the Rev. William Cowie, was minister for thirty-five years.

So Mabel Cowie was a typical Maud *quine*, except that she went on to become one of the leading British playwrights of the twentieth century, under her pen name of Lesley Storm. As I grew up, there were still plenty friends and boyfriends from my parents' generation to fascinate me with stories of her fame and fortune, the only person from our village who had gained an international reputation.

She had gone to Aberdeen University and onwards to London, a glamorous figure who became one of the favourite writers of my future boss, Lord Beaverbrook. As a Scot himself, the old Beaver did not rest till his *Daily Express* in London was matched by a *Scottish Daily Express* in Glasgow, and when that paper was launched in November 1928 Lesley Storm was the face emblazoned on the front page of that very first edition, welcoming the paper to her homeland.

By then she was establishing a reputation as a rather daring novelist, with titles like *Lady, What of Life?* before finding her true vocation in the theatre. There she caught public imagination with *Black Chiffon*, a powerful psychological play about a mother's jealousy of her future daughter-in-law, to the extent of copying the latter's black chiffon nightdress. Psychology was never far from her themes, in plays like *The Day's Mischief*, till she hit the financial high spots with *Roar Like a Dove*, for which she allegedly sold the film rights for £90,000, a substantial sum in those days.

All of this intrigued my young mind till I decided I must try to meet her. From 1950 onwards I had taken advantage of an offer from two grand aunts in London to stay with them any time I liked. That enabled me to explore the West End theatreland and catch up with every American musical from *Oklahoma*, *Annie Get Your Gun*, and *Carousel* to *South Pacific*, *Kiss Me Kate* and *The Sound of Music*, as they flooded into Drury Lane and elsewhere in the 1950s.

On the first of those annual visits, having found that she lived at 25 South Terrace, Kensington, I plucked up the courage to ring the doorbell of Lesley Storm. She answered the door herself and listened to my rather clumsy explanation that I was "Jackie Webster fae Maud!" She kindly took me at my innocent face value and invited me in for afternoon tea. And what an afternoon I had. She was every bit as much "the Maud quine" as I was "a Maud loon", filled with affection for the place and full of questions about her old friends, including one of my teachers at Maud School, Belle Duncan, and so many others.

She was interested in what I was doing in London, including the plays I had seen, but showed particular enthusiasm when I told her where I had been the previous evening. I had taken my grand aunts to see a very funny film called *Tony Draws a Horse*. It was about a little boy who loved to draw horses but made a rather exaggerated feature of their private parts.

I didn't need to tell her the story. "Yes, I know," she said. "That was a play I wrote back in 1939 – and they have now made it into a film!" I might have guessed, since here was another of her psychological studies.

In the sophisticated heart of Kensington, where her husband was a doctor, here was Lesley Storm, famous playwright, genuinely delighted to welcome somebody from Maud with whom she could exercise her native tongue. It was such a natural and reassuring visit, leading to future contact when I would interview her for the *Daily Express* about her later plays.

Flora Garry

By yet another of those coincidences, Lesley Storm was related through marriage to Flora Garry from New Deer, who used to cycle the three miles to Maud every morning to join her on the train for Peterhead Academy. Alongside those great North-east poets, Charles Murray and J.C. Milne, Flora Garry stands out as the most authentic female exponent of Doric verse.

In all truth, our North-east dialect is better suited to the spoken word than to writing, on account of its phonetic structure, the spelling of which depends on how the writer hears it. The result can become a mishmash of spelling and grammar, some of which can puzzle even the practised Doric speaker. Too often it ends up with a range of attempts, running from mediocrity to utter rubbish. So, when you come across the Murrays, the Milnes – and the Flora Garrys – you quickly recognise the genuine article and know they are there to be cherished.

Once again we meet someone who left it so late to reveal her talent that we were lucky to have found her at all. She was a contemporary of my own mother so from an early age I heard her described as the great Buchan beauty of her day. She began life as Flora Campbell from the farm of Mains of Auchmunziel (pronounced Auchmingel) near New Deer, whose farming parents were writers as well. Her mother, previously Nellie Metcalfe, had been the great beauty of her own day, who played the leading lady in my great-grandfather's first play, *Mains's Wooin'*, in 1894. It was there that she met Flora's father, Archie Campbell, flamboyant character, fine athlete at Highland Games and nimble dancer, who became a well-known freelance writer in North-east newspapers such as *The Buchan Farmer*. Archie was also the long-time election agent for Robert Boothby, that flamboyant MP for East Aberdeenshire.

Like Boothby, Flora Campbell was born in 1900 and went from Peterhead Academy to an honours degree in English at Aberdeen University. As a student she would wander down the Chanonry, that most picturesque of streets in Old Aberdeen, solidly populated in those days by professors and their families. And there through uncurtained windows she would gaze in at swell dinner parties, hosted by the professor's wife in her "low-neckit goon". The result, as we would discover much later, was her classic Doric poem, "The Professor's Wife". From her own vastly different background in rural Buchan she would observe the contrast:

> *"Fine," says I to masel*
> *"Fine to be up in the wardle"*
> *An thocht wi a groo, on the brookie pots*
> *In the kitchen at Glenardle*

In the poem, she ends up with the irony of becoming one of those professors' wives herself. But not only in the poem, for Flora married her own cousin, Robert Garry, who gained early fame as the young doctor at Glasgow Western Infirmary who, by his own initiative, introduced insulin to this country. Garry went on to become Regius Professor of Physiology at Glasgow University (1947–1970) and Flora Garry became the supportive wife rather than the well-known poet she deserved to be.

Though she was writing privately, Flora was an old-age pensioner before her work appeared in book form and we realised what we had been missing. She perceived beauty in the rolling, if unspectacular, farmlands of Buchan, an area not over-blessed with woods and hills. But there was always Bennachie, away to the west, as well as her own Bennygoak, the title of an early poem. Here is just a whiff of her language in those opening verses:

It was jist a skelp o the muckle furth
A sklyter o roch grun
Fin granfadder's fadder bruke it in
Fae the hedder an the funn
Granfadder sklatit barn and byre,
Brocht water tae the close
Pat fail-dykes ben the bare brae face
An a cairt road tull the moss

Bit wir fadder sottert i the yard
An skeppit amo' bees
An keepit fancy dyeuks an doos
'At warna muckle eese.
He bocht aul wizzent horse an kye
An scrimpit muck an seed;
Syne, clocherin wi a craichly hoast,
He dwine't awa, an deed

Thus, Flora Garry came into her own at an advanced stage in life and at least had the consolation of living into her one hundredth year. She shared my fears for the survival of the spoken Doric, which lost the vast majority of its everyday vocabulary during the twentieth century. The distinctive accent would survive but the richness of the words was disappearing.

I have a story about each of her two brothers, Frank and Jimmy. With a glorious baritone voice, Frank was also as handsome as his sister was beautiful but, like so many young Scots, he left the farm work for the adventure of becoming a policeman in Shanghai in the 1920s. A few days before he was due home on leave, he was sent in pursuit of some robbers and tracked them to a house where they were hiding. From under a bed, one of them pulled a gun and shot at Frank. As he fell, he managed to fire his own gun and shoot a robber dead. But Frank himself died in the ambulance.

Back home in Buchan his father and mother were just leaving for Catterline, south of Aberdeen, with the concert party of which

Frank had been a popular member. They arrived in time to hear the news as it came over the wireless. Incredibly, they carried on with the concert and it was not until the end that Archie Campbell stepped forward and told the audience what had happened.

"Frank was father's ideal type of man," Flora remembered. "He felt the tragedy more than anybody and never got over it."

The happier story of her brother Jimmy is simply that he courted my own mother and very nearly became my father. So Flora might well have been my aunt. We felt an affinity nevertheless and I did deliver the eulogy at her memorial service in New Deer Church in 2000, that year of her centenary.

I mentioned my pride in three women writers from central Buchan. But the last of those three requires a chapter to herself.

CHAPTER THIRTY-SIX

LORNA HEADS FOR HOLLYWOOD

If I had personal experience of those two Buchan ladies I did not have that privilege with the third, a girl from the nearby village of Strichen called Nora Low. But the fact that I have now attempted to write a play about her life story indicates my fascination with Lorna Moon, the pen name which took her on the road to Hollywood.

Nora's father, Charlie Low, was one of life's characters, perhaps the only socialist in Strichen, striking up a friendship with another North-east socialist, Ramsay Macdonald from Lossiemouth. Both illegitimate, the two men corresponded regularly, Ramsay humorously addressing his early letter to "Charles Low, 10 Downing Street, Strichen," a compliment Charlie was able to reciprocate in 1924 when Ramsay did indeed become Britain's first Labour Prime Minister.

Charlie and his wife, Maggie, ran the Temperance Hotel in Strichen, where daughter Nora fell in love with one of their guests, a travelling salesman from Yorkshire called Will Hebditch. Sharing a wanderlust, Will and Nora eloped to marry in Aberdeen on Christmas Eve 1907, en route to a life in Canada. So Charlie lost his favourite child, a beautiful girl who showed an early talent for writing and with whom he used to read and debate. But Will's dream of farming in bare Alberta did not suit Nora's more romantic notions and soon she was striking up a liaison with another passing Yorkshireman, Walter Moon, who persuaded her to elope once more.

By now she had little Billy to think about but he was Will's boy and it would be not be fair to take him. So the boy was left with a neighbour, while she and Walter Moon settled across the United States border in Minneapolis. As a devotee of the fictional Lorna

Doone, Nora Low now decided to call herself Lorna Moon, working as a film and theatre critic for the *Minneapolis Journal*.

One night she went to see a film called *Male and Female*, starring Gloria Swanson and produced by the great Cecil B. DeMille, who had taken a famous play by Scotland's J.M. Barrie, *The Admirable Crichton*, tarted it up with an orgy, given it a new title – and made a dog's breakfast of it, according to Lorna Moon. Back home in a fury, she wrote to Cecil B. DeMille in defence of her fellow Scot: "How dare you take that wonderful play and make such a filthy mess of it?"

DeMille's reply was swift: "It's *admirable* of you to defend your fellow Scot. But if you think you can do any better – and you're not just a smart aleck – why don't you come to Hollywood and try?"

That was enough for Lorna: "Of course I could do better than some of that rubbish. And can't you just see his face if I turn up on his doorstep?"

She and Walter Moon were not married but they did have a daughter, Mary. Walter knew there was no stopping her. He simply surrendered, drove Lorna to the station, kissed and waved her a last goodbye. She had now left a second child behind.

As planned, she stepped off the train in Los Angeles and headed for her first stop: Paramount Studios. With that knock on his door, Cecil B. DeMille was confronted with the charming young lady from Aberdeenshire.

"I love your Scots accent," he said. What's more, he would put her to the test, giving her a major part in writing the screenplay for his next film, *The Affairs of Anatol*, starring Gloria Swanson. Lorna Moon passed the test but she and DeMille didn't see eye to eye and she was soon on her way to another top producer, Jesse Lasky. It was the age of the silent movie and soon she was turning out four films in six months, earning big money and heading for the top.

At a Los Angeles party one night Lorna set her sights on the most handsome man in the room. She would soon be joining him as one of the three top screenwriters in Hollywood. And being Lorna, she would also be joining him in bed – producing the son he dearly wanted.

There were complications, of course. For a start he was married, with two daughters. And his name happened to be William DeMille, brother of Cecil B.! The baby would have to be spirited away for adoption and the whole affair kept secret. In fact, Cecil B. and his wife managed to engineer it so that they would adopt the child and William would become "Uncle" to his own son. But by the time the boy was born Lorna was already in a sanatorium, suffering from tuberculosis. Part of the deal was that she would never have contact with her son. She saw him through a glass panel before he was taken away – and never saw him again. For once, she was not guilty of desertion. This time she didn't even have the chance to hold her own baby. It would have made a Hollywood screenplay.

In 1984, an American gent came walking down the main street of Strichen. His name was Richard DeMille and he had come to see the village which had produced his secret mother, Lorna Moon. It was a very private visit and I didn't catch up with him then but I did pursue him to California and he was waiting to meet me as I stepped off the Los Angeles train at Santa Barbara, where he lived. I dined with Richard and his charming wife, Margaret Belgrano (yes, a close relative of the Argentinian general who gave his name to that ship we sank in the Falklands). She was also the rehearsal dancing partner of Gene Kelly in his days of *Singin' in the Rain*. Very little of this story was known to the public, since Richard was keeping it close to his chest, with a view to writing his book. But he did put me in the picture to a considerable extent and left it to my discretion.

William DeMille had died in 1955, when Richard was thirty-three, and it was only then he discovered that "Uncle Bill" had actually been his father. The name of his Scottish mother was a complete mystery to him, thus the intention to visit her native village of Strichen one day.

There was no happy ending to the story, as Richard related it over lunch. In 1930, at the age of forty-four, Lorna died of TB but not before she had fallen for a handsome young actor in the sanatorium, a toy boy in today's terms. Everett Marcy carried out her last wish and brought her ashes back to Scotland, back to the village of Strichen, which lies in the shadow of Mormond Hill, seen for miles around with its historic White Horse laid out in stone. Everett brought the request that her doting father, old Charlie Low, who had not seen her since she eloped, would scatter her ashes up there on Mormond. And that is what happened.

She had never forgotten her beloved Buchan, with all its family ties, nor could she understand why she had never been back to see it. Well, she was back now, as old Charlie, accompanied by Everett Marcy, carried the casket up Mormond Hill and scattered his beloved daughter's ashes to the wind, like a farmer hand-sowing his corn in spring: they settled gently on the heather.

The enigma that was Nora Low, alias Lorna Moon, a woman of stunning good looks, immense talent and a voracious appetite for the excitements of life had come home to rest in the rolling land of Buchan, where this very strange story had begun.

CHAPTER THIRTY-SEVEN

FROM BURNS TO OSCAR WILDE

In that lifelong pursuit of people with interesting stories to tell, I was always keen to track down living descendants of the famous. For example, with fifteen children, legitimate or otherwise, our beloved national bard, Robert Burns, must surely have spread his genes widely to succeeding generations. Then one day I found a direct descendant of Burns in the most unlikely of families. The present Lord Weir, whose family firm at Cathcart in Glasgow became the biggest manufacturer of industrial pumps in the world, comes in a direct line from Burns, albeit from one of his illegitimate daughters.

I well remember his grandfather, the first Viscount Weir, who was still alive in the 1950s, and it is astounding to think that he was just four generations down from Robert Burns himself. It brings home to us our own proximity to the lifetime of the national bard. That fact had already come clear to me in my very first job at the *Turriff Advertiser*. I went to visit old Mrs Macdonald, who thought she was approaching her centenary, though she wasn't really sure. When she was born in the 1840s, the compulsory registering of births had not yet arrived. The story which fascinated me concerned her grand uncle who took her on his knee when she was a small girl and told her about being present at the death of Nelson at the Battle of Trafalgar in 1805. That same grand uncle, whose life went well back to the 1700s, remembered Robert Burns.

It intrigued me to think that I had spoken to a lady who had spoken to a man who was alive at the same time as Burns. (Incidentally, having made some inquiries in Edinburgh, I was able to tell Mrs Macdonald that, far from reaching one hundred, she was about to enter her 102nd year.)

But back to direct descendants. Like Weirs of Cathcart, another world-class business based in Glasgow is run by a man with a rather special pedigree. In modern times, Rupert Soames has made a phenomenal success of the company he created under the name of Aggreko, which takes its mobile generators to major events all over the world and has supplied power to everything from the London Olympics of 2012 (a contract worth £50 million) to that biggest of all sporting occasions, the annual Super Bowl of American football. Mr Soames is, of course, the son of Mary Churchill, youngest daughter of the legendary Sir Winston, his grandfather, from whom he has inherited so much drive and determination.

In another direction, I had learned a lot about the life of that great Irish poet, playwright, wit and controversial character, Oscar Wilde, but through all his fascinating story I had failed to pick up on his possible offspring. At last I found a clue. So heading across south London, not far from Clapham Common, I reached a suburban house through a veil of foliage, beyond which lay an air of mystery.

I paused to remind myself of the wit of Wilde, not least the occasion when he arrived for a lecture tour of America and answered the usual question of the customs officer by saying, "No, I have nothing to declare but my genius!" The cultured gentleman who had agreed to see me had the name of Merlin Holland, which disguised the fact that he was the only grandchild of Oscar Wilde. I was there to discuss the tragedy of his grandfather, that wasted genius who rotted in jail at the end of the nineteenth century for the crime of homosexuality.

In the aftermath of the court case, as he faced hard labour, his wife Constance took their two sons to Switzerland, where she found that the disgrace had followed them. The hotelier made it plain her name was bad for business and asked her to leave. That was how Constance Wilde took on the surname of Holland and passed it to son, Vyvyan, who in turn passed it on to his only son Merlin.

As we sat in the shade of his secluded garden, I asked if there was any temptation to cast aside the cover and resume the name of

Wilde. Yes, there were times, said Merlin, when he felt he should acknowledge who he really was, not just for Oscar but for previous generations, like Oscar's father, Sir William Wilde, a physician of international repute who was the top eye and ear specialist of his day.

"Of course there will always be someone ready to accuse you of cashing in on the name," he said, "but maybe the day will come when we can change it back."

There was a facial likeness to his grandfather but the first impression on meeting Merlin Holland in the 1990s was that he was too young to be the grandson of a man born in 1854. His own father was born in 1886, became a widower during the First World War and didn't remarry until 1943. So Merlin was only in his fiftieth year but emerging more and more as the caretaker of the family legend. How soon did Oscar Wilde come into the consciousness of his grandson?

"My father didn't speak much about him but he did read me some of his stories when I was about seven or eight. Then there was the centenary celebration at the Savoy Hotel in 1954 and gradually I became aware of a famous ancestor in the family."

Merlin grew up in Chelsea but in that centenary year his father, Vyvyan, repeated one of Oscar's misfortunes and went bankrupt.

"Rebecca West was an old friend and said she and her husband would help with my education," he recalled. "So I went to Eton and on to Oxford – yes, to Oscar's old college of Magdalen – where my friends knew about the connection but there was no need to tell anyone else.

"As my father always said, you shouldn't go around trumpeting things like that. In fact, I didn't like it when someone would introduce me as Oscar Wilde's grandson."

Merlin went into industry, with Wiggins Teape in Beirut, and then into publishing in London but the 1990s brought an enormous surge of interest in Oscar Wilde, to the extent that his grandson was more and more drawn into the picture. That included a challenge on Wilde's biographer, Richard Ellmann, who thought the cause of his death was syphilis, whereas the medical evidence said it was cerebral meningitis.

"In the last fifteen years," said Merlin, "I have read my way under his skin and I believe he will yet be seen as someone of much greater stature than was previously thought. The academic world is seeing a more profound influence on the theatre and a greater depth to his work than he was given credit for."

The end of the story was quite tragic. The Marquis of Queensberry, incensed by Wilde's relationship with his son, Lord Alfred Douglas, unleashed a fury which prompted a disastrous course. Sued by Wilde for criminal libel, Queensberry was acquitted and his place in the dock was taken by Oscar Wilde himself, charged with the crime of homosexuality and sentenced to two years in prison in 1895. There he wrote a remarkable letter about their relationship to Lord Alfred Douglas, which came to be known as *De Profundis*.

In 1896 his wife Constance went to tell him of his mother's death.

"There was a feeling that Constance was the only person who could save this lost soul," said their grandson. "They nearly did get back together but I suspect that friends pointed out the social implications. He desperately wanted to see his two sons and there was a lot of to-ing and fro-ing in letters. But he never saw them again."

He wanted to leave letters, explaining his conduct to his sons when they were twenty-one but the guardians made it plain that the letters would be torn up.

The full range of his work came better into focus in the 1990s when Merlin Holland wrote the introduction to *The Complete Works of Oscar Wilde*. There were moves to pardon him – and the gay community wanted him as their patron saint – but the family distanced themselves from all that, accepting that he was convicted according to the law of the time and doubting if he himself would have approved. Wilde was indeed a substantial scholar and not just a wit and bon viveur and spendthrift of his own genius, as he put it.

Merlin showed me a moving letter from Oscar to a lady friend, summing up his final tragedy in Paris:

You don't know how poor I am. I have no money at all. I live, or am supposed to live, on a few francs a day. Like St Francis of Assisi I am wedded to poverty but in my case the marriage is not a success. I hate the bride that has been given to me.

I see no beauty in her hunger and her rags. I have not the soul of St Francis; my thirst is for the beauty of life, my desire for the joy.

Released from jail in 1897, he went to live in France, wandering idly around the continent. And there in Paris he died on 30 November 1900. What a sad end to the forty-six years of Oscar Wilde.

CHAPTER THIRTY-EIGHT

THE HORROR OF LOCKERBIE

As I flew back from the Far East in time for Christmas, our plane was approaching Heathrow just as another jumbo took off for New York. It was December 1988 – and that plane was PanAm flight 103. Less than an hour later came the Lockerbie Disaster, which would start the biggest mass-murder investigation in all history. Back in Glasgow, I was soon hot-footing it to the Border town, surveying the fuselage of a plane now deeply lodged in what had once been Sherwood Crescent, with 259 bodies from the plane and another eleven from the town now spread around me.

I remember standing there, bewildered and gazing up from a broken fuselage to an empty sky, trying to reconstruct in my own mind the last conscious moments of those passengers as they realised what was happening at 31,000 feet. Medical experts told me those passengers would have lost consciousness within seconds of the bomb exploding but younger ones would have regained it as they neared the ground. A frightening thought.

I was thinking in particular of the forty American students from Syracuse University, heading home from a semester in London, with so much to tell their families of the British adventure. Their bodies lay in a field at Tundergarth Mains farm, with individual stories which were truly heartbreaking. I came to know, for example, the background of twenty-one-year-old Alexander Lowenstein from New York, a handsome lad who was going to tell his parents of a romance with a fellow student which had blossomed in London.

When the grieving parents began meeting as a body to discuss their mutual plight, I flew to Boston to write about these highly-charged gatherings. There I met Alexander's father, Peter Lowenstein, who had a story to tell.

At their first meeting, Peter recognised a lady who had been his girlfriend in high school. What was she doing here? Well, her daughter Sarah was another of the students. Wasn't that a coincidence? But when the personal belongings of the dead were eventually delivered, there was more to come. The diaries of the two youngsters revealed that Alexander and Sarah had not only met in London but had fallen in love and were coming home to break the good news. With all the millions of people in America, how far can coincidence test our belief?

At that same Boston gathering, my fellow Aberdonian George Esson, who had only recently become Chief Constable of Dumfries and Galloway, addressed the parents and received an overwhelming ovation for the splendid efforts of his policemen in pursuing those responsible for that bomb on PanAm 103. For George it was no new experience. In his previous position with Grampian Police he had had to deal with the Chinook helicopter tragedy of 1986 when forty-three people died while, two years later, he was in charge of the police operation when 167 people were killed in the Piper Alpha disaster, the biggest oil-field catastrophe of them all. In the case of PanAm 103, all suspicion led to Colonel Gaddafi of Libya, two of whose intelligence men would be charged with placing an explosive in a suitcase at Malta Airport, just across the water from Libya.

Those American parents, who had already been to Lockerbie, were also full of praise for the kindness of the Scottish people, regarding them as the greatest race on earth. As I sat quietly at the back of the room in a Boston hotel, absorbing this moving occasion, I was aware of a lady who, like myself, was not part of the gathering. But during a tea break I could see her engaging parents in animated conversation, which I could not help but overhear. And what I heard defied belief.

In answer to her questions they were falling over themselves to assure her that, yes, they were contributing every Sunday at chapel

– to Nor-Aid, the American support group of the IRA! I could take it no longer. As the lady left, happy with her mission, I confronted those parents to confirm what they were saying. Giving money to Nor-Aid? Well, were they not supporting the Irish people? Yes, the Irish terrorists who were spending their American money on weapons to kill young British soldiers on the streets of Belfast. One recent victim, in fact, had come from Lockerbie. And, what's more, those weapons were bought from the very man who had just killed their children – Colonel Gaddafi! Their mouths fell open. I have a lot of time for the American people but their naivety can astonish. They had no idea and were now thanking me for letting them know, promising they would never do it again.

So who was that lady, anyway? Oh, she came from the office of Senator Edward Kennedy, brother of the assassinated President and at that time supporting the IRA, though he later thought better of it. I hope that played some small part in the subsequent demise of Nor-Aid.

Alexander Lowenstein's mother Suse was a brilliant sculptress and, when I later visited them in Long Island, New York, I was able to view an astonishing array of life-size models – the mothers of those Syracuse University students. Suse had asked each one to recall their pose at the moment of hearing the news of Lockerbie. Some fell to the ground in prayer and despair. Others screamed or begged or threw hands to the heavens, pleading or cursing a God who could let this happen. Peter Lowenstein then offered me a flight in his small private plane, for an aerial view of Manhattan island. As we came down over Central Park and wove our way past the Empire State Building and down through the Twin Towers towards the Statue of Liberty, I glanced at Peter's rather florid complexion and had an awkward moment, wondering how I could cope in this plane if by chance he took a heart attack. However, we landed safely on Long Island and I thought no more about it. That was, until I heard some time later that he did in fact have a heart attack!

As for Lockerbie, the conspiracy theories were still rumbling on a whole generation later, with the well-meaning Dr Jim Swire giving vent to his frustration over the death of his daughter, sadly one of the PanAm victims. But his friendly visits to Gaddafi and his refusal to believe in the guilt of the convicted Al Megrahi gained him little. Of course there were others involved, like Iran and Syria as well as Gaddafi, but demands for further inquiries were unlikely to uncover anything.

In this nasty world, while the Mr Bigs go scot-free, the messenger generally bears the brunt. In this case, the man convicted of the mass murder of 279 people, Al Megrahi, a leading security man for Libya who allegedly placed the bomb, was no doubt doing what he was told by his evil master. Gaddafi paid out countless millions in compensation to the next of kin. At least he himself got a suitable comeuppance in the end.

CHAPTER THIRTY-NINE

THE NORTHERN LIGHTS

Through the dim-lit streets of a London suburb I went in search of a legend. I still had to be convinced that she could possibly be alive but there she was, in a bare room-and-kitchen, the little old lady who wrote the anthem of my native corner, "The Northern Lights of Old Aberdeen". It had always seemed like a traditional song that had been around forever, so she came to me like a spirit from the distant past – and confirmed that she had, in fact, written her masterpiece as recently as 1952. Indeed, Kenneth McKellar, that greatest of Scots tenors, later described it to me as one of those natural melodies that hover in the heavens, waiting for someone with the musical antenna to pluck them into reality.

That lady was Mary Webb. And here I was, in her plain little room with its two-bar electric fire, a bed in one corner, a wardrobe in another and, occupying pride of place, the old John Broadwood piano upon which she composed "The Northern Lights". The scene had a touching simplicity. I had brought a bottle of whisky and there we sat with a dram as she unfolded the story of her life, a tale of constant toil that had brought little reward, except the satisfaction of having written a song that will live forever.

Mary Webb began life on Boxing Day of 1906 as Norah Mary Eugenie Butler, daughter of a bootmaker in the town of Leamington Spa, near Stratford-upon-Avon.

"I had played the piano since childhood," she told me, "but when I was fourteen I started my own amateur concert party. My father said, 'Don't be silly. You can't do that.' But I did. Our local MP was Anthony Eden, the future Prime Minister, and I used to play at his party functions.

180

"When I left school I began appearing as a singer and dancer in musical shows and took some acting parts, appearing with Robert Morley and Russell Thorndike, brother of Dame Sybil."

But she was touching forty when she met and married a journalist, Bill Webb, and moved to London, where he worked for the BBC. Mary took a job in the kitchens of West London Hospital and it was there that she met a girl from Aberdeen who became the catalyst for her most famous composition.

"Winnie Forgie was her name and I could see that she was homesick," said Mary. "So I invited her round for tea at our house in Matheson Road and said I must write her a song.

"Having heard of those northern lights, the aurora borealis which you see in the northern sky, I asked her about them and she said they were lovely. That was how I struck on the theme of 'The Northern Lights of Old Aberdeen' and there and then gave my husband a few ideas for the words.

"With his hands shaking from Parkinson's Disease, he scribbled out some lines. I crossed to the piano and could feel a tune that would fit."

In no time at all she was sitting down for the very first performance, bursting forth with words and music:

> *The Northern Lights of Old Aberdeen*
> *Mean home sweet home to me*
> *The Northern Lights of Aberdeen*
> *Are what I long to see*
> *I've been a wanderer all of my life*
> *And many a sight I've seen*
> *God speed the day when I'm on my way*
> *To my home in Aberdeen*

"From the moment I found that tune," said Mary, "I didn't change a single note."

Believing she may have struck a winner, she sent it to Robert Wilson, then riding high with his series of "Down in the Glen". The

181

famous Scots tenor wasted no time in bringing it into his reper-
toire. He was due to sing for Scottish exiles at the Royal Albert Hall,
London, on a night that would become the second most memorable occasion in the life of the kitchen worker from West London
Hospital.

When Wilson burst into "The Northern Lights" the audience
immediately sensed the excitement of a new song that was here to
stay. They rose to their feet and joined him in the chorus, leaving a
starry-eyed lady in her seat, transfixed and bewildered. Silencing
the uproar, Robert Wilson then announced: "The lady who wrote
that song is here in the audience tonight. Will you please stand up,
Mary Webb."

The spotlight turned on a lady the world had never heard of
but at that moment her place in musical history was assured. If
that was a big occasion, however, there was one other night to
cap it. As she told me: "Though I had written this song about
Aberdeen, I had never seen the city itself nor the northern lights.
It was therefore arranged that I should pay a visit, so I set out by
train on a journey I thought would never end. I had no idea it was
so far away.

"I was due to make an appearance on the stage of the Tivoli
Theatre and that is what I did. I played and sang my song and the
theatre company appearing that week joined me in the chorus.

"I'll never forget the scene in the Tivoli that night. The audience
got up and applauded and shouted. It was a highly emotional occasion and, without doubt, the night of my life. Here I was, at last, in
Aberdeen.

"I had just had a nervous breakdown and when I stood to take
my bow I felt giddy and had to hold on to the piano. The people
of Aberdeen were lovely to me. I have had a hard struggle in life
and they have really been my only friends. And me not even a
Scot!"

With a stroke of good luck, on that one and only visit to the city
of her song Mary Webb did actually see the northern lights, those
merry dancers in the sky which become more visible the nearer

1946 – The day I
touched Winston
Churchill

Interviewing
Prime Minister
Alec Douglas-Home

1967 – American
Vice President
Hubert Humphrey

Malcolm Forbes,
Forbes HQ, New York

With Frederick
Forsyth (Day of
the Jackal)

With George Best and
Michael Parkinson

With Omar Sharif

At Cole Porter's
piano, Waldorf
Astoria, New York

With Kate and
Rikki Fulton

1983 –
John Hewitt's goal,
Dons beat
Real Madrid!

1983 – Willie Miller
holds Cup-Winners' Cup

On the team plane home
– carrying the Cup

Union St, Aberdeen –
100,000 welcome the
team back

My literary hero
– Lewis Grassic
Gibbon

Lewis Grassic Gibbon

With Vivien Heilbron
and David Rintoul, who
both appeared in my play

2009 – Gibbon play at
Maud: Steve Robertson
and Eileen McCallum

Scotland the What?
Steve, Buff and George

1996 – Centenary
Day at Maud School,
unveiling the plaque

1997 – Founder's Day Oration
at Gordon's College – the same
school that showed me the door
when I was fourteen

2000 – Honorary Degree,
Aberdeen University

2009 – Doctor Webster,
I presume!

My son Keith with his wife Carol and their children, Sinead and Fraser

My daughter-in-law Louise, with my grandsons Murray and Lorn

Ayliffe with her family: Fiona, Rod and Cameron

My son Martin and his wife Catherine

Me, Ayliffe, Louise, Geoff, Carol and Keith

My grandson Jack

Jack, with Murray and Lorn

With my five grandchildren

2012 – My latest
grandchild, Eden,
daughter of Catherine
and Martin

you reach to the North Pole. Perhaps the gods arranged a special performance in her honour.

Surprisingly, Mary Webb gained the limelight only twice in all her days – at the Albert Hall in London and the Tivoli in Aberdeen. Thereafter, it was virtual oblivion, a baffling situation in an age of high profiles and publicity. Like me, everyone seemed to think that Mary Webb was now bound to be dead. Her husband lived long enough to hear the song just once on the radio and she managed to keep in touch with the Aberdeen girl for whom she wrote the song. Winnie Forgie had emigrated to Australia but returned to live in Aberdeen, by this time as Mrs Winnie Noble.

On this memorable evening, as I absorbed the fascinating story of Mary Webb, she showed me the rather paltry cheque which arrived twice a year for the sales and performing rights of her famous song. Somebody somewhere was not looking after her best interests but she counted her success in the appreciative letters which she turned out with pride. Her fans ranged from Queen Elizabeth, the Queen Mother, to the Mayor of New York.

In view of a stroke which had impaired her right arm, I wondered if I could ask her to play the tune. That should not be a problem, she said. By chance, it was one of the rare occasions when I had taken a tape recorder. So she crossed to the John Broadwood piano and proceeded to give me a delightful rendering of "The Northern Lights of Old Aberdeen". It was another of those special moments.

Turning from the piano stool she said, "I'm very proud of my song. I think it will be here long after I'm dead and gone."

I had come to write a newspaper column about Mary Webb but by now my thoughts were turning to that more recent part of my career: television documentaries. After the success of two programmes, *Webster's Roup* and *As Time Goes By*, surely my next venture should be *The Northern Lights*, centred on Mary Webb. The ideas were buzzing in my head. I would negotiate with the Lord Provost of Aberdeen to give her the freedom of the city. Then I would bring her north for the great occasion, reminding

Aberdonians that this local heroine was still alive and giving her a day that would overtake all others as the greatest of her life. With Mary's final arpeggios ringing in my ears I walked into the darkness of that soulless London suburb, excited about the programme that must surely lie ahead.

Back in Glasgow I submitted the scenario to BBC Scotland and awaited clearance from producer David Martin. When that arrived a few weeks later, I dialled her number to break the news. But there was no reply. I knew she attended Charing Cross Hospital for regular checks on her stroke. Perhaps this was the day. So I tried the next day and the next but still no reply. Now fearing the worst, I finally tracked her down to that same hospital to be told that Mary Webb had been lying there dead for three weeks and only now had they managed to trace a distant relative.

I had left it too late. A final stroke ended her life on Easter Monday of 1989 and now they were preparing a cremation. Putting sadness aside, I turned my thoughts to the John Broadwood piano in that bleak little flat and wondered what would happen to it. Mary had told me she was under pressure from a certain type of nasty landlord, trying to oust her from her rented home so that he could sell it. I managed to contact her only relative to see if I could possibly acquire the piano, in the hope that it would find a home by "The Northern Lights of Old Aberdeen".

To her great credit, she refused my offer of a cheque but emphasised that the piano would have to be removed by the end of that week. A lorry was duly despatched and arrived in the nick of time. As the landlord appeared, Mary's furniture was about to be cast out to the pavement. Instead, her famous piano was now on its way north. I had one more request: If there were no other plans, could I perhaps have custody of her ashes? Of course.

The funeral went ahead, back in her native Leamington Spa – a rather pathetic finale, with just half a dozen people gathered at Oakley Wood Crematorium to hear the vicar express a few sentiments about a lady whose name meant very little, even in her own home area of Warwickshire. At least the organist managed to raise a quiet rendering of "The Northern Lights". Thus my hopes of giving Mary Webb that grand finale to her life, complete with the freedom of Aberdeen, were gone forever. But I was determined to keep the title and to construct some kind of documentary that would include as much of her as possible.

With her piano now lodged at the Beechgrove studio of the BBC in Aberdeen, that well-known motorcycle fanatic Kenneth McKellar came roaring north from Glasgow to stand by the old John Broadwood, talking about the song and its composer, before giving us the kind of beautiful performance that only Ken could give. We recorded it all for television and were lucky enough to unearth an invaluable piece of cine-film which emerged from the distant past. It was the only time Mary had faced a movie camera.

The BBC documentary duly appeared and was nominated for a Royal Television Society award. The final scene took place in the grounds of the old Kaimhill Crematorium in Aberdeen, where we scattered the ashes of Mary Webb.

"God speed the day when I'm on my way / to my home in Aberdeen."

It could have been a better homecoming, of course, but at least her remains now lie in the place that changed the shape of her life, the Granite City of Aberdeen, which she had long regarded as her spiritual home. As for her piano, I presented it to the city, on the understanding that they would find a suitable venue where it could be seen by the general public.

They complied with my request – but only for a short time. It then disappeared from view and it took some time before I traced it to a council shed at Kittybrewster. What on earth were they thinking? The subsequent story does no credit to the civic authority at all.

Repeated assurances from the Lord Provost's office came to nothing. Disgracefully, it took twenty years before the promise was fulfilled – and for that, all credit to Lord Provost Peter Stephen, who, along with Duncan Hendry, that greatly gifted head of His Majesty's Theatre and the Music Hall, found the perfect solution.

As a result of their efforts, the piano upon which Mary Webb composed "The Northern Lights of Old Aberdeen" is now to be seen at the Music Hall, appropriately in an alcove of the Mary Garden Room, where two great ladies of music are commemorated. At long last the public can file past this piece of local history, together with its picture of Mary Webb herself, and pay their own small tribute to the lady who may have died lonely and penniless but who deserves to be remembered as the one who gave us our very own anthem of Aberdonianism.

Quite incredibly, the story doesn't end there. Before making the television film, I tried to find Winnie Forgie, the Aberdeenshire girl for whom Mary wrote the song. With Mary now gone, Winnie would become a central figure in the film. After all, without her, there would have been no song. Knowing nothing of her background, except the Mary Webb connection, I tracked her down to a flat in 11 Raeburn Place, Aberdeen, and rang the doorbell. When she answered on the intercom, I tried to explain my purpose. Could I come up to talk to her about it?

No. Sorry. She didn't want to be involved.

But surely—

No. Sorry.

Completely puzzled, I had to walk away, wondering what on earth could have stopped her from at least speaking to me. Had there been some fallout with Mary Webb? So the film was made without Winnie Forgie – and for the next twenty-three years this mystery festered at the back of my mind. I hadn't even met the woman.

Then, one spring evening in 2012, I was about to address a gathering at the Haddo House estate of Lord and Lady Aberdeen, at which I planned to tell the story of Mary Webb, then we would round off the evening by singing her song. Before I reached the platform, however, a man touched my arm and said, "I always intended to tell you about Winnie Forgie. She was my sister." Until afterwards, there was no time to hear the rest of it but when I told the audience the story of Mary Webb from the 1980s, I was then able to bring it right up to date and say, "Just half an hour ago, in this very hall, I met the brother of Winnie Forgie." They found it a fascinating tailpiece to "The Northern Lights".

George Forgie was indeed Winnie's younger brother. They were brought up on a croft at the Esslemont estate, near Ellon, where George worked as a salesman for the well-known agricultural company of Neil Ross. Most of the audience seemed to know him but nothing of sister Winnie. While working in London with Mary Webb, she had met a well-known chef called Danny Noble, who became her husband, but she was already a widow before my approach of 1989.

Now, at last, I was gaining some hint of why Winnie didn't want to speak to me. Evidently she felt that Mary had gained all the publicity – and likely all the money – from her bestselling song about Aberdeen. But if only she had listened to my story I could have told her that, whoever gained financially, it wasn't Mary Webb, a fairly innocent old soul who must have been "taken in" by some middleman.

As for the publicity, well, I was then about to make a television film in which she, Winnie Forgie (Noble), would get even more exposure than Mary Webb herself. This would have been her own big moment. So, what an opportunity missed.

CHAPTER FORTY

WOULD YOU BELIEVE IT?

Coincidence keeps coming back to astonish me. Due to have dinner at the Beverly Hills home of 20th Century Fox boss Bill Immerman, I went to buy flowers on Santa Monica Boulevard. On the previous night the Scottish football team had scored a sensational victory over world champions France and at the counter of the flower shop two men were exchanging banter about the game. One was a Scot, the other a Frenchman. I couldn't resist joining in. The little Scot had a Glasgow voice and as he turned to welcome me he gave me a second look and said, "Wait a minute, you are the journalist. Jack . . . Jack . . . "

Yes, that's me.

"You're not going to believe this," he went on. "When I was a teenager I did something unusual for a boy from the Gorbals. I wrote a novel. So you came to interview me and I told you my ambition was to write a film. You encouraged me with the story of a reporter on the *Daily Express* who was always going to be writing a film. But everybody laughed. He was not that good."

Yes, I remembered that. The man's name was Larry Forester.

"After he left the *Express*, you saw a memorable film called *Tora! Tora! Tora!* about Pearl Harbour – with screenplay by Larry Forester! So you said if Larry could do it, I could do it too. I never forgot that.

"I then met Rod Stewart at Celtic Park one day and told him I was taking your advice and was coming to Hollywood to try my hand. I had been coaching the Celtic boys so, until I found my feet, Rod said I could coach his football team in Los Angeles.

"That's what I did and gradually I worked my way into

Hollywood, writing and directing films – and here I am. My name's Mick Davis. By the way, I've never had the chance to thank you, so . . . " He held out his hand.

Mick Davis is indeed a highly successful Hollywood director, with a six-million-dollar house in Beverly Hills, a Rolls-Royce and a Bentley! I invited him for a drink at the Beverly Hills Hotel and asked if he was still in touch with Rod Stewart. No, he hadn't seen him for ten years.

With that, who should emerge from the dining room but Rod and his wife Penelope.

"Rod!" exploded Mick. "Remember me?"

Of course he remembered.

"How's this for a coincidence? I haven't seen you for ten years and have just met Jack after twenty-five years. The two men responsible for my career in Hollywood."

What a reunion we had. Needless to say, Mick became a friend, with whom I meet up every time I'm in Los Angeles.

CHAPTER FORTY-ONE

SCOTLAND THE WHAT?

Though my recent television film was based on the story of Mary Webb, it also provided me with an opportunity to tell of another musical legend in the social history of Aberdeen. That great comedian, Harry Gordon, had carried the particular humour of Aberdonianism from his own Beach Pavilion to the far corners of the earth in the first half of the twentieth century. But his day was drawing to a close by the early 1950s, when another phenomenon arose to take his place, in the strange way that these things happen.

It had its roots in the student shows of Aberdeen University, which were benefiting from the writing genius of a young student recently arrived from Robert Gordon's College. For the annual show at His Majesty's Theatre William D. Hardie, commonly known as Buff, was gathering around him a talented cast, which included Steve Robertson, a product of Aberdeen Grammar School and a natural song-and-dance man.

When the student days were over it seemed a waste to abandon such a successful team, so they continued under the postgraduate name of the Aberdeen Revue Group. That was when they were joined by a brilliant pianist, George Donald, who had come into town from Huntly and became a teacher at Robert Gordon's College. That continued through the 1960s, by which time, with family and professional commitments, they decided to call it a day. For their farewell comedy show Buff, Steve and George chose to appear at the Edinburgh Festival Fringe, competing for attention with hundreds of companies – and giving themselves the brand new title of "Scotland the What?", a satirical response to the national boast of "Scotland the Brave!"

As Buff, Steve and George took to the stage at a church hall on Leith Walk, I discovered that our *Daily Express* show business writer, Neville Garden, had never seen them. Well, this was his last chance. Neville went along and was so bowled over by the tuxedo-clad Aberdonians that his extensive audience of *Express* readers was told that this was the funniest show in town. The response was so overwhelming that the three lads now had to reconsider their decision to bow out. So instead of a farewell, "Scotland the What?" found themselves embarking on the greatest phase of their career, a further twenty-six years that would take them from Aberdeen to London's West End and earn them fame that was rewarded with honorary degrees from Aberdeen University, MBEs from Her Majesty and finally the freedom of Aberdeen.

In the course of their phenomenal success they bade goodbye to full-time careers elsewhere. Buff had been secretary of Grampian Health Board, Steve was an Aberdeen lawyer and George was now assistant rector of Perth Academy. In 1995, however, they returned to their spiritual home of His Majesty's Theatre, Aberdeen, for a whole month of capacity audiences. But this time it really was farewell for "Scotland the What?" though George and Steve would still be found on cruise liners and elsewhere thereafter.

As it happened, I had had a rare connection with Buff Hardie from the beginning of his career. Making his very first appearance on a stage, Buff shared a scene with me in the school play at Robert Gordon's College in 1946. On that same weekend we had seen Winston Churchill receiving the freedom of Aberdeen. But how could I have guessed, as we gave our modest performance, that the boy on stage with me that night would one day follow our wartime leader in receiving the Freedom of the City? Or, for that matter, having witnessed the entire span of his career, that I would be proposing the toast on that Freedom night, recalling the story of Buff, George and Steve as they rounded off a phenomenal partnership, guaranteeing their special place in the social history of Aberdeen and the North-east.

Sadly, Steve Robertson, who had become rector of Aberdeen

University and a great favourite with the students, died at the end of 2011. The memorial service, held some weeks later at Queen's Cross Church, was such a celebration of his life that music and laughter took a very natural place in remembering him.

That was followed in April 2013 by a variety show that drew a capacity audience to His Majesty's Theatre – on what would have been his eightieth birthday. From his old school and university they came with their various talents to provide a truly memorable night. There on stage too were his widow, Eva, daughter, Sally, and his four highly talented grandchildren. In the audience were his two partners from "Scotland the What?", Buff Hardie and George Donald, for what was billed, appropriately, as a tribute to "A Wonderful Guy".

CHAPTER FORTY-TWO

SAD END FOR TCHAIKOVSKY

If music be the food of love, said Shakespeare, play on. He could have added that it was also the great consolation of life, there to soothe the aches of troubled times when nothing feels worthwhile. In its various forms, music is the only truly universal language we know. You could not have conversed with Tchaikovsky without a knowledge of Russian. Yet you can hear and absorb into your soul those wonderful melodies and understand every musical word he is saying. The composer's art, in fact, is the one that intrigues and delights me above all others.

Just as I sought to explore the writing art of Lewis Grassic Gibbon, I am constantly seeking the minds of Rachmaninov, Puccini, George Gershwin and, nearer home, Edward Elgar, Eric Coates, Ivor Novello or John Barry – and many more – each one in his different way a master of melody. How did they reach the frame of mind to discover that particular form of notes, often so simple that you feel you could have done it yourself, except that you didn't? Just as easy reading is said to be damned hard writing, I suppose the same applies to composing.

Once again, it all comes down to genius. I have stood by the grave of Pyotr Tchaikovsky in that cemetery in St Petersburg and marvelled at the gift which could give us *Swan Lake*, *The Nutcracker*, *The Sleeping Beauty* and so much more. Above his gravestone stands a bronze bust, with those eyes that follow you. I found it hard to tear myself away. They are the sad eyes of a man who was said to have brought disgrace on the Conservatoire because of an affair with a young aristocrat. Evidently they advised him to end his own life and that is almost certainly what happened in 1893. Tchaikovsky was only fifty-three and those eyes seem to be saying, "You could have had another thirty years of my music." And so we could. In today's world his deviation would hardly have been noticed.

At least he has the immediate company of two other great composers, Alexander Borodin in the next grave and, in the one after that, Nikolai Rimsky-Korsakov, who completed Borodin's unfinished opera, *Prince Igor*, when he died. I'm a bit of a sentimentalist, as you can see. Just as I stood by Tchaikovsky, I can still be found paying homage at Ivor Novello's house at No.11 Aldwych in London, or at George Gershwin's old home at No.1019 North Roxbury Drive, Beverly Hills.

As well as a great composer of light music, Novello was the most powerful stage presence I ever witnessed. After *Glamorous Night*, *The Dancing Years* and *Perchance to Dream* I saw him perform in *King's Rhapsody* at the Palace Theatre, London, in late 1950. I just missed him at the stage door afterwards but his leading lady, Vanessa Lee, said of course I could catch up with him another time. But in the early morning of Tuesday, 6 March 1951, he went home from the Palace to that flat in the Aldwych and was having supper with Tom Arnold, the impresario, when he complained of chest pains. A few hours later my landlady in Northfield Place, Aberdeen, wakened me to say, "Guess who's dead." I tried Churchill and the King. But I never thought of Novello, who was still only fifty-eight.

When I hear the adulation that is showered upon Andrew Lloyd Webber in this fickle world, it saddens me that Ivor Novello is all but a forgotten man. Lloyd Webber is of course a highly successful entrepreneur of the theatrical scene but as a composer of original music, he is not a Novello.

As for George Gershwin, my admiration has always been so high that I coincided my annual stay at the Beverly Hills Hotel with the centenary of his birth on 26 September 1998. I looked forward to suitable celebrations, perhaps with a concert in the Hollywood Bowl, so imagine my disbelief when I found not a single event to mark the event. To think that I had come all the way from Scotland to honour Gershwin and Los Angeles could do no better than a single paragraph in the *LA Times*. So I stood outside his house in North Roxbury Drive, by then occupied by singer Rosemary Clooney (George Clooney's aunt) and remembered how he had come back from a Sam Goldwyn party one night in 1937, stepped out of the taxi and promptly sat down on the pavement, exactly where I was standing now.

The fact that he was holding his head in despair was the first clear sign of a brain tumour, said to have been caused when, in his concern about a bald patch, he ordered a machine to suck blood to his scalp, believing that poor circulation was responsible. What a waste of a musical genius who had given us everything from melodies like "Embraceable You", "The Man I Love" and "Someone to Watch Over Me" to his semi-classical "Rhapsody in Blue", which he played for the first time at the Aeolian Hall in New York in 1924. Rachmaninov and Stravinsky were apparently in the audience that night and went backstage to tell him that now was the time for that final leap towards classical music, which came with his wonderful "Piano Concerto in F" and then his 1935 opera, *Porgy and Bess*.

Remembering all this, I then wandered round the corner to Whittier Drive, in time to see President Clinton being driven to a fundraising lunch. More importantly, however, I saw a gentleman emerging from Jerome Kern's former home, which was next on my "homage" list. I couldn't resist explaining myself and asking if I could possibly see the inside of that great man's house.

Americans are so trusting. So he took me into Kern's wood-panelled music room, where he had preserved the grand piano and piano stool, and there I stood, sensing the tunes that seemed to come from those walls – "Smoke Gets In Your Eyes", "The Folks Who Live on the Hill", "The Last Time I Saw Paris" and all those melodies from *Show Boat*, like "Ole Man River", "Why Do I Love You?" and "Can't Help Lovin' Dat Man o' Mine". I was in my element!

Previous mention of Rachmaninov reminds me of a story about a concert he gave in the Carnegie Hall, New York, in partnership with Fritz Kreisler, regarded by many as the greatest violinist of all time. But not everybody agreed about Kreisler. Max Jaffa was among a number of distinguished violinists who much preferred Jascha Heifetz. And it was Max who drew my attention to the fact that Kreisler's flamboyance of style was sometimes the reason (or cover-up?) for the fact that he didn't always strike the right note!

Rachmaninov, on the other hand, all six foot seven inches of him with massive hands to match, was not only one of the great composers but also the finest pianist and conductor of his day. The story goes that, during their New York duet, a desperate Kreisler, having tied himself in a musical knot, suddenly drew close to Rachmaninov at the piano and, in a loud whisper, pleaded, "Where are we now?"

An unsympathetic Rachmaninov replied, "In the Carnegie Hall!"

CHAPTER FORTY-THREE

IN LOVE WITH JULIE AND THE WIT OF DOROTHY PARKER

Piano music in particular has always fascinated me – and Mary Webb's old John Broadwood was not the only one to catch my attention. In fact, I have been intrigued by the syncopating rhythms of the keyboard since I was a boy, when I heard a relative playing Cole Porter's "Night and Day". I was hooked forever.

The interest came no doubt from my mother, herself a pianist, who sent me to music lessons when I was six. But like so many children of that age, I didn't stick with it and that remains the big regret of my life. Among other obsessions I have always been fascinated by big hotels and sometimes the two interests have come together.

During that spell in New York in the 1960s I was a regular client of the famous Waldorf Astoria Hotel in Park Avenue, my favourite street in Manhattan. One of the attractions was the piano which was played every night in the cocktail bar – by a little man from Glasgow. More importantly, however, was the fact that the piano was the one on which the same Cole Porter composed his great array of magnificent melodies.

After a riding accident in 1937 Porter suffered a leg amputation and moved into the private apartments of the Waldorf, where he remained as something of a recluse until his death in 1964. He then bequeathed his piano to the hotel lounge where, with the permission of the wee man from Glasgow, I was able to sit down and run my fingers over the keys. Thankfully, however, Cole Porter's withdrawal from public life did not end his composing days. Two of his best musicals were yet to come – *High Society* for Grace Kelly,

Bing Crosby and Frank Sinatra and, best of all, *Kiss Me Kate*, which I had seen at the London Coliseum in 1951.

On that occasion I fell madly in love with that wonderful singer, Julie Wilson. Exactly fifty years later I was staying at the Algonquin Hotel in West 44th Street when I noticed that *Kiss Me Kate*, based on Shakespeare's *Taming of the Shrew*, was enjoying a revival on Broadway. There was nothing for it but to see that great show once more. Of course it would no doubt have dated so I prepared myself for disappointment. Instead, this turned out to be just as wonderful a production as I had seen all those years ago. More astonishingly, the capacity audience was predominantly that of my own children and grandchildren – and at the end they were on their feet with a standing ovation, just as enthusiastic as I had been fifty years earlier. What a pleasure to find that Cole Porter's talent was proving as fresh as ever. There was only one omission, of course. No Julie Wilson. Ah well, you can't have everything.

Back at the Algonquin Hotel, I was enjoying my nightcap but lamenting the decline of New York's late-night cabaret rooms, which had gone out of fashion. In fact, this hotel had one of the very few remaining ones, the famous old Oak Room. Glancing at its doorway, I was reading the name of this week's late-night cabaret star. Well, well, what a coincidence. Who would have thought there could be two Julie Wilsons in a lifetime? Anyway, I would venture in to see how this one shaped up to my one. In she came, all sultry and seductive, in the mould of a Marlene Dietrich . . . but wait a minute . . . could it be? Surely not . . . yes, it was! It was MY Julie! Who would have believed it? In a state of pleasurable shock I sat back and took it all in. And with the intimate atmosphere of a cabaret room it was not difficult to speak to her at the end.

"The last time I saw you, Miss Wilson, was in *Kiss Me Kate* at the London Coliseum, 1951. I hadn't seen that show again until tonight, fifty years later – and now within an hour I'm meeting you!"

"Oh my goodness," she exploded. "I was twenty-seven then – I'm seventy-seven now!"

The voice may have lowered to musical speech but she was still

198

wonderful. So we talked over the years between and agreed that this crazy phenomenon of coincidence had astounded us both once more.

I'm not yet finished with the Algonquin Hotel, one of the oldest in Manhattan. Apart from the Oak Room and the clientele of famous names like Mary Pickford, Douglas Fairbanks Snr, John Barrymore and H.L. Mencken, its fame has rested largely on the Round Table, a memorable institution of the 1920s, in which some of America's most prominent writers gathered round the table for lunch, exchanging ideas and gossip. They were mostly well-known critics and columnists from *The New Yorker* and *Vanity Fair* magazines, situated just a few doors away on West 44th Street.

Central to the discussions was the outrageous Dorothy Parker, drama critic of *Vanity Fair*, authoress and film writer, who didn't mince her words, with wisecracks and back-handed compliments – and well known as the wittiest woman in America. The thirtieth President of the United States, Calvin Coolidge, was sometimes portrayed as a man who said very little, a bit dim and uninspiring. When Dorothy was told that he was dead, her characteristic response was, "Gee, how can they tell?" Along with fellow writers Robert Benchley and Robert Sherwood she formed the Round Table, which became an attraction for nosey people who just dropped in, hoping to catch some of the wit.

Among the writers who joined the group was Edna Ferber, who wrote the book of *Show Boat*, from which Jerome Kern composed the operetta of that name, greatly influencing the course of the American musical. In turn, the opinions and utterings of the Round Table influenced writers like F. Scott Fitzgerald and Ernest Hemingway. Dorothy would attend the kind of Long Island parties which Fitzgerald immortalised in *The Great Gatsby*.

After all the hell-raising of her high and low living, which included failed marriages, one-night stands, drinking bouts and suicide attempts, Dorothy finally died when I was working in New York in 1967. By then she was a poor lonely soul of seventy-four with no one for company but Troy, her pet poodle. The actual Round Table, incidentally, is maintained in the Algonquin dining room to this day, with the names of its famous founders. As well as dining there, Dorothy actually lived in the hotel.

On one of my visits I was not happy with the size of my room and asked for something bigger. I was given suite 1115, which immediately took me by surprise. For a start, it included an upright piano, not what you expect in your bedroom. Around the walls were the playbills for some of the great musicals – *My Fair Lady*, *Gigi*, *Camelot* and *Brigadoon*. Then I spotted a small plaque which explained it all. Between two of his eight marriages the brilliant Alan Jay Lerner, who wrote those plays and lyrics, moved into this suite. Meanwhile, his composer friend Fritz Loewe, who was also having marital problems, moved in down below. And here, in this suite – and on this piano – they wrote *My Fair Lady*, one of the most successful stage and film musicals of all time. Needless to say, once again I was running my fingers over these ivories from which so many wonderful tunes were created.

CHAPTER FORTY-FOUR

MY DREAM OF BEVERLY HILLS

If New York was one of my favourite cities, I had become even more at home in Beverly Hills, California, influenced no doubt by those fantasies of the 1930s when, as a little boy, I sat in the Peterhead Playhouse and surrendered to the charms of this sophisticated city. It was a dream to be there one day – and the dream became reality, measuring up to all its promise as the social centre of the Hollywood film scene. More precisely, that centre was to be found at the Beverly Hills Hotel on Sunset Boulevard, which became firmly rooted as my favourite hotel in the world. The heyday of Hollywood, from the '30s to the '40s, may have slipped away before I got there but the magic lingered on, with plenty of witnesses to reconstruct it for your benefit.

The history of the Beverly Hills Hotel will go some way to explaining my fascination with what I had come to regard as my home from home. It was built in 1912 after a property developer from Massachusetts called Burton Green surveyed a stretch of open land which lay between Los Angeles city and the Pacific Ocean at Santa Monica. Mr Green and his colleagues planned to build a luxurious development of tree-lined streets and envisaged a spectacular hotel as its focal point. To that end, they offered financial assistance to a prominent divorcee, Margaret Anderson, to exchange her ritzy Hollywood Hotel for one of even greater potential. Her father, the Rev. Robert Boag, had studied at Glasgow University before emigrating to America. And now Mrs Anderson, a substantial lady, was taking up the challenge, bringing her privileged clientele with her from downtown Hollywood – and creating the Beverly Hills Hotel that became the luxurious centrepiece of a burgeoning community.

Within a few years this community had attracted enough residents to become no longer an extension of Los Angeles but a city in its own right. So what would they call it? Well, what better than to call it after the hotel? And that was how, quite uniquely, the Beverly Hills Hotel gave its name to a city. The rich and famous were among the early residents. Film stars like Rudolph Valentino, Charlie Chaplin, Gloria Swanson and Buster Keaton moved in, as well as Mary Pickford and Douglas Fairbanks Snr, who built their luxurious Pickfair mansion close by the hotel. Down the years guests at the hotel included our own Duke and Duchess of Windsor, Princess Margaret and Lord Snowdon, while Elizabeth Taylor's father had an art gallery there.

It was, of course, the perfect backdrop for films and came into its own in productions like *Designing Women*, starring Gregory Peck and Lauren Bacall. It had an even more prominent part to play in Neil Simon's *California Suite*, which told of the misadventures of four groups of guests at the Beverly Hills Hotel.

In 2012, along with singing stars like Dionne Warwick, I joined the quite memorable centenary celebrations in the Crystal Ballroom. Within the grounds there are more than twenty bungalows, for those who wish that kind of privacy. Personally I much prefer the atmosphere of the Pink Palace itself, as the hotel is affectionately known. But the bungalows have not been without their dramas. What intrigued me most of all was what happened when Marilyn Monroe and Yves Montand moved into bungalows twenty and twenty-one while filming *Let's Make Love* in 1960.

Taking their cue from the title, Marilyn and her man didn't waste time when the day's filming was over. When word reached Montand's delectable actress wife, Simone Signoret, back home in France her response was characteristically cool and sophisticated: "Oh really? Well at least she has good taste." But she didn't leave it at that. Hot-footing it to Beverly Hills, she tore a few strips off that husband of hers!

Less than two years later, Marilyn was dead, aged thirty-six, becoming the most discussed, analysed and perhaps misunderstood star of all time. A good friend of mine, Dan Dworsky, a distinguished architect who courted her for a year, assured me that she was by no means the dumb blonde of legend. Nevertheless, he much preferred the delightful Sylvia, who had in turn been pursued by Elvis. She became Dan's wife.

I have stood by Marilyn's grave in Westwood Cemetery, where their methods of burial are many and varied. In her case, she is slotted into a vertical wall, like a large chest of drawers, each drawer containing a coffin. At head-high, hers is invariably covered in the lipstick of kisses. Dean Martin is just a few drawers away. Some crazy creature offered the earth to secure the drawer immediately above the glamorous star, to satisfy his fantasy of spending his eternity on top of Marilyn Monroe!

Reaching that bizarre note, you may have gained some understanding of how I became bound up in the history of Beverly Hills Hotel. It had changed hands several times since Burton Green's day but was now owned by the Sultan of Brunei, for long regarded as the richest man in the world, whose hotel empire was centred on the Dorchester in London's Park Lane. With a little imagination, I found you could still mosey into the hotel with the hint of a Humphrey Bogart, order up a double Scotch in the Polo Bar and cast around, nonchalantly, at neighbouring tables.

Movie moguls were there for the early morning Power Breakfast, ensconced in their plush alcoves where you could eavesdrop on the beginnings of major film projects. I had just seen a magnificent portrayal of that outrageous actor, John Barrymore, given in a Hollywood theatre by Christopher Plummer, who happened to be staying in the hotel, and was able to engage him in a reminiscence of *The Sound of Music*. (That title would crop up at a later date.) Faces familiar or half-forgotten came into focus. Was that Richard Harris crossing the lobby? The lady on the sofa, uncrossing those gorgeous legs, was undoubtedly Ann Miller, exquisite dancer. And that voice from behind was surely worth verifying. Of course, it really was Gregory Peck.

It was here that I met Michael Douglas and Richard Gere on Oscar night and, on the following day, had a long chat with Elizabeth Taylor. Unfortunately, the invitation to her Oscar party came too late. It did, however, remind me of her passionate affair with Richard Burton, with whom she was twice married and twice divorced.

And that led to another memory. I had gone to meet one of her successors, Sally Burton, who proved to be the last of Burton's wives. After his death she wrote a book about that marriage and turned up for our interview accompanied by the well-known media figure Melvyn Bragg, who seemed to be taking care of her. Very properly, Melvyn withdrew to the other end of the hotel lounge to give us privacy for the interview.

All went well until I raised, as discreetly as possible, Richard's previous marriages to Elizabeth Taylor. I thought she would be sufficiently mature to deal with that. But without warning, Sally Burton went hysterical, shouting to Melvyn Bragg for help, as if I was accosting her. No doubt with some knowledge of the lady, Melvyn arrived to calm her down and give me the wink of understanding when I explained what had happened.

In more recent times Sally took the risk of releasing the explicit Burton diaries for public consumption and confessed to her frustration at having to live in the shadow of Elizabeth Taylor. As most of us knew, there was really only one woman in Burton's life, stormy though that relationship might be. It was the old story of an extreme passion which meant they could neither live with nor without each other.

But by now, I was remembering why I was here on this occasion. This particular visit to Beverly Hills takes us back to our old friend Alistair MacLean and the first of his thrillers to be filmed, the book having been written at his home in Hillend Road, Clarkston, Glasgow, when he was still a teacher in Rutherglen. *The Guns of Navarone* was taken up as a film by distinguished Hollywood producer Carl Foreman who, like Charlie Chaplin, had been driven out of America by the ghastly McCarthy witch-hunt, seeking refuge in Britain. But Foreman was rather taken aback when he finally met MacLean. He said later, "My image of the man who had written so robust, so dynamic and so vast an adventure story was on the same scale. Instead, I met a rather small, quiet, modest man, his charm and erudition hidden behind an almost impenetrable Glasgow accent. Later I learned that his shy exterior belied unbounded courage and tenacity."

Foreman's first choice as director was the man who made his name with Compton Mackenzie's *Whisky Galore* and went on to further his reputation with *The Maggie, The Man in the White Suit* and *The Ladykillers*. Alexander Mackendrick had then been whisked off to Hollywood, where his star rose even further with *The Sweet Smell of Success*. So he seemed the right man to direct *The Guns of Navarone*, which would be produced by Foreman. I had already learned that the director is the most important person in any film. The producer may be the money man and the actors gain the glory but it is the director who will finally determine the success or failure.

Mackendrick was a substantial figure, deeply cultured, superbly intelligent, a handsome Scot who, like MacLean himself, was a former pupil of Hillead High School, Glasgow. Drama had followed him all the way since the whole family emigrated from Glasgow to America, where he was born in 1912. His father died of the flu epidemic at the end of the First World War and within weeks his father's brother was murdered by a maniac in Los Angeles. Grandfather Mackendrick, who had also gone to America, was so appalled at losing his two sons that he brought the family back to Glasgow.

After Hillhead High and Glasgow School of Art, Alexander Mackendrick became a director in time for those famous Ealing comedies of the post-war period, starting with *Whisky Galore*. But it was his involvement with *The Guns of Navarone* that occupied our discussion as we sat in his magnificent garden in Beverly Hills. As MacLean's biographer, I needed to know what happened to cause a rift between himself and Carl Foreman.

"I wanted to take what was essentially a typical action-packed wartime melodrama and give it some pretentious overtones," he explained.

As a scholarly man, his interest in Greek mythology enabled him to find a symbolic significance in MacLean's twin guns of Navarone. But classical allusions were not in Foreman's plans. Damn it, man, he just wanted an all-out wartime thriller.

As Mackendrick the perfectionist was spending six months seeking locations in the Mediterranean and developing his theme, the producer ran out of patience – and sacked him. By then, stars like Gregory Peck, David Niven and Anthony Quinn were already on hand to start shooting. So who would take over as director? Gregory Peck had recently seen *Northwest Frontier* and told Foreman that his preference would be the director of that film. That man turned out to be another Scotsman, J. Lee Thompson, of Perth background, but having already made his name as a writer in the 1930s when, at the age of eighteen he saw his first play, *Double Error*, performed on London's West End. He then became a screenwriter at Elstree Studios.

Meanwhile his second play, *Murder Without Crime*, reached Broadway and he went on to direct it as a film. Here was a small man with a big talent who was by then writing the screen version of Ivor Novello's *Glamorous Night* and Ian Hay's *The Middle Watch*, which included one of his own relatives, the great song-and-dance man Jack Buchanan, whose Helensburgh family was connected to the Thompsons of Perth. Having gained attention with *Ice Cold in Alex*, J. Lee Thompson was now receiving this emergency call from Carl Foreman.

So, for the next part of the *Navarone* story I bade goodbye to Alexander Mackendrick and crossed Beverly Hills to another beautiful garden and resumed the story.

Yes, Lee Thompson had received the call at a very late stage, with little more than a week to work out the sequence of scenes. So, unlike Mackendrick, he didn't have time for arguments with Foreman. That would come later.

Small in stature, he found himself dwarfed by his collection of top actors and under some pressure to do it their way.

"I had carefully worked out every shot in my own mind," he told me, "and I knew that on this occasion I could not be flexible. I had to be firm and simply say, 'No, let's do it my way.' "

At the end of the first day's shooting Gregory Peck put an arm round his shoulder and said, 'Well done, wee man. Folks, we're in good hands."

From then on, it was teamwork that produced *The Guns of Navarone*. The cliff scenes were shot on the island of Rhodes and the rest took place at Pinewood Studios, built as part of Britain's answer to Hollywood. Hailed as one of the best action films of all times, it had its highly publicised premiere at the Odeon, Leicester Square, on 27 April 1961, when Gisela and Alistair MacLean were presented to the Queen and the Duke of Edinburgh.

J. Lee Thompson did manage to make another film for Carl Foreman. Once again, Gregory Peck led the cast in *McKenna's Gold* but that was where the producer and director fell out. Thompson told me, "I think I was the only director who ever made a second film for Foreman. He was an excellent producer and an excellent, if lazy, writer but he did interfere with directors."

So what happened to Alexander Mackendrick? He moved towards the academic world, becoming Dean of the Film Faculty at the Californian Institute of Arts, where he came to be revered by everyone from Steven Spielberg to our own Bill Forsyth. If we failed to get the full benefit of his cinematic genius, at least he inspired a whole new generation of actors and directors. But the family tragedies of his early days in America followed this great gentleman to the end of his life. Before he died in 1993, his granddaughter, Merry Mackendrick from Lochwinnoch, newly qualified as a doctor, was travelling with her boyfriend in Africa, helping villagers with medical advice, when they were set upon by bandits – and murdered. It was the ultimate heartbreak.

CHAPTER FORTY-FIVE

SO WHO SHOT JR EWING?

That earlier mention of Christopher Plummer, leading man in *The Sound of Music*, was a reminder that not everything goes right in a journalist's pursuits. In 1980 I had flown to America for the Presidential Election, choosing Jimmy Carter's home base of New York in the belief that he would be returned for a second term. How wrong can you be? As I sat in the cocktail bar of the Walford Astoria, glued to the television as the results came in, it became clear that I was in the wrong place. For Jimmy Carter, the Democrat, was being slaughtered by the Governor of California, veteran film star of fifty movies, the irrepressible Ronald Reagan. It was the first time a sitting President had not been returned since 1932, when Herbert Hoover was unseated by Franklin D. Roosevelt.

Carter's defeat was due mainly to the bungled attempt to rescue fifty-two Americans taken hostage at the US Embassy in Iran. Reagan, who had failed even to secure the Republican nomination in 1968 and again in 1976, had not only gained the ticket in 1980 but was sweeping his way into the White House.

I was on the first plane next morning for Los Angeles, where I happened to know that the new President lived in the very up-market district of Pacific Pallisades, near the ocean front. Now that was handy, I thought. I had an old Gordonian friend from Aberdeen, Alexander Gray, who had done well in America and was a near neighbour of Reagan. So Alex would be my first stop. Great idea. By the time I reached Pacific Pallisades, however, the security ring around the Reagan home district couldn't have been breached by a division of tanks. So bang went that idea.

While the Reagan story rumbled along, I settled in the neighbouring Santa Monica and lined up some other ideas for this trip to California. The big talking point of the time concerned that greatest of television soap operas, *Dallas*. The whole world had gone insane over the mystery of "Who shot JR?" JR Ewing was the villain of the piece, married to the gorgeous Sue Ellen but with so many enemies it was hard to guess who had fired the gun. Bookmakers offering attractive odds were inundated with customers. Nothing like it had ever been seen before.

Another member of the *Dallas* cast happened to be Sue Ellen's sister, played by Bing Crosby's daughter Mary. Through my previous contact with Bing, by then sadly gone, I had managed to fix an interview with Mary and was just about to leave for the appointment when the phone rang. It was the producer of *Dallas*.

Yes?

"Mr Webster? You are due to see Miss Crosby?"

Yes, yes.

"Well, sorry. The interview is off!"

But . . . but . . .

The man had already gone. So what was this all about?

With a little more thought, I should have guessed. In fact, I should have been hot-footing it to the bookies with as big a bet as I could muster. For the finger that pulled the trigger on JR Ewing – soon to be revealed – was none other than my girl, Mary Crosby! The director had obviously been afraid that the secret might leak out in our interview. Ah well, you win some and lose some.

Next bright idea: How about that loveable character actor, singer and composer of great songs like "Stardust", Hoagy Carmichael, whose screen appearances usually found him at the piano, with a cigarette drooping from the side of his mouth? In those days, would you believe, it was not uncommon to find celebrities in the phone directory. Much less of this ex-directory stuff, and Hoagy's number was there. He was just the kind of delightful man you would have expected. As for an interview, he hadn't been too well recently and, sadly, he didn't feel up to it. I wasn't sure if this was just a gentleman's polite way of saying no but we parted on the friendliest of terms. I should have known better. Poor Hoagy really was unwell. In fact, he died a few weeks later.

Was there a jinx on this Californian visit? My last call each evening was at the Bob Burns Bar in Santa Monica, a shrine to our national bard, where I enjoyed my nightcap to the accompaniment of a splendid pianist. On one of those evenings a rather substantial elderly lady walked into the cocktail bar, accompanied by three rather scruffy-looking youths, an unlikely combination it seemed to me.

As they settled to their drinks I could see the lady tapping her fingers to the music and taking an intense interest in the piano. When the pianist rose for his break, she crossed to speak and I could hear her asking if he minded her playing in his absence. Pianists don't like this kind of thing. If the strangers are mediocre amateurs they will be an embarrassment. If by chance they are very good they will seem like competition. Reluctantly, the pianist agreed and she sat down at his keyboard. After an impressive run of arpeggios she broke into George Gershwin's "The Man I Love", giving it the most magnificent performance I had ever heard. This was top-class professionalism. I was beginning to have thoughts about who the lady might be and by the time she had finished I was pretty certain.

I went across to congratulate her and to say, "You know, the last time I saw you was at the Tivoli Theatre, Aberdeen, in 1943." Her eyes lit up. Yes, that would be right. The act was the magnificent tenor tones of Ted Andrews, accompanied by his pianist wife. They were billed as "Ted Andrews and Barbara – and introducing eight-year-old Julie." I had witnessed the very beginning of Julie Andrews, destined to be one of the great musical comedy stars of all time, leading lady in *Mary Poppins*, *The Sound of Music* and so much else. She sang like a lark in Aberdeen that evening. And her mother played just as she had played tonight. Barbara Andrews from England could not believe that she had been recognised in California. So we enjoyed a drink and had a wonderfully informal conversation.

Being the journalist, of course, I wanted to follow up with a more formal interview. That would be fine. She was staying with Julie and gave me the address for our appointment. She departed with the three youths – presumably detailed to be her minders – and I duly turned up at the house next day and rang the intercom. The voice that answered did not belong to Barbara. It was stern and emphatic that there would be no interview. I could picture an embarrassed Barbara in the background, no doubt having been given a severe warning about speaking to strange men in pubs.

Julie is known as a formidable woman, once described by Moss Hart, who directed the stage version of *My Fair Lady*, as possessing "that terrible British strength that makes you wonder why they lost India". In more recent times she has revealed a skeleton in the cupboard which took everyone by surprise. She was just four when her parents divorced and she greatly missed the father she adored. But it turned out that he was not her father at all. She was evidently the love child of a passionate liaison that Barbara shared with another man. So we never know what upsets people, do we?

What upset me was that I was having no luck with my 1980 sojourn in California. There would be one last throw of the dice. As already mentioned, I was said to be a fairly good ballroom dancer, pretending to be the Fred Astaire of Aberdeenshire. Well . . . maybe the Fred Astaire of Maud. My girlfriend and dancing partner Margaret Cassie and I could glide across a dance floor to some effect, folk said. So I couldn't resist the appearance of Ginger Rogers at the Wilshire Theatre in Beverly Hills. I had no plans, except to seek her out in the dressing room afterwards. Journalistic experience can usually get you that far.

As with Barbara Andrews, I did have a good chat with Ginger but she was leaving town that night, with no time for an interview. My regret was that I didn't at least ask her to dance a few steps with me. So I headed back from California, by which time Ronald Reagan was on the steps of Capitol Hill, being sworn in as the fortieth President of the United States.

Surely the fates could never treat me as badly as this again. And

211

thankfully, they never have. Mind you, Jimmy Carter was having an even worse time. After fourteen months – and on the very day after Reagan's inauguration – Iran's Ayatollah Khomeini piled further humiliation on the ex-President by releasing the fifty-two American hostages.

CHAPTER FORTY-SIX

WITH MORECAMBE AND WISE

If Hollywood was the undisputed capital of filmland and American movies tended to dominate, the British film industry was making its own pitch from the 1920s onwards. As Britain's answer to Hollywood, major studios sprang up at places like Pinewood, Elstree and Ealing, the last named becoming famous as the home of the "Ealing Comedies", created by Sir Michael Balcon. It was much associated with directors like Alexander Mackendrick and his *Whisky Galore*. But it was the first visit to Pinewood in 1964 that gave me an insight into the amount of effort, tension, shouting – and sheer boredom – involved in the making of a film.

Pinewood itself is a handsome mansion in the Buckinghamshire countryside, twenty-four miles from London, with a minstrel gallery where each door bears a familiar name who has a base there. Even Hollywood producers keep a toehold in the British film scene. At any given time several films are in production and at lunchtime you find actors and directors meeting up in the wood-panelled dining room, enjoying a drink and discussing their respective films. From an early start, the first half of their day is already past but even when it is completed they may have done no more than two or three minutes of the film, such is the repetition until they all get it right. It is easy to understand why actors prefer the theatre, with its live audience and stimulating atmosphere.

At the bar counter that day were people like Harry H. Corbett, at the height of his fame in *Steptoe and Son*, and the hell-raising Oliver Reed, on his way to becoming the highest-paid actor in Britain before descending into heavy drinking and bar room brawling.

So I absorbed this fascinating encounter, bade them farewell and headed for one of the studios, in search of two other characters who would be waiting for me. Only bullet holes lingered to remind us that it was here they made *Goldfinger* and *From Russia With Love*. But there was no sign of James Bond. Instead I ran into a couple of amateur sleuths who had taken over from Bond. They were better known as Morecambe and Wise, by then at the top as comedy kings of television, and now venturing into a very different world, clearly wondering if they could find international fame as film comedians. This was their first-ever attempt, called *The Intelligence Men*, and technicians had been telling me of an unusual hazard while filming; they couldn't stop laughing.

They were on location near London one day when a housewife, leaning from a sixth-storey window, called out "Ee, look! There's Eric Morecambe." Eric waved up to her and called "Hello, luv. My, what long legs you've got."

As I joined them, the studio phone rang and Eric lifted the receiver. "Sorry, luv," he said. "We're not on the phone here."

I knew what kind of day we were going to have. At close quarters, Morecambe's face was an interesting study. The weeks of his mouth were upturned, the nose was poised for fun and the whole expression teetered on the brink of laughter. For a moment he was serious: "We sometimes wonder how long our success can last. If someone comes along with something brand new, well it can make you look old-fashioned."

Ernie joined in to discuss newcomers. It sounds strange now to recall the latest arrivals of the early-1960s: "There's this Jimmy Tarbuck, for example. He is bringing in the Liverpool brand of comedy that has followed the popularity of The Beatles . . . "

"And humour will always have its fashions," said Eric. "Sick humour was just a fashion and there have been others. Remember, there were the elephant jokes?"

"Well, how could you forget them?" said Ernie, retreating from the threatening elbow of his partner.

"Next thing may be a fashion for gags about fish," said Eric, at which point I ventured a feeble crack of my own, suggesting that the sting would surely be in the tail!

Film extras were curled up with paperbacks, wearily awaiting their next turn. But now it was time for Eric and Ernie to perform again. I watched as they went through the ritual, then repeated it so that it could be dubbed in Chinese. I was joined by the film's director, Robert Asher, who enthused about his new stars and his high hopes that they would become great film comedians in the tradition of Norman Wisdom.

For all their previous success, however, it didn't happen. *The Intelligence Men* was followed by two others but in a different medium; there was to be no fame in films.

Eric Morecambe had told me, "You can be a funny man but if you don't have the right material you are liable to be a mediocre funny man." That, sadly, was the fate of two men who remained legends of television only.

But if Pinewood was dominated by the Rank Organisation and Ealing was the creation of Michael Balcon, there is no more fascinating a story than that of Elstree, the success of which belonged to two Scots. In an age of obsession with celebrity it is astonishing how little we know about some of our significant figures. The name of Robert Clark never reached the headlines yet he became a major figure in turning Elstree into a world-class film studio, an unlikely happening when you consider his origins.

Clark was born in 1904 into a working-class family at 3 Clavering Street in Paisley, the last of thirteen children. Out of school at fourteen, he was engaged as an office boy to the Glasgow law firm of Maxwell Waddell in Hope Street, where John Maxwell spotted the potential of a young lad who should have gone to university. Guiding him to that end, Maxwell was delighted when Robert Clark eventually graduated from Glasgow University with his MA and LLB, rejoining the firm to become a fully qualified solicitor.

John Maxwell, who had a family connection with the famous Pollok estate in Glasgow, was a man of vision who became deeply involved in the budding film industry of the 1920s, to the extent that he not only had a stake in several picture houses but started a film production company in the city. Sensing that he needed to be in London, he headed south to take over an ailing company which he turned into the Associated British Picture Corporation.

Now establishing himself in what became the Elstree Studios, he engaged a young director called Alfred Hitchcock to make his first talkie, *Blackmail*, in 1929. But Maxwell would need help to expand this business. And that was when he remembered young Clark, back in Glasgow. Was he interested in coming to Elstree as his assistant?

Clark already idolised Maxwell for what he had done for his career and promptly jumped at the offer. So off he went to renew his working relationship with his old boss, at the same time making the extraordinary decision to read for the English Bar, making him a qualified lawyer in England as well as Scotland. But apart from returning to Paisley to marry his sweetheart, Mary Lang, his main focus was now on movie production. In the 1930s he was responsible for films like *Blossom Time*, which brought him the friendship of that famous tenor, Richard Tauber.

The Second World War interrupted film-making and that was compounded by the tragedy of John Maxwell's premature death in 1940. Robert Clark was now a director and driving force of Associated British Pictures, ready for the heyday of his own career, which coincided with that golden age of British films, running from the end of the war until the late 1950s. He was now the man responsible for a whole range of popular films, from *The Hasty Heart*, featuring Ronald Reagan, to *Laughter in Paradise* with Alastair Sim, Ivor Novello's *The Dancing Years* and the wartime thriller *Ice Cold in Alex*, for which he brought together two of his fellow Scots, J. Lee Thompson as director and Tom Morrison, to write the screenplay. Morrison, a former reporter on the *Glasgow Herald*, came from High Burnside, on the outskirts of Glasgow, one of a family of five, all of whom became distinguished writers, not least sister Nancy who wrote *The Gowk Storm*.

But Robert Clark's greatest satisfaction lay in his production of

The Dam Busters, that 1954 film in which Michael Redgrave played the part of Sir Barnes Wallis, the inventive genius who gave us the bouncing bomb that burst the German dams and flooded Hitler's munition factories during the war. So Robert Clark, the wee lad from a Paisley backstreet, had become a major figure of British film, lunching with Marlene Dietrich or putting stars like Audrey Hepburn under contract.

Still remaining well out of the limelight, he was building up a private fortune as a property developer, not just in London but back in Glasgow city centre and even in his hometown, with the Paisley Piazza. He was also a director of London Weekend Television and a founder of Caledonian Associated Cinemas, with its large chain of picture houses in Scotland.

So that was how John Maxwell and Robert Clark came to be involved in the creation of Elstree Studios, a major feat of which very little is known in Scotland. But if Clark was virtually unknown in his own land, Glasgow University did at least catch up with his success just before his death in 1984, when he was awarded an honorary degree of LLD. Happily, that day coincided with an honour for another distinguished Scottish film-maker Bill Forsyth, who had given us films like *Gregory's Girl* and *Local Hero.*

When Robert Clark died there wasn't a line of obituary in the national newspapers, not even *The Times.* The only trace of his passing was to be found in the local paper in Paisley. Well, he did come from Clavering Street, after all.

CHAPTER FORTY-SEVEN

THE HELL OF NORTHERN IRELAND

If my career leaves the impression of a joyful romp through the glamour and excitement of the celebrity circuit, there were occasions when it was a very different story. The troubles of Northern Ireland from 1969 onwards became a major news story for years to come, not only for news reporters but for feature writers trying to convey the atmosphere of Belfast and elsewhere. The long-standing animosity between Catholics and Protestants had broken into a new age of extreme violence, with a variety of causes, not least the demand of Catholics for their voting rights. Among the early conflicts, police in Londonderry used water cannon to disperse hundreds of Catholics who had trapped their arch-enemy, the Rev. Ian Paisley, and his supporters at the Guildhall. Paisley's car was overturned and set on fire, with the crowd shouting, "We want Paisley."

Elsewhere in the world at that time Neil Armstrong became the first man to land on the moon, Richard Nixon was sworn in as President of the United States and the great Judy Garland was found dead in her flat, aged forty-seven.

By 1970, as a *Daily Express* feature writer, I was on my way to Northern Ireland for my first real taste of trouble. The main flash point tended to be the annual Orange Walk in July, when the Protestants paraded to Finaghy Park, passing through Catholic districts where conflict was always liable to break out. Journalists were there from all over the world, most of them choosing to stay at the Europa Hotel. But that had become a target for IRA bombers, with frequent explosions blowing guests out of bed in the middle of the night. I preferred the Royal Avenue Hotel on the main thoroughfare, which managed to maintain a semblance of normality, with an orchestra playing for dancing in the dining room and only the distant boom of a bomb to remind you where you were.

On the eve of the Orange Walk, the IRA had given warning that bombing would begin at the stroke of midnight. Mobile phones were unheard of in those days, so an hour before the promised outbreak I crossed to the main post office building to phone the day's story to the *Express* in Glasgow. Whatever else was going to happen would have to come later. The phone boxes were built into the outer wall of the post office and from there I strolled down Royal Avenue, just wondering if the IRA would stick to their promised mayhem.

I didn't have long to wait. The first blast came at the far end of the Avenue, on the very stroke of twelve. The second and third came at equal distances, causing a dilemma. Was it wise to run away from this sequence or run towards it, in the hope that it would bypass you? There was little time to make up your mind. All I know is that the last bomb in this frightening display was lodged in one of those telephone kiosks from which I had so recently sent my story to Glasgow. So they weren't there to take my later news, reporting that all hell had broken loose in Belfast.

Such narrow escapes became almost routine. I soon discovered that Scottish journalists were regarded with suspicion by the IRA, apparently through their belief that we were sympathetic to the powerful Loyalist element from Glasgow, some of whom crossed regularly to engage in the troubles. So, observing the nightly encounters, you had to be careful where you landed. I suppose in my Humphrey Bogart belted raincoat and felt hat I was something of a giveaway. I shouldn't have been too surprised, therefore, when I was put up against a wall by a gang one night and questioned about who I was and what I was up to. I wasn't making a good job of it and there was some discussion about what they should do with me. (There had been previous cases of my breed getting a rough time.) Now, physical courage and quick thinking were never my strong points but it is amazing what fear and alarm can do in an emergency.

For my Catholic captors, surely every one of them a fanatical supporter of Celtic Football Club, I suddenly had a brilliant idea. Had they read *Fire In My Boots*, the recent autobiography of that great Celtic hero, Jimmy Johnstone? Yes, of course. And so what? Well, Jimmy was a football genius but he wasn't a writer, you see. He needed what you call a ghostwriter, someone who would write it for him. And I was the person who wrote it – and in doing so, I became a friend of Jock Stein, that greatest of football managers who had achieved the apparently impossible by taking a bunch of local lads in Glasgow and turning them into the Champions of Europe in 1967.

They fired a few questions to test my authenticity. But it was all true. And suddenly there was a change of expression. I was really a friend of Jock Stein? Yes, and I had stories to prove it. Abandoning their previous intentions, they were now beaming in wonderment and wanting to shake the hand that had shaken the hand of Jock Stein. I was a pal!

I breathed a sigh of relief – and later told Big Jock about how he had spared me an unpleasant experience, if not my life. But that didn't stop me landing in another nasty spot a few nights later. This time, while the British soldiers were in face-to-face battle with the IRA, I somehow managed to get myself behind the Irishmen. The Army was firing in CS gas to quell their attackers – and I found myself with a bellyful of the dreadful stuff. I had no idea it could be so debilitating. Blinded and choking, I turned and ran till an old lady grabbed me and guided me to a saucer on her window sill. Evidently, vinegar was the antidote to CS gas and in those Catholic areas on a night like this, the women were well organised with saucerfuls of it. The lady just called for my handkerchief, soaked it in the stuff and covered my face till I was breathing again. Whether or not it was my imagination I don't know but for a year or two thereafter I could have sworn that my lungs were not entirely clear.

But Belfast could offer a variety of nasty moments. Still staying at the Royal Avenue Hotel, I was having breakfast one morning with

Cyril Ainsley, a veteran journalist and war correspondent with the *Daily Express* in London. Cyril, who had seen it all, suddenly rose and went cautiously towards a potted plant by the window. He had spotted something. "Call the bomb disposal squad!" he shouted. Sure enough, an incendiary device had been lodged in the potted plant – and the military arrived just in time. I thought the charming old Royal Avenue Hotel might be spared the worst of the troubles but while it survived that particular incident, they got it in the end.

I followed the countless thousands to Finachy Field for the Orange Walk of 1971, bewildered as always by the fervour of this colourful Protestant parade, the jaunty flute bands playing "The Sash My Father Wore" and the drum majors tossing their maces in the air. Once there, I was interviewing the Rev. Ian Paisley, that extraordinary figurehead of the movement who had formed his own church and held a magnetic influence over his people. The sheer power of this huge, loud man gave the impression that he must be indestructible. I had always wondered why one so detested by the IRA had managed to avoid assassination. But meeting him face to face, I now entertained the thought that bullets would most likely bounce off him.

Talking of bullets, I also realised that he and I were standing dangerously near a range of flats in a Catholic area, from which a sniper could so easily have a pot at him. I didn't prolong the interview. Considering the sworn hostility between Paisley and men like Martin McGuinness on the other side, I came to the conclusion that, while there is supposed to be a solution to every problem in life, the Northern Ireland situation might turn out to be the exception.

It certainly astounded me when a form of peace and understanding was reached in the new century, to the point that Ian Paisley and Martin McGuinness could be seen in jovial partnership in the new administration. The only explanation must surely be that, after thirty years of undiluted misery, the people of Ulster had reached a point of utter exhaustion, when, in their private moments, even the warring politicians could not face the prospect of passing on to their children and grandchildren the kind of madness they themselves had perpetuated down the years.

Having said all that, however, with bitterness still simmering under the surface, I would not bet that the peace will be everlasting. I only hope I'm wrong.

CHAPTER FORTY-EIGHT

ALONE WITH CHRISTINE KEELER

John Profumo and I had at least one thing in common – we had both been in a bedroom alone with Christine Keeler. For those too young to remember, Miss Keeler was an attractive girl of twenty who used to sleep with men for money. John Profumo, on the other hand, was a distinguished politician, Minister for War in Harold Macmillan's Conservative government from the late 1950s. But rumour had it that he had been to bed with Miss Keeler. His prospects were not improved by the fact that we were at loggerheads with the Soviet Union in what was known as the Cold War – and Miss Keeler was also said to have been to bed with a Russian spy, officially known as the Naval Attaché at the Soviet Embassy in London. So what about the pillow talk?

When the whole story exploded in 1963 it was widely accepted as the scandal of the century. Christine Keeler took her place in history as the woman who brought down the Tory government. When challenged originally, Profumo had denied the story in the House of Commons but later admitted to the Prime Minister that he had, in fact, lied about his mistress. He resigned in disgrace and was followed by Macmillan himself, who handed over the Premiership to Sir Alec Douglas-Home. Within a year the Tories were out of power.

The shenanigans had been centred on the estate of the aristocratic Astor family at Cliveden, where a prominent London osteopath and artist, Dr Stephen Ward, had a cottage. It was there that John Profumo first met Christine Keeler. For whatever reason, it was also Dr Ward, the son of a vicar, who tipped off MI5 about the Russian spy connection but he himself was soon in court, charged with living off the immoral earnings of Christine Keeler and her flatmate, Mandy Rice-Davies. Adding to the drama, as the jury was ready with its guilty verdict, Dr Ward committed suicide. Miss Keeler went to jail on a perjury charge – and John Profumo resumed married life with his forgiving wife, the glamorous West End star Valerie Hobson. He spent the rest of his days in the quiet penance of social work in the east end of London, for which he received much gratitude.

So where did I come into this murky story of a twilight world where the rich and famous consorted with prostitutes, perverts and drug addicts in a notoriety of orgies, violence, suicide and security risks? We didn't know about things like that in Maud.

Some years later, when the dust had settled and the main characters had largely withdrawn to privacy and silence, my journalistic instinct was to wonder if Christine Keeler might be prepared to talk it over with me. I could only try.

I traced her address to a bleak council flat in Chelsea, where she lived with a son, wholly dependent on social security. I gathered that her subsequent life had brought little luck. But yes, we could meet. The rendezvous was the Russell Hotel in central London, where I happened to be staying. The fragile figure that came through the swing doors did not exactly fit the picture of a woman who could bring down a British government. But she settled elegantly on a cocktail bar stool as I gained my first impressions. The resonant voice and the bone structure of her face gave some hint of what it was that attracted men in high places.

I learned that her working-class background was tempered with a Scottish aristocratic connection and could see that the eyes and cheekbones owed quite a lot to the fact that her long-lost father was the son of a full-blooded Native American. But how did it all seem to her now? Did she recognise herself in the image of 1963? Was Stephen Ward himself a spy for the Russians? And, most intriguingly, had she ever seen John Profumo again? I didn't expect such a frank interview. It was true that at one time she did sleep with men for money but not any more, she said.

But let her speak for herself: "The fact is that I don't believe in permissiveness and have always had to be involved with someone to have sex. One-night stands do nothing for me at all. I need a few weeks to get to know the man. Yet I don't think I have ever been in love. I have known lust but not love. I had a big ego and have been very jealous, even of the two men I married but didn't love.

"Looking back on those events of 1963 I still cannot believe that my frolicking was in any way responsible for the collapse of a government. I was just a pawn. There were some Labour people very anxious to get rid of the Tories and the more they could put on me the better they thought they could succeed.

"It has not been easy living with the name of Christine Keeler. For the first few years after coming out of Holloway jail I was paranoid, like a wounded creature. In 1965 I married James Levermore, an ordinary working-class man, not that I was in love with him but because I wanted to establish that I was ordinary too. Do you understand that? It was a case of finding a man who could make love to me properly and was ordinary and would marry me.

"I had one son but the marriage didn't last. Then I married Antony Platt, a wealthy man with a big house in Chelsea and I was immediately pregnant again. But that marriage didn't last either. In between those marriages I had the best three years of my life, years in which film stars like Robert Mitchum and Clint Eastwood came to my parties."

So what about Dr Stephen Ward, the social adventurer who put her in touch with so many of the wrong people in life? A smile broke over her face.

"Despite all, Stephen was a wonderful man to me, the best friend I ever had. He was a charmer, an artist, as well as a famous osteopath who could cure my headaches with a click of the neck. I lived with him when I was nineteen and he was forty-six but I didn't fancy him sexually. And although we slept together we never once made love. We were touchers. Don't you think it's about time we stopped this old-fashioned idea of thinking that people must be having sex if they are together?

"Stephen said he was pleased we never had sex because it would spoil a good friendship. Actually, he wasn't a very sexual man. But he was intrigued with prostitutes and their way of life. He was so intrigued, in fact, that he took me out in his car in London and made me walk along a street to see how many men would accost me."

Well, well, I was getting it all! But was Dr Ward a Russian spy?

"Yes, I am in no doubt about it. He was a communist sympathiser and admitted as much. He used to tell me to ask John Profumo about when the Americans were going to give the bomb to Germany. I told him I couldn't ask a question like that and, in any case, he wouldn't be likely to tell me. But whenever I came back from being with Profumo he would cross-examine me and I had to tell him all we had been talking about.

"Because I knew I had asked nothing, I was the one who knew for sure that there was no security risk involved in the Profumo Affair. It was just a load of nonsense."

Of her affair with Profumo, she said it first took place at his house in Regents Park where he lived with his actress wife, Valerie Hobson. He told her they often had the Queen there for dinner and he pointed out the scrambler telephone on which he could phone the Prime Minister directly.

"We then went into the bedroom, where he proved to be a strong, forceful lover, the kind of man who knows what he wants. He was also very humorous and impressive."

Had she ever seen him since?

"I have never bumped into him but I was in a club in Soho one night when the pianist turned out to be his godson. He passed me a message to say Profumo wanted to see me. I think he just wanted to be friendly and to clear the air but I said I had had enough trouble and didn't want to see him.

"Am I sorry for him? Not really. He was a very wealthy man and while we both suffered, he still ended up with his money and I had nothing."

Before this interview began, we were due to have dinner. But first, a drink. A glass of wine? No, she would rather have a large whisky. When that was finished I motioned towards the dining room. No, she didn't feel like eating. She would prefer another large whisky. There were three large whiskies, by which time the veneer of sophistication had rather peeled away. I had occasion to go along to my room but as I made to return, Miss Keeler was at my bedroom door.

By now she was raging about a lawyer and his mishandling of a book that had been written. As I retreated into my bedroom she was telling me what she would do if she could lay her hands on him. It would not have been pleasant. That was when it struck me that here I was, alone in a bedroom with the notorious Christine Keeler! I also got the feeling she rather liked me. She then signed a copy of that book, dedicating it to "Jack, the only interviewer who has interviewed me properly." It made me wonder how many had interviewed her improperly.

Finally I managed to escort her back to the lounge bar and as she drifted out through those swing doors, a legend in a white, high-necked blouse and calf-length skirt, she was heading home to a corner of Chelsea known as World's End, hoping that the name held no particular significance for the years that lay ahead. From what I can gather, the fates have not been kind to her.

As for the significance of the Profumo Affair, coinciding as it did with rock 'n' roll, The Beatles and the new age of youth rebellion, there is little doubt that it opened the floodgates of immorality in British life and established the so-called Permissive Society. With the titillation of such a hot subject, even the middle-aged and elderly felt suddenly free to talk about it, with something not far from orgasmic fervour. And if that was how people behaved in high society, well, what was good enough for them . . .

CHAPTER FORTY-NINE

BERTIE FORBES COMES HOME

If it is hard to keep America out of my ramblings it is even harder to do likewise with the Forbes family of New York, with their origins in my own small corner of Buchan. The daredevil that was Malcolm Forbes, by now well established as head of the family publishing house and a colourful celebrity across America, had spread his empire to include the luxury yacht called *The Highlander*, a private Boeing 727 called *Capitalist Tool*, an island in the South Pacific, a Christopher Wren house in London, the stately Chateau Balleroy in France and a 174,000-acre ranch in Colorado, not to mention the world's biggest collection of Fabergé eggs – and the cloth with which they mopped up the blood at Abraham Lincoln's assassination!

Malcolm was nothing if not adventurous. To that motley collection he had added the former Governor's Palace in Tangier, which explained his invitation to the birthday party of Morocco's King Hassan. In his various exploits, the hot-air ballooning Malcolm had diced with death more than was sensible. Shot and wounded at the D-Day landings in Normandy, he was decorated for his bravery, and that was just the start of his escapades. But this was different. A great social occasion lay ahead. As he joined other guests awaiting the king to signal the start of lunch, there was a sudden burst of firecracker noises, suggesting that the fireworks display had started too soon. But this was no fun show.

A convoy of trucks came hurtling up the Casablanca road, swung into the palace gates as 1,200 military cadets began firing in all directions. Led by King Hassan's own military adviser, this was an attempt to overthrow his royal personage. By the time this attempted coup was over, more than a hundred guests lay dead in the palace courtyard. The Belgian ambassador died in the arms of the French ambassador. The famous cardiologist Jean Himbert was crawling to the aid of the injured when he was callously machine-gunned to death.

Word reached Malcolm's own palace that he had been murdered. In fact, the survival instinct had taken him on a leap over the palace wall and down on to the sands, where he crawled away on his belly. But pursuing soldiers found him and he was brought back and forced to lie face down among the dead and dying. This time it seemed his moment had finally come. But miraculously the revolt petered out, the leaders were caught and later executed – and Malcolm Forbes had survived once again. The king joined him among the survivors.

In that same decade of the 1970s, he had sent his only daughter, Moira, to study at Aberdeen University, though he himself had been rather out of touch with his father's native patch, what with the war and his political activities, including his successful attempt to bring General Dwight D. Eisenhower back from Europe in 1952 to become the thirty-fourth President of the United States.

When he was awarded an honorary doctorate from Aberdeen University in 1986 he asked me to accompany him on graduation day. He was full of questions about the famous Forbes Picnics back in the old parish, which had come to an end with his father's death in 1954. Could I help to restart them?

In the following year he and the family flew into Aberdeen Airport on *Capitalist Tool*, before heading to a field beside his father's old school at Whitehill of New Deer. What an event it was. The whole parish turned out to meet the man who had not been there since 1937, when he was eighteen. As Malcolm addressed the gathering, *Capitalist Tool* came flying low over Whitehill in a spectacular salute to the folk below. There was tug o' war for the adults, races for the children, pies and pints in the marquee and a great sense of rural community. As I drove him back to Aberdeen Airport at the end of the day, I pointed out the New Deer cemetery, where his ancestors lay, all except his own father, who was of course buried at Englewood, New Jersey, just across the Hudson River from Manhattan. I could see a spark of interest in New Deer cemetery.

He was no sooner back in New York than he came on the phone. He had called a family gathering and suggested they should dig up father Bertie and bring him home to Buchan. His marriage had ended a long time ago so there was no reason for him to stay in America.

I arranged for the old kirkyard at New Deer, by then no longer in use, to be opened up for a day. Sandy Ritchie, the local joiner-cum-undertaker, took delivery of the formidable American-style coffin as the entire Forbes family flew in once more in *Capitalist Tool*. After a service at the kirk in which Bertie and his nine siblings had worshipped every Sunday, we crossed the street and lowered him into the family grave, where the poor boy who became a legend of American journalism would spend the rest of his eternity. Meanwhile, having attended the fiftieth birthday of *Forbes* magazine in the '60s, I expected the next milestone to be the seventy-fifth, so it was a surprise to receive an invitation to the seventieth anniversary, which turned out to be an even more lavish affair than the earlier one.

Once more at his estate in Far Hills, New Jersey, the marquee shaped like a Scottish castle was filled with every known face in America, to the extent that I found myself at one point in conversation with Rupert Murdoch (that other Buchan man), diplomat Henry Kissinger and Sir James Goldsmith, the man whose financial manoeuvring had recently sparked off the infamous Stock Exchange crash of 1987.

By now Malcolm was divorced from his wife, Roberta, and enjoying a highly publicised romance with film star Elizabeth Taylor, who was by his side at the top table that night. But his ex-wife was elsewhere in the company, keeping discreetly at a distance as the evening broke into a spectacular fireworks display and dancing to the famous Lester Lanin orchestra. When it came to the last waltz, Roberta was sitting alone as Malcolm and Elizabeth led the way. So

I asked her to dance – and managed to give them a gentle dunt or two on the way round the floor!

Like his father, who advanced the timing of his last visit to Scotland for no apparent reason, Malcolm had a rare gift of instinct. That may have explained why he brought forward the next big anniversary to the seventieth. He would not have been alive for the seventy-fifth.

In late February 1990, he flew back from London to New York one night, was driven out to Far Hills – and was found dead in bed next morning. After all those near-death experiences, which included a total recovery from bladder cancer, it was a sudden heart attack that got him in the end. He was seventy. It was all over the news bulletins in this country and it was not long before I had a phone call from his eldest son, Steve. The funeral would be an Episcopal affair but they would like me to bring the minister from the Church of Scotland at New Deer to participate in the service. Transport would be no problem. They would send the Forbes *Capitalist Tool* to Aberdeen Airport to pick us up and take us back!

But there was another problem. The Rev. Russel Moffat had never had a passport and would need to present himself in person at the Glasgow office – but the North-east was in the midst of a snowstorm, with all roads blocked. However, the Grampian snow-ploughs came to the rescue and Mr Moffat was back from Glasgow in time to join the plane at Aberdeen. There we were, lording it across the Atlantic in the world's most luxurious private Boeing, complete with plush lounge and bedrooms, before being whisked off to our hotel. He had never imagined anything like this.

To break him in gently to the New York experience, I took Mr Moffat on an evening stroll down Fifth Avenue and round to the high-domed Church of St Bartholomew on Park Avenue, where he could attune himself to the setting of the funeral next morning. All 2,500 seats would be occupied by the elite of America as Mr Moffat took his place at the altar, suitably different in the black robes of Presbyterianism, in contrast to the more flamboyant whites of the Piskies.

Facing him in pride of place from the front pew was Elizabeth Taylor and next to her none other than the seventy-seven-year-old President Richard Nixon, come to say farewell to his Republican colleague. From across the aisle, studying him discreetly as he smiled benignly to fellow mourners, I tried hard to fit the scandal of Watergate upon his quite distinguished head. And so it went on. But none of it fazed the wee minister from New Deer, who played his part admirably and later joined the reception at the Forbes Building on Fifth Avenue.

In his address to the congregation, Steve Forbes told them pointedly: "My father had no difficulty with women. He simply married the best."

Well, he didn't marry Elizabeth Taylor, for whom the party was now over, but he did spend thirty-nine years with Roberta, who sat further back in the congregation. It was she who walked with dignity from that magnificent church, wishing no doubt that matters had turned out differently but comforted by the presence of her four sons and one daughter. And Steve had given the last word to his mother.

CHAPTER FIFTY

ON THE FLOOR OF THE SENATE

Back in the 1990s, through those various connections, I became an honorary patron of the American-Scottish Foundation, a charitable organisation which not only fostered goodwill between our two countries but raised money for Highland crofters and other cottage industries in need of help. In my own time we had also brought the much publicised Tartan Day into existence in America. Its founder in 1956 was the well-known Scottish aristocrat, Lord Malcolm Douglas-Hamilton, brother of the same Duke of Hamilton who was sought out by Hitler's deputy Rudolf Hess when, sensationally, he flew to Scotland in 1941 in the belief that the Duke could act as intermediary in gaining a peace settlement between Hitler and Churchill.

In 1964, however, Lord Malcolm, a distinguished wartime pilot, was flying his own plane over Africa when it crashed. It was some time before the bodies of him and his son Niall were discovered. His widow took over the running of his foundation but later handed over to Alan Bain, a Scots-American lawyer in New York, who recruited me to his team.

The idea of a Tartan Day in America had to be formalised and it was a moving experience in 2000 to stand on the floor of the Senate and hear Senator Trent Lott propose the resolution that "From this day forward, and in perpetuity, the date of 6 April will be regarded in America as Tartan Day." That date, of course, was taken from the Declaration of Arbroath in 1320, giving Scotland independence in the aftermath of Bannockburn. On that same day, on the steps of Capitol Hill, Senator Lott became the first recipient of the William Wallace Award for his efforts to establish Tartan Day. Despite a cynical response in some sections of the Scottish press, I found it quite a moment in history. The celebrations were hosted at the British Embassy by Sir Christopher Meyer, our Ambassador to the United States.

In 2001 the second recipient of the Wallace Award was none other than Sir Sean Connery, regarded by some as the best-known Scot in the world. On the eve of his award ceremony in Washington he and his wife were guests at another of the Embassy receptions when Alex Salmond, now Scotland's First Minister, took me aside and suggested that I look out for Sir Sean's acceptance speech next morning. I gathered it would be something special.

Well, the speech itself may have been good enough but that could hardly be said of Connery's delivery. Decked out in full Highland dress, he came to the podium with a swatch of large pages, from which he proceeded to read as if he had never seen them before. For a professional actor it was less than impressive, prompting the thought that the speech might have been prepared by somebody else. Alex Salmond, perhaps?

The award ceremony of 2004 was moved from Washington to New York's Broadway, where the honour was extended to take in the entire Forbes family, who had certainly made a major contribution to the relationship between Scotland and America. Due to give the speech of introduction, I followed my usual practice of checking out the venue in advance. So here I was on the stage of the famous old Hudson Theatre, testing the microphone and familiarising myself with the surroundings, when a thought suddenly occurred to me: Was there anybody around? No. Had it not been one of my secret ambitions to appear on the Broadway stage? And since this opportunity would never arise again, what was there to prevent me from doing my Fred Astaire act?

Accompanied by nothing but the music of my imagination, I broke into a dance routine that had me spinning across the stage of the Hudson Theatre, lost in a dream of what-might-have-been when, all of a sudden, I was disturbed by a rustling in the wings. Two cleaning ladies, leaning on their mops, were standing puzzled and amused by the antics of this visiting idiot, whoever he was. So I made my embarrassed apologies and slunk out of sight, knowing, if nothing else, that I could now say in all honesty that I had appeared on the Broadway stage!

CHAPTER FIFTY-ONE

WHAT OF CHARLES AND CAMILLA?

With the tragic end to the life of Princess Diana in 1997 the Royal Family faced its biggest-ever threat. She had so ingratiated herself with an adoring public that there was bound to be a backlash. People are like that. There must always be somebody to blame. The fact that she was being driven through Paris at speed, by a chauffeur who had been drinking – and that she was wearing no seatbelt – was not enough of an explanation. Diana was allegedly escaping the so-called paparazzi, who were trying to snatch a photograph as she drove off with her escort, Dodi Fayed, from the Ritz Hotel.

In the newspaper world we all knew that, in fact, Diana was not averse to the paparazzi and the attendant publicity. In fact, she gloried in it. Just days before her death, while lazing on Dodi's yacht in Monte Carlo, she was on her mobile phone to a favourite photographer, checking that he was getting her best angle. But the conspiracy theories abounded, to the farcical point where her father-in-law, Prince Philip, was accused by Dodi's father, Mohammed al Fayed, of having plotted her murder. The inevitable target of public frustration was Prince Charles, with whom she had figured in a marriage that was ill fated from the start. On the requirement that the future king should marry a virgin – and considering the difficulty of finding such a rarity in the modern world – he had been denied the love of his life, Camilla Parker-Bowles. So the marriage of Charles and Diana, largely engineered by both their grandmothers and with the best of intentions, descended into disaster, which led to well-documented affairs on both sides.

The Royal Family was on its knees for a decade or more, rescued largely by the romance of Prince William and Kate Middleton which blossomed at St Andrews University and was fulfilled in the wedding of 2011 – and by Queen Elizabeth herself as she headed steadfastly towards her Sixty Glorious Years on the throne. As the immediate heir to that throne, Prince Charles would face the major task of re-engaging with an unforgiving public. That would not be made easier by his inevitable return to the lady he truly loved. Camilla Parker-Bowles would have to share the hostility that was coming their way, faced with ridicule and insult, portrayed as a woman without a redeeming feature.

At a dinner party in London I set that picture against the woman I was observing across the table. It was early days in their resumed association, when they had not yet been seen together in public. But here was a most attractive lady, totally without the horsey image presented by her detractors and emerging instead as a figure of promise.

When we met, that promise was more than fulfilled, for she turned out to be a substantial figure of quiet charm, intelligence and no small measure of wit and personality. There may not have been the instant glamour of a Diana but there was so much more than that. The occasion was the fiftieth birthday party of our mutual friend Christopher Forbes, from that third generation of the Forbes family of New York, held in the splendour of their London home, Christopher Wren's magnificent Old Battersea House.

When Camilla wanted to know my connection with the family, I began by saying in my everyday Buchan accent that I came from Aberdeenshire. Quick as a flash, she winked and said, "I would never have guessed!" Unlike Diana, who detested Balmoral, Camilla was already well acquainted with North-east folk and how they spoke. So we entered into as natural and delightful a conversation as you could wish. Even as a fairly small, intimate company, we followed dinner by taking to the floor, Prince Charles dancing with Christopher's wife Astrid (of German aristocracy) and Camilla with Christopher, generally known as Kip. When the music changed to "Pretty Woman" they switched to their own partnerships and it was there that you could see the natural and loving affinity between Charles and Camilla. You can tell so much on a dance floor.

Coming off the floor, I remarked that she was cutting quite a dash, to which she replied, "Not half as much as you!" We joked about my Fred Astaire aspirations. So I was getting to grips with the reality of a lady who was being so unfairly reviled by a public that neither knew her nor wanted to give her a chance. But after those years when she took all the brickbats with an air of dignity, it did not surprise me in the least when she finally won over the majority, many of whom had now met her – and realised what an impressive and thoroughly delightful lady she was.

Never was that more evident than in June of 2013 when I joined in the procession of honorary graduates of Aberdeen University for a very special occasion at that magnificent complex of King's College in Old Aberdeen. The University was installing Camilla, Duchess of Cornwall, as its latest Chancellor in a long line of the highly distinguished. She accepted that new role as head of the university with a deep sense of gratitude, enlightening the audience on her North-east roots, through her father's family, the Shands, who came from near Banff.

On a glorious summer's day she then mingled freely with 600 guests in the large marquee, confirming once more her suitability as the first member of the Royal Family to occupy such a major position in the life of Aberdeen and the North-east.

CHAPTER FIFTY-TWO

DRAMA AT THE EXPRESS

Most of the adventures described in this book took place within my twenty years at the *Scottish Daily Express*. Having spent the early part of my career in the North-east of Scotland, it was the move to Glasgow that opened up a whole new horizon of opportunity. It was also my good fortune to arrive as the heyday of print journalism was reaching its peak. The appearance of television in the 1950s had not yet begun to impact on newspapers and the further invention of the Internet was a distant dream for only a few. So newspapers still reigned supreme, with Lord Beaverbrook's *Daily Express* leading the field as the biggest-selling daily newspaper in the whole world. But sometimes you have to pay for your success and what happened to its equally prosperous sister paper, the *Scottish Daily Express*, is an extraordinary tale.

Beaverbrook, whose own name was Max Aitken, was the son of a Scottish minister who emigrated from Torphichen, near Edinburgh, to Canada, where young Max had made a fortune in the cement business by the time he was thirty. Returning to Britain in 1910, he found his way into Conservative politics and sensationally captured an English seat from the Liberals. By the end of the First World War, however, having started his own newspaper in Canada when he was just fourteen, he took over the ailing *Daily Express* in London. But just as his father had gone from Scotland to speak to the Canadians, Max Aitken cherished a dream that one day he would return with "a word for Scotland".

That dream was finally realised in 1928, when he bought a former tobacco factory in Albion Street, Glasgow, not far from George Square, and launched his *Scottish Daily Express*. If hardly the best time to start a new venture, it survived the Wall Street Crash of 1929 and the Great Depression of the early 1930s and began to establish itself as the biggest-selling paper Scotland had ever seen, eventually reaching a figure of 650,000 copies a day.

Having arrived on Leap Year night of 1960 from *The Press and Journal* in Aberdeen, I found myself adjusting to the vast open-plan of a bigger paper, with a level of noise and frenetic activity that made me wonder how anyone could concentrate on their work. I learned in time, of course, that this fair imitation of madness could provide its own stimulus and I was soon joining in the general excitement of working for the *Express*. I have already mentioned the freedom to suggest your own ideas and to find yourself on a plane that afternoon, en route to Paris or New York, Singapore or Hong Kong. Money was no object. I had struck a wonderful way of life and for more than a decade the last thing on my mind was that anything could happen to interrupt it. But you never know what's round the corner.

Colleagues with whom I became friendly at the *Express* included an engaging Glasgow character who seemed like a throwback to an earlier age, when a colourful bunch of Scottish left-wing politicians at Westminster became known as the Red Clydesiders, led by men like James Maxton and Manny Shinwell. More than ten years my senior, Denny Magee had all the attributes of an orator, complete with long, flowing hair and that craggy face not uncommon in Glasgow. He told me how, as a soldier during the war, his unit had been one of the first to discover the horrors of the Belsen concentration camp. Local people claimed they knew nothing about such a place and when Denny and his colleagues put up graphic posters in the town square, they laughed it off as British propaganda, so the soldiers prodded bayonets in their backs and said, "Right. You, you and you, get into this truck." They drove them to see for themselves and, incredible though it may seem, those local people seemed genuinely shocked.

Denny was full of stories. After the war he returned to Glasgow and followed his comedian's instinct towards the stage, becoming a comic's "feed" to people like Lex McLean at the Glasgow Pavilion. But the old music hall was losing its audience and Denny was looking around for something else to do.

Nobody at the *Express* could remember how it happened but he found his way into the editorial department, quietly learning how to sub-edit features. But Denny Magee had another agenda of his own. Gaining in confidence, he began to stir up union activity where hardly any existed and in time became Father of the Chapel (chairman of the union branch). That was when I began to fear what Denny was up to. Gradually this likeable man was calling chapel meetings and presenting all kind of problems on the slightest pretext. His charisma demanded attention, as he blossomed into an orator of undoubted skill. The staff at the *Express* had been a happy bunch, well paid and certainly not overworked, but in those prosperous times of the 1960s the management had made one mistake that came back to haunt them. With the paper at its height of success, they readily engaged more and more people, to the point that they were clearly overstaffed.

With leaner times threatening in the early 1970s, they were keen to reduce that Scottish staff of 2,000, which began to look like a ridiculous number. The editor in Glasgow was a gloriously flamboyant and heavily bearded eccentric called Clive Sandground, who made light of the fact that he lost a leg to polio in boyhood and managed to hop about with his artificial limb at alarming speeds. Sandground was asked by the London management to draw up a reasonable staffing level, assuming that a paper like ours was starting from scratch. At that stage it was no more than a hypothetical exercise and he assessed the required number at around 1,800, with which few could have disagreed.

This confidential document was duly sent to London but by some mysterious means a copy of it landed on the desk of you-know-who. This played right into the hands of Denny Magee. Yet another of his emergency meetings was summoned. With great enthusiasm, this was presented to the open-mouthed journalists not as an early assessment but as a *fait accompli,* a major disaster about to happen.

241

The outcome of all this was that Clive Sandground, still in his late thirties, was "sent to Coventry" by Denny and his night-desk followers, to the point that he could no longer operate effectively as an editor if his staff wouldn't speak to him. He left Albion Street with the consolation of a handsome payment, enabling him to buy himself a yacht which he duly named *The Golden Handshake*.

So who would take over as editor of the *Scottish Daily Express*? With the announcement that he would be Ian Brodie, a Scot who had recently returned from the *Express* office in New York to become Foreign Editor in London, Denny was back on his soapbox, in full flight. Having got rid of Clive Sandground as editor, he was now ready for his successor. Who was this man Brodie, anyway? Only recently appointed Foreign Editor in London, had he perhaps failed in that task? Was this what was being foisted upon us?

In the intimidating atmosphere, there was a silent majority who hardly dared raise a voice. We were, after all, into the era of Arthur Scargill and his like, who were, in my opinion and so many others', quickly running Britain into the ground. Denny Magee had already boasted to some union officials that he would "bring Beaverbrook to its knees". And now, in his total ignorance of Ian Brodie, he was embarking on yet another disgraceful display of irresponsible trade unionism.

This finally brought me to my feet to question his remarks. Since he obviously knew nothing of the man, would he listen to someone who could tell him about Ian Brodie? As it happened, in my spell in the New York office of the *Express*, I had worked with the man and knew that he was a first-class journalist as well as a splendid human being. Far from having failed in his London job, he was coming to Scotland for the obvious reason that we needed an able editor to cope with the farcical situation developing before our very eyes. So, in view of his obvious ignorance, what right did Denny have to undermine this man before he had even arrived? Oh, he had reason to believe that Brodie did not approve of the four-day week and other reductions which were being negotiated. Well, many people had doubts about all that.

So, after this farce of a meeting, I returned to my desk, only to be surrounded by Denny and his henchmen, saying they were "concerned about my attitude". Concerned about *my* attitude? What about theirs? Did they not see that they were endangering the jobs of all two thousand of us? That they were turning a happy office into a place of misery, where morale was at rock bottom?

Ian Brodie duly took over but the trouble continued. Within the next year there were no fewer than fifty-six nights of interrupted production, including sixteen when there was no publication at all. Unlike other industries where lost production can be made up with overtime, newspapers don't have that privilege. The day's sales and advertising are lost forever. When some of us argued with Denny Magee that this could not go on and that the *Express* would surely reach a point of closing us down altogether, he dismissed it as nonsense. They would never do that, he assured us. In fact, it later emerged that he had already been warned of that possibility.

It all blew up on a March day of 1974. It was announced from London that the great *Scottish Daily Express*, started by Lord Beaverbrook in 1928 and still the biggest-selling daily newspaper Scotland had ever seen, would close its Albion Street operation on the last day of the month. Of the 2,000 employees, a skeleton staff of 200 would be retained to prepare a paper which would now be printed at the Manchester base of the *Express*. The other 1,800 would collect their redundancy money and go.

Of course it set off a massive uproar about the *Express* "deserting" Scotland and going off to England. Sadly, the Scottish public fell for all the propaganda and no amount of rational explaining could convince them otherwise.

That last evening turned into a nightmare. The building itself was in chaos, with some in tears of disbelief, while others mobbed the famous Tom's Bar next door, before spilling out to an Albion Street where television cameras were whirring into action, recording the death throes of a great newspaper. The editor, Ian Brodie, had decided to go down with his ship and would be leaving when the printing presses fell silent early next morning.

When he arrived in the case room as the front page was ready for printing, he found it had been hijacked by the "Action Group", who were inserting their own front-page story, appealing to the public to support their plan for a workers' cooperative newspaper which they would call the *Scottish Daily News*. As Brodie courageously tried to prevent this outrage, he was punched and pummelled by the mob – in the very last hour of his distinguished career with the *Express*. They did set the presses rolling for 3,000 copies, though the despatch overseer managed to prevent the papers from leaving the building. In such horrific circumstances, Denny Magee, with the help of his cohorts, had realised that boast that he would "bring Beaverbrook to its knees".

Incredibly, the *Express* handed over its now defunct printing plant to the workers' cooperative – and Sir Max Aitken (son of the founder) even gave them loans of £725,000, for which he did not receive a word of thanks. It took more than a year before the *Scottish Daily News* appeared on the street, with self-imposed conditions that there would be no four-day week, no restriction on working hours, no extra pay for overtime, no demarcations; in fact, none of the things that had so recently been their fighting principles. But they would have the satisfaction of all pulling together in their idealistic dream of a workers' cooperative. They did, however, welcome that most controversial publisher of the time, Robert Maxwell, to add his experience of running a newspaper.

The big-time capitalist, always good for a publicity stunt, joined the band – and slept on a camp bed on the sixth floor in Albion Street. But what about staffing levels for the new paper? Naturally for a lesser operation, they wouldn't need as many as their 1,800 redundant colleagues. In fact, they employed around 500 – and the *Scottish Daily News* finally hit the streets in May 1975, with a lot of misplaced goodwill from a public that had been severely hoodwinked. But soon they would face the reality of running a newspaper in difficult times, experiencing the same conditions which prompted the Express to seek a modest reduction of labour in the first place.

Within six months the much-vaunted workers' co-operative had not only fallen out with Robert Maxwell but their *Scottish Daily News* had disappeared down the drain altogether, now leaving all 1,800 out of work. To add to the tragedy, many of them had invested their redundancy money in this disastrous venture. (I subsequently entered a taxi one night and found that my driver had previously been one of our best reporters.)

The skeleton staff retained by the *Express* moved to an office in Park Circus Place and, in time, the printing of the paper returned to a plant in Glasgow. Denny Magee and his admirers had not destroyed the *Express* altogether but they had certainly inflicted such damage that the ambitious venture of Lord Beaverbrook, creating the greatest journalistic experience in Scottish newspaper history, would never be the same again.

Was it all worth it? When I met Denny Magee in later times he was unrepentant. He told me he had used his redundancy money to buy a couple of corner shops. He was still of such charm and personality that it was difficult to dislike him as a person. And of course he was not alone in destroying a great newspaper but as the man with theatrical aspirations which eventually found him a new audience beyond the Glasgow Pavilion, he was undoubtedly the catalyst of an industrial drama which ended in disaster.

Despite my joy in working for the *Express*, the experience was greatly lessened by all that had happened and by the time I reached my twenty years on the paper I sought to take advantage of a redundancy scheme which would release me to the world of freelance writing. My intended departure, however, became a matter of unbearable irony. The story was told by the trade journal, the UK *Press Gazette*, revealing that, "the *Daily Express* managing director in London, Jocelyn Stevens, has stepped in to try to stop two top Scottish writers from leaving the organisation. When the management received redundancy requests from Dorothy-Grace Elder and Jack Webster they refused to accept them. In an unusual move, Mr Stevens appealed to the Glasgow executives to block the loss of the big two. The union was told that the loss of both writers would damage the future of the *Scottish Daily Express*."

The National Union of Journalists was now threatening to bring the whole *Express* organisation to a standstill if Dorothy and I were not released. On the day when the others were leaving, the union bosses gave Jocelyn Stevens thirty minutes to change his mind. He now had no option.

It pained me to think that the union which had done so much damage to the livelihood of so many was now facilitating my own departure. On 12 September 1980 I was given the news at one o'clock and had just four hours to look around and realise that I was saying goodbye that very afternoon to the paper that had done so much to revolutionise my career – indeed my whole life. It was heartbreaking.

CHAPTER FIFTY-THREE

LIFTING THE LID

When I wrote my first two *Grains of Truth* in the 1980s a lady who came to interview me said that, while I dealt with events and people I had met, I had not revealed very much about myself. So that fell short of being autobiography. The lady may have been right. I kept her words in mind when it came to this book and hopefully a more personal slant has already revealed what kind of creature I am. If I bare my soul a little further there may be more clues.

Far from being born with the drive and outgoing nature required of a journalist, I was painfully shy as a boy, partly due no doubt to the bad stammer which dogged me for a large part of my life. It is a daily burden you must learn to live with. I certainly wasn't your rough-and-tumble type and avoided schoolboy fights, to the extent that I cannot remember ever having been in one.

As for my childhood home at 2 Park Crescent, Maud, we spoke nothing but the so-called Doric, a name for the dialect of North-east Scotland, sometimes called "the Buchan tongue" because it was spoken at its purest in rural areas like Buchan. Although the capital of the North-east, the city of Aberdeen had a watered-down version, sometimes delivered with a glottal-stop not unlike that of Glasgow. Doric simply took the standard speech of Lowland Scotland and baffled outsiders by broadening the vowel sounds. Thus English words like *stone* became *slune* in Scots but *steen* in Doric. Whereas the English language would settle for the single word *have*, no such simplicity was countenanced in Buchan. You could choose from two words, *hiv* and *hae*, though in fact you had no choice at all because they had different connotations. Where an Englishman might say, "You have to have something in your stomach," the Buchan man would say, "Ye hiv tae hae something in yer stammack." Yet, trans-posing those two forms of 'have' would sound a nonsense. But change that same sentence into the future tense and it becomes "Ye'll hae tae hae something . . . " Don't ask me about the logic. You simply knew by growing up with it. And I grew up with it all.

Until I went to school aged four-and-a-half, my counting from one to eight was "een, twa, three, fower, five, sax, seiven, acht." Like so much else in our North-east tongue, the *acht* came straight from German. We also followed the Germans in matters like telling the time. While other Scots followed the English in their slovenly use of "half-eight" for "half past eight", our North-east phrase of "half-acht" came straight from the German "halb-acht". But that didn't mean "half past eight." We meant "half-past seven" – one half of the eighth hour! A much more logical usage, I would sug-gest, though I would be surprised if many people are using it today.

I began to learn English at Maud School in April 1936 (unlike every-body else, our school year started at Easter) but even to this day, nearly eighty years later, I still think in the Doric tongue and frequently find myself translating into English. If most of what I'm saying is in the past tense it is because, like many another dialects, that North-east one is dying. Of course in rural areas there are still some good Doric speak-ers but their grandchildren have lost the vocabulary.

From their accents, you will always know an Aberdonian from a Glaswegian, though even that becomes neutralised among the young, exposed as they are to the globalisation of everything, not least their pop culture. Whereas the Gaelic of the west receives a massive amount of Scottish government money in a dubious attempt to keep it alive, the Doric receives nothing at all. Not that that kind of expenditure makes much difference in the end. A language lives or dies by the willingness of a sufficient number of people to speak it in a natural and everyday manner. And that number is diminishing by the day.

So what else do I reveal about myself? Well, I make my porridge every morning and take a large whisky every night. Between those defining moments, I still think of meal times in the language of my childhood. What most people call their lunch, around one o'clock, is "my denner", while the later meal is "my tea", meaning high tea, which always landed around 5.30 or 6 p.m. The idea of dinner in the evening was unknown to us, much too posh for the plain folk of Buchan. I didn't pick up these sophistications until later in life.

Elsewhere, I listen more to radio than television, though I've been a faithful follower of *Coronation Street* from that very first episode of 9 December 1960, and defend its durability, smooth introduction of plots and characters and some brilliant acting. I reckon its unbroken run for more than half a century is quite the most remarkable feat in the entire history of television. Needless to say, I have visited the Street and walked the cobbles, from the days of Ena Sharples and Elsie Tanner, Stan and Hilda Ogden, Alf and Audrey Roberts, through to Steve and the gorgeous Becky Macdonald and, of course, "Hot-pot" Betty, who I remembered as Betty Driver, a big-time dance band singer during the war.

If I can tear myself away from Weatherfield, the people who continue to entertain me elsewhere include Stephen Fry, Gyles Brandreth, Rowan Atkinson, Maggie Smith, Judy Dench, Celia Imrie, Burt Bacharach, the John Wilson Orchestra and yes, the much maligned Ken Dodd, the last of the old-time comics, as well as that magnificent satirical duo who called themselves Kit and the Widow (now Kit and McConnel), without whom the Edinburgh Fringe would be much the poorer. Add to that the name of my tennis hero, Andy Murray (he escaped in the massacre of schoolchildren at Dunblane in 1996), and what an array of treasures we have. From the past, my favourites range from Frank Sinatra, Ella Fitzgerald and Karen Carpenter to Jimmy Durante and the incomparable Fred Astaire, representing the sheer height of elegance. Fred would never reveal his favourite dancing partner. Ginger Rogers? Cyd Charisse? His own sister Adele? But I discovered after his death that, privately and perhaps surprisingly, his favourite was none other than the lady I met in Paris – Rita Hayworth, in films like *You Were Never Lovelier*.

On the radio I have kept a special place for David Jacobs, whose

Sunday night hour from 11 till midnight on Radio 2, playing my kind of music, has been a sheer delight for years. I have met up with David in London from time to time and know that Sunday nights would not be the same without him. If these are some of the people whose talents have delighted me, there are others I could well do without. That list includes the insufferable Dame Edna Everage or Barry Whatever-his-name-is!

And just as there are people who grate, there are words and phrases I cannot bring myself to use. In the 1960s everybody had to be "with it", though some of them were clearly without it. The years bring their own fashions and you wonder how they arise. I have never heard anyone claim they were the first to say "at this moment in time" when they really meant "now". Nor do we know who plagued us with "iconic" or "prioritise" or "judgemental" or "staycation" or "twenty-four-seven" or "too little, too late" or a thousand and one other clichés. Is there something in the ether that simultaneously sprinkles verbal absurdities into the minds of so many? We'll never know.

Before I begin to sound like a grumpy old man, I must say I am really quite slow to anger. I have neither the energy nor the inclination and tend to take a fairly cheerful and optimistic view of life but when I am finally roused to action, I keep it short and sharp. A classic example arose when I set out to gain an honour for my old editor at Aberdeen Journals, a splendid man called George Fraser – a former colleague of Grassic Gibbon, his rival for the girl who eventually became George's wife. As a youth in the village of Newmachar, near Aberdeen, George had suffered a heart condition exactly like my own, both of us anticipating that we might not see much of a lifespan. He was thirty-six years older than me so I kept an eagle eye on him, as a possible guide to my own prospects of survival.

To my mounting pleasure, he reached his centenary in 1995, by which time he had been writing a weekly column in the Aberdeen *Press and Journal* for a record-breaking seventy-seven years. I used to commend it to budding journalists as a model of how to write a column. So I phoned his local Member of Parliament for South Aberdeen, Mr Raymond Robertson, in the hope that he might recommend George Fraser for the Honours List (MPs could do that in those days) but Mr Robertson was not available. In the absence of a response, I persevered with calls till the charming lady in his office asked if I could tell her what it was about.

Well it was really confidential but I explained my purpose. In time the good lady came back on the phone, clearly embarrassed, to say that Mr Robertson didn't know the gentleman – and therefore couldn't do anything about it. He didn't know George Fraser, a lifelong, prominent journalist in his own constituency? Well if he didn't know him, he damned well ought to!

That was when I rose to anger. I lifted the phone and called Dover House in London, asking to speak to the Secretary of State for Scotland, Mr Michael Forsyth. Mr Forsyth came on the phone immediately, listened to my story but said it was deadline time for the next Honours List. However, if I could fax him one A4 page with that story right now, he would see what he could do.

When the List appeared, George Fraser became a Member of the Order of the British Empire. Michael Forsyth took many a brickbat in his political life but in the case of George Fraser he rose so far in my estimation that I have never forgotten him. George's longevity was, of course, giving me great hope for my own survival. In fact, still with a mind of great clarity, he lived to a resounding 104!

CHAPTER FIFTY-FOUR

THOSE EARLY MEMORIES AND 100 YEARS OF MAUD SCHOOL

In my later years it amused me no end to find that, physically, I was often mistaken for that popular actor John Thaw, better known as Inspector Morse. Though older and taller, I was frequently stopped for my (his) autograph and, not wishing to disappoint, I simply signed "Best wishes, John Thaw", and hirpled away with his characteristic limp! By coincidence, my granddaughter Sinead was running the reception desk at the famous old Randolph Hotel in Oxford which was, of course, the favourite haunt of Inspector Morse.

Before the days of Morse and television and the more modern wonders of technology, all ears were for "the wireless". I still cannot get accustomed to "the radio". All information and entertainment came from the BBC at Broadcasting House in Langham Place, London, not least during the Second World War, when we followed every news bulletin to update ourselves on what was happening. So I gained a great affection for that building which, when I first visited it, seemed rather like the old *Queen Mary* in full sail. That war was not only the biggest event in all history but also the great dividing line in the lives of those who experienced it. Everything was defined by whether it was before or after it, and most of the good things seemed to come before. To my child mind, the symbols of Britain during that war were Winston Churchill, Big Ben and Broadcasting House, three major voices that seemed to stand between us and destruction by Hitler. It was Britain, not Scotland, that was at war with Hitler, which may explain why my generation is less inclined towards political independence, much as we value our Scottish traditions and take it as an insult when people cast doubt on our patriotism.

I listened to that wireless from a very early age, when the rhythms of the '30s must have embedded themselves in my subconscious, to the extent that popular tunes which were born in the same year as myself, 1931, remain among my favourites today. For the record, they included "Stardust", "Dancing in the Dark", "Dream a Little Dream of Me" and "River Stay Away from My Door", sung by Paul Robeson as a dam on the River Yangtse burst its banks during a typhoon and hundreds were killed and twenty million Chinese were made homeless.

If these were the tunes of my year, I also found it interesting to pinpoint the people who were exactly my age. The fairly diverse list ranged from Russia's Mikhail Gorbachev and his successor, Boris Yeltsin, to Larry Hagman (JR Ewing of *Dallas*), Rupert Murdoch, novelist John le Carré and the American heartthrob James Dean. Throw in the 1931 building of London's Dorchester Hotel and the Empire State Building in New York and I begin to feel my age.

I remember the '30s as a decade of mellow saxophones, syncopating pianos, summers that went on forever – and sophisticated ladies smoking from cigarette holders when smoking was considered the fashionable thing to do. I remember Henry Hall and his orchestra broadcasting weekly from Gleneagles Hotel and Reginald Foort entertaining at the BBC Theatre Organ. Impressions lingered.

At four-and-a-half I was off to Maud School, never among the top few in the class though, curiously, when I was eleven, I did well in an IQ test, prompting my teacher, Miss Morrison, to suggest I should be sent to Robert Gordon's College in Aberdeen. She meant well; and it was not her fault that it turned out to be the disaster I have charted elsewhere.

I can claim no more than average intelligence and was not of an academic mind, which may explain why in my subsequent career I wrote much more from the heart than the head. Thankfully, that did me no harm at all, since the majority of people respond more to the emotions than the intellect. The various columns had a big following and in 1996, while working for *The Herald* in Glasgow, I was voted Bank of Scotland Columnist of the Year.

In that same year I was invited back to Maud School to unveil the centenary plaque, in one of the more moving days of my life. Resplendent in Victorian garb, the modern children were reflecting on the scene of 1896, sitting respectfully as their headmistress spoke. The memories of childhood unfolded before my very eyes. Former pupils came from far and near to share in this experience and from my own class I could pick out nine of us who came here that April day of 1936. Once more we were under the watchful eyes of Miss Morrison, Miss Duffus and Miss Hunter, whose married names peeled away. I recalled our infant classroom with roaring fire, where we arrived during the brief reign of Edward VIII, clutching glossy picture books of the king who would never be crowned.

Then came the Coronation of his brother in 1937 and soon the crisis of Munich and Hitler's war. Our village life was disrupted, as local lads who had volunteered for the Territorial Army were off to war, waving emotional farewells from train windows, some never to return. On the same day that other train steamed in from Glasgow, carrying 200 pupils from Dowanhill and Hyndland Schools, evacuees they called them, with labels round their necks. Our school roll was doubled for as long as they would choose to stay.

As city children set free from grimy tenements to the fresh air of rural Aberdeenshire, they were energised to the point of pumping cows' tails to see if milk came out. In time, our village population of 700 people was more than doubled by succeeding battalions of soldiers training for the eventual D-Day of 1944. Our favourites were the men of the 4th Battalion, King's Own Scottish Borderers, welcomed into village homes, where Pipe Sergeant Jock Gray from Kelso taught me to play the bagpipes. In later years Jock was transferred to what became the Royal Scots Dragoon Guards, for the purpose of forming their pipe band – the band which gained world recognition for its memorable recording of "Amazing Grace" and later the unbearably beautiful "Highland Cathedral". So I was well taught.

Of course there were liaisons between the soldiers and local women, the evidence of which, as a young lad, I witnessed with wide-eyed wonder from a special vantage point. With our own men gone to war, my uncle Gavin was scarce of musicians for his dance band. So at the age of ten I was drafted in as the drummer in his Rialto Band, beating and brushing my way through drums and cymbals, every Saturday night earning ten shillings (50p) for my efforts – and watching the goings on of the dance floor. The accordionist by my side was a local farm servant called Arthur Glennie, who later married the organist at New Deer Church, Isobel Howie from Auchnagatt, two average performers. As their claim to fame, however, they proved that the reproductive power of average can, on occasion, result in genius. Their daughter became the world's leading percussionist, Evelyn Glennie, who later appeared in one of my documentary films, *Webster Goes West*.

It was all coming back to me on this centenary day at Maud School, when I told the children about a brush with history which intrigued them. As a boy in the 1940s, already with an ambition to be a journalist, I started that magazine called *The Maud Review*, for which I interviewed the very first headmaster, Mr John Law. By then long retired to a house overlooking the school playground, Mr Law gave me a vivid description of that opening day in 1896. And here I was, passing on to the children a first-hand account of that day, exactly a hundred years later. So history was not some dull and dreary subject but a living fascination which we were creating at that very moment.

There would be another day like this in the year 2096, looking back on today in the same way as we were looking back on 1896. To that end, I then helped to bury a time capsule, to be dug up by future generations.

As a youngster in this village of Maud which I loved so much I had wondered if we were perhaps a backwater, speaking in a local tongue which might be a disadvantage in that world beyond. But I had since discovered that a Scottish rural education was superior to most – and that my plain Buchan accent turned out to be as rich an asset as I possessed. Nor was it a coincidence that so much of my writing in journalism, books and television had been about this locality which shaped my life. What I had regarded as "local" turned out to be universal in a way I had not considered.

I received a letter one day from a film producer in Hollywood who said he happened to pick up a copy of my *Grain of Truth* in Los Angeles. It seemed of no special interest to him but his eye caught one story after another, which compelled him to write and say, "You may have thought your book belonged to Maud and Buchan alone but I can tell you – it might as well have been about my little village in middle America!" He could rattle off the similarities of the cattle mart, the railway junction, the village school, right down to the sweetie shop which corresponded to mine. Yes, he had a Lizzie Allan too! That gave me a whole new perspective on a world where, in those days at least I suppose, so much of rural life was pretty much the same.

What memories came alive on this centenary day. After I unveiled the plaque we moved inside the school hall, which seemed little different from my own day. The pupil register for a hundred years was there for all to inspect. Yes, by my Sunday name, John Barron Webster was there from 1936 until 1943. And so was Doris Symon, the girl with whom I fell madly in love at the age of five. (Never underestimate the emotional depths of a child!) It was here in this hall that an Eastern European lady called Marguerite Feltges came to teach us dancing and discovered that I had enough rhythm in my body to become a good dancer. Victor Sylvester and his ballroom orchestra had me gliding across the floor to great effect. And if television's *Strictly Come Dancing* had a section for over-80s I would still be willing to have a go. Miss Feltges' particular type of instruction was called "eurythmics", a word that does not find its way into every dictionary. Her main employment was at Aberdeen High School for Girls and it was there a generation later that she gave similar instruction to a lively pupil called Annie Lennox. Destined to become one of the world's most popular singers, the same Annie Lennox chose an unusual name for her partnership with Dave Stewart. Yes, in honour of Margeurite Feltges, they were known as The Eurythmics.

We hung about Maud School in joyous recollection that day, unwilling to part with it and knowing that for certain we would never see this kind of gathering again. With a last nostalgic look, I drove off south with a thousand echoes in my head, the adrenalin flooding every inch of my being. Of all the events of my life there had never been a more meaningful day than this.

CHAPTER FIFTY-FIVE

AN OCTOGENARIAN?

If I have still failed to reveal myself I should probably leave it to my eldest son, Geoffrey, who spoke at my eightieth birthday party, held at Cromlix House near Dunblane, now owned by my tennis hero, Andy Murray. It is interesting to know how your children have regarded you. In the modern manner, his speech referred to his father and mother as Jack and Eden and this is a condensed version of what he said:

"When I was a teenager and Dad was in his mid-to-late forties I referred to him as 'the old man'. But having now gone past that stage myself I realise I may have aged him prematurely. But tonight, as we celebrate his eightieth birthday, he's the last person to be referred to as 'the old man', such has been the vigour, passion and enthusiasm he has shown for life.

"Let me take you back to the autumn of 1981 when *A Grain of Truth* was published, with the sub-title 'A Scottish Journalist Remembers'. Do you remember those opening words? 'In the searing heat of 1947, that most glorious of twentieth-century summers, they carried my bed to the front green of our council house in the village of Maud, Aberdeenshire, in the hope it would hasten recuperation from a serious heart condition. I was just a boy in the sixteenth summer of life and there, under the cool of a garden shelter, I lay pale and limp, still smarting from the long series of cardiographs and blood tests, the shaking of heads and vague talk of leaking valves and murmurs which seemed like a fair concoction of doom. How psychologically damaging to discover that your life has apparently been defused before it has properly started; on top of which I was burdened with a painful stammer.'

"That was all of sixty-four years ago – and he's still here. Medics apparently debate whether this was the first-ever recorded case of 'man flu'! Eventually he rose Lazarus-like from that sickbed and the rest, as we like to say, is history. A lifetime with Aberdeen Journals, the *Daily Express* and the *Glasgow Herald*, books, plays, television programmes and DVDs have all been amassed along with awards as UK Speaker of the Year and Columnist of the Year. Not bad for 'a loon fae Maud' who overcame the indignity of being shown the door by Robert Gordon's College for academic underachievement but who returned to the city in 2000 to collect an Honorary Degree from Aberdeen University – and in 2009 for an Honorary Doctor of Letters from the Robert Gordon University.

"And then there is his memory. His power of recall is remarkable – names, dates, places have all been stored over the years. Mention the name of an interviewee any time in the last sixty years and he'll tell you where and when they were born, how they got where they are; and he'll even throw in for good measure what their father did too. And he can do that for thousands of people.

"There was a strange imbalance in our house for Keith, Martin and myself. Mum Eden, the bedrock of the family, always there, working away quietly with supreme efficiency to make sure everything ran smoothly. Then there was this man who would come in at night and tell you how he'd spent the day in Aberdeen with Charlie Chaplin. Or how he'd been on the golf course with Bing Crosby, or how he'd been sparring a few hours earlier with Muhammad Ali. I don't know what happened when he met Sophia Loren but he's never stopped talking about her.

"When other boys boasted about having footballers such as John Greig or Billy McNeill in their autograph books, we could open ours and show them Pelé and George Best. While some homes are filled with music, art and books, the Webster household was more about news, current affairs, sport and show business. And looking back, the penny must have dropped that if this world was accessible to our father – that Great Neap of the North as fellow columnist

Jack McLean once referred to him – then surely, in some form, it must be accessible to us.

"So perhaps little wonder that Keith, Martin and myself all followed. Jack was either the master of the soft sell or he'd bred three sons without an ounce of originality. It has all changed over the years though, hasn't it? In Jack's day twitter was something the birds did, hacking was associated with dirty footballers and not mobile phones, and spam came out of a tin and had nothing to do with something called e-mail.

"One thing we did learn from him was his passion for words, grammar and spelling. He would say, 'Why use ten words when one will do?' – the one exception being football referees, for whom ten words were never enough, some of which I'd never heard before! This brings us to his love of football. Little could he have imagined the impact his history of Aberdeen Football Club would have when he took on the role of fan-turned-historian. It culminated, of course, in 1983 with Aberdeen beating the mighty Real Madrid in Gothenburg to win the European Cup Winners' Cup, in what Jack described as the greatest night of his life. Greatest night? This is the man who had sailed to New York on the old *Queen Mary*, dined with presidents and royalty, ridden on horseback across the Badlands of America, flown over the Arctic in the cockpit of the very first Concorde and yomped his way through Malaysian jungles with the army. And there were the births of three sons and five grandchildren. But a night of football tops all that? How I wish Eden had survived to bring a bit of rational balance to that statement tonight.

"This birthday, more than any other, Keith, Martin and I were faced with the dilemma of what to get for the man who seems to have it all. Thoughts of a Black and Decker toolkit or How to Make Your Garden Bloom all came to mind but were quickly dismissed. But a gathering of his nearest and dearest seemed just right.

"After all, this is a man who has spent a lifetime getting to know people, discovering what makes them tick and passing that on through the spoken and written word. So tonight is our gift to him, while his gift to us has been words. By his own reckoning, millions of them have spilled down the decades. On filming *Webster's Roup* for BBC Scotland, there was the sale of Honeyneuk: 'When the last of the drams went down and the handshakes were clasped I took leave of old friends and neighbours, assuring them I would always come back to Maud. And maybe, in a sense, I have never been away.' Writing about Lizzie Allan's sweetie shop in Maud: 'Lizzie was the arch-priestess of the lollipop, goddess of gastronomy, dispensing politics with peppermints, philosophy with fags, never yielding a principle in the cause of business.' When writing about Eden: 'Whoever created the cliché about no one being indispensable must surely have forgotten about mothers.' On arriving in New York for the first time: 'As the *Queen Mary* finally edged into her berth on the Hudson River, New York unwrapped itself all right, the teeming noise of the city suddenly breaking over you like a tidal wave in a cacophony of dockside din, hooters blaring, porters shouting and yellow cabs screeching to a halt.' And there was the attention-grabbing opening lines to one of his columns: 'John Profumo and I have at least one thing in common. We have both spent some time alone in a bedroom with Christine Keeler.' Who could fail to read on?

"This is a night no one wanted to miss and a night like this cannot pass without mention of Ayliffe. They are a formidable team who treat age as merely a number to be dismissed as irrelevant and have visited all corners of the world since losing their partners in that dark November of twenty-one years ago.

"I'm sure Jack will reveal the secret of reaching this landmark birthday. For my part, I reckon it has a lot to do with a boyish enthusiasm for life, never entirely growing up. He has reached this stage without ever having learned to swim or climb a mountain; and the complexities of wiring a plug or ironing a shirt have somehow always been beyond him. He's a man who lives in the present, has a romantic fascination with the past but cannot wait to see what tomorrow brings.

"No reflection on Jack's life could be complete without a mention of the man who inspired and influenced him so much, Lewis Grassic Gibbon. In 1991 he wrote about a visit to his grave at Arbuthnott: 'I read again the words on his headstone, moving words from *Sunset Song*: The kindness of friends, the warmth of toil, the peace of rest.' I ask everyone now to join me in a toast on your eightieth birthday – Happy birthday, Jack."

Geoffrey delivered his speech with great charm and just as he took stock of me, I was prompted in replying to take stock of my descendants, realising that it was the very first time they had all been together under one roof. The fact that the three boys had grown up so well was due entirely to Eden, with her good guidance, fine intellect and calming influence. My contribution, as Geoffrey said, was in pointing them towards journalism, however unwittingly.

Not that that was always the first choice. Geoffrey wanted to be a jockey and left school to be a stable lad to Sir Hugh Fraser at Drymen but he grew too tall and the rewards were too small so he joined the *Troon and Prestwick Times*, en route to the *Evening Express* and Northsound Radio in Aberdeen, before settling as a BBC producer and sports broadcaster. Keith's sport was cricket, playing for Clydesdale, but he switched that allegiance to American football when that sport raised its head in Scotland and he became a quarterback for the Glasgow Lions. His encyclopaedic knowledge of the game and its history led to a career with *First Down*, the American football weekly for Europe, of which he became the editor, with annual visits to the SuperBowl in the United States. He will also be one of the last people to say that he worked in Fleet Street, before that great institution broke up.

When Eden and I took the boys on a novelty flight from Glasgow to Aberdeen in the 1970s we never dreamt that that would fire an ambition in Martin to be a pilot. First, however, he went to the media college in Preston and joined the *Burnley Express*, being voted Young Journalist of the Year for the North-west of England. From there he worked in London before switching to the BBC, where he became a senior producer in Southampton. But that flying bug never left him. Quietly he took lessons and, into his forties, passed out as a fully-fledged pilot, licensed to carry passengers, though maintaining his job at the BBC. Any Sunday you will find him taking his plane from Bournemouth to Cherbourg for lunch and a walk along the beach with his wife, Catherine, arriving home in time for tea.

So they all made their own way without an iota of help from the old man. I thought that would be the end of it. But no. Into the next generation, Geoffrey's eldest boy, Jack, went to media college in Edinburgh, while Keith's son, Fraser, did likewise at Oxford, with ambitions to be a film director. Outwith the media, Keith's daughter, Sinead, was making a career in hotel management, with the Randolph Hotel in Oxford. And Geoffrey's two younger boys, Murray and Lorn, were doing well at Glasgow High School. As I had always said, I never boast about my offspring! But this was a special night – and I could do what I liked.

The postscript to all this was the arrival of a very late grandchild, born in 2012 to Martin and Catherine, who named her Eden, after her grandmother. And yet another of my coincidences: like my other granddaughter, Sinead, she was born on 19 November.

CHAPTER FIFTY-SIX

WHERE DID WE COME FROM AND WHATEVER HAPPENED TO SOCIETY?

The older I grow the more fascinated I become with the origin of the species. Where did we come from? How did it all begin? Considering the vastness of space and the multiplicity of suns and galaxies, was there ever a time when nothing at all existed? It may be late in the day to go philosophical but that doesn't stop us from wondering. The belief in God has taken a severe battering within my own lifetime. Scientific evidence may point in one direction and human faith in the other but the plain fact is that nobody can know for sure. If He does exist then believers can expect a comfortable eternity – and atheists can literally prepare for one Hell of a shock! For them, the cry of "I didna ken, I didna ken" may well be met with another cry: "Well ye damned well ken noo!" But the dismissal of God does little to solve the mystery. The famous Charles Darwin, grand uncle of composer Ralph Vaughan Williams, gave us a theory about the survival of the fittest, which helps to explain our development.

I can understand that our planet Earth came as a spark from the sun and after a journey of ninety-three million miles spun itself into an orbit by which it circumnavigates the sun once every 365¼ days. That in itself is remarkable. But my own bewilderment comes later – and centres not only on the amazing spectrum of animal life (who decided there should be everything from a mouse and a butterfly to a giraffe and an elephant?) but on the sheer magnificence of the human body, such a feat of clever planning as to demand the identity of the architect. What a piece of work, even if we did begin as monkeys.

That well-known atheist, George Bernard Shaw, cantankerous old devil though he was, did concede that there is a "life force" at work. In other words, if not the God in heaven, then some other creative force must have existed. That is surely the very least of it. And if that life force is simply some mysterious trick we call Nature, then I'm prepared to stand in awe of that force with as much wonder and enthusiasm as those who worship their God in heaven. That doesn't mean that I dismiss the deity altogether. He deserves consideration, if only because we are such pygmies in the whole scheme of things that we may not have the capacity to grasp the full story.

In all truth, I'm the kind of coward who believes in taking no chances. So here comes the confession. From time to time I turn to prayer, without any certainty that somebody is listening. My overtures are more general than personal and have much to do with gratitude. Yet, as I hinted in an earlier chapter, I have been astounded by the power of prayer, starting with my own heart condition when I was a boy. Just coincidence? It may well be. But I keep an open mind.

So now to a summary of the whole spectrum of my lifetime to see if I can make any more sense of it. My earliest memories are of 1934, when I was three and lived at the place of my birth, Fedderate Cottages, Maud. Two minor events remain clear: our family flitting from there to the neighbouring 2 Park Crescent, for which I carried the biscuit tins; and the wedding reception of my aunt Nan in the village of New Pitsligo, when I was alarmed to see couples dancing. I thought they were fighting.

Before I was five, my mother delivered her only child to Maud School and embarrassed me by bursting into tears as she left. I consoled her by saying, "Dinna greet, Mam!" I was so happy at Maud School, with its air of warmth and camaraderie among new-found acquaintances and the first stirrings of love for that girl at the next desk. There was the annual school picnic to Fraserburgh Beach, one of Britain's best, and the excitement of Coronation Day in 1937, when King George VI embarked on his short reign and his eleven-year-old daughter Elizabeth could not have imagined that she would follow him in her own time to Sixty Glorious Years and more.

Then came the Forties, with the bewildering fear-cum-excitement of war, which would deprive us of so many young men from our village. During that war I was heading for failure at Robert Gordon's College, Aberdeen, ending my schooldays at the age of fourteen, before developing the heart condition which dashed my hopes of a future. But the fates came good and opened up a writing career beyond my wildest dreams, taking me from the *Turriff Advertiser* to Aberdeen Journals, the *Daily Express* and *The Herald* in an adventure which enriched the rest of my life.

After the war and the depressing consequence of austerity, the 1950s gave promise of a better life, except that the political power of Communism now threatened to dominate the world. Branches of the party were everywhere in this country, even in the small rural town of Turriff, where the Provost was a leading Communist. The subsequent collapse of that ideology was one of the most unexpected happenings of the twentieth century.

Socially, by the 1950s the joy of my life was ballroom dancing, spinning around to those rhythms of Victor Sylvester and his strict-tempo orchestra. But my kind of melody was soon swept aside by the arrival of rock 'n' roll, brought to us by Bill Haley, an American band leader who explained to me that he had taken four types of music – Hillbilly, Rhythm and Blues, Jazz and Dixieland – and bound them into one rhythm which proved acceptable to the followers of all four. It certainly changed the course of popular music, even if that great orchestral conductor, Sir Malcolm Sargent, dismissed it as "nothing more than an exhibition of primitive tom-tom thumping which they have been doing in the jungle for centuries". But life moves on; and when I met Bill Haley much later in his life he was suffering just as I had done in the '50s, with his rock 'n' roll now threatened by other forms of so-called music.

The Swinging Sixties of The Beatles had brought a revolution of youth that cast aside all restraint in its demand for freedom. Parents lost control and family life went into decline, under siege from the so-called Permissive Society, in which the scourge of drugs was now playing a major part. Even simple good manners became a thing of the past. We looked back to wartime, the biggest emergency the world had ever known, and remembered with nostalgia that human behaviour had never been better. A common danger binds people together.

This collapse of modern society, with its extremes of violence, cruelty, abuse and moral turpitude has been the most depressing change of my lifetime. In the general decline, people we used to respect have become cheating politicians, cheating bankers and, yes, cheating media men and women, who have left honest people with very little to respect. That, plus the strangulating effect of the suicide bomber establishing a whole industry of so-called "security" which, I cynically suspect, will ensure its own survival and plague our descendants for evermore.

CHAPTER FIFTY-SEVEN

MY DAY WITH MRS THATCHER

So to the 1970s, a weird decade characterised by one trade unionist, Arthur Scargill, the miners' leader who was virtually running Britain, with one disruptive strike after another. Even Prime Ministers like Harold Wilson, Edward Heath and James Callaghan could do little to stop him. It took a woman, the controversial Margaret Thatcher of the 1980s, to defuse Mr Scargill. Whatever her shortcomings, if she did nothing more than that in her time as Prime Minister, Mrs Thatcher deserved gratitude.

As a *Daily Express* journalist I spent a day in her private plane as it hopped around Britain, marking her arrival as leader of the Conservative Party in 1975. There were just three of us on the plane, with Mrs Thatcher on my right side, showing me a new style of laying out her speeches, and husband Denis on my left, complete with customary gin and tonic. It was then that I came to realise what a funny man he was. He told the story of arriving at St Pancras Station one day to find that his train was completely full. Then he noticed that the very front carriage was empty so he took a chance and boarded, putting his briefcase up on the rack. As he took his seat, he saw a notice which said that this carriage was reserved for the annual outing of some mental institution. Sure enough, they were soon crowding around him and the lady superintendent began a head count to make sure they were all there. She went, "One, two, three, four . . . " then came upon Denis.

"Who are you?" she asked.

With his airy manner, Denis said "I am the husband of the Prime Minister."

The lady continued "Five, six, seven!"

My personal proximity to Mrs Thatcher on that plane produced a surprise which may have explained the behaviour of her cabinet members when she became Britain's first-ever woman Prime Minister in 1979. That coterie of men, I noticed, seemed to cluster round her like bees to a honeypot. Well, my discovery had been – if I can put this delicately – that she gave off such a musky odour as could only be described as highly sexual. Disbelieve it if you like . . . but true. Men know about these things. [Since I wrote this chapter her official biography has confirmed every detail of my observation, with novelist Kingsley Amis being even more explicit about her sexuality!]

Her subsequent career of course turned her into the longest-serving Prime Minister of the twentieth century, as well as a powerful lady who made her mark around the world. As we know, when she died in April 2013 at the age of eighty-seven there was an astonishing outburst of hate towards the lady, largely from those who had suffered from the closure of declining industries like coal mining. Even young people not born when she was in power were among those who joined the bandwagon of distasteful street parties to "celebrate" her death, whatever they would have known about her. With just a little more thought, those same people might have questioned how she became such an international figure if she was truly as bad as they said.

Future historians will take a more measured view, putting facts before myths. Faced with industrial anarchy and led by people like Arthur Scargill, Britain had become the laughing stock of the world, commonly known as "the sick man of Europe". So what were the facts? From her arrival as Prime Minister in 1979 Margaret Thatcher set about removing that stigma. By 1982, faced with Argentina's invasion of the Falklands, she chose to go to war on the other side of the world. It was a bold decision but it paid off – and she was rewarded with a return to power in the 1983 election. By now she was dealing with Arthur Scargill, who vowed that he would bring down her Tory government. Of course that was not for him to decide and Mrs Thatcher skilfully put him in his place, with such public support and admiration that she became the first Prime Minister in over a century who faced the prospect of winning a third term of office.

Once again she swept to a decisive victory in the 1987 General Election, hardly the expectation of an unpopular Prime Minister. Her personal downfall came in 1990, not on the vote of the public but from her own party, which was hell-bent on entering Europe, while she was firmly against it. She held the veto so they had to get rid of her. Of course she was deeply hurt, just like Winston Churchill, who had led us to a magnificent victory over Hitler in the Second World War when he too was discarded as Prime Minister, even before that war was over. You must not expect gratitude in politics.

Denied the chance of a sensational fourth term in 1992, Mrs Thatcher nevertheless saw her party cruise to victory once more, this time under the Premiership of John Major, stretching that length of so-called Thatcherism to eighteen years. As she slid quietly into retirement, Mrs Thatcher had certainly changed the face of British politics forever. Old age took her into the realms of dementia, a sad old widow who deserved a decent departure, but it was not to be. With the news of her death the old venom resurfaced in large measure, the wider world looking on in bewilderment, wondering what kind of people we were. However, for her funeral procession to St Paul's Cathedral the silent majority turned out in their tens of thousands, cheering her all the way from Westminster, up Whitehall and down the Strand towards St Paul's.

The service itself would have been memorable if only for the tribute paid by the Bishop of London. It was one of the finest speeches I have ever heard, constructed and pitched to perfection.

The Iron Lady was finally on her way.

CHAPTER FIFTY-EIGHT

AND FINALLY – THE QUEEN

By the time we reached the 1990s I was well established as a columnist on *The Herald* in Glasgow. Strangely, that final decade of the century proved to be my most productive as an author. Having written two volumes of memoirs in the '80s and embarked on that successful series of television documentaries for the BBC, I would produce nine more books in the '90s, including three volumes of my collected columns, as well as the biographies of hotelier Reo Stakis; the Director of Kelvingrove Art Gallery, Dr Tom Honeyman; and the world's biggest-selling novelist of his day, Alistair MacLean. There was now a sense of accelerating towards retirement in 1996, when I was voted Bank of Scotland Columnist of the Year. But like policemen, it is a case of once a journalist always a journalist.

The weekly column in *The Herald*, which had brought me a whole new range of readers, was extended for several years after retirement. Into the new century, I was also commissioned to write an extensive history of the city of Aberdeen as well as the centenary volume of Aberdeen Football Club. Then came the big surprise. A letter from Robert Gordon's College was asking if I would consider writing the entire 250-year history of the college. Yes, the school that kicked me out at fourteen for academic inadequacy was now asking if I would undertake this formidable task. Mischievously, I was tempted to write back to ask, "Where are all your fancy historians now that you have had to come to one of your biggest academic dumplings to write your history?" Of course, good manners prevailed and I was delighted to oblige. The book was called *The Auld Hoose*, after that original building, dated 1732, which still stands as the central focus of the college to this day. This was the building that was commandeered as barracks for his troops by Butcher Cumberland on his way north to defeat Bonnie Prince Charlie at the Battle of Culloden in 1746.

It was all happening now – an honorary Masters degree from Aberdeen University, followed by that honorary Doctor of Letters from the Robert Gordon University, the sister of Gordon's College. Evidently the lifelong writings about my native heath had done Aberdeenshire and the North-east of Scotland no harm at all. So considering the health hazards and poor prospects of my boyhood, these latter-day accolades proved, if nothing else, that life is full of surprises.

And there was an even bigger one to come. In that remarkable London Olympics year of 2012 Her Majesty gave me an Honorary British Empire Medal for services to journalism.

CHAPTER FIFTY-NINE

LONDON'S DELIGHT

Despite what many people say about London, it remains one of my favourite cities in the world, so brimful of history, architectural magnificence and cultural delight. I have been going there since my youth, just walking the streets to absorb its special atmosphere and catching up with the latest musicals, but there could have been no more memorable visit than that of August 2011 when I went to see George Gershwin's *Crazy For You* at the Regents Park Open Air Theatre, Bernard Shaw's *Pygmalion* at the Garrick – and then Tchaikovsky's *Swan Lake* at the Royal Opera House, Covent Garden. That performance by the famous Mariinsky Ballet Company of St Petersburg was the delight of a lifetime, sending me out to the streets of London on an emotional high. So I was unprepared for what happened next.

Some incident in Tottenham Court Road that evening had sparked off one of those unthinkable riots in which the youth of the city went on a rampage, burning down shops and embarking on such an orgy of violence, looting and general disorder as London hadn't seen in years. It was a frightening scene, which seemed to confirm that view about the malaise of our modern society. It looked as if we had reached the bottom of the pit. And yet . . . exactly a year later something extraordinary happened. In the face of our national doubt and cynicism, for which we have a special talent, London 2012 brought us the Olympic Games that showed a side of our society I thought had gone forever.

From an official opening that was surely the greatest show on earth, we were suddenly presented with a whole raft of British competitors who, much to our shame, were names we knew little or nothing about. Apart from Andy Murray, who had a magnificent gold-winning victory over Roger Federer, and cyclist Chris Hoy, who was about to be Britain's most decorated Olympian of all time, they were strangers. Had we never heard of fellow Scots like the rowing champion Heather Stanning from Lossiemouth, who won our first gold of the Games, or Katherine Grainger from Aberdeen, who gained another gold? Further afield, until the week before the Games how many of us knew about Bradley Wiggins, the first Briton to win the Tour de France, before coming straight home to win an Olympic gold for cycling? Or what about Mo Farah, a refugee from Somalia who came from nowhere to win both the 5,000 and 10,000 metres races, cheered on by 80,000 people in that wonderful stadium – and declaring himself so proud to be British.

Within days, the magnificence of those and many more athletes had sparked a burst of pride that united the nation in a joy that was as palpable as it was unprecedented. In the most unexpected of circumstances, Great Britain seemed to have rediscovered itself, to the point that even the most disinterested found themselves glued to the television as our competitors streaked towards a total of sixty-five medals, twenty-nine of them gold. After the USA and China, we claimed third position in the league table. Gloom and doom were cast aside and that sense of patriotism that had been discarded so long ago was back in fashion. Hearts were beating for Britain. The nation was uplifted.

As the chairman and organiser of the Games, Sebastian Coe, himself a distinguished Olympian runner and double gold medallist at Moscow in 1980 and Los Angeles in 1984, had masterminded a triumph beyond belief. Whether that sudden burst of patriotism, such as we had not experienced since VE Day of 1945, would linger as a legacy for the future only time would tell but those amazing athletes had shown the nation something we didn't know – that we were still blessed with young people possessing not only exquisite skills in a whole range of sports but with a glowing honesty and integrity, sportsmanship and humility, an air of common decency

– and a determination to succeed for themselves and their country. The fact that most of them were doing it for a minimum of financial reward was a lesson for the bonus-grabbing and self-serving creatures in higher places who needed to take a fresh look at themselves in the mirror.

There might even come a day when I would have to eat my words about a declining society – and rejoice in the fact that the Olympic Games of 2012 marked a turning point in the behaviour and general quality of life in this country. It was also a reminder of my two favourite Olympians from distant times, whose names will surely remain with us forever. From the Berlin Olympics of 1936, America's Jesse Owens will be remembered not only for his record-breaking feats but for the fact that Adolf Hitler turned and left the stadium in disgust, to avoid having to congratulate a black non-Aryan athlete.

Nearer home, we had a hero of our own, the deeply-religious Eric Liddell, favourite to win the 100 metres at the Paris Olympics of 1924 but who refused to run in the heats because they were held on a Sunday. Instead, he ran in the 400 metres, in which he had little experience but sensationally won the gold medal. Liddell was hailed on his return to Edinburgh University, before heading out east as a missionary in China. Captured by the Japanese during the war, he did wonderful service to his fellow prisoners before dying of a brain tumour in 1945, still only forty-three. His story was told very movingly in David Puttnam's 1981 film *Chariots of Fire*, the music of which became the theme tune of London 2012. But there had always been a mystery as to the burial place of Eric Liddell and on a visit to Hong Kong in 1988 I met a fellow Scot who was determined to find it.

Charles Walker from Prestwick was working as a civil engineer in the colony when, through sheer perseverance and some good fortune, he met an old man who could tell him precisely where it was. In fact, this gentleman had helped to bury him. In the old prison camp in China, now a children's playground, he could guide him on how many paces in one direction and

275

how many paces in another. And that would be the spot. So Charles Walker not only pinpointed the hidden grave of Eric Liddell but ordered a granite stone from the island of Mull – and provided a suitable memorial to one of the great Scots of the twentieth century.

CHAPTER SIXTY

LET'S GRASP THIS LIFE

Looking back from the autumn of my years, that long and winding road has led to a totally unexpected and wonderful life. I treasure every moment of it. From time to time I have revisited Fedderate Cottages in Maud to stand again at the place of my birth. With the permission of the occupants I have seen again the room where I was born, then gone to the front door and considered that this was where I got my very first view of the world. With a quick mental montage, I've thought of all I have done since leaving this door-step, the places I have seen and the people I have met – and here I am, back where it all began. It is a therapy which gets your life into perspective.

I have a favourite photograph of myself at three years old, stand-ing outside that door with a saucer and a penny in my hand, await-ing the arrival of Luigi Zanre, the ice cream man from Peterhead. I look at that sad little face and wonder what it was thinking. For sure, it had no hint of the random adventures that lay ahead – trav-elling the world; flying over the Arctic in the very first prototype of Concorde, three years before it went into service; thrilling to watch the sheer magic of the centre court at Wimbledon; sitting with Roy Williamson as he told me how he composed "Flower of Scotland"; standing by the Washington Memorial on 4 July 1976, the 200th anniversary of the United States; meeting the great entertainers of the twentieth century, from Muhammad Ali and Charlie Chaplin to Elizabeth Taylor, Bing Crosby and Bob Hope, not to mention the grand finale of Frank Sinatra at the Desert Inn of Las Vegas. All that and so much more lay ahead for that sad little face.

The last time I stood by that doorway I was remembering those

famous words of John Donne: "And never send to know for whom the bell tolls. It tolls for thee." And I was reminded that life is a pretty tenuous business, a short run. The past is history, the future is mystery, but today is a gift and appropriately we call it the present. I believe it is a gift to be grasped and made the most of, so that when we come to the folding of our own tent there will be just rich memories and, as Frank Sinatra used to sing in "My Way", regrets I've had a few but then again too few to mention. And if you and I can achieve that in our lifetime, I think you will agree that we will have been well and truly blessed.

Danks Street Depot

Acknowledgments

Putting together a book is something that can only really be achieved with the combined efforts of a large group of people, so I would like to pass on my thanks to everybody at Murdoch Books, in particular Kay, Vivien, Mary, Juliet, Alan and Zoë 'Questions' Harpham.

I would also like to thank a group of people whose tireless efforts in the food industry are an absolute inspiration to me. People like Ray and Kerry from Cornucopia Farms, Lynne Tietzel, Tony Papas (who first opened my eyes to how to cook), Penny Williams and my very dear friend Michael Klausen.

To my team at Danks Street Depot: I thank you for for putting up with these past crazy 3 years; for your hard work and for having faith in Melanie and me.

A special thanks to the most beautiful and inspirational person I know, my wife Melanie. And not to forget Charlie, my son, for reminding me how much fun life can be.

And, finally, thanks to the person who started all of this...mum.

Danks Street Depot

Jared Ingersoll

MURDOCH BOOKS

Contents

Have you ever heard the saying 'You can't make a silk purse from a sow's ear'? Well, I say 'Forget the silk purse, give me the rest of the sow's head—I want brawn'. The point is that when you know how to treat produce to get the best out of it, you'll be eating well. A pig's head when treated correctly is as good an ingredient as a well-aged piece of beef, or foie gras, or a perfectly ripe plum. And you'll find that the best ingredients are often the least expensive. The simple equation to good food is wonderful produce coupled with a bit of guidance (which will later develop into knowledge) and a heavy dose of passion.

And what constitutes wonderful produce? Well to answer that is a book in itself! But here are a few hints for getting great produce: buy locally, buy seasonally and buy what you feel like eating. Try to buy produce from someone who knows the products and can tell you where they came from. I get really frustrated with obscene-looking mounds of artificially ripened, dull and flavourless produce that has been flown in from all over the world. These are presented by companies who then tell me that their products are what 'I' the consumer wants…rubbish, give me flavour. A brown paper bag of perfectly ripe, perfumy local strawberries that need to be eaten within a day or two is absolute perfection, whereas a little plastic tray of nasty green strawberries from the other side of the world with the red side facing up in an attempt to trick me into buying them is not. If fresh produce seems expensive, it is generally because you are trying to buy it out of season or it has been freighted a great distance and overhandled. My tip to you is, if you have never been to your local market put it on your 'to do' list, and when you are there talk to a store holder about what they are selling — then taste, smell, feel and live a little.

I have a great fondness for, and a head full of memories of, food from almost every part of my life. Memories that involve large groups, like the time I cooked paella for 500 people. Memories of great celebration, such as our wedding dinner. Simple, beautiful memories like the time I ate cheese, tomatoes, bread and wine with my future wife while looking at the distant shores of Turkey. Sneaky memories like scoffing whole spoonfuls of caviar while working at a restaurant in London (sorry Phil…I couldn't help myself). Funny memories like the time when I was 7 or 8 years old and making my sister dessert but getting custard and mustard mixed up. There are memories of flavours, smells and textures. Memories of successes and failures, memories that continue to inspire me and others I would rather forget. And I owe it all to food.

This book is the product of a life dedicated to the pleasure of food and my number one message is that above all food should be fun. I want you to look at this book as my humble way of showing you a few dishes that hold a special place in my heart and that scream out for your own personal touch.

Eat well, Jared

Snacks and nibbles

Life is good with food in one hand and
   a glass in the other.

Pickled cauliflower, carrots or whatever
snacks for about eight

If you are going to pickle anything always do more than you need. That way you have plenty of leftovers and one of my greatest joys when cooking is having tangy pickles on hand either to complement a dish or to munch on while waiting for dinner to finish cooking.

Once you feel confident with the basics of pickling, it is time to experiment with some other vegetables. There are a few basic guidelines for success. Hard root vegetables such as carrots, kohlrabi and swede (rutabaga) should be partially cooked before adding to a cool brine. Beetroots (beets) should be cooked whole in the brine (use the quantities below but add an extra 200 ml/7 fl oz of water), then peeled afterwards. Cucumbers, qukes (a type of small cucumber) and zucchini (courgettes) need only be immersed in the cool brine, then left for at least 48 hours. Slicing, peeling and seeding is a matter of personal preference. Pickled vegetables will keep in the fridge for at least 1 month.

Fills a 2 litre (70 fl oz/8-cup) jar

For the pickling brine
330 ml (11¼ fl oz/1⅓ cups) white wine vinegar
400 ml (14 fl oz) dry white wine
500 ml (17 fl oz/2 cups) water
325 ml (11 fl oz) extra virgin olive oil
80 ml (2½ fl oz/⅓ cup) mustard seed oil, optional
4 large red chillies, split but left whole
16 black peppercorns
8 cloves
8 allspice berries
a touch of freshly grated nutmeg
1 bunch of thyme
12 bay leaves
4 stalks of rosemary
a good pinch of salt and double that of sugar

To make the pickling brine, put all the ingredients together in a small saucepan and bring to the boil over a high heat. Continue to boil for 10 minutes—you should end up with about 1.25 litres (44 fl oz/5 cups) of brine. Remove the pan from the heat.

For the pickles
1 cauliflower (about 1 kg/2 lb 4 oz), cut into florets, or
3 bunches of baby carrots, peeled (I like to leave about 1 cm (½ in) of stalk on, purely
    for the look—if some of the stalks fall off it doesn't really matter)

To pickle the cauliflower, put the florets in a large bowl (at least 2 litres/70 fl oz/8-cup capacity) that is large enough to take the vegetables and all of the brine.

Pour the hot brine over the florets. Take a piece of plastic wrap or baking paper and place it on top of the cauliflower to ensure that everything remains submerged. Allow to cool completely, then transfer to a sterilized 2 litre (70 fl oz/8-cup) jar or airtight container and store in the fridge. For best results allow the cauliflower to sit for at least 24 hours before eating.

To pickle the carrots, bring a large saucepan of salted water to the boil and cook the carrots for about 2–3 minutes. When you test a carrot, it should be very crunchy and only half cooked. Strain and run under cold water until completely cool. Allow the brine to cool completely, then pour it over the cooked carrots. They are now ready to store either in a sterilized 2 litre (70 fl oz/8-cup) jar or an airtight container. They are best stored for at least 48 hours before eating.

Cauliflower and caper tapenade
for a party

You will see a recurring theme throughout this book—I have a soft spot for cauliflower and I think I have my mum to thank for that. Mum was different from other mothers when I was a kid because she thought that cooking vegetables very briefly, until only just done meant they would retain goodness and flavour. All the other mothers I knew used to cook their vegetables to death and, unfortunately, cauliflower is the smelliest vegetable of them all when overcooked!

I like this recipe because it utilizes the sweet flavour and crunchy texture of cauliflower. Take this tapenade and serve it on anything from croutons to seared scallops.

200 g (7 oz) cauliflower, cut into florets
80 g (2³/₄ oz) salted capers, rinsed
60 g (2¹/₄ oz) pitted green olives
a few sprigs of thyme, leaves only
1 small bunch of flat-leaf (Italian) parsley
¹/₄ teaspoon grated lemon peel
150 ml (5 fl oz) extra virgin olive oil
salt and ground black pepper

Blanch the cauliflower, then chop. Chop the capers, olives, thyme and parsley separately (chopping the thyme quite finely), then put all the chopped ingredients in a bowl with the lemon peel and oil. Mix well and taste for seasoning. This tapenade will look fairly rustic. It is best served soon after being made, but it will keep quite well for 4 or 5 days in the fridge.

Taramasalata
for a party

This is the one recipe that I am most nervous about including in this book. Whenever you make and serve this, beware of the taramasalata police. You will recognize them immediately as they move towards your bowl of taramasalata. They will give it a poke and a taste, then quietly smirk because the one that they make is either more lemony/oniony/bready/uses potato/uses Spanish, Greek or some other type of olive oil, or even an extra virgin oil.

There are hundreds of slightly different recipes for taramasalata. This one suits me most as it is well balanced and is a pretty pink colour. I prefer not to use a flavoursome extra virgin olive oil in taramasalata as the taste can be too strong—instead use either a light olive oil or a mixture of 270 ml (9^1/2 fl oz) canola oil and 80 ml (2^1/2 fl oz/^{1}/3 cup) extra virgin olive oil.

If you are about to serve a large meal, don't put out too much taramasalata, as it is extremely moreish and quite filling. However, if you are going to eat this with roasted olives (page 15), pickled vegetables (page 12) and beer on a sunny day, then don't be stingy as it is a great lazy lunch. For the adventurous, try finishing a seafood risotto with taramasalata instead of butter, or when you cook a thick chunk of blue eye cod, barramundi or other firm white fish, brush over just a little taramasalata when you rest your fish and let the flavours melt together before serving.

200 g (7 oz) very stale white bread with the crusts removed (don't use sourdough)
1 large onion, finely diced
juice of 2 lemons
salt and ground white pepper
100 g (3^1/2 oz) tin of tarama roe (pasteurized red mullet roe)
350 ml (12 fl oz) light olive oil

Break or cut the bread into chunks. Put the bread in a bowl, cover with water and soak for at least 20 minutes. When your bread has softened, squeeze out as much liquid as you can.

Depending on the size of your food processor, you may need to do this recipe in batches. If this is the case, divide everything into two and do as two different recipes, then combine both in a bowl afterwards to check for seasoning and consistency. Put the onion, lemon juice, salt and white pepper in a food processor. Blend until you have formed a paste, then add the tarama roe and blend until well combined. Add the softened bead and continue to blend, stopping to scrape the sides of the bowl from time to time.

With your food processor running, and once everything is well combined, slowly and carefully drizzle in the oil to allow the ingredients to emulsify. Once you have added all of the oil you should have a thick and creamy pinkish dip. Taste and adjust the seasoning as required—if your taramasalata is too thick you can adjust the consistency by carefully adding water a few drops at a time.

Olives roasted with rosemary and orange for a party

pictured page 16

You've got to love this recipe. Make it when you have a couple of moments to spare and keep the olives in a jar in the fridge until you want them. They taste great and look awesome and are as versatile as any olive. I like to keep the oil even after the olives have been eaten and use it to make dressings or to pour over bruschetta.

Like many of my recipes, use the quantities given as a guide. I am more interested in opening you up to opportunities than dictating to you how much rosemary or garlic you should like to eat!

Fills a 1.5 litre (52 fl oz/6-cup) jar

1 kg (2 lb 4 oz) manzanilla olives in brine (you can use kalamata olives, ligurian olives
    or whatever takes your fancy but don't use pitted olives)
1 bulb of garlic, broken into cloves, with the skins left on
3 stalks of rosemary
a generous pinch of ground black pepper
about 500 ml (17 fl oz/2 cups) extra virgin olive oil
the peel and juice of 2 oranges, peel cut into strips

Start by rinsing the brine off your olives. Put the rinsed olives in a large saucepan with the cloves of garlic, rosemary stalks, pepper, oil and orange peel. Bring up to a very gentle simmer and cook for about 10 minutes. Add the orange juice and cook for another 15 minutes or so until you have soft cloves of garlic and olives that are just starting to wrinkle. The cooking time will vary slightly depending on the type and size of your olives—large kalamata olives will take slightly longer, tiny ligurian olives will take no time at all.

Cool slightly, then transfer everything to a 1.5 litre (52 fl oz/6-cup) sterilized jar: it is always advisable to use sterilized containers when storing food. If stored correctly (in a sterilized jar out of direct sunlight, preferably in the fridge) these olives should last for months. The oil will solidify, but this is okay as it will liquefy when brought to room temperature.

Chive tarts with enoki mushroom salad
for a party

This is a great recipe that is easily adapted to suit just about any soft herb, and then you get to change the toppings. For instance, you could try chervil tarts with a small dollop of sour cream, or parsley tarts with salmon roe. I have made the assumption that you don't want to spend too much time on these so I am using pre-baked tartlet cases; these are pretty easy to find these days but if they are not in your local delicatessen ask if they can get some in for you.

I like enoki mushrooms for the salad not only because of their great texture but also because these tiny little mushrooms are very attractive. They don't have a lot of flavour though, so I help them along with a few other ingredients. The salad makes enough to mound on top of each of the tarts. A word of caution, once dressed the mushrooms will only hold for around 5 minutes so dress them just before serving.

This will make around 50 tartlets. I can easily scoff half a dozen before a meal.

For the chive tarts
50 x 3 cm (1^1/$_4$ in) ready-made tartlet shells
2 bunches of chives, finely chopped
185 ml (6 fl oz/^{3}/$_4$ cup) milk (full-cream/whole milk gives the best results; skim milk
    tends to foam too much during the blending process)
1 whole egg and 2 egg yolks, lightly beaten together
30 ml (1 fl oz) cream (whipping)
^{1}/$_2$ teaspoon dijon mustard
salt and ground black pepper

Preheat your oven to 120°C (235°F/Gas ^{1}/$_2$). Lay out the tartlet shells on baking trays. You get the best results for the custard if you have a good-quality, high-speed upright blender that will allow you to completely pulverize the chives. Put the chives and milk into your blender or food processor and purée. Don't let the mixture blend for too long as you do not want to heat or curdle the milk.

If you feel you have to strain the mixture do so into a bowl, being sure to squeeze as much as you can from the chives, otherwise just throw it all in. Use a spatula or wooden spoon to add the egg, cream and mustard to the chive milk. You don't want to mix too much or you will aerate your custard—mix until well combined, no more. The easiest thing to do now is to transfer your mixture into a pitcher or bowl with a spout, and from there pour it into your tartlet shells.

Bake for about 8–12 minutes. What you are looking for is a 'just set' custard. One test is to tap the edge of a tart shell with your finger—it is ready if the custard doesn't wobble twice. If the tarts require longer, then check them often as they will cook fairly quickly because they are so small. If the custard starts to rise, you have gone a little too far and they need to come out of the oven promptly—don't despair, they will still be lovely to eat. Allow to cool completely, but don't refrigerate.

For the enoki mushroom salad

200 g (7 oz) enoki mushrooms
1 tablespoon truffle oil or good-quality extra virgin olive oil
2 tablespoons freshly grated parmesan cheese
a dash of lemon juice
a sprinkle of chopped chives
salt and ground black pepper

Starting from the caps of the mushrooms slice them into 5 mm (1/4 in) pieces, cutting as far as the stems are separated—discard the 'clump' at the bottom. Gently toss all of the ingredients in a bowl and season with salt and pepper.

For serving

Just before you are ready to serve, place small tidy mounds of the enoki mushroom salad on top of each cool tart, using all the salad. Serve immediately.

Poached and crumbed duck wings with pickled cauliflower sauce

Use this recipe as a guide to quantities—it's a very loose recipe. Either serve two duck wings per person for an appetizer or canapé or allow six wings per person for great beer and TV food. The idea with this recipe is that when you are cooking duck, you remove the wings and pop them in the freezer. Once you have collected a few you can defrost them and prepare this crunchy treat.

For the pickled cauliflower sauce
100 g (3¹/2 oz) pickled cauliflower (either bought or home-made
    from page 12), chopped
1 egg yolk
1 teaspoon dijon mustard
a dash of brine from the pickles
80 ml (2¹/2 fl oz/¹/3 cup) vegetable oil
1 bunch of chives, chopped
salt and ground black pepper

Put the cauliflower in a food processor and pulse until coarsely chopped. Tip the cauliflower out but don't worry about cleaning the food processor as it is all going back in there again.

Add the egg yolk, mustard and pickling brine to the food processor and blend well. While the motor is running, very slowly drizzle in all of your oil. Stop the blender and add the chopped cauliflower and chopped chives and mix by hand. Taste and adjust the seasoning and consistency if needed—I prefer it to be only just bound together and fairly loose.

For the duck wings and sherry sauce
12 duck wings
300 ml (10¹/2 fl oz) sweet sherry (you don't need to use anything fancy
    or expensive)
a dollop of dijon mustard
about 300 g (10¹/2 oz/3³/4 cups) fresh or 300 g (10¹/2 oz/3 cups) dry
    breadcrumbs (Basics)
500 ml (17 fl oz/2 cups) vegetable or canola oil
salt

When you look at your duck wings, you will see that they are made up of three segments joined by two joints. Cut through the joints to make into three pieces, then throw away the wing 'tip' as there is not really anything there worthwhile eating. Place the wing pieces in a saucepan that allows them to fit snugly, then cover with the sherry.

Bring the sherry up to a very gentle simmer and cook for about 45 minutes. If you are using a gas stove be careful that the sherry doesn't catch on fire. If you do flambé the poaching liquor don't panic—as soon as the alcohol has burnt away the flames will die, this will only take a moment.

Remove the pan from the heat and allow the wing pieces to cool in the sherry. When they are cool enough to handle but not completely cold, lift the wings out of the liquid. The middle segments of wings have two bones: remove one of the bones by taking the nugget of skin in one hand and gently twisting out the bone with the other.

Once you have removed all of the wings, put the liquid back on the stove and reduce for 10–12 minutes over a high heat until you have a thick syrup, then set to one side. Take your wings and brush with a little of the mustard, then toss in the breadcrumbs.

You are about to deep-fry—please be careful! A good safety tip is to only fill your pan by one-third—this will give the oil room to boil up without spilling over the side of the pan. Heat some vegetable oil in a large saucepan. One way to tell if the oil is hot enough is to place the handle of a wooden spoon into the oil; if little bubbles appear, your oil is ready.

Deep-fry the duck pieces until golden—you may need to do this in batches. Using a slotted spoon remove them from the oil and drain on paper towels, then season with salt. Transfer to a plate.

For serving
Drizzle a little of the reduced sherry over the duck wings and place next to a dollop of pickled cauliflower sauce. Serve immediately with a bottle of good ale.

Warm goat's cheese salad with chapons and fried rosemary for four to share

This is a sweet, rich and delicious way to start a meal—simply place the salad in the middle of your table to share. It's great served with a really chilled cool-climate riesling or a dry rosé. I like to use a log of fresh chèvre from Woodside Farms because it is a soft, young goat's cheese with a sharp, nutty flavour and delicate chalky mouth-feel.

I like to serve this salad with *chapons*, which traditionally is a crust of bread that has been dipped in garlic oil, then rubbed inside a salad bowl prior to tossing a salad—it imparts a beautiful flavour to the salad. The name comes from the French word for hat, *chapeau*, because when you shave off the crust of bread it looks a little like a hat. This recipe makes the chapons the main focus and is a really great way to use the delicious crust from your old sourdough loaf, leaving the inside part of the loaf for your panzanella (page 58) or ribollita (page 78). You can make the chapons in advance and store them in an airtight container. Serve them in a bowl or smear them with goat's curd and serve as a canapé. There are no tricks to this recipe; change the quantities to suit your taste and the amount of bread that you have available.

For the chapons
1 slightly stale loaf of good-quality sourdough bread
80–100 ml (2^1/2–3^1/2 fl oz) extra virgin olive oil
a good dash of red wine vinegar, to taste
2 cloves of garlic, thinly sliced
salt and ground black pepper

Preheat your oven to 120°C (235°F/Gas ^{1}/2). I like to cut the bread so as to remove only the crust and as little of the inside loaf as possible, and make pieces from the crust that are about 1 cm (^{1}/2 in) wide and 2–3 cm (^{3}/4–1^1/4 in) long—don't even try to be neat, just start shaving your loaf!

Place your crusts in a large bowl, then add the oil, vinegar and sliced garlic and season well with salt and pepper. Toss everything together, then put onto a baking tray that is large enough that your crusts are spread evenly—don't mound them on top of each other. Now into the oven, which is coolish because you don't want to toast them as much as you want them to get really dry and crispy (dry or really stale bread holds liquids much better than toasted bread). The freshness of your bread and how much oil and vinegar you use will determine your cooking time. As a rule of thumb allow 20 minutes, but check and roughly stir about every 5 minutes.

For the olive dressing
120 g (4^1/4 oz) ligurian olives
3 tablespoons honey
1 tablespoon truffle oil
ground black pepper

Make your dressing by placing everything in a small saucepan and gently warming through, then set to one side and allow to cool a little.

For the fried rosemary
enough vegetable oil to fry
1 stalk of rosemary, leaves only
salt

Heat the oil in a frying pan and fry the rosemary leaves until they start to become golden and crispy. Drain on paper towels and season lightly with salt.

For the warm goat's cheese
2 tablespoons vegetable oil
6 x 40 g (1^1/$_2$ oz) pieces of fresh chèvre (goat's cheese)
enough plain (all-purpose) flour to dust

In a frying pan large enough to take all the cheese, heat a little oil over a high heat. You want your pan to be nice and hot but not smoking. Lightly dust the cheese with flour and fry until coloured. Flip it over, being careful as the cheese will start to soften, then colour the other side. Working very quickly, lift the warm cheese onto a platter.

For serving
Drizzle the olive dressing over the top of the goat's cheese and sprinkle with the fried rosemary. Use your chapons to scoop up the cheese.

I love spring and new beginnings

There is nothing more exciting than the change of season. At times like these a cook requires equal measures of passion and patience.

Three omelette recipes

One of my main concerns in the café is to monitor and take care of the single most important piece of equipment in our kitchen—the omelette pan. To the best of my knowledge our omelette pans have been washed only twice: once when we bought them and the second time when they were mistakenly used to cook something else (the thought still sends a shiver through me). At home you don't need to be quite as precious as us; we have to be because on an average Saturday morning we sell anywhere from 30 to 50 omelettes and there is no room for error. The point is that if you go to the trouble to 'season' your pan, take good care of it and it will take good care of you.

About the pan. Some people prefer to use a non-stick pan, which will produce a perfectly fine omelette. My only problem is that non-stick pans generally don't last very long, and they are too non-stick and slippery for my liking. The best omelette pan is a thick, cast-iron pan that is around 18 cm (7 in) in diameter and about 3.5 cm (1 1/4 in) deep; it also needs to have sloping sides to help shape your omelette. To season your pan you should rub it with a little oil, then sprinkle well with table salt until it has a thin layer of salt on every surface of the pan. Place the pan into a very hot oven and leave for about 40 minutes. If your pan doesn't have a heatproof handle, put it on the stove instead. Remove the pan from the heat and, using a thick cloth, brush all of the salt into your sink (careful, the salt is also very hot); it may need a bit of a firm rub. Now, use a cloth to rub a generous amount of oil into the pan and then put it back into the oven for about 10–15 minutes. Take the pan out of the oven and use a clean cloth dipped into a little clean oil to give your pan a really good rub down. Your pan is now seasoned and you should avoid getting it wet. After you use your pan, simply wipe it clean with a dry cloth. One thing to know is that the first omelette will stick a little—don't panic, you shouldn't have any worries after that.

One last tip—simply remember to work quickly and don't let your omelette sit in the pan for too long!

For one plain omelette
3 fresh eggs
salt and ground black pepper
a small knob of butter

Place your pan on a high heat—you don't want the surface of the pan to start smoking, but it will need to be quite hot. Break your eggs into a small bowl and gently whisk with a fork—don't overmix, your eggs should be well incorporated but you should still be able to make out bits of yolks and bits of whites. Season.

Add the butter to the pan. It should start foaming but don't let it brown too quickly. Add the egg and, using your fork, stir it briskly in a circular motion until it resembles a very wet scrambled egg, this will happen very quickly, so don't walk away! Using the back of your fork, patch any holes and shape your omelette, then tilt the pan and slide one-third of the omelette up the side of the pan. If you are filling your omelette, add the filling to the middle of the omelette, then fold the bottom third over the filling. Now roll your omelette onto your plate ensuring that the 'seam' is on the bottom. Serve immediately.

For the basil and goat's cheese filling

20 g (³/4 oz) fresh chèvre (goat's cheese)
2 large basil leaves

For the best results, bring your cheese to room temperature before using. Add the basil and cheese to your omelette just before folding.

For the roasted button mushroom filling

100 g (3¹/2 oz) button mushrooms
a pinch of chopped thyme
a knob of butter
a dash of olive oil
salt and ground black pepper

Preheat your oven to 190°C (375°F/Gas 5). Button mushrooms have copped a bit of flak lately; people are saying terribly hurtful things such as they have no flavour. This is not true, there is good flavour in just about everything if you know how to bring it out, and roasting is one of the best ways to coax the best out of your mushrooms. Put all of the filling ingredients on a baking tray and cook in the oven for at least 15 minutes until the mushrooms start to become crisp. Stir them often while you're cooking. Add to your omelette just before folding.

For Charlie's artichoke omelette

1 large firm artichoke
a wedge of lemon
a splash of olive oil
freshly grated parmesan cheese, optional

Take the artichoke and start removing the outer leaves, one at a time. Keep going until you reach the yellow, tender leaves. Place the artichoke on its side; you should be able to see where the leaves finish and the heart begins. Using a sharp serrated knife cut off the leaves. Pick up the artichoke and place it in the palm of your hand with the stem pointing towards your wrist. Using a sharp paring knife or small vegetable knife trim away the dark green exterior of the artichoke. Working carefully, cut the stem about 2 cm (³/4 in) down from the base of the heart. Now, using a spoon, scrape out all of the spiky 'choke' from the centre of the artichoke heart. Rinse under cold water, then rub the heart well with a piece of cut lemon to stop the artichoke from turning brown.

Shave or slice the artichoke heart as thinly as you can. Heat your omelette pan and briefly fry your artichoke in the oil until it's soft and golden. Pour your egg over the artichoke and cook the normal way. You can add a little grated parmesan cheese if you wish. This is the first meal my son Charlie ate by himself with a fork!

Swordfish with asparagus in bagna caôda for six

A good family friend of mine, Mr Nick, is a great hunter who has won many prizes for his skill. He only brings home the best meat—that which he is able to kill with a 'clean shot', which bleeds quickly making for a quick death and superior meat. After he goes hunting a group of friends gather at his place for a cook-up. All are welcome, cooking is done by whoever wants to, and everyone brings some raw ingredients. You can end up with wild boar, paua (a type of abalone), fresh pine mushrooms, beautiful limes, wild berries, fancy vinegars and homemade cheeses. It's an amazing experience as I get to cook with my mate Ben, and we use it as an opportunity to have some no-holds barred fun with food. I have some great memories of those afternoons, and some great recipes to boot. This is one 'experiment' that I loved so much it was served at my wedding. The bagna caôda sauce is nothing new, but is traditionally used as a dipping sauce for raw vegetables. It's so versatile it can be used for almost anything. I like to buy a whole piece of swordfish and cut it into cubes at home. Allow 185 g (6 1/2 oz) of fish per person and ask your fishmonger to cut you one piece according to how many people you are feeding. This recipe will feed six people.

For the bagna caôda
100 ml (3 1/2 fl oz) extra virgin olive oil
4 cloves of garlic, thinly sliced
10 anchovy fillets
a pinch of chilli flakes
200 ml (7 fl oz) milk
150 ml (5 fl oz) cream (whipping)

Put the oil, garlic, anchovies and chilli in a saucepan and cook over a high heat until it is sticky and golden. When you get an amazing toasted garlic aroma and the colour looks good, add the milk and cream. Heat through but don't let it boil—it will look slightly curdled but this is fine. Set to one side.

For the swordfish and asparagus
about 1 kg (2 lb 4 oz) chunk of swordfish (mid-cut, skin removed)
a dash of vegetable oil, enough to lightly coat the fish
salt and ground black pepper
24 spears of asparagus, cut into 2 cm (3/4 in) long pieces
a few sprigs of chervil

Dice your swordfish into 1.5 cm (5/8 in) cubes, trying to get the pieces as uniform as you can. Rub the fish with a little of the oil, salt and pepper. Now get a large frying pan nice and hot and, working very quickly, colour the fish on all sides, then remove from the heat—you want the fish to be quite raw inside.

Wipe your pan clean, then add the asparagus and bagna caôda and place back over the heat. When your asparagus is tender, after about 5 minutes, return the fish to the pan and gently fold everything together and remove from the heat. The heat from the sauce should be enough to finish cooking the fish. Serve in shallow bowls so you can have puddles of the delicious sauce in the base. Garnish with sprigs of chervil.

Spinach, avocado and chapons salad
for four

This is another use for the chapons that I use in the warm goat's cheese salad (page 24). Smear them with goat's curd or pâté or whatever takes your fancy.

2 French shallots, thinly sliced
salt
55 ml (1³/₄ fl oz) aged red wine vinegar
90 ml (3 fl oz) extra virgin olive oil
a dozen or so chapons (page 24)
goat's curd, pâté or whatever you like on your chapons
2 ripe avocados
4 large handfuls of baby English spinach leaves, picked and cleaned

Start by placing the sliced shallots in a large bowl and sprinkle with a generous amount of salt and the red wine vinegar. Leave this to sit for about 20 minutes. Slowly whisk in the oil to finish the dressing.

Smear your chapons with whatever topping you have chosen.

Use a teaspoon to remove 'scoops' of avocado flesh, then add these to the dressing and gently combine. Add the spinach leaves and roll about—the avocado will start to break up, but this is fine as it will all become part of your dressing. Gently lift your spinach into your serving bowls and top with the chapons.

Asparagus with a warm
coddled egg dressing for four

I like to serve this as a nice and easy starter and, when Mother Nature permits, I use green, white and purple asparagus. White asparagus is really the only one that I would ever be tempted to peel, as it tends to have slightly bitter skin. Purple asparagus loses a lot of the purple colour as it cooks, but it does have a sweeter, milder flavour than green asparagus.

Let the asparagus tell you what to trim off; do this by taking hold of the bottom end and bending—it will break where it needs to. Never throw away your asparagus bottoms because they are perfectly good for soup. Or, to make asparagus stock, simply bring enough water to cover the asparagus to the boil, add your stems, boil for 10 minutes, then leave to infuse overnight in the fridge. Next day strain off for a fragrant and green asparagus stock.

2 anchovy fillets
a pinch of chopped rosemary
60 ml (2 fl oz/¼ cup) pickled shallot vinegar (Basics)
8 large eggs
80 ml (2½ fl oz/⅓ cup) extra virgin olive oil
salt and ground black pepper
16 pieces of thick asparagus or enough for four people
a few sprigs of chervil, chopped

Have all of your ingredients ready because once you begin things will move pretty quickly and there will be no time for delays. You will need two pots of boiling salted water, one large enough for the eggs and the other large enough for the asparagus.

Using the back of a fork start crushing the anchovy fillets and rosemary with the vinegar in a small bowl.

Put the eggs (in their shell) into one of the pots of boiling water and cook for 4 minutes. By this stage the whites should be just about cooked and only a little runny while the yolks will be completely runny. Drain the eggs and hold the hot eggs with a cloth while you use a spoon to break them in half and scoop the egg whites and yolks into a bowl. Mash together lightly with a fork, leaving it slightly chunky. You must do this promptly, as you want your dressing to be served warm, and reheating is not really an option. Add the anchovy mixture, then slowly pour in the oil while mixing. Taste for seasoning.

Now, cook the asparagus in your second pot of boiling water—thick asparagus will need about 8 minutes, thinner less time. It is always a good idea to test the asparagus after a couple of minutes, this will give you an idea of how quickly it is cooking. One thing about asparagus—you want it to have a firm texture, but it should not have a 'crunch' to it. Asparagus that is undercooked has a slightly acidic flavour.

Once cooked, drain well and arrange on a platter, then add the chopped chervil to the dressing and pour over the top of the asparagus. Serve immediately.

Cured cucumbers
for four

It's a really hot day. My son Charlie is splashing away in his paddling pool, my wife Mel is walking around in her 'comfy clothes' and I am sweating away in front of a fan. We have just had lunch and a long cold drink, but I still feel like something…something crunchy, refreshing and invigorating.

Three cheers for the easiest recipe in the book!

This recipe is very loose—use one cucumber per person and adjust the quantities of the other ingredients to suit.

4 Lebanese (short) cucumbers
salt
sugar
lemon juice
finely chopped chives

Cut the cucumbers lengthways into quarters or sixths. Sprinkle the cut side with a little salt and sugar, then squeeze on a little lemon juice. Leave to sit like this in the fridge for a couple of hours. When you go to serve them remove from their liquid and sprinkle with a few finely chopped chives. They look particularly great standing up in an icy cold glass and placed next to a great big pitcher of Pimms!

Orechiette with broccoli, bitter greens and pecorino cheese **for six**

I love it when you discover a recipe that takes an everyday ingredient, broccoli in this instance, and turns it into a flavour that leaves you making appreciative noises after each mouthful. It's good for a couple of reasons: first, because the taste is great; second, because it makes you stop and truly appreciate how good food can be if you look at it in a different way. The thing you want to pay attention to in this recipe is the browning of the garlic—when you get it 'just so' you will create an amazing nutty flavour that carries along wonderfully with the broccoli.

1 bunch of cavolo nero or other bitter green leaf
1 bunch of rocket (arugula)
2 heads of broccoli
1 bunch of broccoli sprouts or broccolini
4 cloves of garlic, crushed and 2 cloves of garlic, thinly sliced
a good pinch of chilli flakes
100 ml (3½ fl oz) extra virgin olive oil
2 anchovy fillets
500 ml (17 fl oz/2 cups) dry white wine
500 g (1 lb 2 oz) good-quality orechiette or casarecci pasta
300 g (10½ oz/3⅓ cups) freshly grated pecorino cheese

Chop the cavolo nero and rocket together. Slice off the broccoli florets as close to the flower as possible and cut the florets to the same size as the pasta. Then peel and slice the stem into 1 cm (½ in) pieces. Cut the broccoli sprouts to the same size as the pasta.

In a saucepan cook the sauce base by gently frying the crushed garlic and half the chilli flakes in half of the oil until golden and tender. Add the anchovy fillets and the raw sliced broccoli stems and cook for 2–3 minutes. Pour in the white wine and cook until the broccoli is tender and the wine has all but cooked away, about 10–12 minutes. Scoop the mixture into a blender and blend until smooth, then set aside.

Bring a large pot of salted water to boil. Have a large frying pan next to it because once you begin cooking you want to have everything you need in place. When the water has started to boil, blanch the broccoli florets and broccolini. After 2 minutes lift the vegetables out of the water with a slotted spoon and let sit on a plate until you have everything else ready.

Now drop the orecchiette into the same water as the vegetables. While the pasta is cooking (it will take 10–12 minutes) you want to finish your sauce. In your frying pan cook the sliced garlic and remaining chilli flakes in the rest of the olive oil until toasted and a 'nutty' aroma is released. Add your chopped cavolo nero and rocket and allow to wilt slightly. Add your broccoli sauce, blanched broccolini and broccoli. You may want to splash in some water to help combine things nicely but don't add too much as you want this to be a fairly dry sauce.

By now your pasta should be cooked and you simply lift your pasta out of the water using a slotted spoon or sieve, drop it into your pan of sauce and toss about. Add most of the pecorino, reserving some to sprinkle over the top of the finished dish.

Duck, lime and broad bean soup
for eight

Duck is often thought of as a winter food and that's when you generally see it on menus around town, but I find a well-flavoured duck broth balanced with wonderful fresh broad beans a great spring-time dish.

This recipe calls for a whole duck for neatness alone (no leftover bits) but it is perfectly suited to whatever cut you have, such as breast or legs (however, you get the best results when cooking on the bone). Cooking the duck in the oven is preferable to on the stove as it's a gentle cooking method that doesn't let the broth reduce too much, so you'll end up with a nice, light flavour.

For the duck broth
2.25 kg (5 lb) whole duck (Use the neck, wings, everything. If the head is attached
    even better, but you will want to rinse out the mouth and throat cavity really well.)
3 stalks of celery (you may need to trim these to fit into the dish)
1 leek, split and rinsed free of dirt
1 onion, peeled but left whole
1 carrot, peeled but left whole
1 bunch of thyme
1 clove of garlic
peel and juice of 1 lime, peel cut into strips
salt and ground black pepper

Preheat your oven to 170°C (325°F/Gas 3). Remove the innards from the duck and pat the duck dry, making sure that the cavity is free of blood. Put the duck and vegetables, thyme, garlic, lime peel, lime juice, salt and pepper in a large casserole dish (approximately 4.5 litres/156 fl oz/18-cup capacity) that has a tight-fitting lid. Add enough water that the duck and vegetables are submerged to prevent them from drying out. Cook the duck in the oven for about 2 hours, or until the flesh is just starting to fall away from the bone. Check it a couple of times during the cooking process to make sure that everything is covered with liquid. Add more water if necessary.

If you are using a whole duck, there will be a layer of fat sitting on top of your broth. As gently as you can, ladle this off; if you are precious about your duck fat, this can be clarified and kept to use later—but for now its job is done as we want a clean, light duck soup.

Let everything cool just enough so you can handle the duck, then carefully lift out the duck, reserving the flavoured broth. Put the duck on a chopping board and remove all of the meat, throwing away any skin, fat and bone. As you are removing the meat, pull it apart into bite-sized pieces and place these in a clean saucepan. Strain the duck broth over the top. Bring up to a simmer over a high heat and skim once more. Taste for seasoning.

For the broad bean and celery salad

3 stalks of celery
600 g (1 lb 5 oz) broad (fava) beans in the pod
a few sprigs of chervil, coarsely chopped

While the duck is in the oven, you want to prepare your salad. To do this peel the veins out of your celery, cut in half lengthways, then slice crossways on the diagonal into diamond shapes. Blanch the celery diamonds in salted water for about 3 minutes or until just tender, then rinse under a cold tap to cool.

For the broad beans, remove the beans from the pod, then blanch the beans in hot water for about 1 1/2 minutes. Run them under a cold tap; once they are cool, gently squeeze them to pop the bean out of the pale green skin. Combine the broad beans, celery and chervil.

For serving

a tiny drizzle of good grassy extra virgin olive oil
a squeeze of lime juice

Place a scattering of the celery and broad bean salad into the bottom of your soup bowls. Ladle on some of the hot duck broth, making sure to get some of the meat, then drizzle on a tiny amount of your olive oil and a little squeeze of lime juice.

Seared scallops with steamed artichoke butter

Allow as many scallops in their shell as you want for each person. For each scallop you will need about 1 teaspoon of butter. This recipe depends on how much artichoke purée you will yield from your artichoke—don't stress if you end up with too much; just put it into the fridge and use at a later date—it will keep quite well for 2 to 3 weeks. If there isn't quite enough, just apply it a little more sparingly to each scallop. You should end up with enough butter to cover three to four dozen scallops. If fresh artichokes are out of season, you can use 120 g (4¼ oz/heaped ½ cup) drained good-quality artichokes in olive oil.

For the steamed artichoke butter
4 artichokes
1 lemon
a pinch of salt and ground black pepper
a dash of honey
about 250 g (9 oz) butter

Put the artichokes in a steamer basket over a saucepan of simmering water until tender when pierced with a knife. For large artichokes you'll need 25–30 minutes. Allow to cool completely. Keep removing the leaves of the artichoke until you reach the yellow, tender leaves. Place an artichoke on its side; you should be able to see where the leaves finish and the heart begins. Using a sharp serrated knife cut off the leaves. Pick up the artichoke and place it in the palm of your hand with the stem pointing towards your wrist. Working carefully, use a sharp paring knife or small vegetable knife to trim away the dark green exterior of the artichoke. Cut the stem about 2 cm (3/4 in) down from the base of the heart. Using a spoon, scrape out all of the spiky 'choke' from the centre of the heart. Rinse under cold water, then rub the heart well with a piece of cut lemon to stop it from turning brown. Repeat with the other artichokes.

Using a fork mash the artichoke heart into a bowl. Grate over a little lemon peel, then add a pinch of salt and a dash of honey. In a separate bowl whisk about the same amount of butter as you have artichoke purée and keep mixing until it is creamed. Add the butter to the artichoke purée and whisk until well combined. Taste for seasoning.

For the scallops
scallops in the shell
vegetable oil, optional

If you are cooking a lot of scallops, place a dollop (about 1 heaped teaspoon) of steamed artichoke butter on each scallop and place under a very hot grill (broiler). They will take no more than 2 minutes to cook.

Another method is to fry the scallops, but this works best if you are only cooking a few. Remove them from their shells, reserving the shells, and place into a bowl, then drizzle with a little oil. Heat a frying pan until very hot and start adding the scallops—you need to work very quickly as timing is critical. When the scallops are golden on the bottom, add a generous dollop of the butter to the pan. When the butter starts to melt, turn the scallops over. Be sure to scoop some butter over each scallop. Lift each scallop onto a shell and spoon over some of the butter, adding more butter to the pan if needed. Serve immediately.

Sardines with fresh bean salad
for four as a light lunch

The morning of writing this recipe I walked through the cool room of my supplier to see what was fresh. Use the same principle when you make this salad—buy whatever fresh beans look best on the day. I had a selection of juicy, yellow butterbeans; thick crunchy roman beans; the haricot vert were a little marked so I left them and instead used delicate baby green beans, broad beans, sugar snap peas and snow peas.

For the green bean salad
250 g (9 oz) yellow butterbeans (Lima beans)
150 g (5^{1}/2 oz) baby green beans
150 g (5^{1}/2 oz) roman beans
500 g (1 lb 2 oz) broad (fava) beans in the pod
100 g (3^{1}/2 oz) sugar snap peas
100 g (3^{1}/2 oz) snow peas (mangetout)
one batch of tomato dressing (Basics)
a few torn basil leaves

For the butterbeans and baby green beans, I like to pinch the stem off but leave the tail attached. Use a knife to 'grab' the top of the roman beans and pull out the vein, then repeat on the other end. Cut into 1 cm (^{1}/2 in) long diamonds. Remove the broad beans from the pod. Using a knife, grab the stem of the sugar snap peas and the snow peas and pull off the vein and repeat for the other side. I like to julienne the snow peas and cut the sugar snaps in half lengthways.

As each of the beans cooks at different rates, I recommend cooking them separately, then removing with a slotted spoon and rapidly cooling under cold water. You can use the same pot of water to cook all the beans, making sure to keep it on the boil. Cook the broad beans last as they will discolour your water. Cook the butterbeans for 4 minutes, the baby beans for 2–3 minutes, the roman beans for 5–6 minutes and the broad beans for no more than 2 minutes. Once the broad beans are cooked, cool, then squeeze each one out of the pale green skin to reveal the brilliant green bean. Leave the sugar snap peas and snow peas raw. Combine all of the beans in the bowl with the tomato dressing and torn basil and leave it to sit for a couple of minutes while you cook the sardines.

For the grilled sardines
12 sardine fillets, butterflied
4 tablespoons tomato base (Basics) or tomato paste (concentrated purée)

Brush the sardines with a little of the tomato base, then cook, skin side up, under a very hot grill (broiler) for 5 minutes or cook on a hot barbecue, skin side down, for 3–4 minutes.

For serving
a scattering of herbed breadcrumbs (Basics)

Arrange the salad on four plates and then top with the cooked sardines. Scatter with the breadcrumbs.

Poached duck breast in green peppercorns and gewürztraminer with salad for four to six

This is a clean and fresh duck dish, perfect for a hot day when you want something satisfying.

You can adjust the amount of peppercorns to suit yourself—I like this dish with a peppery bite so if you have a sensitive palate reduce the amount of peppercorns. If you can't get fresh peppercorns you can use 25 g (1 oz) dried peppercorns instead.

For the poached duck breast and dressing
4 good-sized duck breasts (about 120 g/4¼ oz), skin on
300 ml (10½ fl oz) gewürztraminer or medium-bodied white wine
300 ml (10½ fl oz) duck or chicken stock (Basics)
70 g (2½ oz) fresh green peppercorns (or 25 g/1 oz dried peppercorns)
100 ml (3½ fl oz) extra virgin olive oil

In a hot frying pan, seal the duck breasts starting skin side down—all you want is a nice golden colour, then flip them over and quickly seal the flesh side.

Pour the gewürztraminer and stock into a saucepan that is wide enough to fit the duck breasts side by side. Add the peppercorns. Bring to a gentle simmer, then gently add the duck breasts and poach for about 15 minutes—this should give you slightly pink flesh.

When the duck is cooked to your liking, remove it from the poaching liquid and keep boiling the broth until it is reduced to a glaze—you should end up with about 150 ml (5 fl oz). Remove the pan from the heat and, while still warm, whisk in the oil. This is the dressing for the salad.

For the salad
100 g (3½ oz) peas in the pod
2 heads of celery
2 artichokes
a wedge of lemon
4 radishes
100 g (3½ oz) sugar snap peas, coarsely chopped
100 g (3½ oz) pickled vegetables (either bought ones or home-made from page 12)
1 bunch of chervil, coarsely chopped

Pod your peas, then blanch them in salted water for about 3 minutes until they are tender and sweet. Rinse under cold running water to stop the cooking process.

Remove all of the dark green outside stems of the celery; don't throw these away as they are still great to eat but it is the celery heart that is better suited for this salad (celery hearts are the small pale green insides of the celery).

Take the artichokes and start removing the outer leaves, one at a time. Keep going until you reach the yellow, tender leaves. Place one artichoke on its side; you should be able to see where the leaves finish and the heart begins. Using a sharp, serrated knife cut off the leaves. Pick up the artichoke and place it in the palm of your hand with the stem pointing towards your wrist. Working carefully, use a sharp paring knife or small vegetable knife to trim away the dark green exterior of the artichoke. Cut the stem about 2 cm (3/4 in) down from the base of the heart. Using a spoon, scrape out all of the spiky 'choke' from the centre of the artichoke heart. Rinse under cold water and then rub the heart well with a piece of cut lemon to stop the artichoke from turning brown. Repeat with the other artichoke.

Wash your radishes well, but leave on some of the stem—these are useful to hold on to as you slice your radish.

Using a mandolin or a sharp knife and a keen eye, slice the celery, raw artichoke hearts and radish as thinly as you can, then place in a bowl with the peas, sugar snap peas, pickled vegetables, chervil and about two-thirds of your dressing. Gently toss together.

For serving
Divide the salad among your plates. Slice the duck thinly and layer the strips over the top of the salad, then drizzle with the remaining dressing.

Summer and holidays

This season is all about cooking for a group
while keeping things simple and light.

Fresh tomato salad
for four

This is how you make a really great tomato salad. Go to the market and look for the best tomato you can buy. There are a few things to look for but I honestly believe that deep down in our brain there lurks the food gland, and the job of this gland is to help guide us towards the best possible produce. Trust your senses. Use your eyes—avoid damaged, split or wrinkled skin; ask yourself if the colour is good (though be aware that not all varieties depend on a deep red colour; if you are unsure, ask your grocer). Use your sense of touch—don't poke your finger into every tomato you see, but don't hesitate to pick them up and feel them for ripeness. Use your sense of smell—do the tomatoes smell nice? And, when you can, use your taste buds—I am lucky to be in the position where I buy a lot of fresh produce, so a walk around my suppliers' stores to taste everything is essential. But I don't think you should feel shy about asking your local grocer if you could please taste something; the worst thing they can do is say no.

There is one more sense to employ, and that is common sense. Ask where the tomatoes came from; I guarantee that almost without exception, when tomatoes are in season the best tomatoes are ones that are grown locally rather than interstate or overseas. Ripened naturally is better than picked green and ripened on trays; and organic is generally better. Don't fall into the trap of buying carefully designed plastic trays of perfect looking (and really expensive) tomatoes—anyone who has grown a tomato would agree that size and shape are not necessarily guaranteed, and why appearance has become the most important characteristic of produce is completely beyond me. Hands up anyone who has gone to their shop and said 'I can't buy those tomatoes, they are not identical to each other'? It is interesting how companies make us believe that's what we want! Not me. I want flavour pure and simple.

This is a very simple recipe for a great tomato salad. Right now this is my favourite, but it may change next year—I may prefer different vinegar, or a different tomato—but right now, this is me…

For the dressing
110 g (3³/₄ oz/¹/₂ cup) sugar
1 clove of garlic, crushed
80 ml (2¹/₂ fl oz/¹/₃ cup) aged red wine vinegar
1 sprig of thyme, leaves only
125 ml (4 fl oz/¹/₂ cup) extra virgin olive oil
salt and ground black pepper

Put the sugar in a clean, dry saucepan. Place over a high heat and stir gently until it has formed a pale caramel, then remove from the heat and add the rest of the ingredients while the sugar is still hot—please be careful here, it will spit all over the place for a second or two. The sugar will not instantly dissolve and it may form a clump; if so, don't worry, most of it will dissolve in a few minutes, just stir from time to time. Allow to cool completely. This will keep for ages, so you can easily make double the recipe and keep some for another day.

For the salad
1 kg (2 lb 4 oz) perfectly ripe, tasty ox-heart or beefsteak tomatoes
salt and ground black pepper
1 tablespoon dried oregano

Chop the tomatoes, then put them in a large bowl. Season with salt and pepper and sprinkle with the oregano. Pour on the dressing, let it sit for a few minutes, then serve with a piece of bread and a glass of semillon—perfect.

Pickled and spiced cherries
enough for your leg of ham

For the best results here you need to have patience, which I find to be the most difficult thing. I get really excited when the cherry season starts and Jamie, my produce supplier, gets a little frustrated about my need for a constant cherry update. Are they any good? What size are they? How much are they per box? When I feel they are perfect, usually about 5 to 7 weeks after the first box goes on sale, I start to pickle as many as I can.

There is a nice annual tradition at my local vegetable markets to auction off the first box of cherries of the season and donate the proceeds to charity—last year it went for about $50 000.

Fills a 2.5 litre (87 fl oz/10-cup) jar

1 kg (2 lb 4 oz) cherries, left intact, with the stems on
750 ml (26 fl oz/3 cups) red wine vinegar
500 g (1 lb 2 oz/2¾ cups) soft brown sugar
6 cloves
6 juniper berries
4 allspice berries
1 star anise
the peel and juice of 1 lemon, peel cut into strips
1 stick of cinnamon
2 green cardamom pods

Pick through the cherries for any less than perfect ones, then give them a rinse. Put all the other ingredients in a large saucepan and bring to the boil. Boil for about 5 minutes, then add your cherries and cook for a further 5 minutes before removing the pan from the heat. Allow to sit overnight before transferring everything into sterilized jars. These will keep for months.

Glazed leg of ham
for the family

In my neck of the woods Christmas is smack bang in the middle of summer and for me Christmas isn't Christmas without a leg of ham. In my family it is considered a complete failure of the festive season if there is not still some leftover ham, hidden under a tea towel until at least January 14th. In fact, by then you must have had fried ham and eggs at least twice, eaten half a dozen ham and cheddar sandwiches, made a couple of ham pizzas, come home late and chewed on the bone while drunk and still have mum in the background saying 'I wish you lot would finish this ham so I can make soup!'.

This ham has a good glaze that I am sure that you will enjoy whether at Christmas or any other time of year. The ham will easily serve 14 people at one sitting with some left over for a great soup.

8 or 9 kg (18 lb or 20 lb 4 oz) leg of ham, bone in
2 teaspoons black peppercorns
2 juniper berries
4 cloves
1 allspice berry
2 cm (3/4 in) piece of cinnamon
300 g (10^{1}/2 oz/1^{1}/3 cups) demerara sugar
100 g (3^{1}/2 oz/heaped ^{1}/3 cup) dijon mustard
300 ml (10^{1}/2 fl oz) apple juice

Take your ham and gently peel away the skin, making sure that you leave all the fat where it is. I will slap your hand if I catch you removing the fat before it is cooked—it has a job to do during the cooking process; you can take it off (if you must) after the ham has cooked and cooled.

Preheat your oven to 180°C (350°F/Gas 4). Gently toast your spices in a dry frying pan, then pound them together in your mortar and pestle. Mix this with the sugar.

Now it is time to get messy: use your hands to rub the entire ham in dijon mustard. Wash and dry your hands. Sit the ham on a wire rack in a roasting tin, then pat on your spiced sugar—some of it will fall off into the pan, which is fine. Pour in some water to keep the bottom of the pan from burning. Bake for about 20 minutes, then remove and baste with a little of the apple juice; repeat this process every 10 minutes, basting with the apple juice and pan juices, for about 1 hour or until you have a beautiful, fragrant ham with a lovely golden glaze. Allow to cool completely. You can keep the basting glaze as a sauce to serve with the ham.

To store your ham, do not cover with plastic wrap as this will cause your ham to sweat; instead use a tea towel, or even better, a pillowcase with 'Merry Christmas' or a picture of a smiling Santa on it. I like to serve my ham simply with just a potato salad and pickled and spiced cherries (page 51).

Whole poached salmon
for ten

To poach a salmon you really need only two things. The first, a fish. The second, a pan that will fit the fish comfortably—you do not want your fish to be bent in the pan, it must remain flat. The choice of poaching liquid is up to you—if you have a nice fresh fish stock use that, otherwise use the following poaching liquid. You can also salt bake the salmon (see page 97), allow it to cool and serve it the same way. One 3 kg (6 lb 12 oz) salmon will feed ten.

If you don't have the luxury of a large pan, you can easily refine this recipe to cook individual portions of salmon by poaching in the same liquid. A piece of fish that weighs 165 g (5 3/4 oz) will take 4 to 5 minutes when cooked on a gentle simmer. Or, if it is steamed it will take 5 to 6 minutes.

When serving the salmon, pick your favourite accompaniment from the opposite page.

For the poached salmon

7 litres (245 fl oz/28 cups) water
1 litre (35 fl oz/4 cups) dry white wine
1 1/2 bunches of flat-leaf (Italian) parsley
1 1/2 lemons, sliced
1 1/2 stalks of celery
1 1/2 onions, cut into quarters
plenty of salt and ground black pepper
3 kg (6 lb 12 oz) whole salmon that has been gutted and scaled
chopped herbs, optional

Place the water, wine, parsley, lemon, celery, onion and salt and pepper in a pot that is large enough to fit the fish without it being bent. Bring the poaching liquid to the boil and gently simmer for about 15 minutes, which is just long enough to blend all the flavours together.

Gently lower in the fish and ensure that it is completely covered. Do not let the liquid boil; just simmer very gently. A fish of this size will take around 20–22 minutes of cooking. Take the pot off the heat and allow your fish to cool completely before removing from the poaching liquid.

If you have never served a whole fish like this before now, take a deep breath and relax; it is not difficult and there is nothing to worry about. Sure, it may seem a little daunting, but there really is nothing to it. Remove the fish from the poaching liquid and very carefully remove the skin from the top fillet. Using a rubber spatula in each hand (or simply your hands), very carefully start to lift the top fillet away from the fish, then place on a board. Now, take hold of the head and gently pull up and backwards towards the tail—you should be able to remove the head, spine, all the bones and the tail in one easy go, then any stray bones can be easily picked out. Using the spatulas again, remove the bottom fillet, leaving the skin behind. Place the bottom fillet on a serving platter, season the fillet with plenty of salt and pepper and, if you wish, sprinkle on some chopped herbs, such as parsley, chervil or chives. Place the top fillet back to present the 'whole' fish.

For the caper and egg dressing

6 hard-boiled eggs, removed from their shells and chopped

3 tablespoons salted capers, rinsed and chopped

3 tablespoons chopped flat-leaf (Italian) parsley

a squeeze of lemon juice

90 g (3¼ oz/⅓ cup) mayonnaise (Basics) or enough to bind

salt and ground black pepper

chopped herbs, optional

Combine all the ingredients and taste for seasoning. I like to leave my dressing fairly chunky and for it to have a good lemony bite. You can also add other herbs to this if you wish—if you have stuffed herbs inside the salmon, why not use the same for this dressing.

For the grilled asparagus with capsicum jam

12 thick spears of asparagus, trimmed

vegetable oil

capsicum (pepper) jam or chilli jam

extra virgin olive oil

Brush the asparagus with vegetable oil and cook on a really hot chargrill plate or barbecue hotplate for 2–4 minutes, depending on the thickness of the asparagus. Chop into 2 cm (¾ in) long pieces, dress with capsicum jam and drizzle with extra virgin olive oil.

For the salsa verde

1 bunch of flat-leaf (Italian) parsley

1 bunch of basil

1 bunch of chervil

1 bunch of chives

120 g (4¼ oz/1 cup) chopped pickled vegetables (either bought cornichons or
    home-made pickled cauliflower from page 12)

about 325 ml (11 fl oz) extra virgin olive oil

salt and ground black pepper

Use a very sharp knife to chop your herbs; resist the temptation to use a blender as it will bruise the herbs rather than chop them. I prefer mine to be coarsely chopped as you can then pick up the individual flavours of the herbs. Put all the herbs and the pickled vegetables in a bowl and then stir in your olive oil until the salsa verde is just wet enough to slide off your spoon; finish by tasting and adding salt and pepper as required. Best served as soon as it is made, but it will easily keep for a few days in the fridge.

For serving

Serve the salmon with one of the above accompaniments or with pickled vegetables (page 12) and some fresh radish, perhaps with a wedge of lemon.

Panzanella
for four

I am all for taking a classic dish and tweaking it in new ways; in fact I get a lot of inspiration from the old classics. My only complaint about people doing this is when they don't stick to the basic rules of what a dish is about. Now, I'm not saying that this is the best recipe for panzanella ever—I would never be that arrogant (at least not in the public domain). But it does bring to your attention what panzanella is all about: perfectly ripe tomatoes and the best-quality sourdough left to go very stale. If your tomatoes aren't particularly ripe and your bread is too fresh, then make yourself a nice toasted sandwich with a good piece of cheese and a delicious chutney.

This recipe uses ox-heart tomatoes, which are my favourite for panzanella, but you can substitute other types, such as beefsteak. Simply remember to use juicy, ripe tomatoes that taste good and are more than just red and shiny—if in doubt always buy locally grown tomatoes.

I usually start stockpiling my sourdough at the start of spring, taking advantage of any sunshine I can. I rip the inside of sourdough loaves into bite-sized pieces, spread them out onto wire racks and leave them in direct sunshine until they have become completely dry (this may take 2 to 4 days depending on the weather). Only then can they be stored in airtight containers—if you try to store bread that is not completely dry you run the risk of mould appearing and ruining your hoard. Another approach is to take a loaf of bread that is a few days old, rip it into pieces and leave it to dry out—you can then store it until you are ready to make breadcrumbs (Basics), ribollita (page 78) or any other recipe that requires dry bread.

For this salad you need an equal volume of tomato to dry bread.

For the tomato dressing
3 large, perfectly ripe ox-heart tomatoes, coarsely chopped
2 anchovy fillets
45 ml (1½ fl oz) red wine vinegar (a nicely aged vinegar is preferable)
salt and ground black pepper
185 ml (6 fl oz/¾ cup) extra virgin olive oil (the best you've got in the cupboard)

Put the tomatoes, anchovies, vinegar and salt and pepper into a blender and purée—ox-heart tomatoes will purée to juice really easily. You should end up with about 350 ml (12 fl oz) of liquid. When the tomatoes have blended to a juice, strain off all of the solids, then whisk in the oil. Your dressing should be quite thin and not too oily. Taste the dressing and adjust the seasoning and vinegar as required. You'll be using a lot of dressing for each serve so you want the flavour to be generous but not too overpowering—think along the lines of a well-flavoured tomato juice.

For the salad

1 large red capsicum (pepper)
about 1 loaf of dry sourdough bread, ripped into bite-sized pieces and dried
4 perfectly ripe ox-heart tomatoes, coarsely chopped
a few basil leaves
a few flat-leaf (Italian) parsley leaves
some slivers of anchovy fillets, as many as you like
salt and ground black pepper
a chunk of parmesan cheese

Start by roasting your capsicum. Do this by placing it directly onto an open flame until the skin starts to blister and burn; keep moving the capsicum around to 'burn' it evenly all over. If you don't have a gas burner, the same results can be achieved under a really hot grill (broiler). Once this is done, put it in a small bowl and cover with plastic wrap and leave until cool. Once the capsicum is cool enough to handle, scrape off the skin, pull out the stem, rip the capsicum in half and scrape out the seeds and membrane. Rinse under a cold tap; there's no need to dry it.

Place the bread in a large bowl—you want to have an equal volume of bread to tomato. Add most of the dressing, then leave to sit for a minute, or about as long as it takes to pour four glasses of a nice dry Alsatian riesling (my weapon of choice for this dish).

Add your roughly chopped tomato, herbs, torn pieces of capsicum, anchovies, salt and pepper to the bowl. Gently toss the salad together and serve onto your plates. Splash on the remainder of the dressing and use a vegetable peeler to shave parmesan over the top.

Roasted scotch fillet with watercress and beetroot salad for six

Scotch fillet is a great roasting meat, but only if it is of exceptional quality and has been allowed to hang, otherwise it can be a little tough. If you are roasting it don't serve it too rare, you want the heat to penetrate right through the meat. Cook until about medium–rare and allow to rest for a long time (at least half of your cooking time). This recipe suits a hot day when you need to feed a lot of people but don't have much time on your hands.

To roast it perfectly, for every 1 kg (2 lb 4 oz) of meat, cook in a preheated oven at 240°C (475°F/Gas 8) for 20 minutes. Then turn the oven down to 220°C (425°F/Gas 7) and cook for time below to get the desired result.

Rare: 15–20 minutes

Medium–rare: 25–30 minutes

Medium: 35–45 minutes

Medium–well done: 50–60 minutes

Well done (but please don't): 70 minutes and over

Remember to allow your meat to rest for anywhere up to half of the total cooking time. A couple of things to keep in mind. You can always cook rare meat for longer but you can't cook overcooked meat less! And, if you are cooking for a group, offer well done cuts from the outside and rarer cuts from the middle.

For the scotch fillet
salt and ground black pepper
1 kg (2 lb 4 oz) whole piece of scotch fillet
1 large onion, thinly sliced
2 cloves of garlic, thinly sliced
1 stalk of rosemary, leaves only

Preheat your oven to 240°C (475°F/Gas 8). Start by seasoning the beef well, then seal it all over in a hot frying pan until really well coloured. Remove the meat from the pan and put it in a large bowl.

Add the onion, garlic and rosemary to the bowl and squash and roll the onion onto the meat. Now place the beef along with the onion in a roasting tin and put it in the oven for 20 minutes. Turn the oven down to 220°C (425°F/Gas 7) and cook for a further 25–30 minutes for medium–rare or for as long as suits you. The trick is to keep turning your meat every few minutes to ensure even cooking and to caramelize the onion onto the outside of your beef.

When cooked to how you like (I recommend medium–rare to medium–well done) take out of the oven and allow to rest, reserving any cooking juices and the onion. Now, because of the nature of this dish, the beef does not need to be piping hot so this will give you plenty of time to make the salad and the dressing.

For the dressing

100 ml (3¹/2 fl oz) red wine vinegar
1 tablespoon wholegrain mustard
150 ml (5 fl oz) extra virgin olive oil
salt and ground black pepper

To make the dressing, pour off the roasting juices from the roasting tin into a small saucepan, place over a gentle heat and allow to reduce until almost a glaze. Remove from the heat and whisk in the vinegar, mustard and oil. Season with salt and pepper.

For the salad

6 kipfler (fingerling) potatoes
6 baby beetroot (beets) with their leaves
1 bunch of watercress, picked from the stem
1 avocado, chopped
a few dried tomatoes (You can make these yourself by cutting roma/plum tomatoes in
    half, placing on a rack and putting into your oven with just the pilot light on (or
    into a very low oven) overnight. Repeat the following night if not dry enough.)

Boil the potatoes in salted water for 5–10 minutes, until tender—the time needed will depend on the size of your potatoes. Drain, then slice into 5 mm (1/4 in) thick slices.

If you're worried about staining your hands when working with beetroot, it's a good idea to wear gloves. Remove the stems from the beetroots, keeping the leaves aside. Scrub the beetroots well. Pour most of the dressing into a large bowl. Using a mandolin or a sharp knife thinly slice the beetroots and add to the dressing, then add the beetroot leaves and allow to sit for a moment.

Add the watercress, sliced potato, pieces of avocado, dry tomatoes and the onion that was roasted on the beef and gently fold the salad to mix the dressing and ingredients evenly.

For serving

Slice your meat neatly and thinly. Serve by putting down a couple of thin slices of beef on a plate, then make a stack with alternating layers of salad and beef—you can either have two or three layers. To finish, drizzle with the remainder of the dressing.

Danks Street prawn cocktail
for six

You'll need a mouli for this recipe—it is the best thing to 'squeeze' the flavour out of the prawn shells. It is a great piece of equipment that every well-equipped kitchen needs.

For the prawns
a handful of good-quality salt (I like sel gris from France or pink salt from the Murray
     Basin in Victoria)
about 1 kg (2 lb 4 oz) large raw prawns (shrimp)
iced water

Bring a large saucepan of water to the boil and add the salt. Boil the prawns for as little time as you can—large prawns will take 3–5 minutes. Plunge the prawns into iced water until completely chilled. Clean the prawns by removing the head and peeling the shell away from the body, but leave the tail on; you may wish to devein them. Keep all the heads and shells for the sauce.

For the cocktail sauce
50 g (1³/₄ oz) butter
a few sprigs of thyme
2 cloves of garlic
1 strip of orange peel
1 tablespoon orange juice
3 ripe tomatoes, chopped
80 ml (2¹/₂ fl oz/¹/₃ cup) brandy
1 large red chilli, split and seeded
125 g (4¹/₂ oz/¹/₂ cup) mayonnaise (Basics)
salt and ground black pepper

In a large saucepan melt the butter, then add your reserved prawn heads and shells, the thyme and garlic. Cook this until the butter and prawns brown slightly, then add all of the remaining ingredients except the mayonnaise. Turn down the heat of your pan so everything stews nice and slowly. After 15–20 minutes of cooking and occasional stirring, your mixture should start to get a little dry, but if it is too dry add a little water—you want your mixture to look juicy but not too wet.

Now take everything and push as much as you can through a mouli to extract a concentrated paste. Allow to cool slightly then mix this paste through the mayonnaise. Taste and adjust the seasoning—you are looking for a nice and powerful, prawnie cocktail sauce with just a hint of chilli.

For serving
iceberg lettuce
6 lemon wedges

To serve, cut a big fat wedge of iceberg lettuce, pile your prawns on top of that, then add a dollop of the cocktail sauce. Serve with lemon wedges.

Pickled coleslaw
for eight as an accompaniment

In my part of the world coleslaw conjures images of limp cabbage in a watery, gloopy mayonnaise on an all-you-can-eat buffet. But Michael Klausen, a very dear friend and an inspirational cook, showed me this recipe and changed my world for the better even though I don't like eating cabbage as a salad and can't abide the flavour of green capsicum. I make this at home often, and crave it when I don't have any made in the fridge. It goes really well with ham, pork and roast chicken.

1 litre (35 fl oz/4 cups) cider vinegar
800 g (1 lb 12 oz/3^2/$_3$ cups) sugar
1 tablespoon celery seeds
1 onion, finely diced
2 green capsicums (peppers), finely diced
800 ml (28 fl oz) water
1 large white cabbage, shredded
salt and ground black pepper

To make the brine, pour the vinegar into a large saucepan and add the sugar, celery seeds, onion and capsicum. Bring to the boil for 15 minutes then add the water.

You will need a non metallic container large enough to hold all of the ingredients. Start by scattering a layer of cabbage, salt and pepper in the base of the container and spoon on some of the brine. Then add some more cabbage, salt, pepper and brine. Keep going until everything is used—you will probably have to really push the cabbage down towards the end. You want to place a weight on top of the cabbage to make sure that it stays immersed; I normally use a dinner plate or tray.

Cover and allow everything to pickle for at least 24 hours at room temperature or 48 hours in the fridge. This will keep perfectly fine in your cupboard for a couple of weeks; it will last indefinitely in your fridge.

Slow-roasted pork shoulder
for eight to ten

Here is the thing about this recipe: it takes a long, slow cook so use this to your advantage; by that I mean if you are cooking this for a Sunday dinner at say 7 o'clock, pop it in the oven while you are preparing your lunch then take the rest of the day off. Or, if you have a really full day and can't get out of that dinner you promised put this in the oven and get on with your chores. I would recommend that the first time you do this, you pick a day that you'll be home during the whole cooking process as it is in the oven for such a long time, and temperatures do differ from oven to oven and you'll want to keep a close eye on it. When you do cook it again you'll have a better understanding of how this recipe will work in your oven and have the confidence to walk away and leave it.

2.7–3.25 kg (6 lb–7 lb 1 oz) whole pork shoulder (preferably one that has been allowed
   to hang for a day or so to allow the skin to dry out)
vegetable oil
salt
2 tablespoons fennel seeds
1 teaspoon chilli flakes
6 cloves of garlic, peeled
juice of 2 lemons
200 ml (7 fl oz) extra virgin olive oil

Preheat your oven to 200°C (400°F/Gas 6). To prepare the meat, pat it dry, then score the skin with a sharp knife, taking care not to cut into the flesh. Brush the pork with vegetable oil and rub a good amount of salt into the skin. Put the pork on a wire rack in a roasting tin that will be able to catch any juices. Cook in the oven until nicely coloured and the skin becomes crispy, this can take up to 1 hour. While that is happening make your paste.

Lightly toast the fennel seeds, then scoop them into a mortar and use the pestle to grind them with the chilli. Add the garlic and a little salt and keep grinding until it forms a paste. Slowly add your lemon juice and olive oil, mixing well.

Carefully remove the pork from the oven and reduce the temperature to 110°C (225°F/Gas 1/2). Brush the paste all over the pork. Pour a little water into the roasting tin to prevent the pan from burning. Return the pork to the oven.

Check your pork from time to time, adding a little more water to the tin if needed. You can tell when your pork is cooked when the meat starts to give from the bone when you push it with your finger—this will take between 5 and 6 hours.

I like to serve this meat with pickled coleslaw (page 65) and some boiled potatoes.

Boiled crab with lime butter
for four

Crab has some great memories for me but the strange thing is that I really do find it hard to put crab on the menu. The reason is that I find it difficult to spend time mucking around with such an incredible animal—I prefer to take the animal from its environment, acknowledge it for the amazingly unchanged creature it is, then respectfully kill it and consume it. I have this theory that the crab wouldn't mind going to such a worthy cause as my personal, yet humble, enjoyment.

Here are some of my best crab moments. My friend Ben and I fishing on the Oregon coastline, getting frustrated because every time we cast the fishing line we ended up with a great big crab on the end of our line. We threw three or four crabs back in frustration before we finally clicked—crabs are delicious, especially when cooked over a camp fire.

Catching some mud crabs with friends of mine, Rob and Julianne, on their island in the Yamba River on the coast of New South Wales. We then boiled them in sea water in a large tin over hot coals on the shoreline while in the eye of one of the most awe-inspiring electrical storms I have ever seen.

Swapping a pair of boots for a bucket of crab claws with a Mexican fisherman in San Quentin, then boiling them and serving with a simple lime butter.

This is the recipe we used on the beach in San Quentin, Baja California. We had one bowl, a campfire, and a cool box for a fridge (getting ice was a trek across a desert). So if we could make the recipe work there I am guessing that you should be able to pull it off anywhere. You can use mud crubs or blue swimmer crabs to make this recipe, but if you can get them, mud crabs are better.

For the lime butter
125 g (4¹/₂ oz) butter
3 limes
¹/₂ bunch of coriander (cilantro)
3 large red chillies (keep the seeds in if you like things hot)
a drizzle of honey
salt and ground black pepper

Soften the butter slightly and whisk it in a bowl until it is white and creamy.

Grate the lime peel, then squeeze the limes so you get all the juice. Chop all of the coriander except for the root. Remove the seeds and membrane from the chilli, then dice the flesh. Add all of the ingredients to the bowl with the butter and keep mixing together until really well incorporated. Taste for seasoning.

For the crab

2 x 600–800 g (1 lb 5 oz–1 lb 12 oz) whole live crabs (either mud crabs or blue
swimmer crabs)
sea water (if you happen to have it on hand) or water seasoned really well with
mineral salts or good sea salt
sea salt

Bring a large pot of water to a rapid boil—you need a large pot or the water temperature will drop too much when you add the crabs.

I prefer to kill crab by using a heavy knife, a keen eye and a firm hand—drive the tip of your knife into the top of the head, just above and in between the eyes, then cut all the way through in one swift movement; this will kill the crab instantly. I prefer this to any slow killing such as freezing, drowning or just plain boiling as I believe it is better for the crab, better for the meat (as there is no time for shock to damage the flesh) and better for my conscience.

Cook the crab in the pot of rapidly boiling water for 12 minutes, then take out of the pot and rest for 6 minutes before serving.

For serving

coriander (cilantro) leaves

When you are ready to serve, remove the head by taking a firm grip on the crab, and with your other hand lift the side of the head up and away. Remove the gills (sometimes known as dead man's fingers); those are the brown-grey strips that lay on either side of the head. Using the back of a heavy knife or a hammer, crack the shell, but keep it intact, then place the crab in a large bowl and toss in some of the butter—allow the flavours to settle in. Sprinkle with coriander and serve while still hot with a dish of sea salt and the rest of the butter in a little pot.

A break in the heat

In autumn, things are just starting to cool down, new season root crops are fragrant and wonderful, and eating rich food feels good again.

Radicchio di treviso with fried onions, parmesan and balsamic for four

For simple meals like this salad, it's important to use great ingredients. So, with that in mind, use as good an extra virgin olive oil and balsamic vinegar as you can. Ideally you're looking for a thick, peppery olive oil and an aged vinegar—trust me, the flavour will be well worth the expense.

Also, don't use anything other than a mature parmesan that you shave off the block just before you need it—the flavour is not only wonderful but it will also give you a delicious 'crunchy' mouth feel. It is a sound investment in pleasure whereas pre-grated or pre-shaved stuff is just plain nasty and a waste of perfectly good milk. If you buy a good block of parmesan, keep it wrapped in baking paper, not plastic wrap. And don't waste any—when you're finished with the cheese, keep the rinds to use in your ribollita (page 78). To store them, put them in a jar and cover with olive oil. You'll find that you'll not only preserve your rinds this way, but you will end up with a delicious parmesan-infused oil that you can use in salad dressings.

There are a couple of different types of radicchio. Radicchio di verona is the rounder, looser type of radicchio and it can have slightly tougher leaves. Radicchio di treviso is narrower, tighter and has more tapered heads that I prefer for this dish because they are easier to eat and look better on the plate. Radicchio should be readily available throughout autumn but it can taste very bitter at other times of the year, so keep this as a strictly autumnal dish.

I would allow one small head of radicchio for each person. The recipe opposite will give you an idea of how much other ingredients you'll need to serve four people, but like many of my recipes it is written intentionally vague, so taste the final salad and adjust where needed. This salad is hearty and flavoursome and well suited to the cool change in the weather when autumn arrives.

Radicchio di treviso with fried onions, parmesan and balsamic

2 red onions
1 teaspoon salt
1 teaspoon sugar
vegetable oil, for deep-frying
4 heads of radicchio di treviso
100 ml (3¹/₂ fl oz) thick, peppery extra virgin olive oil
80 ml (2¹/₂ fl oz/¹/₃ cup) aged balsamic vinegar
1 bunch of flat-leaf (Italian) parsley, coarsely chopped
black pepper
a block of mature parmesan cheese

Thinly slice the onions, then put them in a bowl. Season with the salt and sugar, toss together, then let it sit like this for a couple of hours. Squeeze out as much liquid from the onion as you can.

You'll need a heavy-based saucepan for the next step. Heat enough vegetable oil in the pan to deep-fry the onions, but don't overfill the pan because you are working with hot oil. As a general rule, only fill your pan one-third or one-half full of oil when deep-frying. Put the onion in the oil as it is warming up—don't wait for the oil to become hot. Cook the onion over a high heat, stirring often, making sure to keep an eye on it as it will do nothing for ages and then colour quickly towards the end. When it becomes a pale golden colour (it will continue to colour after you have removed it from the oil) work quickly and carefully to remove it with a slotted spoon and drain on crumpled paper towels. Gently toss the onion a couple of times to ensure the pieces don't clump together. When the onion is completely cool taste it for seasoning and add more salt or sugar accordingly.

Take the radicchio and remove and discard the thicker outside leaves, then cut in half lengthways, shred finely and put in a large bowl, trying to keep it all together and tidy. If it comes apart it doesn't matter too much. Drizzle on your olive oil, splash in your vinegar and sprinkle on the onion and parsley. Grind in some black pepper and, using a vegetable peeler, shave in a generous amount of parmesan. Instead of tossing your salad, gently 'roll' it with your hands, this will incorporate all of the ingredients but will keep it tidy. Taste your salad and make adjustments where needed. To serve, grab a 'bundle' of the finished salad and place it next to a wedge of good bread. Shave a little more parmesan over the top to finish.

Leek polenta with asparagus
for four

Polenta is often seen in restaurants and cafés in the form of a wedge or a block. What you don't realize is that when the polenta is being made the chef has gorged himself on the wonderful, creamy, soft polenta before pouring it into a pan and letting it set. At Danks Street Depot, we cook our polenta to order to ensure that the end result is fresh, light, creamy and delicious, like in this recipe.

For the leek polenta
6–7 leeks
1 clove of garlic, crushed
800 ml–1 litre (28–35 fl oz) milk
100 g (3¹/₂ oz/²/₃ cup) fine polenta

Remove the roots and the green parts of the leeks, then cut the leeks lengthways and rinse them to ensure they are completely free of dirt. Chop the clean white part of the leeks into 2 cm (³/4 in) pieces—you should have about 500 g (1 lb 2 oz). Put into a saucepan with the garlic and 800 ml (28 fl oz) of the milk and cook until the leek is very soft, about 8–10 minutes of simmering.

Using a wooden spoon, vigorously stir in the polenta. Keep stirring and cooking for about 15 minutes. If your polenta starts to become too dry, add the rest of the milk—you want a nice soft polenta, like runny porridge. While this is happening, cook and prepare the asparagus.

For the asparagus
12 spears of asparagus, trimmed
a splash of red wine dressing (Basics)
a great big pinch of freshly chopped herbs (parsley and chives work well)

About 10 minutes before you're ready to serve the polenta, cook the asparagus in a saucepan of boiling salted water. You'll know the asparagus is ready when it is tender but has no crunch when you bite into it. People often cook asparagus too little, which leads to asparagus that tastes a little acidic—perfectly cooked asparagus should be delicate, sweet and only slightly *al dente*. Put it into a bowl with a little red wine dressing and the freshly chopped herbs.

For serving
40 g (1¹/₂ oz) butter
60 g (2¹/₄ oz/scant ²/₃ cup) freshly grated parmesan cheese
salt and ground black pepper

When you are ready to serve everything, beat the butter and most of the parmesan into your polenta. Stir vigorously, then taste for seasoning. When you are completely happy that your polenta is rich and creamy and the asparagus is tender, pour your polenta onto plates, divide up your asparagus and put it on the polenta. Splash over the dressing and the herbs from the bowl, then top with some more parmesan.

Ribollita (Bread and bean soup) for four hungry people with leftovers

I really do hate throwing away flavour. I keep my parmesan rinds as well as any prosciutto and pancetta rinds, which is one of the reasons I love this soup—it is one of the best ways to utilize these flavoursome treasures. To keep parmesan rinds I place them into an airtight jar and cover with olive oil, which both flavours the oil for dressings and preserves the rinds themselves. To store prosciutto or pancetta rinds keep them in your fridge where they can breathe; don't cover them with plastic wrap or they will sweat and go mouldy, instead wrap them in a piece of baking paper. I find the egg tray on the fridge door is the best spot to store them; they will sit there comfortably for a couple of weeks at least.

This is a thick, hearty dish full of flavour best served to famished friends. It does require a little bit of work and a bit of planning to cook, which is why it is so important to cook more than you need as it really does taste better the next day. Just keep in mind that when you reheat it the next day it will be thicker and may require a little more liquid.

It is a good idea to start with your beans and while they are cooking prepare the rest of your soup. The beans are wonderful by themselves or as a side dish for anything from barbecued lamb shoulder to steamed blue eye cod.

For the beans

150 g (5½ oz) fresh shelled borlotti (cranberry) beans (Depending on the beans, you'll need 200–350 g/7–12 oz fresh borlotti beans in the pod. If you are using dried beans, soak 135 g/4¾ oz beans for 24 hours.)
2 overripe tomatoes
2 cloves of garlic, peeled
1 bay leaf
a few sprigs of thyme
a splash of parmesan-infused olive oil or good-quality extra virgin olive oil

Preheat your oven to 200°C (400°F/Gas 6). Put the beans in a casserole dish and crush the tomatoes onto the beans with your hands. Add the rest of your ingredients and cover with cold water. Do not add salt yet as it can cause the beans to become coarse and chalky when cooked. Seal your dish with a lid or wrap well with foil and bake for 1½–2 hours. Start checking the beans after 1½ hours, you want them to be delicate and tender, almost creamy in texture. If you are cooking dried beans you may need to top up with more water and cook for about twice as long. Drain, reserving the cooking liquid and fishing out the bay leaf and sprigs of thyme.

For the soup
2 stalks of celery
1 bulb of fennel
4 carrots, peeled
1 red onion, peeled
a small head of celeriac, peeled
2 cloves of garlic, peeled
a few sprigs of thyme, chopped
a few stalks of rosemary, leaves only, chopped
a pinch of chilli flakes
a pinch of coriander seeds, crushed
salt and ground black pepper
100 ml (3^1/$_2$ fl oz) extra virgin olive oil
pancetta, prosciutto or parmesan cheese rinds
2 litres (70 fl oz/8 cups) water or any type of stock you have on hand
500 g (1 lb 2 oz) tomatoes, peeled and chopped
200 g (7 oz) cavolo nero or other bitter green leaf, coarsely chopped
200 g (7 oz) sourdough bread, torn (I prefer no crusts)
100 g (3^1/$_2$ oz) rocket (arugula), coarsely chopped
a drizzle of parmesan-infused oil

Coarsely chop the celery, fennel, carrots, onion, celeriac and garlic and put in a food processor with the herbs and spices. Blend until a very coarse paste forms; depending on the size of the bowl of the food processor you may need to do this in batches. Scoop into a bowl.

Since you've got the food processor out, give it quick a rinse, then blend one-third of the cooked beans with enough of the cooking liquid to form a paste and set to one side.

Heat a large heavy-based saucepan or stockpot over a high heat and add the olive oil and your vegetable mix. As your mixture starts to heat, it will release its liquid; keep cooking and stirring until the mixture becomes dry and starts to give off a sweet roasted vegetable aroma. It is fine to let the mixture colour slightly but be careful not to let it stick. Now add your pancetta, prosciutto or parmesan rinds, water and tomato and bring to the boil and let simmer for 30 minutes.

Add the cavolo nero, cooked borlotti beans, bean purée and sourdough. Cook for another 15 minutes, then just before you serve your soup throw in the chopped rocket and check your seasoning—don't be shy with the salt and pepper, this soup requires a good amount. Fish out your rinds, then pour the soup into your serving bowls and then add a final drizzle of your parmesan-infused oil. Serve with a wedge of bread with good butter.

Potato soup with gorgonzola
dolce latte for four as a light lunch

I owe this recipe to Lynne Tietzel who supplies, educates and inspires me with her wonderful cheeses—it is impossible not to get caught up in her enthusiasm. One thing people may not appreciate about cheese is that like any ingredient it has a point when it is 'ripe' or perfect; depending on the cheese this can take anywhere from 24 hours to 3 years. Once the cheese has reached the point of ripeness it really is a race against time to use it. One day Lynne popped into the café with some absolutely perfect gorgonzola dolce latte (gorgonzola dolce latte or gorgonzola dolce is the younger, softer and milder version; gorgonzola picante is older, sharper and stronger). It was the first really cold day of the year, and the idea of a hearty warming soup made me excited. This soup became so popular (one day we sold it to every second person who walked through the door) that *The Sydney Morning Herald* came in to film it being made so they could put the recipe on their web site. I believe this to be a testament to both the importance of good ingredients and cooking to suit the day—I wouldn't serve this in the middle of summer.

You need to take care with fantastic cheese—if you complicate the flavours you will lose the individual characteristics. The rule of thumb is to keep the flavours simple and complementary.

1 white onion
1 large all-purpose potato (such as desiree)
a knob of butter
salt and freshly ground black pepper
900 ml (31 fl oz) skim milk
at least 200 g (7 oz) gorgonzola dolce latte cheese
1 bunch of chives, chopped

Peel the onion and potato, then slice separately as thinly as possible—it is important for the texture of the soup. I like to use a mandolin; if you don't have one use a sharp knife, but take it slowly.

Put the onion, butter and salt in a heavy-based saucepan with a tight-fitting lid. Add the lid and put on a very gentle heat on the smallest hob. You want to take care to not let anything colour. When the onion has become very soft and juicy (about 13 minutes), add the potato and stir well. Put the lid back on and sweat the potato with the onions. Be careful when cooking the potato as it will stick to the bottom fairly easily. After about 10 minutes the potato should have started to soften; it still needs more cooking, so a little crunch is fine. Add the milk, stir well and bring up to the simmer, only allowing it to simmer for about 5 minutes at which time everything will be well cooked. If it takes longer it doesn't matter too much, but I find that the soup is lighter in texture the less the milk is cooked. Taste your soup for seasoning, then blend really well—a stick blender in the pot is easy or you can pour it into a blender, then pass through a fine sieve. If your soup is too thick it can be thinned down with some more milk.

To serve, put a blob of gorgonzola into each soup bowl and cover with loads of chopped chives. Reheat your soup if needed (but do not re-boil) and, if you have a stick blender, blend your soup well before serving, or you can achieve the same results by using a whisk—you are simply putting a bit of air into your soup. Now, pour your foamy, flavoursome, creamy soup over the cheese and serve immediately.

Duck confit for four, or for two with enough left over to make rillettes

The French term *confit* refers to food that is preserved in any number of ways. Sugars, syrups, alcohol and vinegars are used to preserve fruits and vegetables while fats are used to preserve meats such as pork, goose, turkey, rabbit and duck. You could fill a book on the subject of confit.

Duck confit is regarded as a French classic, but its origins go way back to the ancient Greeks and Romans. Today, chefs have science on their side and have worked out everything from the exact temperature of the fat to the pH level of the salted meat, but it really needn't be so complicated. Often restaurants only preserve the duck leg. I have put together this recipe because it is easy to do at home and uses one whole fatty duck so you have no bits left over.

I like to use Murray River golden salt for my confit because it has a coarse texture and will not dissolve completely, so it prevents the meat from becoming overly salty. Also, because it is refined inland it has a slightly mineral-rich flavour. It has two other very important qualities—it is pretty and easy to use. If you can't get it, any coarse salt such as flossy salt or kosher salt will do.

1 fat duck, about 2.5 kg (5 lb 8 oz) (if you have an obliging butcher, ask to have the
  duck cut into four pieces)
250 ml (9 fl oz/1 cup) water
120 g (4¹/4 oz/1 scant cup) coarse sea salt
2 juniper berries, crushed
2 cloves, crushed
4 bay leaves
1 bunch of thyme, leaves only
2 cloves of garlic, crushed
vegetable oil, optional

Collect all the fat you can from the cavity and any fat on the offal of the duck, then remove the skin from the whole duck including the neck—this will take a good bit of pulling and a little trimming with a sharp knife. Place the fat, skin and water in a heavy-based saucepan. Boil over a high heat and stir from time to time. After about 20 minutes you need to start watching the fat—it should be a milky, bubbly mass. As the water evaporates the fat will start to become clear and after 30–40 minutes the fat will become completely clear and golden. Remove from the heat and pass through a fine sieve. Refrigerate until needed.

If your duck is whole, cut it into four pieces. Start by removing the legs, leaving the thigh and drumstick together, then split the breast down the middle and chop away the bones on the leg side of the duck. Leave all of the meat on the bone. Mix the salt, spices, herbs and garlic together and sprinkle over the duck meat, cover with plastic wrap and leave to sit in the fridge overnight.

The next day, rinse the duck in plenty of cold water—do this over a sieve so that you are able to catch the spices and put them back onto the duck.

Put the duck along with its reserved coating of herbs and garlic in an ovenproof dish that is large enough to take the duck and duck fat but only come halfway up the side of the dish (a 3 litre/104 fl oz/12-cup dish will suffice).

Preheat your oven to 110°C (225°F/Gas 1/2). Melt your duck fat but don't let it get too hot. The temperature of the fat should be around 75–80°C (165–175°F). You can test this with a candy thermometer or by very carefully touching the fat—it should feel hot but not burn you. Pour the fat over your duck, making sure that the meat is completely submerged (you can cheat by topping up with vegetable oil if you don't quite have enough fat, but it is preferable to use pure duck fat). Once you have poured on the fat, cover it with a sheet of baking paper to ensure the duck is completely covered during the cooking process.

Put the duck in the oven. The confit is ready when a knife inserted into one of the legs reveals that the meat is tender all the way down to the bone—this will take about 21/2–3 hours.

Remove the duck and place it in a wide-mouthed 1.5 litre (52 fl oz/6-cup) sterilized ceramic pot, glass jar or container that you wish to store your confit in. Strain the fat into a clean saucepan, place on a high heat and boil until it has become clear again, then pour it over the duck until the duck is completely covered. Any extra fat can be kept in a sterilized jar in the fridge and used for cooking or for your next batch of confit. Allow to cool completely before covering. The duck meat, if covered correctly, will keep for at least 3–4 weeks in the fridge. Your confit is ready to serve straight away, but it is best if it is allowed to sit in the fridge for a few days. When you use the meat, keep the fat and re-use for the next batch of confit or to roast potatoes.

Duck confit is best eaten warm. To reheat it you can simply pull the duck out of the fat and place in a hot oven or under a hot grill (broiler) for a few minutes. Duck confit has a hearty flavour that goes well with braised cabbage, red wine, mustards and pickles. A really easy suggestion is to warm the duck then combine it with some crushed walnuts, rocket (arugula), shaved slices of pear and a splash of your favourite vinaigrette. Allow one piece of duck per person.

Confit is preserved meat, which means that there is danger of bacteria that can cause spoilage—don't worry as it is a very low risk if you make sure that all of your equipment and your hands are clean and dry and that your raw ingredients do not sit at room temperature any longer than necessary.

Duck rillettes
for eight to ten

Rillettes (pronounced ree-yeht) is best thought of as a coarse meat pâté. It is the big boy of duck dishes as it is extremely rich and is best enjoyed in small quantities on warm toast alongside some pickles or cornichons. I like to make it from the confit leg instead of the breast meat, which tends to make the rillettes pasty.

To make rillettes, you start by making confit (page 84) so you are effectively making two different dishes at the same time. By that I mean that if you preserve a whole duck you can store the breast meat for later use, then use the legs to make your rillettes. If you end up with slightly more or less meat than this recipe calls for, just adjust the fat and seasoning accordingly.

200 g (7 oz) duck confit meat (page 84), removed from the leg and allowed to come
    to room temperature
salt and ground black pepper
150 ml (5 fl oz) clarified duck fat (Basics), at room temperature

Temperature is the trick with this recipe—you want the fat and the meat to be coolish, but not so cool as to start to set when you start working the rillettes. Put the duck meat in a large, clean, dry bowl and, using a clean, dry, stiff spatula, start to mash the duck meat until completely shredded. You may need to single out some stubborn pieces and give them a bit of extra work. A sign of a well-made rillettes is that there are no pieces of duck, just a smooth pâté of meat. You need to keep mixing your meat for the duration of this process, which can take 30 minutes to an hour—you'll get a sore arm, but just think of it as burning off the calories before ingesting them!

When you are happy with the consistency of the meat, add your seasoning, then start to pour in the fat a dash at a time, you will need to mix in around 100 ml (3½ fl oz) or half fat to the amount of meat. When everything is well combined check the seasoning again; I prefer mine to have lots of salt and to be quite peppery, but that's up to you.

When you're completely happy put the rillettes into a very clean, dry 300 ml (10½ fl oz) ramekin, pot or jar and refrigerate to allow to set. Leave the remainder of the clarified duck fat at room temperature, then place in a large bowl and use a whisk to whip until creamy and white. Use a spatula and place a layer of the fat over your rillettes—this layer of fat can be scraped off before serving; its job is to preserve your rillettes. If unopened this will keep perfectly well in the refrigerator for at least 2–3 weeks even though it usually gets eaten well before then.

Pasta stuffed with roasted pumpkin with ox-heart tomato and pecorino cheese for six

This is a real fun-looking dish, hearty and bold. One thing to keep in mind here is that when you go to finish your pasta in the ox-heart tomato mixture you may think the sauce doesn't look quite right. But what happens is that the tomato will break down as the pasta heats up. The end result is a juicy looking pasta sauce that isn't too wet.

For the roasted pumpkin filling
1 small butternut pumpkin (squash), peeled and cut into large dice
2 cloves of garlic, sliced
a large pinch of chilli flakes
1 stalk of rosemary, leaves only
salt and pepper
a good dash of extra virgin olive oil

Preheat your oven to 200°C (400°F/Gas 6). Heat a roasting tin in the oven to get it nice and hot. Combine the pumpkin, garlic, chilli flakes, rosemary leaves and salt and pepper in a bowl with a good dash of extra virgin olive oil. Tip the pumpkin into the roasting tin, then put into the hot oven. You want to get a golden roasted colour on your pumpkin and to cook it until it is soft—this will take about 20 minutes. Allow the pumpkin mix to cool slightly, then transfer to a bowl and use a wooden spoon to mash the mixture until a coarse purée forms.

For the filled pasta shells
400 g (14 oz) lumaconi (or large macaroni, rigatoni or conchiglioni)
a dash of extra virgin olive oil

Boil the pasta in plenty of salted water for about 8 minutes until *al dente*, then strain it into a colander and give it a little shake, being sure to get off as much water as possible. Tip the pasta onto a tray, drizzle with a little oil and give a very gentle toss to lightly coat the pasta. Allow it to cool completely.

You now want to stuff your pasta shells with the pumpkin filling. To do this you can either use a spoon or a piping bag. Be gentle as the shells are now quite delicate—if you lose a couple don't worry too much as you should have plenty of pasta.

For the pecorino sauce
80 g (2³/4 oz/scant 1 cup) freshly grated pecorino cheese
125 g (4¹/2 oz/¹/2 cup) sheep's milk yoghurt
a dash of lemon juice
a tiny pinch of chilli flakes
salt and ground black pepper
cream (whipping) or milk, optional

Put the pecorino and yoghurt in a bowl and season with the lemon, chilli, salt and pepper. Combine everything together until you have a smooth paste. You are looking for a thick sauce, so you may need to adjust the consistency with a little cream or milk.

For serving

45 ml (1¹/2 fl oz) extra virgin olive oil

a few ligurian olives

2 large very ripe ox-heart or beefsteak tomatoes, chopped

1 bunch of basil

a wedge of pecorino cheese

Put the oil in a large frying pan, add the olives and place over a high heat; as the pan heats up the olives will begin to fry and their juices will start to come out—when this happens add the chopped tomatoes and allow them to heat through.

Add your filled pasta shells to the pan and turn down to a gentle heat. Use your eye to tell you how much moisture is required in the pan, this will depend largely on the tomatoes: you may need to add a little water to keep the pan moist, but not too much so the sauce is thin and watery. Put on the lid, then cook the pasta for 8–10 minutes, just long enough for the flavours to infuse and the pasta to heat up—you will need to gently stir from time to time to ensure everything heats evenly and make sure they don't stick.

Just before serving tear up the basil and toss it through the pasta. Transfer the pasta to your plates and finish with a dollop of the pecorino sauce. Use a vegetable peeler to shave shards of pecorino cheese over the top.

Family, food and friends

Serving delicious food to loved ones is the most rewarding thing a cook can do.

Roasted chicken, corn and stuffing sandwich for six

The popularity of something like this sandwich really humbles a chef—we can spend a lifetime trying to create the next most talked about recipe and then a simple chicken sandwich steals the limelight. At Danks Street Depot we sell a lot of these sandwiches for the simple reason that they are delicious. We use the best organically grown chickens we can find, the freshest, sweetest corn and great bread. You must use a good-quality chicken or you will not get a good-quality sandwich. Avoid at all cost a chemically pumped, hormone-bloated battery hen. If you buy an organic chicken or a reputable free-range chicken the little extra money will produce a great deal more pleasure.

Although you can easily substitute any of the components here for pre-made products, by doing everything yourself you will be eating about as good a chicken sandwich as you can get, other than buying it from me (wink-wink). Now, before you start thinking 'that's a lot of work for a sandwich' why not double this recipe and serve roasted chicken with roasted corn and stuffing. Bake a couple of potatoes and wilt down some spinach for a wonderful dinner, then you have everything on hand for scrumptious chicken sandwiches tomorrow!

For the stuffing
1/2 an onion, finely diced
2 cloves of garlic, crushed
50 g (1³/4 oz) butter
1 bunch of thyme, leaves only, finely chopped
1/4 loaf (approximately 300 g/10¹/2 oz) of stale, good-quality sourdough bread, crumbed (Basics)
2 eggs
salt and ground black pepper

Sauté the onion and garlic together in the butter, add the thyme and, when soft, mix in the breadcrumbs. Allow to cool, then while still in the pan, mix in the eggs and salt and pepper.

For the roasted corn
1 tablespoon extra virgin olive oil
50 g (1³/4 oz) butter
4 ears of corn, husks removed, kernels cut off with a sharp knife
1 clove of garlic, crushed
a few sprigs of thyme, leaves only
salt and ground black pepper

Preheat your oven to 180°C (350°F/Gas 4). Heat the oil in a frying pan over a medium heat, then add the butter so it starts to melt, then add the corn kernels, garlic, thyme, salt and pepper. Toss about until all well coated, put onto a roasting tray and into the oven for 10 minutes, or until golden. Allow to cool. Turn the heat up to 220°C (425°F/Gas 7).

For the roast chicken

1.4 kg (3 lb 2 oz) good-quality whole chicken
a knob of butter
salt and ground black pepper
about 185 g (6½ oz/¾ cup) mayonnaise (Basics)

Pat the chicken dry to remove any excess moisture inside and out. Fill the cavity with a handful or two of your stuffing, enough to fill the bird, keeping the rest for later. Rub the skin with a little butter, then season well with salt and pepper. Place in a roasting tin. Roast for around 35 minutes, then drop the heat to 160°C (315°F/Gas 2–3) and cook for a further 30 minutes. When cooked, remove the chicken from the oven, turn the chicken upside down so it is sitting breast side down and allow to cool—this will help keep the breast meat juicy.

When the chicken has cooled, remove the skin from the breast and slice it thinly (discard the skin from the legs as it tends to be too fatty). Shred the chicken meat. Put the skin and shredded meat into a bowl along with your stuffing and roasted corn kernels. In the roasting tin there should be some fat and juice—carefully strain off the fat, then tip the rest of the juices onto the chicken mixture. Add just enough mayonnaise to bind together.

For the sandwich

2 big handfuls of rocket (arugula)
45 ml (1½ fl oz) red wine dressing (Basics)
1 loaf of crusty white bread, cut into thick slices allowing 2 slices per person
about 2 tablespoons mayonnaise (Basics)

Start by tossing your rocket with the red wine dressing in a large bowl. Lay out the bread and spread some mayonnaise on each slice. On half of the bread place your chicken salad, then a mound of rocket, add a little seasoning and top with the other slice of bread.

Three salt-baked recipes

Cooking in a salt crust is good fun. After you have done it a couple of times and got the hang of it, you'll find yourself salt-baking almost anything. I have found that you get the best results by making a salt dough instead of simply using a layer of salt, plus the cooked salt dough looks very impressive. A salt dough also has one other advantage over a salt crust, which is that you effectively create a small portable oven around your food. This means that you can start the cooking process at home, then the heat inside the dough will finish the cooking while you're on the way to your picnic or friend's house. Both easy and impressive.

Use coarse flossy or kosher salt rather than table salt; table salt dissolves quickly and can make your meat taste salty. Fancy sea salts are better used elsewhere as for this process it is a waste. Baking in a salt dough works best for whole cuts of meat (for example, leg, shoulder, veal rump) or for whole animals (for example, fish, chicken, duck). I wouldn't cook anything under 600 g (1 lb 5 oz) in a salt dough as you want the crust to have time to cook but you don't want to overcook your meat. Also, you'll find that if you cook a small portion of meat in a salt dough it will become so salty as to be inedible.

Preheat your oven to somewhere around 190–220°C (375–425°F/Gas 5–7) as a general rule, or as specified in the recipe. Make sure to cover the meat completely and check that the crust is intact—patch any little holes that may appear. When you cook, the crust should go nice and brown and bake as hard as clay. Do not eat the salt crust— you may have to try it at least once because it does look lovely but you will want a spittoon on hand and plenty of drinking water. When you are ready to serve you will need to open your crust. Do this by using the heel of a large heavy chopping knife and hack into the dough near the base, working all the way around; you will then be creating a 'dish with a lid'. Take this to the table and remove the lid.

For the salt dough
1 kg (2 lb 4 oz) plain (all-purpose) flour
1 kg (2 lb 4 oz) flossy salt
about 550 ml (19 fl oz) water (enough to make the dough malleable)

In a large bowl, combine the flour and salt. Make a well in the middle and add most of the water. Don't add all the water—it is easier to add more water to a dry dough than to add more flour to a wet dough. What you are looking for is a firm yet malleable dough. Start to form a dough by kneading with your hands—this will take a bit of work. Once your dough is made, place it in a bowl and cover with plastic wrap; it will need to rest for about an hour. If you refrigerate your dough, remove it from the fridge and allow it to come to room temperature as this will be easier to roll.

Roll out your dough on a well-floured bench until about 5 mm (1/4 in) thick; you may want to do this in two pieces for ease. Place the dough on a baking tray.

For salt-baked salmon

3–3.5 kg (6 lb 8 oz–7 lb 10 oz) whole salmon that has been gutted and scaled
1½ quantities of the salt dough

If you would like to, you can fill the cavity. If so, I recommend using flavourings such as lemon, fennel, garlic, bay leaves and parsley. Wrap the salmon in dough, making sure it is completely covered. Cook at 200°C (400°F/Gas 6) for 45 minutes. Rest for 30 minutes before eating. Serve with salsa verde (page 55). Serves 8–12.

For salt-baked chicken

1.8–2 kg (4–4 lb 8 oz) whole organic chicken
1 quantity of the salt dough

Twist the wings of the chicken to sit under the bird and gently pull the legs away from the body slightly; now pat dry inside and out. If you want to stuff the cavity, use the squeezed blood orange and lemon peels from the dressing (see below) and a small head of fennel with the fronds attached (it's fine if the fronds stick out a bit).

Put the chicken, breast side down, onto the middle of your dough and wrap it completely, making sure that it is totally covered. Roll the chicken over so it sits breast side up. Cook at 190–200°C (375–400°F/ Gas 5–6) for 50 minutes to 1 hour. Rest for 30–40 minutes before eating. Serve with the dressing (below). Serves 4–6.

For salt-baked leg of lamb

1 tunnel-boned leg of lamb, shank left on (ask your butcher to do it for you), about
    1.4 kg (3 lb 2 oz) boned weight
1 quantity of the salt dough

Similarly to the salmon, there's no need to flavour the lamb but it's a nice touch to stuff the cavity left by the bone with herbs such as rosemary, thyme and garlic. Cover the lamb in the dough so there are no gaps. Cook at 200°C (400°F/Gas 6) for 55 minutes. Rest for 45 minutes before eating. Serve with the dressing (below). Serves 6–8.

For the dressing (for chicken and lamb)

2 tablespoons fennel seeds, toasted
1 clove of garlic, peeled
3 tablespoons sugar
1 tablespoon salt
juice of 1 blood orange and 2 lemons
a good dash of extra virgin olive oil

Grind the fennel seeds with a mortar and pestle, then add the garlic, sugar and salt and crush into a paste. Add the juice from the orange and lemons and the oil. Taste for seasoning—you want a good balance of salty/sweet/sour.

Lamb shoulder and cardamom curry
for four

I spent a short while working in a Indian restaurant in New Zealand, both as a waiter and in the kitchen. I was often mistaken for a 'nice Kashmiri boy' by our Indian customers and if I kept my mouth shut and smiled a lot they would tip well! This recipe was shown to me by a Danish chef and the flavour is stunning. I have made a few adjustments to the original by using ingredients and techniques taught to me by the Indian boys in the restaurant.

If you don't know what some of these ingredients are, it's about time to venture to your local Indian spice shop. Take this recipe with you and point out what you want; while you are there, buy a couple of other things that you have never seen before—have some fun! Don't forget to ask lots of questions; these little adventures are a great way to pick up secrets.

Start by making your curry base, this needs to be done at least 1 day in advance so you can marinate the lamb in it overnight. The base will keep for 2 weeks.

For the curry base
5 green cardamom pods
2 black cardamom pods (these look similar to, but are larger and uglier than, green cardamom pods and they have a sweeter and 'meatier' flavour)
1 teaspoon onion seeds or nigella seeds
1 teaspoon fenugreek seeds
$^1/_2$ teaspoon fennel seeds
$^1/_2$ teaspoon cumin seeds
150 g (5$^1/_2$ oz/1 scant cup) ghee
2 onions, finely diced
1 cm ($^1/_2$ in) piece of fresh ginger, grated
2 cm ($^3/_4$ in) piece of fresh turmeric, grated
2 cloves of garlic, grated
3 large red chillies, chopped with the seeds left in
2 bay leaves
$^1/_2$ teaspoon ground asafoetida (be careful with this spice, a little goes a long way—too much will ruin your curry)
1 tablespoon salt
60 g (2$^1/_4$ oz) jaggery, grated or pounded in a mortar and pestle
500 ml (17 fl oz/2 cups) malt vinegar

Use a mortar and pestle to roughly grind together the cardamom (both types) and the onion, fenugreek, fennel and cumin seeds.

Melt the ghee in a heavy-based saucepan over a high heat, then add the ground spices. Cook until they are golden or popping. Add the onion, ginger, turmeric, garlic, chilli, bay leaves, asafoetida and salt to the pan. Cook until the onion is nice and soft and a rich brown colour, about 5 minutes, stirring often as it will stick easily.

Turn down the heat, add the jaggery and vinegar and let everything cook down until you have a rich curry base; it will take about 20 minutes. Taste for seasoning; you want a powerful, hot curry base that is well balanced in flavour. Taste for salt (do you need to add more salt?), sour (add more vinegar?), sweet (add more jaggery?), heat (add more chilli?). Allow to cool.

For the lamb
1.3 kg (3 lb) lamb shoulder, bone in (leave the fat on—you need it)
500 ml (17 fl oz/2 cups) chicken stock (Basics)

Rub the lamb with the curry base (use it all), cover and let it sit in the fridge overnight.

Preheat your oven to 170°C (325°F/Gas 3). Place the lamb and all of the curry base in a roasting tin and cover to halfway up the shoulder with chicken stock, then put in the oven. The lamb will take about 3 hours to cook, but throughout the cooking process you need to keep topping up the liquid if it reduces too much; also, you'll need to keep turning the lamb—as one side darkens expose the other. If you get to the point where your lamb is well coloured all over, the sauce is rich but the lamb still needs a little more cooking, just cover it with foil for the remainder of the cooking time. As a guide, cook uncovered for 2 hours and covered for 1 hour or when it starts to get dark. The lamb is cooked when the flesh falls off the bone.

For the tahini dressing
2¹/₂ tablespoons tahini
30 ml (1 fl oz) lemon juice
45 ml (1¹/₂ fl oz) water
salt and ground black pepper
sugar, optional

Put the tahini in a bowl, then whisk in the lemon juice, water, salt and pepper. As soon as you start to incorporate liquid it will thicken—adjust the consistency with water until it resembles pouring cream. I really like the slightly bitter flavour it has, but if you prefer you can adjust with sugar.

For serving
250 g (9 oz/5 cups) baby English spinach leaves, picked and cleaned
confit tomato (Basics), optional
tempuring (Basics), optional

To serve, scatter some baby spinach leaves over a platter, rip off the meat and place on top of the spinach, then pour on the curry sauce. I then like to squash some confit tomato over the top, letting all the tomato juice incorporate with the curry. Now, drizzle with some tahini dressing and scatter some tempuring over the top. Serve alongside a big bowl of basmati rice.

Salted, spiced and roasted whole duck
for four, or two with leftovers

I like to call this recipe 'How to roast a duck and have time for your wife'. I came up with it when I wanted to cook something special for my wife on our third wedding anniversary. We were brand new parents (Charlie being only 3 months old) and were running a busy café, so time out was precious and I wanted to be sipping wine together in our candle-lit courtyard rather than slaving over a hot stove.

The duck was so delicious that we have it as a regular feature on the dinner menu, even doing special duck dinners with this being served as the main. This recipe has been adapted for the oven, but if you have a coal- or wood-fired barbecue, give it a go in there—the results are stunning.

The duck benefits greatly from being able to salt for at least 24 hours before cooking (tech speak, allowing for reverse osmosis). The beauty of this recipe is that it is almost impossible to stuff up; unlike chicken, which can become dry and tough with just the slightest overcooking, duck, with all that delicious juicy fat, is more forgiving.

You can alter the salt mix to suit yourself or the seasons and what you are serving with the duck. I like to use Murray River golden salt in the spice mix, but you can use any good-quality sea salt or mineral salt. That special anniversary night I simply cooked the duck in my kettle barbecue over coals with some potatoes and served a salad of beautiful ripe tomatoes (page 50) and lightly cured cucumbers (page 35).

For the spice mix
1 teaspoon black peppercorns
1/4 teaspoon pink peppercorns
1/4 teaspoon green peppercorns
4 juniper berries
1 allspice berry
1 bay leaf
3 1/2 teaspoons sea salt or mineral salt
a few sprigs of thyme, leaves only
finely grated peel of 1 lemon and 1 lime

To make the spice mix, pound together the peppercorns, juniper berries, allspice berry and bay leaf with a mortar and pestle; keep pounding until you have a rough powder. Add the salt and thyme and continue to pound, then add the grated lemon and lime peel and pound some more until all the ingredients are well incorporated and you have a beautiful spice mix.

For the duck

2.25 kg (5 lb) whole duck
as many bintje (yellow finn), kipfler (fingerling) or other waxy potatoes as you like

Take the duck and fold the neck flap under the carcass, then fold the wings under to fully expose the breast. Take the legs and give them a gentle tug (don't pull them off)—this 'opens' the bird up to the heat and flavour. With a sharp knife, lightly score the skin of the breast and leg but don't cut into the meat of the bird; think more along the lines of gently scratching through the skin, which will help the spice mix penetrate the duck. Now, rub the entire duck with the spice mix, being sure to get some inside the cavity as well. Place in a roasting tin to catch the juices that will come off the bird and place in the fridge, uncovered, for at least 24 hours but no longer than 48. Leaving the duck uncovered will allow the skin to dry out, which will give you nice crispy skin.

Preheat your oven to 200°C (400°F/Gas 6) and place your duck on a rack, then into a deep roasting tin. Cook for at least 1 1/2 hours. If you are roasting potatoes, cut them to size and place them under or around the duck after the duck has been on for 40 minutes, basting from time to time with the duck juices. The duck is cooked when clear juices run out when a knife is inserted into the leg joint; don't worry too much if the skin on the breast splits. When the duck is cooked allow it to rest, breast side down, for at least 20 minutes before serving.

For serving

To serve, simply take the duck to the table and carve off some breast and leg for each person. Serve with potatoes and, if you like, pour on some of the cooking juices. I like to serve it with pickled and spiced cherries (page 51) or cured cucumbers (page 35).

Cockie-leekie
for eight hungry people

This dish is as Scottish as bagpipes, haggis and blokes in skirts. It is a great feel-good family dish that always lasts for at least two meals and the name makes kids laugh. Could you ask for anything more? I like to add a little pearl barley to mine which is not quite sticking with tradition but I find that it provides a little more body. This recipe uses a boiling hen, which is preferable to chicken as it has a stronger flavour—a boiling hen is basically a tough old chicken that responds really well to long cooking to soften the meat. You should be able to order a 'boiler' from your butcher. If you can't get one, use a good-quality organic chicken that has been grown for flavour rather than size.

Brisket is the only cut of meat that I'll ever consider for cockie-leekie or any other slow-cooked or pot-roasted dish. It is also great salted or corned; or perfect for slicing thinly, seasoning and oiling and very quickly cooking on a hot barbecue and serving very rare. The golden rule with this piece of beef is to either cook it briefly and serve it rare, or cook it really slowly. The meat is sweet and fatty with a beautiful grainy texture —it is my favourite cut of beef.

500 g (1 lb 2 oz/2¼ cups) pitted prunes
165 g (5¾ oz / ¾ cup) pearl barley
1 kg (2 lb 4 oz) piece of brisket, cut in half
1.5 kg (3 lb 5 oz) leeks, the best white bits thinly sliced, the green bits tied together
   to flavour the stock
1 litre (35 fl oz/4 cups) chicken stock (Basics)
2 litres (70 fl oz/8 cups) water
2 teaspoons salt and a little ground black pepper
1.8 kg (4 lb) whole boiling hen

Cover the prunes with water and soak overnight. Cover the pearl barley in water and also soak overnight.

The next day strain, then rinse both the prunes and barley. In a pot large enough to also take the chicken later (you'll need one of about 4.5 litres/157 fl oz/18-cup capacity), put in the beef, tied leek ends, stock and water. Season with the salt and pepper. Bring the heat up but try not to let it boil, you want a nice gentle simmer. Skim off the grey bubbles as they rise but leave any fat on the surface of the broth. Fat carries flavour, so skimming off the fat at the early stage of cooking means that you are throwing away perfectly good flavour. If you maintain a gentle simmer that does not allow the fat to boil back into your broth you will have a perfectly clear and well-flavoured broth; you can skim it off at the end if you like.

After about 1 hour of simmering add the soaked and rinsed barley—you will need to very gently stir the barley from time to time throughout cooking. Half an hour later, add the chicken. At this stage you may also need to add another litre (35 fl oz/4 cups) of water if it has evaporated too much. An hour later remove the leek ends, then add the prunes and cook for 10 minutes before adding the white part of the leeks and cooking for a final 10 minutes—ideally the leeks should retain a slight crunch to them.

The proper way to serve cockie-leekie is in a shallow bowl: place a piece each of beef and chicken and some leeks, barley and prunes in a bowl and pour on the broth. The lazy and fun way to serve it is by taking the pot to the table with a carving fork, sharp knife and a ladle and letting your guests eat way too much.

Beef shin with dry gremolata
for six to eight

This recipe can be taken to the table whole, then cut and the sauce added, which is great fun as it pretty much guarantees some admiring comments. Another approach is to remove the meat from the bone after cooking, add the meat to the rich and sticky sauce, then pour it over strong, hearty pasta such as orechiette or casarecci.

You can adapt this recipe to other beef cuts such as the forequarter flank, but it is best not to use two different cuts together as they do take different times to cook.

I like to serve this with a mixture of strongly flavoured greens such as cavolo nero, rocket (arugula) or silverbeet (Swiss chard) that has been simply sautéed in olive oil, chilli and garlic alongside a puddle of freshly made polenta.

Gremolata is a type of spice mix that is used to flavour a meal. This recipe uses dry gremolata, which can be made well in advance and stored in an airtight container or jar—it is one of those great things to have on hand as it can be used with seafood, such as barbecued octopus, or sprinkled over meat, pasta or salads. There are many ways of drying the gremolata out completely. The nicest is to leave the mixture in direct sunshine for a couple of days. If you are lucky enough to have a shelf above your oven to spread out the gremolata, it will dry out as the oven is running; another option is to use a dehydrator, which is a device that uses warm air to extract moisture from food. Or, if you are making it at the same time as your beef shin, follow the recipe on the facing page.

For the marinade
the peel and juice of 1 orange, peel cut into strips
the peel and juice of 1 lemon, peel cut into strips
1 bunch of rosemary, leaves only
2 bay leaves
3 cloves of garlic, crushed
1 bottle of decent red wine
salt and ground black pepper

To make the marinade, combine the peel and juice of the orange and lemon with the rosemary leaves, bay leaves, garlic, wine and salt and pepper in a large bowl.

For the beef
1.6–1.8 kg (3 lb 8 oz–4 lb) frenched beef shin ('frenched' basically means that your
    butcher has cut the top of the knuckle off)
750 ml (26 fl oz/3 cups) chicken stock (Basics) or beef stock
6 ripe tomatoes, coarsely chopped

To prepare the beef, coat the shin with the marinade ingredients and leave for at least 2 hours, preferably overnight. Bring the meat to room temperature before cooking.

Preheat your oven to 200°C (400°F/Gas 6). Place the shin and all of the marinade in a large casserole dish or deep roasting tin. Add the stock and tomatoes (you want the liquid to come about halfway up the piece of beef), then put in the oven. What you want is to allow the beef not covered by the liquid to colour, then roll the meat over to expose the other side. Keep repeating this process every 15 minutes or so, this gives flavour and colour to your sauce and also keeps your meat moist. As the amount of liquid will reduce during cooking, pay close attention to this as you near the end of the cooking. You want a rich, sticky sauce—if you find that the sauce is reducing too far, simply add more liquid; if it is looking too watery but the beef is perfectly cooked, strain the sauce into a saucepan and reduce until you have the desired consistency. The shin should take around 2¹/2 hours to cook.

For the dry gremolata

4 cloves of garlic, chopped
2 tablespoons olive oil
1 bunch of rosemary
1 bunch of flat-leaf (Italian) parsley
the finely grated peel of 1 orange
the finely grated peel of 1 lemon
the finely grated peel of 1 lime
150 g (5¹/2 oz/1 cup) pine nuts, toasted and roughly chopped
salt

In a small saucepan fry the garlic in oil until golden, then strain off the oil.

Remove the leaves from the rosemary and parsley and coarsely chop together. Mix the citrus peel through the herbs and spread the mixture over a piece of baking paper on a baking tray. After removing the beef from the oven reduce the heat to 150°C (300°F/Gas 2). Cover the herbs loosely with foil and cook for 20 minutes while the beef is resting, being careful not to scorch your herbs. Once your herb mix is completely dry, pound into a powder using a mortar and pestle, then combine with the pine nuts, fried garlic and salt.

For serving

To serve, place the beef on your serving platter and pour on some of the sauce, pouring the rest of the sauce into a jug to add to the cut meat at the table. Sprinkle a good amount of the gremolata over the beef and have some more gremolata on the table alongside the salt and pepper as an additional seasoning to be added as desired.

Pot-roasted rabbit with tomato and butter for four

Buying rabbit takes a bit of care. It is becoming more popular as a farmed meat as more people are enjoying this wonderful sweet, lean meat. However, like any farmed product, there are those who deserve your support because they are producing a wonderful product in the right conditions and those you should avoid. If I can get it I do prefer wild rabbit, but I am extra cautious about where it comes from and the condition it is in. A good fresh rabbit should not smell bloody or gamey; it should be dry and not too floppy. Look into the stomach cavity for the kidneys and livers, which should be present. The fat should be a bright white and the organs intact and healthy looking. You will feed four people from one large white rabbit.

1.3 kg (3 lb) whole white rabbit
salt and ground black pepper
a dash of oil
1 bunch of baby carrots, peeled, stalks removed
4 baby onions, cut in half
50 g (1³/₄ oz) piece of pancetta, cut into matchstick-size 'lardons'
4 cloves of garlic, peeled but left whole
200 ml (7 fl oz) verjuice or sweet white wine and a dash of cider vinegar
500 ml (17 fl oz/2 cups) chicken stock (Basics)
a few sprigs of thyme
250 g (9 oz) cherry tomatoes, cut in half
100 g (3¹/₂ oz) good-quality butter or the artichoke butter from page 41
1 handful of flat-leaf (Italian) parsley, chopped

Preheat your oven to 180°C (350°F/Gas 4). Cut your rabbit (or ask your butcher to do it for you) into the following pieces: remove and divide the legs, remove each of the shoulders, cut off the belly flap and cut into strips, chop the saddle and neck into four. Season with salt and pepper.

In a flameproof 4.5 litre (157 fl oz/18-cup) casserole dish add some oil and heat on top of your stove over a medium heat, then add the seasoned rabbit pieces, carrots, onions, pancetta lardons and garlic and cook for about 10 minutes. When everything is a nice colour, deglaze the casserole with the verjuice (which basically means pour in your verjuice so that it lifts off the colour and flavour from the bottom of the casserole dish), then add the chicken stock and thyme, season and cover with a lid or foil and place into the oven for about 35 minutes. Halfway through the cooking stir everything.

Poke your rabbit legs with a sharp knife, the meat should be tender to the bone and the juice run clear. Take the rabbit, vegetables and garlic and place them on a serving platter. Pour all of the remaining juice into a saucepan, add the tomatoes and bring to the boil. When the sauce has reduced slightly, start to whisk in small pieces of the cold butter. When it is all incorporated and looking foamy, remove from the heat, throw in the parsley and pour all of the sauce over the rabbit—it should sit in a little puddle of sauce. Serve in a deep bowl with lots of the sauce, a knife, fork and a spoon and a wedge of bread. I like to serve this dish alongside a fresh bean salad (page 42).

Food to warm the cockles

Nothing is as warming as a loving embrace, except perhaps, for a bowl of soup.

Celeriac and port soup
for six

I loooove celeriac—it's a lumpy, warty-looking beast with a sweet, aromatic delicious flesh—beauty in the beast!

1 small onion, sliced
a knob of butter
salt and ground black pepper
1 small all-purpose potato (such as desiree), peeled and sliced
1 head of celeriac around the size of 2 clenched fists (800 g–1 kg/1 lb 12 oz–2 lb 4 oz),
    peeled and thinly sliced
1 litre (35 fl oz/4 cups) milk
a dash of cream (whipping)
300 ml (10^1/$_2$ fl oz) port

You need a heavy-based saucepan with a tight-fitting lid to make this soup. Put the onion and butter in the pan and add a little salt. Put on the lid and sit the pan over a low heat, stirring from time to time to prevent sticking, but keep the lid on as much as possible—you are trying to extract the sweet juices from the onion. Once the onion is soft, add the potato and celeriac, then replace the lid and keep the heat low—you are trying to soften the root vegetables before adding the liquid. Keep an eye on the vegetables as the potato and celeriac will stick easily. When the vegetables are just starting to become tender, about 15 minutes, add the milk and cook without the lid for another 20 minutes or so until everything has become soft. Allow to cool slightly before blending. Using a blender, purée your soup and pass it through a fine sieve. Add a dash of cream and taste for seasoning

While your soup is cooking reduce the port to a syrup that looks like honey. To do this pour the port into a small saucepan and place over a high heat. Keep the port on a rapid boil until it has reduced by about two-thirds. If the alcohol catches on fire, don't panic, it will only burn for a moment and will go out by itself.

To serve this soup I like to leave the celeriac soup smooth and white and ladle this into bowls, then add a drizzle of the port reduction over the top. You can have a bit of fun when you're drizzling on the syrup— we write the word 'danks' on the soup when we serve it at the café.

Toasted reuben sandwich
for four

This sandwich is named after its creator Arthur Reuben, owner of Reuben's Delicatessen, which no longer exists, but in its day was one of New York's more famous delicatessens. I was first shown this sandwich by a Chinese chef in Wellington, New Zealand, so I am sure Arthur would forgive me if it is not exactly how he would do it. When you buy one of these in New York, you usually receive about 2 kg (4 lb 8 oz) of pastrami, a foot-deep pile of sauerkraut stuck together by a mountain of melted Swiss cheese wedged between two bits of rye bread and, just to make it subtle, a foot-long pickle on the side of the plate. I find most people in Sydney are a little concerned about eating that much protein and vinegar in one sitting, so this sandwich is a bit more modest. Instead of Swiss cheese I like to use a beautiful cooked cow's milk cheese from Heidi Farms in Tasmania.

You can buy pre-cooked corned beef for the sandwich but I would recommend cooking yourself a piece for dinner one night and making sandwiches with the leftovers. I prefer to use bought sauerkraut, the reason being that with our very open kitchen we would reek the whole place out if we were to try and make it ourselves.

1 loaf of fresh ciabatta or other crusty white bread
some dijon mustard to scrape on the bread
16 slices of cooked corned beef (page 120)
8 slices of tilsit, gruyère, fontina or Swiss cheese
100 g (3½ oz) drained sauerkraut
salt and ground black pepper
pickled vegetables (either bought ones or home-made from page 12)
a dollop of wholegrain mustard

I like to cut the bread on an angle, which will give you a large, round slice of bread on which to build your sandwich—you'll need eight slices of bread. On each slice add a thin scraping of dijon mustard, two slices of meat, one slice of cheese and some of the sauerkraut. Season with salt and pepper and close your sandwiches up. What you end up with is the sauerkraut in the middle surrounded by cheese, then by corned beef and bread.

To cook your sandwiches either use a sandwich press or, if you don't have one, cook them in a large frying pan that's placed over a medium heat—I don't worry about any oil or butter as they should not stick. If you are using a frying pan, keep squashing the sandwiches down; when golden brown, turn over and repeat on the other side. What you are looking for is a crispy, golden sandwich that is hot all the way through. The best way to tell it is ready is to press the sandwich with your fingers—if the cheese oozes from the sides it is done. Cut in half and serve alongside some of your pickled vegetables and a dollop of wholegrain mustard.

Bacon hash
for four

In 1997 I went to North America with my beautiful girlfriend (now my beautiful wife) and two good friends, Ben and Belinda. We drove across the continent in a 1972 Chevy Beauville van that we nicknamed Margie. She had a beautiful grey and silver exterior and original cream leather and hound's-tooth interior. We bought her in Canada on the merits that she had all the room we needed (two double bench seats that could be removed and placed around an open campfire) and a newly reconditioned V8 engine. Also, the guy dropped his price when we waved some cash at him. Everything was great and we had a ball. Then we got to Los Angeles.

It was in LA where we discovered that the transmission was ruined. After a stressful 10 mile per hour crawl along the freeways of LA, Margie finally died at Redondo Beach at around 6 o'clock at night. We didn't have a clue where we were and knew no-one in the area—all we knew was that there were things called drive-by shootings in LA. We decided to spend the night in the van and to help us sleep in cramped conditions we sought help from a bottle of bourbon (note to potential travellers, this does not work). To cut a long enough story short, next morning we woke feeling pretty rough. After organizing to get the van fixed we stumbled upon The Pot Sticker Café. The place was one big breakfast joint and offered all the coffee you could drink. Every now and then I enjoy a meal so much that all I want to do is recapture the experience of eating it. I had such an experience that morning. The hash I was served was freshly fried and full of flavour and there was a mysterious healing quality to it. Use this recipe wisely as its powers should only be used for good; it is ideal for 'the morning after'.

300 g (10¹/₂ oz) piece of speck, diced into 1 cm (¹/₂ inch) cubes (you'll need to go to a
    butcher or delicatessen for this)
500 g (1 lb 2 oz) onions, diced into 1 cm (¹/₂ inch) cubes
2 cloves of garlic, finely chopped
a few stalks of rosemary
600 g (1 lb 5 oz) all-purpose potatoes (such as desiree), diced into 1 cm (¹/₂ inch) cubes
    (don't peel the potatoes)
a dash of oil

Preheat your oven to 180°C (350°F/Gas 4). Put the speck in a large casserole dish and place in the oven. Stir the speck from time to time to ensure even cooking. As the speck cooks it will release most of its fat—resist the urge to tip this off as it is all needed. When the speck is just starting to give when you press it with a spoon and it has become golden brown, about 30 minutes, add the onion, garlic and rosemary, stir well then put back in the oven. You want the onion to cook right down and start to colour; you will need to stir a couple of times during this stage as it will take another 30 minutes.

Now add the diced potato and fold it through the bacon and onion, then return to the oven. You want to keep cooking until your potato is tender, about another 30 minutes. Remove the rosemary stalks. If you are really impatient this can be eaten straight away, but the best way to serve this is to allow it to cool completely then place into a hot frying pan with a little oil and fry up till nice and golden. I like this served with poached eggs (page 133), toast and confit tomatoes (Basics) or juicy, ripe tomatoes.

Braised lamb necks
for four

I love eating lamb necks. I firmly believe that when you eat them you must gnaw at the bones to get the best out of them—they are full of flavour. I allow around one lamb's neck for two people. Ask if your butcher can clean the sinew off the back of them and cut them into pieces for you.

2 lamb necks, cleaned of excess fat and sinew, each cut into four pieces
seasoned flour, for dusting
about 150 ml (5 fl oz) vegetable oil
4 cloves of garlic, peeled but left whole
2 carrots, peeled and cut in half lengthways
1 large leek, cut into four short pieces
1 stalk of celery, cut into four short pieces
1 onion, quartered
a good splash of red wine
1 kg (2 lb 4 oz) tomatoes, chopped
a few sprigs of thyme
2 bay leaves
1 teaspoon ground coriander seeds
salt and ground black pepper
up to 1 litre (35 fl oz/4 cups) chicken stock (Basics) or beef stock
60 g (2¼ oz/⅓ cup) pitted and chopped kalamata olives
1 tablespoon salted capers, rinsed and chopped
a handful of flat-leaf (Italian) parsley, chopped

Preheat your oven to 170°C (325°F/Gas 3). Coat the lamb necks in seasoned flour. Heat a frying pan until almost smoking hot to start, then turn down just slightly before adding the meat. Fry the lamb necks in oil until well coloured, then turn and colour the other side; you may need to do this in batches. Transfer the browned pieces of meat to a large casserole dish or roasting tin (you'll need one that is about 5 litres/ 175 fl oz/20-cup capacity). Tip off any burnt oil from the pan, add a dash of fresh oil and fry the garlic and vegetables (except the tomatoes) until they too are a golden brown, then add to the meat.

While the pan is still hot, deglaze it with the red wine: tip out the oil, then pour in enough red wine to cover the base of the pan and bring to a boil while using a wooden spoon to scrape up the browned goodness that has become stuck to the bottom of the pan. Pour this over the necks and vegetables, then add the tomatoes, thyme, bay leaves, coriander, salt and pepper and enough stock to almost cover the necks (a few pieces sticking out is okay). Place in the hot oven and braise, uncovered, for about 2½ hours. During the cooking process you will need to turn the meat over from time to time.

Towards the end of the cooking time, start to check your meat. You will know it is ready when the meat flakes away from the bone as you press it, also the sauce should be nice and shiny and have thickened. If you see that the meat is cooked but the sauce is still quite thin, you can tip your sauce into a clean saucepan and reduce over a high heat until you have the consistency you desire. Divide the pieces of lamb neck among your plates and next to it place a piece of each of the vegetables and some of the delicious sauce, then finish with a sprinkling of freshly chopped parsley.

Corned beef with buttered vegetables
for six with leftovers

This is the ultimate nana food! The recipe is written using 2 kg (4 lb 8 oz) of beef, which will feed six people and leave enough for a couple of reuben sandwiches (page 115). Adjust the recipe according to the size of your beef.

For the spice paste
1 tablespoon juniper berries
1 tablespoon black peppercorns
1 clove of garlic, chopped

Grind the juniper berries and pepper with a mortar and pestle, then add the garlic and pound into a paste.

For the corned beef
2 kg (4 lb 8 oz) uncooked, corned silverside
400 ml (14 fl oz) balsamic vinegar
100 g ($3^1/_2$ oz/heaped $^1/_3$ cup) tomato base (Basics) or tomato paste (concentrated purée)
300 g ($10^1/_2$ oz/heaped $1^2/_3$ cups) soft brown sugar
6 bay leaves
200 ml (7 fl oz) chicken stock (Basics) or water
500 ml (17 fl oz) water

Rub your spice paste on to the corned silverside, cover with plastic wrap and let it sit overnight in the fridge.

Preheat your oven to 200°C (400°F/Gas 6). Put the corned beef in a large cast-iron pan or a casserole dish, fat side down, with the vinegar, tomato base, sugar, bay leaves, stock and water. Cover the pot with a lid and cook in the oven for about 1$^1/_2$ hours. Check from time to time to make sure that it doesn't dry out, adding water as needed. While you're in there give your beef a baste with the cooking liquid. After 1$^1/_2$ hours take the lid off the pan and turn the beef so the fat side is facing up and cook for another hour while you cook the vegetables and parsley sauce. It is very important to now baste your beef about every 15 minutes or so.

For the buttered vegetables
12 baby carrots, peeled
8 baby turnips, peeled
8 small new potatoes
1 tablespoon salt
a knob of butter
1 tablespoon wholegrain mustard
a generous pinch of chopped flat-leaf (Italian) parsley
salt and ground black pepper

Boil the vegetables in well-salted water. The carrots and turnips can be cooked together if they are of similar size (8–12 minutes in boiling water), but I recommend cooking the potatoes separately (about 20 minutes starting with cold water). Just before you serve the beef, place all of the hot vegetables in a bowl and gently toss in the butter, mustard, parsley and season with a little salt and pepper—you may need to splash in a little hot water to help things along.

For the parsley sauce

500 ml (17 fl oz/2 cups) milk
1/2 an onion, peeled
a couple of black peppercorns
1 bay leaf
60 g (2 1/4 oz) butter
2 tablespoons plain (all-purpose) flour
a small knob of butter, extra
1/2 bunch of curly parsley, chopped
salt and ground black pepper

You need to make a béchamel sauce—to do this start by warming the milk, onion, peppercorns and bay leaf together in a saucepan as this will allow the flavours to infuse. Strain the milk.

While this is happening melt the butter in a second saucepan, then add the flour and combine using a wooden spoon. Cook this mixture, called a roux, over a gentle heat for about 5 minutes, then start adding the warm, infused milk a little at a time. Each time you add some milk stir until completely incorporated before adding more. To start with the mixture will look a little like a blob of paste, but it will thin with each addition of milk—keep going until all of the milk is added. Let this cook over a gentle heat for about 5 minutes.

Give the first saucepan a quick rinse, then add a knob of butter and place on a low heat. When the butter is melted add the parsley and cook while stirring for about 2–3 minutes. When the parsley has started to soften, strain your béchamel sauce onto the parsley, taste for seasoning and cook for 1 more minute.

For serving

To serve, place a couple of slabs of the beef alongside the buttered vegetables. Splash on a touch of the cooking liquid from the beef and have the parsley sauce in a dish for people to add themselves.

White onion risotto with crispy pancetta and parsley oil for four

This recipe manifested itself in the early days of Danks Street Depot after the busy weeks following our first review. One day we simply had no food in the kitchen; desperate for an interesting risotto and having nothing but some onions, bacon and rice I suddenly became excited about the flavour combination of these simple ingredients. Since then, this has become one of those dishes that people look forward to when they see it back on the menu and one that I eat way too much of.

You can change the stock if you want a different flavour, but keep the technique the same for all your risottos. Every chef has a slightly different way of doing risotto, but for me this is it. Rue the day someone comes into my kitchen with some fancy pants effortless way of cooking risotto.

For the onion stock
750 g (1 lb 10 oz) white onions (these are sweeter and juicier than brown onions and
    work best for this recipe)
2 tablespoons oil
1/2 teaspoon salt
1.25 litres (44 fl oz/5 cups) water

Thinly slice the onions and place in a cold saucepan with the oil and salt. Add a tight-fitting lid and put over a medium–low heat. When you start to get heat through your onions, stir from time to time to ensure that they do not colour—very important! Keep the lid on your saucepan as much as possible; what will happen is that the steam will start to build up and gently pull all of the super sweet onion juices out of the onions. When the onions have become soft, 12 minutes or so, cover with cold water, bring to the boil and simmer for no longer than 5 minutes. Purée this onion stock in a blender, then pass through a fine sieve. The stock can be made in advance and stored in the fridge until you need it.

For the parsley oil
1 bunch of flat-leaf (Italian) parsley, chopped
about 100 ml (3 1/2 fl oz) extra virgin olive oil
a pinch of salt

Put all the ingredients in a blender or food processor and purée until a paste forms. This makes more than you'll need for the risotto, but it will keep for a couple of weeks in a sterilized jar in the fridge and it is great brushed over grilled (broiled) meat or fish or used in dressings. Bring to room temperature before using.

For the crispy pancetta
100 g (3 1/2 oz) long, thin slices of pancetta

Preheat your oven to 200°C (400°F/Gas 6). Put the thin slices of pancetta on baking paper and cook in the oven until crispy (4–5 minutes), then drain on crumpled paper towels before letting cool on a wire rack.

For the risotto

40 g (1¹/₂ oz) butter
1 white onion, finely diced
2 cloves of garlic, finely chopped
220 g (7³/₄ oz/1 cup) arborio rice
a handful of freshly grated parmesan cheese
an extra knob (or as much as you want) of good butter to finish the rice

In a heavy-based saucepan over a medium heat melt the butter, then add the onion and garlic. Keep stirring and do not let colour—when the onion has become soft and sweet turn up the heat, add the rice and stir vigorously. You want to keep stirring the rice over the heat for about 10 minutes—this will improve the flavour of your risotto, also it prepares the rice well for absorbing all that stock and flavour without the grains 'bursting' and looking crumbly.

Have your hot onion stock near at hand and start adding the stock, one ladle at a time, waiting until it is all absorbed before adding the next ladle. During the process you keep stirring, stirring, stirring—a sure sign of a good risotto is an aching arm and little beads of sweat on your forehead. Your rice is cooked when it is tender but not chalky in the middle, this may or may not involve all of your onion stock, and you may even have to add a little extra stock or water. I like to let the rice sit for a couple of minutes before finishing (just enough time to pour some wine and allow your arm to rest before the final effort).

Stir almost all of your cheese and as much butter as you want into the risotto and beat until all is well incorporated and creamy—adjust the consistency with a touch more stock or water if needed. Risotto must be soft and beautiful and slide into your mouth; if it is dry and crumbly it is forgettable, nasty and hard to eat.

For serving

Pour your finished risotto onto plates or a platter and drizzle with as much of the parsley oil as you want. Layer the pancetta over the top and sprinkle with the rest of the cheese.

Spaghetti with cauliflower strascicata
for four

Don't be put off by this recipe—at first glance it looks like way too much chopping and the fried cauliflower may seem a little strange to some people. But as soon as you start cooking and all of the aromas come together, you'll find it very difficult not to start eating it straight out of the pan. One word of advice: the bits that get stuck to the bottom of the pan are best eaten in greedy solitude.

400 g (14 oz) spaghetti
100 ml (3¹/₂ fl oz) extra virgin olive oil
¹/₂ head of cauliflower, chopped into pieces about the size of your thumbnail
3 cloves of garlic, thinly sliced
3 anchovy fillets, chopped
2 large red chillies, chopped (keep the seeds in if you like things hot)
50 g (1³/₄ oz) salted capers, rinsed and chopped
100 g (3¹/₂ oz) pitted olives, chopped
1 bunch of flat-leaf (Italian) parsley, chopped
60 g (2¹/₄ oz) toasted sourdough breadcrumbs (Basics)
200 g (7 oz/2 cups) freshly grated parmesan cheese
1 lemon, cut into wedges

Cook the spaghetti in a large pot of boiling water until *al dente*. Drain, then cool; while cooling drizzle with a little of the oil, then gently toss.

In a large heavy-based frying pan heat the rest of the oil over a medium heat, add the cauliflower and fry until just starting to colour. Add the garlic, mix well, then add the anchovies, chilli, capers and olives. When the cauliflower starts to become tender and has a rich golden colour, add half of the parsley and the cooked spaghetti. When the pasta is hot, add the crumbs, parmesan and remainder of the parsley.

The parmesan will start to stick to the pan; use a wooden spoon to scrape the bottom of the pan (this is where the term strascicata comes from, meaning drag). Remove from the heat, serve immediately with a wedge of lemon.

Roasted forerib with fresh horseradish sauce for four

The forerib is great roasted on the bone and it has nice layers of fat that keep the meat moist during cooking. Also, it is not too large, so a whole piece is not intimidating. Because of the nature of this cut, you can easily take one 'chop' and roast it for two people so use this as a rough guide as to how much to buy from your butcher (or allow 375 g/13 oz with bone per person). You may need to give a little advance warning when buying this cut on the bone so why not plan to get the butcher to hang the meat for a few days before you pick it up—the results are unquestionably better. Make sure that the fat is left on the meat and that the rib is not cut too short; you need to leave about 1–2 cm (1/2–3/4 in) bone from the eye of meat.

Below is a guide to how long you need to cook forerib to get the result you want. For every 1 kg (2 lb 4 oz) of meat, cook in a preheated oven at 240°C (475°F/Gas 8) for 20 minutes. Then turn the oven down to 220°C (425°F/Gas 7) and cook for the period of time mentioned below to get the desired result.

Rare: 15–20 minutes

Medium–rare: 20–25 minutes

Medium: 25–30 minutes

Medium–well done: 30–40 minutes

Well done (but please don't): 40 minutes and over

Another way to judge when the meat is done is the way I was taught when I first learnt to cook meat: I was shown how to 'feel' for doneness. Experience is the only way to guarantee precision on this one. However, I can share a little trick to help you understand this. Look at the palm of your hand relaxed with fingers out. Take the index finger of your other hand and gently push the fleshy part of your palm at the base of the thumb; this is how a rare steak should feel. Now, gently bring the index finger and thumb of your first hand together and touch that fleshy thumb part again; this is how meduim–rare feels. Thumb and middle finger is medium. Thumb and ring finger is medium–well done. Thumb and pinky is well done.

For the roasted forerib

1.5 kg (3 lb 5 oz) forerib, on the bone
salt and ground black pepper
2 carrots, peeled and cut into quarters
1 onion, cut into quarters

Start by taking the forerib out of the fridge a couple of hours beforehand so it comes to room temperature.

Preheat your oven to 240°C (475°F/Gas 8). When you are ready to cook, season the meat all over with plenty of salt and pepper, then seal in a large roasting tin or frying pan until you have good colour all over. Place in a large roasting tin, fat side up and bone side down, either on a rack or on the carrot and onion—this will keep the meat off the bottom of the pan and ensure even cooking. Cook for 20 minutes, then turn the heat down to 220°C (425°F/Gas 7) and cook for a further 25–30 minutes for a medium–rare piece of beef. Now, rest your beef somewhere warm for up to half the total cooking time. You can keep the carrot and onion to serve with the roast, but they are mainly there to add flavour to the meat.

For the fresh horseradish sauce

200 ml (7 fl oz) extra virgin olive oil
100 g (3½ oz/1¼ cups) dry sourdough breadcrumbs (Basics)
1 clove of garlic, finely chopped
300 g (10½ oz) piece of fresh horseradish, peeled and finely grated
60 ml (2 fl oz/¼ cup) red wine vinegar
salt and ground black pepper

Use some of the oil to gently toast the breadcrumbs and garlic together in a frying pan over a low heat until golden and crispy. Allow to cool before using a mortar and pestle to pound into a paste with the horseradish and vinegar. Once you have a paste carefully work in the remainder of the oil. Taste and adjust the consistency and seasoning to your liking—it will look a little like pesto.

For serving

To serve the meat, I like to remove the meat from the bone in the roasting tin—this way you will capture all of the wonderful roasting juices. Start removing the beef from the bones by sliding the knife just under the meat and on top of the ribs. Now slice off a portion by cutting across the meat and when you get to the bottom bone twist your knife sideways to remove the perfectly cooked, well-rested slab of beef.

Place your beef on a warm plate, top with a dollop of horseradish sauce and spoon on some of the pan juices. I like to serve this simply with boiled potatoes and an iceberg lettuce salad.

Sautéed duck livers and prosciutto
on toast for four

This is a great lunch dish—the rich livers are cut with salty prosciutto and peppery rocket. Different breeds of duck and different suppliers will produce livers that vary in size. The ones I've used are about 50–60 g (1³/4–2¹/4 oz) each.

For the dressing
100 g (3¹/2 oz/1 cup) walnuts
1 tablespoon grated orange peel
juice of 1 orange
60 ml (2 fl oz/¹/4 cup) balsamic cider vinegar or balsamic vinegar
80 ml (2¹/2 fl oz/¹/3 cup) extra virgin olive oil
salt and ground black pepper

Toast the walnuts by putting them in a 150°C (300°F/Gas 2) oven for 5–7 minutes until they are just starting to colour. If they become too dark they will taste bitter and will ruin the dish. Rub them with a clean cloth to remove the skin. Put the walnuts in a mortar and pestle or food processor and grind or blend. As you are working the walnuts, slowly add the orange peel and juice and vinegar, then the olive oil. Add your seasoning.

For the sautéed livers and prosciutto
800 g (1 lb 12 oz) duck livers
1 sage leaf per liver
¹/2 slice of prosciutto per liver
seasoned flour
3–4 tablespoons clarified duck fat (Basics) or vegetable oil
4 large handfuls of rocket (arugula)
salt and ground black pepper
4 thick slices of good sourdough toast

Clean the livers free of any tubes and bits, then place each one on a sage leaf. Wrap each liver snuggly in prosciutto, then secure with a toothpick. Lightly coat the prosciutto-wrapped livers in seasoned flour and fry in a hot frying pan with just a little duck fat or oil. Cook on a high heat until well coloured, about 3 minutes on one side, then 2 minutes on the other, this will give you nice pink livers—if you prefer them cooked more, turn one more time and give another couple of minutes.

Tip your livers onto a clean cloth to drain, then remove any excess fat from the pan. Add the rocket and a touch of seasoning to the pan and cook briefly, moving often to ensure even cooking. Place the rocket in a mound on each piece of toast. Add the dressing to your cooling pan as the heat of the pan will loosen the dressing and get the flavours going—return your livers to this and coat them well. Place the livers on your rocket and drizzle with any remaining dressing.

Lyonnaise sausage and lentil stew with a poached egg brunch for four

For this dish I like to use a lyonnaise sausage, which is a peppery pork sausage that is warming and rich. I get them made by a mate of mine who forms the sausage meat into a beef casing called a 'bung'. This is a large piece of intestine that stops in a dead end. When cleaned, salted, rinsed and stuffed it makes a sausage that is around 12 cm (4¹/2 in) in diameter and 50 cm (20 in) long and weighs around 1.5 kg (3 lb 5 oz). I like to be able to serve a big fat disc of sausage topped with a runny poached egg. You may not be able to get a sausage the size I have just described; however, any good pork sausages will do just as well.

For the stew
600–800 g (1 lb 5 oz–1 lb 12 oz) lyonnaise sausage or other pork sausages
2 carrots, peeled and sliced
2 bay leaves
a knob of butter
1 onion, diced
1 clove of garlic, crushed
¹/2 teaspoon fennel seeds
¹/2 teaspoon ground white pepper
185 g (6¹/2 oz/1 cup) puy lentils or tiny blue–green lentils
400 g (14 oz) tin peeled tomatoes, broken up a little, juice and all

Put the lyonnaise sausage or pork sausages in a saucepan with just enough cold water to cover, then add the carrot and bay leaves and bring to a simmer and gently poach. The time you need depends on the size of the sausage(s)—you can test by poking the meat with your finger, it should be nice and firm. Take the pan off the heat. Allow the sausage(s) to cool in the liquid. When cool, remove the sausage(s) and peel off the skin. If you are using a lyonnaise sausage cut it into thick discs; if you are using normal sausages, cut into thick pieces. Reserve the cooking liquid (you won't use the carrot or bay leaves, though).

In a clean saucepan on a high heat, soften a little butter and fry the sausage pieces until they are nice and brown. Remove the sausage pieces and add the onion, garlic, fennel and pepper. Cook until soft, then add the lentils, tomato, 500 ml (17 fl oz/2 cups) of the sausage cooking liquid (don't throw out the rest) and the browned pieces of sausage. The lentils will take around 30 minutes of cooking to get them nice and tender—a little overcooked doesn't matter too much but be sure not to serve any firm lentils. If the lentils look like they need more liquid, add some more of the sausage cooking liquid or water.

When you are ready to serve, taste your stew—I like mine to have a warm white pepper flavour, which will be balanced out with a runny poached egg yolk.

For the poached eggs

4 fresh eggs (A poached egg has only one important ingredient, an egg. So it is
   extremely important that you use the freshest, most beautiful eggs you can find.)
1 part white vinegar to 15 parts water
salt and ground black pepper

Use a saucepan at least 10–15 cm (4–6 in) deep. Almost fill the pan with water, then add the vinegar.

Bring the water to the boil, then turn down so it's not quite simmering, only just moving. If the water is boiling it will knock your egg around a little too much; if the water is too cool it will take too long to cook and your whites may become rubbery.

Break your egg into a ramekin or a teacup, then gently lower it into the water and pour in your egg, this way you ensure that the egg keeps its shape. Don't overcrowd your pan; if you are cooking a lot of eggs it may be better to cook in batches, or use two pans.

Test your egg! Lift out of the water with a slotted spoon and press gently with your finger; this is the best way to feel how cooked your egg is. As a guide a soft poached egg (cooked whites and runny yolk) will take 3–4 minutes, a hard egg (completely firm yolk) will take about 7 minutes.

Using a slotted spoon, gently lift your egg onto a clean dry cloth to drain (it's just been sitting in a lot of water, remember), season with a little salt and pepper, then serve as soon as possible.

For serving

a generous sprinkle of chopped flat-leaf (Italian) parsley

Put your braised sausage in individual bowls with a big spoonful of the lentils and top with a poached egg and a generous sprinkling of parsley to freshen the flavour.

Sweet things

Everybody loves a sweet ending.

Danks Street bread and butter pudding
for twelve

I've included this recipe in the book for the simple reason that I fear the consequences if I don't—my regular customers have been demanding it for a long time. The best thing is that the recipe is very simple, though there are a couple of things to keep in mind: use only croissants that have been made with a really good-quality butter (the ones I use have been made with a Danish cultured butter); also, they have to be stale. The batter looks way too wet before cooking but it does work.

8 eggs
500 g (1 lb 2 oz/2¼ cups) caster (superfine) sugar
600 ml (21 fl oz) cream (whipping)
grated peel and juice of 1 lemon
500 g (1 lb 2 oz) stale croissants and/or pain au chocolat (this is about 5 croissants
    and 3 pain au chocolat), cut into 1 cm (½ in) thick slices
a big blob of rhubarb or strawberry jam
a handful of chocolate melts (buttons)

Preheat your oven to 190°C (375°F/Gas 5). Grease twelve 375 ml (13 fl oz/1½-cup) ovenproof moulds, then line the base and side with baking paper. Alternatively, if you'd prefer to make a large pudding, grease and line a 4.5 litre (157 fl oz/18-cup) ovenproof dish.

In a large bowl, whisk the eggs and sugar together until pale and creamy, then add the cream, lemon peel and juice and gently whisk until the batter is combined. Add the slices of croissant and pain au chocolat and fold together until well covered. Leave to sit in the bowl for a while (10–15 minutes, or even overnight) to absorb the batter, then fold well one more time.

Pour the batter into the moulds, then top with a dollop of rhubarb jam and a few chocolate melts. Put in the oven. If you're making individual puddings they will take about 15 minutes; if you are making a large one it will take 15–30 minutes.

Drunken aunties' plum trifle
for six

This is one of those desserts that I have to do at Christmas purely for sentimental reasons, but it is good whenever stone fruit is in season—try replacing the plums with peaches or nectarines. I make these trifles in individual glass bowls, but you can easily make it into one large trifle. If you are making individual trifles and are cutting the jelly and sponge cake to size, you may find that you have a few scraps left over—don't waste them, just make an extra trifle (it won't be as pretty but it will be delicious) and hide it in the back of the fridge for your indulgence only! This recipe can be adapted to use a pre-made sponge cake, packet jelly, and tinned fruit, but where's the fun in that? All of the components to this benefit from being made a day in advance, which means it is a relatively easy process to serve.

For the jelly (gelatin dessert)
400 g (14 oz) black muscat grapes
200 g (7 oz/scant 1 cup) caster (superfine) sugar
1/2 bunch of mint
1 piece of lemon peel
4 leaves of sheet gelatine

Put the grapes, sugar, mint and lemon peel in a saucepan with just enough water to cover. Boil everything together for about 15–20 minutes and use a whisk or potato masher to squash the grapes as they cook. Pour into a sieve over a bowl. Place a weight on top of the cooked grapes—you want to get out as much of the juice as possible, then allow this to strain until cool. Measure the amount of liquid you have, it should yield 500 ml (17 fl oz/2 cups), but it may vary slightly. Top up with water if necessary.

Soak the gelatine in cold water to soften. While this is happening, bring your grape syrup up to the boil in a saucepan, then turn off the heat. Take your softened gelatine and squeeze out any excess liquid, then add the gelatine to the grape syrup. Stir until dissolved, then pour the mixture into a baking tray that is about 30 x 24 cm (12 x 9 1/2 in). Refrigerate and allow to set; this will take at least 2 hours.

For the plums
45 ml (1 1/2 fl oz) red wine
100 ml (3 1/2 fl oz) sweet sherry
400 ml (14 fl oz) water
100 g (3 1/2 oz/scant 1/2 cup) sugar
small piece of cinnamon
6 ripe blood plums

Put the wine, sherry, water, sugar and cinnamon in a saucepan and bring to the boil. When boiling, add the plums and cook until the skin is starting to split, then lift out the plums and continue to boil the syrup until it has reduced by half. Remove the pan from the heat and allow to cool slightly. When the plums have cooled enough to touch, peel off their skins, then take a small knife and slice in half following the stone, then gently pull away the two halves and remove the stone. Put the prepared plums in a container and pour on the syrup while it is still warm, then allow to cool completely. Keep the cinnamon in for flavour but fish it out before serving the plums.

For the sponge cake

5 large eggs, separated
dash of natural vanilla extract
225 g (8 oz/1 heaped cup) caster (superfine) sugar
60 g (2¼ oz/½ cup) sifted plain (all-purpose) flour
60 g (2¼ oz/½ cup) sifted cornflour (cornstarch)
a pinch of salt

Preheat your oven to 180°C (350°F/Gas 4). Beat the egg yolks, vanilla and sugar with a spatula until thick and creamy. Sift the flour and cornflour together and carefully fold into the egg yolk mix. Whisk the whites and the salt until stiff, then fold your egg yolk mixture into this. Line and flour a shallow baking tray—the size doesn't matter too much as for this recipe you can cut the sponge cake however you like but as a guide use a tray about 38 x 30 cm (15 x 12 in) that's around 3 cm (1¼ in) deep. Bake for 12–14 minutes, or until a toothpick inserted into the cake comes out clean. Remove from the oven and allow to cool slightly in the tin before tipping out onto a wire rack and allowing to cool completely.

For the custard cream

100 ml (3½ fl oz) cream (whipping)
1 vanilla bean, split down the middle
1 piece of lemon peel
3 egg yolks
50 g (1¾ oz/scant ¼ cup) caster (superfine) sugar
80 ml (2½ fl oz/⅓ cup) thick (double/heavy) cream (I use 45%-fat cream)

In a small saucepan gently warm the whipping cream with the vanilla and lemon—don't let this boil, just let the flavours infuse the milk.

Whisk the yolks and sugar together until pale, then add the infused cream. Put back into your pan and cook over a very low heat until the custard is thick enough to coat the back of a spoon, stirring during the cooking process. Strain into a bowl and allow to cool, discarding the vanilla and lemon. When completely cold whisk the thick cream until stiff, then fold it through the custard.

For serving

a few mint leaves
a heavy-handed splash of sherry (think of drunken aunties)

I have old-fashioned, thick clear glass trifle bowls that I use, but you can use whatever you like. Individual servings are easier to make look tidy—you'll need six bowls of about 350 ml (12 fl oz). For each trifle, cut your sponge to fit into the base and a little up the side of the bowl, then splash on some sherry. Pour in some plum syrup until the sponge is well soaked. Add two plum halves, top with a dollop of custard cream and add a couple of mint leaves. Now comes the jelly. Using your eye, cut a piece of jelly that will fit over the trifle but stay within the bowl. Run a spatula under a hot tap, then slide it under the piece of jelly and quickly lift up, then slide on to the trifle. Just before serving pour over a little more sherry.

Peach and cherry casserole
for eight

This recipe can be changed to suit whichever summer fruits you choose. I prefer to make these in individual dishes, but it can easily be made into one larger dish to be shared.

4 small, ripe peaches
100 ml (3½ fl oz) water
300 g (10½ oz/scant 1½ cups) caster (superfine) sugar
40 cherries
the peel and juice of 1 lemon, peel cut into strips
2 vanilla beans, split down the middle into quarters
1 stick of cinnamon, gently crushed

Preheat your oven to 180°C (350°F/Gas 4). Firstly, peel your peaches—treat them the same way you would a tomato by soaking them in boiling water for a few seconds, then lifting straight into cold water. Use the tip of a knife to gently pull away the skins. Now, cut them in half and remove the stones.

Make a light caramel by boiling the water and the sugar together in a saucepan until syrupy. While this is happening put the cherries, lemon peel and juice, vanilla bean and cinnamon in a separate bowl. When the caramel has started to become a pale straw colour add all of the ingredients that are in the bowl to the pan, then remove the pan from the heat and gently fold together. This will 'stop' the caramel.

In small heatproof dishes, place a peach half and five cherries along with a piece of vanilla and cinnamon, then pour on any remaining liquid. Cover each dish with foil and bake for 10–15 minutes. Serve with a dollop of sweetened cream or ice cream.

Hot angelina plum tart
for six

I only discovered angelina plums last year and had an absolute ball playing around with them. This tart is a nice, easy recipe that takes advantage of the cute shape and size of the plums and the robust flavour of their flesh, which holds up against the flavours of the butter, sugar and lemon. The tart is cooked in a similar manner to a tarte tatin.

a knob of unsalted butter
1 kg (2 lb 4 oz) ripe angelina plums
165 g (5³/4 oz/²/3 cup) sugar
the peel and juice of 1 lemon, peel grated
1–2 sheets of bought puff pastry

Preheat your oven to 180°C (350°F/Gas 4). Choose a flameproof pan that will fit the plums comfortably in one layer and can also go into a hot oven. In that pan melt your butter over a medium heat; when the butter starts to foam, add the plums, sugar, lemon peel and juice. Increase the heat so the pan is over a high heat and sauté the plums until the skin just starts to blister, about 2 minutes. Tip out the plums and allow to cool enough to be handled. Don't wash your pan, you will be using this again shortly.

Squeeze out the stones from the plums, trying to keep the plums as intact as possible, then arrange them back into your pan with the prettiest side on the base of the pan. Add any juice that may have come out during the stoning process.

Cut the puff pastry so it is just a little wider than your pan and place on top of your plums—you'll probably need to have two sheets overlapping to cover the whole pan. Tuck the edges of the pastry into the pan. Return the pan to the heat until the plums start to fry, then place the pan into the oven. Cook for about 50 minutes. I was once told that when you cook puff pastry you should cook it until it looks cooked, then give it another 5 minutes because there is nothing worse than half-cooked dough. Undercooked dough is usually caused by people who are nervous about colouring their pastry too much. You don't want it burnt but it does need to be well cooked in order to taste good.

Invert the tart onto a serving plate—the easiest way to do this is to hold your plate over the pan, then quickly flip the pan over. Serve with your choice of custard, cream or ice cream. The way I normally serve it is with a quenelle of whipped thick (double/heavy) cream on the top.

Eccles cakes
for a crowd

This recipe is similar to the ones originally baked in Church Street in Eccles, Manchester. Eccles cakes are typically made from currants that have been steeped in water, then mixed with butter and sugar. I prefer the results you get from cooking muscatel grapes to get their sugar going. These are great on their own but my absolute favourite way of serving them is to serve them at room temperature next to a wheel of ripe cheese.

Makes 24

120 g (4^1/$_4$ oz) unsalted butter
335 g (11^3/$_4$ oz) dried muscatel grapes, picked off the stem, or raisins
135 g (4^3/$_4$ oz/scant ^{2}/$_3$ cup) caster (superfine) sugar
grated peel of most of a lemon
juice of 1^1/$_2$ lemons
about 8 sheets of bought puff pastry (the number of sheets you need will depend on
    the size of your pastry sheets)
1 egg, lightly beaten
an extra sprinkling of caster (superfine) sugar

Melt the butter in a saucepan. Add the grapes, sugar, lemon peel and juice and cook everything over a medium heat until the muscatels start to puff up and the sugars start to caramelize, about 10 minutes. Remove the pan from the heat and allow to cool completely—this will take at least 2 hours.

Preheat your oven to 180°C (350°F/Gas 4) and grease a baking tray. Cut 24 x 10 cm (4 in) discs from the puff pastry—you can use a saucer as a guide. Place a small dollop of fruit into the middle of each disc (using up all the fruit mixture), then brush the edges of the pastry with the egg. Pick up each disc and pull the edges into the middle of the fruit until you have completely covered the fruit and sealed the parcels. Place them on the baking tray, seam side down. Use a very sharp knife to score the top of the cakes. Brush with the egg and sprinkle with caster sugar.

Bake for 10–12 minutes, then sprinkle with a little more sugar and bake for a further 5–10 minutes. Don't worry if a couple of the cakes explode. When they are completely cooked and well coloured remove them from the oven. There will be some sticky juice that has oozed out during the cooking; carefully roll the cakes in that sticky ooze while it is still hot, then transfer the cakes to a wire rack.

Fresh strawberries with
sweet goat's cream for four

It is here I shall admit to a very real problem—I am always looking for perfection in food, and it is something that I have found only a few times. Once was eating freshly caught mud crabs that we boiled in sea water in an old tin over open coals smack bang in the eye of an amazing electrical storm in Yamba, on the coast of New South Wales. Another perfect moment was eating seared goose foie gras at The Square Restaurant in London. Then there were the fish that my friend Ben and I caught in the surf on the night of a full moon in Mexico; we simply floured them, then fried them in butter on the beach. And, of course, not to forget mum's meat loaf!

And I once ate a punnet of strawberries I bought from a market in London; they were the most amazing strawberries I have ever eaten. They were a beautiful, luscious red and had a rich fragrance and perfumy flavour with juice that ran down my chin! I ran back to buy more but they were gone. Whenever I look back on that beautiful and heart-breaking moment I sigh. Unfortunately, every strawberry I have eaten since that day is compared to that perfect punnet, so let's just say I am 'particular' about my strawberries.

This is a great way to finish a summer lunch, but I find that I only end up eating this once or maybe twice a year as the strawberries must be absolutely perfect. I strongly recommend holding out until you get the best as it will make your appreciation of them so much greater.

500 g (1 lb 2 oz) of the best strawberries you can get
80 g (2³/4 oz/¹/3 cup) caster (superfine) sugar, or to taste
a few sprigs of mint
a dash of lemon juice, optional
125 g (4¹/2 oz/¹/2 cup) goat's curd
80 ml (2¹/2 fl oz/¹/3 cup) thick (double/heavy) cream (I use 45%-fat cream)

Halve your strawberries and place in a bowl. Sprinkle with about one-third of the caster sugar, a few pieces of mint and, if you like, a dash of lemon juice. Leave to sit in the fridge for about an hour.

Take your goat's curd and, using a spatula, incorporate the cream and remaining sugar until smooth.

Place a mound of goat's cream in a bowl and spoon on your strawberries and mint. Serve as cold as you can. Smile and enjoy the beautiful day!

Pineapple with cream and
ginger nut biscuits for four

pictured page 148

A very simple recipe that is best when pineapples are at their peak. You've got my mum to thank for this recipe, which is based on one of my favourite childhood desserts (one that I am soooooo looking forward to showing my son). The simple version is a ginger nut biscuit warmed in a muffin tin in the oven; when the biscuit becomes soft you use the back of a spoon to push down on the biscuit to make little ginger nut bowls. Then top with whipped cream and some chopped pineapple. The recipe below is nothing more than a fancy version of mum's dessert.

1 pineapple
2 tablespoons caster (superfine) sugar, plus another 1 tablespoon
100 ml (3¹/₂ fl oz) thick (double/heavy) cream (I use 45%-fat cream) or goat's curd
3 ginger nut biscuits (ginger snaps)

Preheat your oven to 170°C (325°F/Gas 3). Take your pineapple and do nothing to it; if you feel you must you can cut off the leaves but do not cut into the fruit itself. Place the pineapple in the oven for 2 hours or so until it feels soft and gives a little—be sure to turn it from time to time to ensure even cooking.

Add 2 tablespoons of the sugar to the cream or goat's curd.

Allow the pineapple to cool slightly, then use a sharp serrated knife to cut off the top and the bottom, then carefully cut away the skin. Cut the flesh into quarters and remove the core. Place, core side down, on a tray, sprinkle with the remaining tablespoon of sugar and, using a blowtorch (preferable) or a really hot grill (broiler), caramelize the sugar on top of the pineapple. Transfer the pineapple to your plates, place a quenelle of sweetened cream or goat's curd next to it and, using the coarsest side of your grater, grate the biscuits over the top. If you find it easier, you could use a small food processor to chop up the ginger nut biscuits instead of using the grater.

Vanilla panna cotta with fruit
for four

This is my absolute favourite dessert! The simplicity of vanilla, lemon, cream and sugar gives you a flavour foundation that is perfect with any slightly acidic fruit. Rhubarb, tamarillo and quince are all equally good so buy whichever is best and cook it simply to bring out its own distinct flavours. Now that we have discussed flavour, let's talk about the real beauty of a good panna cotta, and that is texture. It should never be firm or rubbery, this is a crime! The sign of a good panna cotta is that it only juuuust manages to hold itself together for you to get your spoon into it; in fact let it sit for too long at room temperature and it will simply melt away. I have spent months and way too much money getting this recipe just so, and it works for me. When you make it, make it your own. If it is too soft, try to reduce your cream slightly; too firm, cut back on the gelatine, but be warned, even the slightest variation will be noticeable.

As this recipe needs to be made a day in advance, the fruit recipes that I have suggested here also benefit from being made at least a day beforehand, so this way you are able to do everything in advance, and simply soak up the glory on the following day. For the baked rhubarb, I prefer to use thin, brightly coloured rhubarb that doesn't require any peeling. Thicker stalks may require a little gentle peeling but keep in mind that a lot of the colour and flavour is in the skin, so I am always tempted to allow a few stringy bits for the sake of better flavour.

For the panna cotta
300 ml (10½ fl oz) cream (whipping)
1 vanilla bean, split down the middle and scraped
the peel from 1 whole lemon, in a single strip if possible
1 leaf of sheet gelatine
70 ml (2¼ fl oz) milk
70 g (2½ oz/scant ⅓ cup) caster (superfine) sugar
an extra 100 ml (3½ fl oz) cream (whipping)

Put the cream, vanilla bean and lemon peel in a saucepan over a very low heat and infuse for 10–15 minutes. Don't allow the cream to boil or leave on the heat for any longer than 15 minutes—you do not want to reduce the cream or you will alter the liquid content of the recipe.

Put the gelatine and milk together in a bowl and allow the gelatine to soften in the milk. Combine the sugar and extra cream using a spatula or wooden spoon, mixing just enough to dissolve the sugar—don't whisk or beat in too much air.

When you have the desired flavour in the infused cream, and your gelatine has softened, then you can combine your ingredients. Add the gelatine and milk mixture to your saucepan of hot cream and stir until the gelatine has dissolved. Then add the creamy sugar mixture and stir to combine. Do not use a whisk or work in too much air. Using a slotted spoon remove the lemon and vanilla, allow the mixture to cool then pour into four moulds. I use plastic 125 ml (4 fl oz/½ cup) dariole moulds, which is the best thing to use if you wish to turn out your panna cotta—spray them with a little oil so they turn out easily. If you don't have these you can just as easily pour everything into a coffee cup or glass and serve in that. These need to sit in the fridge overnight.

For the spiced and poached tamarillos

8 tamarillos
400 g (14 oz/1³/₄ cups) caster (superfine) sugar
600 ml (21 fl oz) water
1 lemon, sliced
1 stick of cinnamon
2 cloves
a couple of grinds of black pepper

Preheat your oven to 120°C (235°F/Gas ¹/₂). Blanch your tamarillos in boiling water until the skin has just started to split, then cool quickly by running under cold water. When they are cool enough to handle, use the tip of a paring knife to peel away the skin—try not to puncture the flesh.

Make a syrup from the sugar, water, lemon, cinnamon, cloves and pepper by boiling everything together for 10 minutes.

Place your peeled tamarillos in an ovenproof dish that is deep enough to take the syrup as well as the fruit. Cover the tamarillos with the boiling syrup, then place a sheet of baking paper over the top to ensure that everything is covered by the liquid. Cook in the oven for about 15 minutes or until the tamarillos are just tender.

Allow everything to cool together. Once cooled, lift your tamarillos out into a container and pour the syrup into a saucepan and reduce by half. Let the syrup cool completely before pouring back over the tamarillos. Allow this to sit for at least 24 hours in the fridge before using; they will also keep perfectly well for a couple of months if stored in a sterilized jar and kept under plenty of liquid.

For the baked rhubarb

350 g (12 oz) rhubarb (about 3 fat stalks), leaves removed, stems washed and cut into
    4 cm (1¹/₂ in) pieces
2 lots of 115 g (4 oz/¹/₂ cup) caster (superfine) sugar
juice of an orange

Put the cut rhubarb on a tray and sprinkle with one portion of the sugar. Gently toss about to make sure that the rhubarb is well covered and let this sit for at least 4 hours, but preferably overnight.

Preheat your oven to 150°C (300°F/Gas 2). Place the rhubarb in a roasting tin—don't stack it on top of each other but allow a little space between. Sprinkle with the remaining sugar and drizzle with the orange juice. Bake for 35 minutes, or until the rhubarb has shrivelled a little but is not overcooked.

For serving

Carefully turn out the panna cottas onto individual plates and put some of your fruit alongside it. Serve straight away.

Basics

Great basic recipes to have on hand.

Breadcrumbs

Fresh or dry breadcrumbs You will find it easier to make crumbs with bread that is a day or two old but you can use fresh bread to make fresh breadcrumbs. Simply place your bread in a blender and blend until well powdered. Shake your crumbs through a coarse sieve to remove larger pieces of crumb.

Toasted breadcrumbs Preheat your oven to 160°C (315°F/Gas 2–3). Make your crumbs as above, but you do not need to sieve them. Spread a layer of crumbs on a dry baking tray and place in the oven. Cook until you have achieved a nice even gold colour; to do this you will need to stir often.

Herbed breadcrumbs Make your fresh or dry crumbs as above, but as you are blending your bread, add some chopped herbs and/or a clove of garlic. Heat a large frying pan with a drizzle of olive oil and a generous knob of butter. When the butter is starting to foam add your crumbs and fry over a medium heat while continuously stirring. Cook until they are well toasted and coloured, then drain on paper towels.

Chicken stock Makes about 1 litre (35 fl oz/4 cups)

3 kg (6 lb 12 oz) fresh chicken bones, rinsed of blood
4 large carrots, peeled but left whole
2 stalks of celery
1 onion, peeled but left whole
1 leek, rinsed
1 clove of garlic, peeled but left whole
1 bay leaf
5 peppercorns
1 bunch of thyme
1 bunch of parsley

Put the bones in a stockpot and pour in enough cold water to cover them by 4 cm (1 1/2 in). Bring up to the simmer and remove the grey foamy scum, but leave the fat on. Add the carrots, celery, onion, leek, garlic, bay leaf and peppercorns. Very gently simmer for 6 hours being sure that the temperature doesn't change under the pot—this is crucial to avoid cloudiness and discolouring. You may need to add more water during cooking to keep the bones covered. During the last hour of cooking add the thyme and parsley. When you are happy with your stock, remove the solids and strain the stock into a container. Leave to cool completely in the fridge, then remove the fat when it forms a solid. Good stock like this one should be gelatinous. Use within a couple of days or freeze for up to 2 months.

Clarified duck fat

1 kg (2 lb 4 oz) duck fat and any skin you have retained (adjust the quantities and
   timing of the recipe depending on how much fat you have on hand)
200 ml (7 fl oz) water

A word of warning before you begin. Because you will be boiling fat use extreme caution—one golden rule is to only fill your pot halfway to minimize any fat boiling over the side. Place the fat and water in a large, heavy-based pot over a high heat. Boil hard, stirring from time to time. After about 20 minutes you need to start watching your fat—it should be a milky, bubbling mass. As the water evaporates the fat will start to become clear and after 35–45 minutes the fat will become completely clear and golden. Remove from the heat and pass through a fine sieve. Stored in an airtight container your fat should keep for at least a couple of months in the fridge, even longer in the freezer.

Confit tomato

1 litre (35 fl oz/4 cups) extra virgin olive oil
12 roma (plum) tomatoes (don't do anything to these)
herb stalks, the more the merrier

Preheat your oven to 120°C (235°F/Gas 1/2). Pour the oil into a roasting tin and put in the oven for 10 minutes to warm. Add the tomatoes to the hot oil and return to the oven. Cook for about 12 minutes or until just starting to soften. You want the tomato to just start to cook down, but to be kept together in the skin—don't panic if the skin does split, it just means that you need to be extra gentle. Remove from the heat and allow to cool in the oil. Put the tomatoes and oil in a sterilized wide-mouthed jar; they will keep in the fridge for a couple of weeks.

Duck stock Makes about 1 litre (35 fl oz/4 cups)

1.5 kg (3 lb 5 oz) duck bones, wings and necks (these don't need to be rinsed)
3 carrots, sliced lengthways
1 onion, halved
1 leek, sliced longthways and rinsed
2 cloves of garlic, peeled but left whole
if you have any, add mushroom trimmings, tomato peel or seeds
salt and ground black pepper

Preheat your oven to 200°C (400°F/Gas 6). Roast the duck bones in a roasting tin until they become a deep brown colour, about 2 1/2 hours. Transfer the bones to a stockpot, tip most of the fat off the roasting tin and then add everything else to the tin. Return the tin to the oven and roast until the vegetables are a nice brown colour and there is a delicious roast vegetable aroma, about another hour. Transfer the vegetables to the pot and cover everything with water. Put onto a high heat and bring to a simmer as quickly as you can, but be sure not to let the stock boil or the fat will be boiled into the stock, which will result in a murky-looking and flabby-tasting broth. Cook for about 8 hours. Taste for seasoning, skim off the fat and strain into a clean saucepan and reduce by about one-third. Use within 2 days or freeze for up to 2 months.

Mayonnaise Makes 250 g (9 oz/1 cup)

1 egg yolk
1 tablespoon white wine vinegar
1 tablespoon dijon mustard
salt and ground black pepper
200 ml (7 fl oz) vegetable oil

Place all the ingredients, except for the oil and water, in a food processor. Start blending; when the egg yolk starts to become pale, slowly drizzle in the oil to allow the mayonnaise to emulsify. You want it to have the consistency of pouring cream—to achieve this you will need to thin out with a little hot water. Keeps for up to a week in the fridge.

Pickled shallot vinegar Makes 250 ml (9 fl oz/1 cup)

100 g (3^1/$_2$ oz) French shallots, finely diced
2 teaspoons salt
100 ml (3^1/$_2$ fl oz) red wine vinegar
100 ml (3^1/$_2$ fl oz) Moscato d'Asti (a sweet sparkling Italian wine) or Champagne

Sprinkle the diced shallots with salt and leave to sit for a couple of hours in a non-metallic bowl to start the pickling process. Add the vinegar and wine and mix together. Cover and allow to sit for at least 24 hours in the fridge. Will keep indefinitely.

Tomato base Makes about 400 g (14 oz/scant 1^2/$_3$ cups)

2 kg (4 lb 8 oz) of the very ripest tomatoes you can get
1 bulb of garlic, cut in half (you don't need to peel the cloves)
300 ml (10^1/$_2$ fl oz) extra virgin olive oil
1 bunch of thyme
a few sprigs of basil
a little sugar (you can taste and adjust later on)
salt and ground black pepper
a splash of balsamic vinegar

Preheat your oven to 170°C (325°F/Gas 3). Chop the tomatoes and put in a roasting tin with all the other ingredients, then place in the oven. During the cooking process stir and mash the tomatoes often, being sure to stir any dark pieces through the sauce—you want the tomatoes to colour, but be careful not to let them burn or there will be a nasty bitter flavour. The length of cooking time will vary on a how 'wet' your tomatoes are but will probably take a good 2 to 2^1/$_2$ hours. You are looking for a thick, oily sauce.

When you are happy with your sauce remove from the oven and allow it to cool slightly, then push through a mouli—do not blend. I know it is easier to use a blender but the result is inferior. If you don't have a mouli you can push the sauce through a very fine strainer or a coarse strainer lined with muslin (cheesecloth). Taste for seasoning and once completely cool, store in a jar in the fridge. This will keep for at least a month.

Tomato dressing Makes 200 ml (7 fl oz)

2 French shallots, thinly sliced
2 tablespoons red wine vinegar
salt and ground black pepper
4 tablespoons tomato base (page 156) or tomato paste (concentrated purée)
80 ml (2½ fl oz/⅓ cup) extra virgin olive oil
a sprinkle of chopped flat-leaf (Italian) parsley

Put the shallots in a bowl with the vinegar and the salt, allow to sit for a few minutes, then whisk in the other ingredients. This will keep for 3 to 4 days.

Red wine dressing Makes 200 ml (7 fl oz)

55 ml (1¾ fl oz) red wine vinegar
150 ml (5 fl oz) extra virgin olive oil
1 clove of garlic, peeled but left whole
salt and ground black pepper

Put the vinegar, oil, garlic and seasoning in a jar and shake thoroughly. Keeps indefinitely.

Tempuring

10 cloves of garlic
5 French shallots
5 large red chillies
300 ml (10½ fl oz) vegetable oil
1 bunch of curry leaves, about 60 g (2¼ oz)
salt

Thinly slice the garlic with a mandolin or sharp knife. Repeat with the shallots but keep them separate Slice the chillies, keeping the seeds in. Set aside separately.

Heat the oil in a deep saucepan. Check the temperature of the oil before you start cooking—to do this dip a wooden spoon into the oil, if you see that little bubbles are forming around the spoon your oil is hot enough and you can start cooking. You need to cook everything separately and when they just start to become crisp use a slotted spoon to remove onto crumpled paper towels to drain. Be careful when deep-frying the leaves, as they will spit fiercely for the first second of cooking. Start with the chilli, then the curry leaves, garlic and, finally, the shallots.

Gently toss everything together and season with a little salt. When cool, store in an airtight container for up to a month. This can be used in a multitude of different ways from using it to liven up a piece of steamed fish, to garnishing a salad.

Index

Published by Murdoch Books Pty Limited.

Murdoch Books Australia
Pier 8/9, 23 Hickson Road, Millers Point NSW 2000
Phone: +61 (0) 2 8220 2000 Fax: +61 (0) 2 8220 2558
www.murdochbooks.com.au

Murdoch Books UK Limited
Erico House, 6th Floor North, 93–99 Upper Richmond Road
Putney, London SW15 2TG
Phone: + 44 (0) 20 8785 5995 Fax: + 44 (0) 20 8785 5985

Chief Executive: Juliet Rogers
Publisher: Kay Scarlett

Design concept, art direction and design: Vivien Valk
Project manager: Paul McNally
Editor: Zoë Harpham
Photographer: Alan Benson
Stylist: Mary Harris
Production: Monika Paratore

National Library of Australia Cataloguing-in-Publication Data:
Ingersoll, Jared
Danks St Depot
Includes index.
ISBN 1 74045 598 3.
1. Danks Street Depot (Restaurant : Sydney, N.S.W.). 2. Cookery. 3. Restaurants – New South Wales – Sydney.
I. Title.
641.5099441

Printed by Midas Printing (Asia) Ltd. PRINTED IN CHINA. First printed 2006.

IMPORTANT: Those who might be at risk from the effects of salmonella poisoning (the elderly, pregnant women,
young children and those suffering from immune deficiency diseases) should consult their doctor with any concerns
about eating raw eggs.

CONVERSION GUIDE: You may find cooking times vary depending on the oven you are using. For fan-forced ovens,
as a general rule, set the oven temperature to 20°C (35°F) lower than indicated in the recipe. We have used 20 ml
(4 teaspoon) tablespoon measures. If you are using a 15 ml (3 teaspoon) tablespoon, for most recipes the difference
will not be noticeable. However, for recipes using baking powder, gelatine, bicarbonate of soda (baking soda), small
amounts of flour and cornflour (cornstarch), add an extra teaspoon for each tablespoon specified.